VALHALLA
pure outfitters
...for the adventure!

- ◆ *Gear You Love!*
- ◆ *Your Favourite Brands!*
- ◆ *Knowledgeable, Friendly Staff!*
- ◆ *Unbeatable Prices!*

Factory Outlet for

 Made In Canada

615 Broughton St, Downtown Victoria 360-2181
6550 Metral Drive, Nanaimo North 390-6883
219 - 5th Street, Downtown Courtenay 334-3963

www.vpo.ca

CLIMBING EQUIPMENT • TRAVEL GEAR • SANDALS

PACKS • BOOTS • TENTS • BAGS • SUPPLIES

You've Read the Magazine...

Now lookout for these new guidebooks from

Wild Isle Publications

www.wildisle.ca

Island Alpine

Island Alpine

A Guide to the Mountains of Strathcona Park and Vancouver Island

by
Philip Stone

First Edition

Wild Isle Publications
2003

Island Alpine
A Guide to the Mountains of Strathcona Park and Vancouver Island
2003 First Edition
© Wild Isle Publications, All Rights Reserved

Published by   Wild Isle Publications
                      PO Box 482, Heriot Bay, BC V0P 1H0 Canada
                      ph: 250 285-2234 fx; 250 285-2236
                      www.wildisle.ca/publications

National Library of Canada Cataloguing in Publication Data

Stone, Philip, 1965-
  Island alpine : a guide to the mountains of Strathcona Park and
Vancouver Island / by Philip Stone.

  Includes index.
  Previous ed. has title: Strathcona Park, North Vancouver Island :
selected rock and ice climbs.
  ISBN 0-9680766-5-3

  1. Mountaineering--British Columbia--Vancouver Island--Guidebooks. 2.
Hiking--British Columbia--Vancouver Island--Guidebooks. 3. Vancouver
Island (B.C.)--Guidebooks. I. Title. Title: Stone, Philip, 1965-
Strathcona Park, North Vancouver Island.
GV199.44.C22V35 2003   796.52'2'097112   C2002-911230-3

            First Edition - first printing January 2003
                      second printing April 2003

Cover Photo: Mt. Colonel Foster and Landslide Lake from the Elkhorn south west approach route in May.
Frontispiece: The Golden Hinde as seen from the north on the summit of 'the Comb'.
Back Cover: top- Paul Agnew at Crown Mountain. bottom- Golden Hinde from Phillips Ridge. © Philip Stone
inset- The author, at Elk Pass © Ryan Stuart, left- climbing 'the Chuck' on Rugged Mountain © John Roberts

"...its peaks offer rich gifts
of graceful line and solid rock to the climber.
Its trailless valleys will still test
the patience of his soul."

- Ferris Neave, 1942
of Strathcona Park

Contents

Introduction	**1**
Southern Vancouver Island	**44**
Central Vancouver Island	**62**
Beaufort Range	110
Strathcona Park	**124**
Strathcona Park East	136
Strathcona Park North	182
Central Strathcona Park	202
Strathcona Park South	278
Strathcona Park West	310

Climbers on the South East Peak of Mt. Colonel Foster. Mt. Tom Taylor behind.

Contents

Northern Vancouver Island — 330
Sutton Range — 336
Tlupana Range — 374
Johnstone Strait — 392
Haihte Range — 416
Nimpkish Lake - Quatsino Sound — 440

Appendix — 462
Sources — 469
Index — 473

Preface

Compiling this guide to the mountains of Vancouver Island has been a labour of love and a longer journey than I ever thought it might be. I remember clearly my first view into Strathcona Park, from the south col of Mt. Colonel Foster. It was June 1988 and looking south into the park, everything was still cloaked in a blanket of snow. What struck me right then was what a seemingly endless sea of peaks there were. And then a heartbeat later, disbelief that there was no definitive guidebook describing these magnificent mountains. I knew right then and there that I would undertake the project but I had no idea it would take fifteen years of 'research' to complete.

Collecting the photographs for this guide was the foil that brought everything else into focus. It meant hiking and climbing off the beaten track for the promise of a new angle of a given summit. Often this meant some shaking of heads by my companions, baffled as to why we needed to go 'this way'. But finally the results are here for all to see and my thanks go out to those who humoured some of my on and off-the-wall trip ideas.

I hope that 'Island Alpine' will serve the Vancouver Island mountaineering community well. Just seeing all these mountains together in one volume is sure to spark plenty of daydreaming, scheming and tripping. As is the nature of guidebooks, those who follow its descriptions are sure to find things differently on their own travels. I have tried to present the information as accurately as possible from first-hand experience, consultation with other climbers and endless research of journals, books and maps. But there are still endless variables. Logging road access is one element that is nearly impossible to ascertain with certainty. Some route information has been described second-hand from sketchy recollections and other details simply deduced from maps, photos and trips to adjacent areas. So this book is not to be considered infallible and if you have any additional or updated information to contribute, please bring it forward so it can be included in a subsequent edition.

What I think we have with Island Alpine is a good first attempt. It opens the door and lays a solid foundation for future exploration and climbing. I hope you find it valuable in your own adventures in the Vancouver Island mountains and that it shows the way to unlocking more and more of the Island's incredible mountain secrets.

Philip Stone

Acknowledgements

The evolution of Island Alpine went through many phases before the final product became reality. It took 15 years of wanton wanderlust through the Vancouver Island mountains to compile sufficent information and photographs to even consider the project. In that endeavour I have to thank deeply the similarly warped individuals with whom I have been fortunate enough to share my passion for the mountains:

My wife Sheahan Wilson, who not only has tackled her share of slide alder but continues to forgive my alpine-absenteeism. Corrie Wright, Greg Shea and Lyle Fast, for just way too many grand adventures to mention. In fostering a love of the mountains which after all is what this is all about, I owe a deep debt of gratitude to Frank and Margaret Dearden and my parents Peter and Patricia Stone.

As the possibility that 'Island Alpine' might actually end up in print became reality, a number of knowledgeable and well-respected Island mountaineeers stepped up to the plate: Lindsay Elms, whom we are all fortunate to have in our midst to chronicle the pioneer work of past and present. Sandy Briggs provided a wealth of information for more obscure places than a person with a day job should rightfully know about. Peter Rothermel, Craig Wagnell, Francis Bruhwiler, Sasha Kubicek, Don Cameron and Chris Sheperd contributed their collective knowledge and photographs, particularly for the South & Central Island areas. Chris Barner and Ryan Stuart chipped in and wielded the mighty red pen. My particular thanks to Rob Wood for penning a poignant foreword.

Lastly thanks to those that helped edit the final proofs especially Susan Lawrence and Sheahan Wilson.

Foreword
by Rob Wood

Everybody knows there are a lot of mountains on Vancouver Island but I didn't know just how many. Nor did I know very much about the relatively few that I was familiar with until I picked up a draft of Island Alpine. What a gargantuan task Philip Stone has accomplished to describe them all! So much has been done and yet we have barely scratched the surface.

Phil and I have quite a bit in common. As well as sharing a passion for the mountains, we are neighbours, eking out a living on 'island time' among the Discovery Islands. We also hail from a part of the world where the mountains have been farmed, hiked and climbed many times over and treading new ground is all but impossible. Consequently we share a deep appreciation of the Vancouver Island alpine where pioneering is de rigeur.

So what exactly is it that is so inviting about this Island alpine that we are willing to trade in the old world charm of the crowded moors, crags and pubs of our homeland? Why is it that so many of us hardened travelers of the world's wild places should choose to settle for this?

For my part, when I first arrived on Vancouver Island almost 30 years ago I was struck not only by the dramatic beauty of the mountain and ocean wilderness, but also by the abundance of opportunities for adventure and the freedom to 'do your own thing'. In fact, in deep wilderness you pretty well have to do your own thing. I soon learned that there is an intrinsic purity about this kind of experience because as everybody else is also happily doing their own thing, nobody makes a big deal about their accomplishments.

Surprised by how little was known about the considerable achievements that had been made, I became increasingly aware of a very unique and refreshing West Coast way of doing things; a very modest, open, laid-back kind of competence and toughness that has evolved from the pioneers and also, I suspect, from the geography. The elements here are so powerful you can't buck 'em. You just get stuck in and go with the flow.

There are so many aspects to the Island Alpine that appeal to a wide variety of interests but I will comment briefly on two that have occupied much of my attention. First, I am tempted into a brief rant about the ice-climbing potential on Mt. Colonel Foster, which is still amazingly undeveloped. Doug Scott described our winter ascent of the Grand Central Couloir as "comparable with the six great North Face routes in the Alps". The ice is better here than in the Rockies because, rather than being frozen water, which is brittle and difficult to sink an ax into, our Island alpine ice is nevé (as is the ice in Scotland), which is formed from snow alternately melting, freezing and compressing into ice which is much softer, more aesthetic and way more user friendly. The East Face of the Colonel is huge and the longest routes are as long as any in the Rockies, with many fine natural lines of all grades waiting to be done.

What is closer to my own experience these days --and probably the icing on the Island alpine cake-- is the hiking terrain found in the pristine alpine meadows and ridges, especially in Strathcona Park. Such a completely unspoiled and diverse array of natural vegetation, in exquisite terrain with crystal-clear streams and pools, is a rare phenomenon and on the Island it is so easily accessible.

Many high mountain areas of the world are pristine above the vegetation zone but most of the so-called 'alpine' areas of the world have been worked by humans and their livestock. These mountains may be beautiful, but they are not pristine. Because the Island alpine has never been affected, it is more than pretty: it has a powerful, welcoming ambiance. Nowhere that I have ever been has given me such a profound sense of being at home. Though considerable effort is often required to get there, the rewards are indeed superlative.

One possible disadvantage of the dispersed West Coast lifestyle is the comparative lack of stimulation that comes from fellow adventurers coming together to share experiences and tell their tales, the climbing 'scene' if you like. Both Phil and I are interested in fostering ways of overcoming this deficiency, particularly as a busy family life leaves less and less time for hanging out at the crags. Story-telling is a huge part of the pub-based climbing scene in Britain and the camp-fire based scene in Yosemite's famous Camp 4 for example. It is to this end that I am proud to support Phil's compilation of this guidebook in the hope of reinforcing and promoting the distinctive Island alpine culture. By spelling out the story we hope to keep it alive and to encourage others to do the same.

XIV　Jan Neuspiel prepares a rappel line on the Summit Traverse of Mt. Colonel Foster

Introduction

Clinging desperately to a wizened cedar branch with feet scratching on the compacted soil high above a rushing creek, you look down to see the creek disappear in a series of cascades to the old-growth forest far below. Clutching bush after bush, you climb higher and higher, out of the vegetation toward the treeline.

Suddenly the exquisite mountain landscape unfolds: Indian paintbrush, asters and lupins adding colour to the heather rimming a beautiful alpine pool in the shade of a cluster of gnarled mountain hemlock and yellow-cedar. All around, as far as you can see, are mountains: the high peaks of Strathcona Park, the tight valleys of the north Island and to the east, the endless Coast Range. And there it is, the peak that is this trip's objective- steep, intimidating and intriguing. So begins another trip into the Vancouver Island alpine.

When rain and wet snow lash the cloud-enshrouded summits, a long hike through one of the Island valleys soothes the yearning for wilderness. When summer soaks the high ground in warmth there is no greater thrill than relaxing after a day's climb to watch the setting sun disappear over the Pacific horizon. Such is the magic of the Vancouver Island mountains, a spell that brings those who have experienced it back time and time again for a new fix.

Among popular Canadian myths, the geography of Vancouver Island must rank up there with Niagara Falls being the highest waterfall. However, as the initiated well know the mountainous interior of Vancouver Island is a wilderness region as beautiful as it is unknown - and includes Canada's highest waterfall! Although only a few kilometres across the Strait of Georgia from their mainland cousins, the Island ranges have a distinctly different character. The juxtaposition of jagged alpine summits, lush temperate rainforest and whitesand beaches pounded by Pacific surf creates a landscape that is unique in the world.

Valerio Faraoni rappelling down the West Couloir on Elkhorn

Huge winter snowfalls dominate the Island mountains, transforming them every year into a wonderland of white. The spring thaw eventually arrives and patches of heather poke through as the snow gradually dissipates. Once liberated from their snowy cloak, wildflowers bloom and the alpine comes alive with colour and the buzz of summer. Cooler nights soon arrive and the first dustings of snow appear on the peaks as the cycle of the seasons continues.

The revolving seasons are a large part of the lure of the Island alpine, with each season being suited to a different style of trip, with an evolving landscape as a backdrop. A matter of a couple of weeks can make the difference between planning a ski tour or a new alpine rock route. This aim of this guidebook is to help plan every outing as a safe and satisfying trip.

Introduction **1**

Mountaineering History of Vancouver Island

The Ellison party nearing the summit of Crown Mountain in 1910.   The Museum at Campbell River #10147

The mountaineering history of the Vancouver Island Ranges is rich with First Nations culture and tradition, magnificent Island scenery, tales of bold first ascents, epic bushwhacks, and lively characters.

For thousands of years First Nation's People criss crossed Vancouver Island on several well worn trading routes such as the Tahsis to Woss Lake Oolichan Grease trail. It is possible that some of the mountain peaks may have been ascended by indigenous people, especially those that are situated on good travelling routes. The abundant food and resources and the far more efficient transportation that the ocean provided made the ocean more of a focus in First Nations' culture. There are however some notable connections with the alpine and First Nations. There is Forbidden Plateau and the legends that surround it and Conuma Peak was an iconic figure and burial place for the Nootka people.

European, Russian and Asian settlers began arriving on the west coast of British Columbia in the late 1700's eager to exploit the region's natural resources. After a hundred years of fur trading, coal mining and settling farmland, the lure of gold and copper began to spark interest in the rugged interior of Vancouver Island. A number of expeditions were dispatched from the booming trading port of Victoria to search for ore deposits throughout the 1800s.

These early forays yielded progressively more and more information about the Island and indeed significant mineral deposits were discovered at a number of locations along the west coast. This brought settlers and their industry to the valleys, mountains and inlets of the Island.

While the map of Vancouver Island began to take shape in the late 1800s there was still very little known about the Island's interior. Finally in 1894 Reverend William W. Bolton led the first of two expeditions from Shushartie at the northern tip of Vancouver Island and criss-crossed an adventurous route all the way south to Victoria. En route Bolton's party climbed Snowsaddle Mountain one of the earliest recorded ascents on the Island.

One of the more significant early ascents on the Island was that of Mt. Arrowsmith. Its prominent location and impressive character would have made it an obvious prize for early European mountaineers arriving on the BC coast in the early 1900s. Although it seems there is no concrete record of who exactly climbed Mt. Arrowsmith for the first time it is safe to assume that it took place before 1910.

2   History

Rev. William Bolton

The expedition report that William Bolton returned with, to the now Provincial capital Victoria, caused great interest among politicians, conservationists, botanists and mountaineers. The transcontinental railway was en route to the west coast of Canada and the powers that be in Victoria saw an opportunity to emulate the great success of the Canadian Pacific Railway's resorts in Banff and Jasper. Bolton's account of the Vancouver Island mountains seemed to describe an obvious location for a National Park an accompanying railway and no less than two hotels, one at Buttle Narrows and one at the confluence of Cervus Creek and the Elk River.

To research the matter further the Minister of Lands, Price Ellison, set off to explore the area on July 7, 1910 with a party of twenty three including his daughter, 20 year old Myra Ellison from Campbell River. Ellison's party travelled up the Campbell River lake chain and were making their way westward when they spied Crown Mountain. They settled on Crown Mountain as their objective and made it to the summit on July 29, 1910. The vista southward from Crown Mountain moved the Minister to decree the area a park and so Strathcona Park came to be.

In August of 1912 the legendary Arthur Oliver Wheeler then president of the Alpine Club of Canada led an expedition from Campbell River to climb the 'Strathcona Matterhorn'. On August 21st 1912 Wheeler and his summit party of nine (A.O.'s son Oliver Wheeler, Albert MacCarthy, D.A. Gillies, A.R. Hart, J.R. Robertson, H.O. Frind, L.C. Wilson and F.A. Robertson) ascended the Northwest Ridge from the Elk River to the summit and christened the peak 'Elkhorn'.

As plans moved forward for the development of Strathcona Park the need for a detailed survey became apparent. Col. Reginald Thomson who was overseeing road construction from Campbell River to Buttle Lake commissioned W.W. Urquhart to lead a survey party along with photographer W.R. Kent. Together Urquhart, Kent and a young immigrant Einar Anderson travelled over, through and to the top of almost every major feature in the park during the summers of 1913 and 1914. They named many of the rivers and peaks and their own names will forever be associated with the mountains of Strathcona Park.

After the meticulous exploration of Strathcona by Urquhart and Kent a period of relative inactivity ensued until the 1930s. The onset of the First World War had seen the elaborate development plans for Strathcona shelved and instead the government turned to the resources of the park to assist with the war effort.

ACC Party on first ascent of Elkhorn, 1912.
(Whyte Museum of the Canadian Rockies V14/AC 328P - 12, Photo: H Frind)

Syd Watts on Mt. Arrowmith   photo: Syd Watts

Access was another factor and climbing activity was concentrated around the Comox Valley both for this reason and because of the relatively high population of the valley communities (Campbell River was a twinkle in Father time's eye until the 1950s).

A second survey in 1934-38 led by Norman Stewart, to gather data for the National Topographical Series maps, generated renewed interest in Strathcona. The accuracy of the information gathered by Stewart is attested to in the fact that many of the readings are still used on the 1:50,000 map series today.

Stewart's measurements of the Golden Hinde, a.k.a. the Rooster's Comb, confirming it as the highest summit on the island prompted Comox Valley mountaineer Geoffrey Capes to attempt what he thought was to be the first ascent in 1937. Capes led frequent trips from his home in Courtenay to the Comox Glacier and climbed many of the peaks around it and the Cliffe Glacier in the early 30s.

Approaching from Buttle Lake up the Phillips Creek valley using a trail marked by Stewart's team who were still working in the area Capes along with Sid Williams and Roger Schjelderup caught up with Stewart on the lower flanks of the mountain. It was then that they were informed that Stewart and his assistant Dan Harris had climbed to the summit of the Rooster's Comb the day before. They graciously accepted Harris' offer to guide them up the next day to make what they still believed to be the second ascent.

In a twist of fate it wasn't until the 1990s that the truth of the first ascent of the Golden Hinde came to light. In researching his historical perspective of the Vancouver Island mountains 'Beyond Nootka' Lindsay Elms interviewed Einar Anderson who had accompanied Urquhart and Kent on their 1913-1914 survey as a teenager. Anderson recounted how he and Kent had in fact climbed the mountain twenty some years prior in 1913 or 1914.

It was members of Norman Stewart's survey party that lay claim to the first significant ascent of Mt. Colonel Foster. In 1936 Alfred Slocomb and Jack Horbury possibly accompanied by Bill Bell climbed to the top of the south east Peak. There has been debate over the years as to which summit these men in fact reached. Some say the south east peak, others argue the slightly higher south west peak while some wouldn't be surprised if they had made it to the main summit. The current thinking seems to confirm that Slocomb and his cohorts climbed the south east peak.

Victoria Peak saw its first recorded ascent by a party led by Otto Winning and Syd Watts in the 1950s. Watts went on to become a pivotal figure in the climbing and exploration history of Vancouver Island roaming over much of its territory, claiming numerous first ascents in the process and becoming a founding member of the Island Mountain Ramblers.

During the 1950s and 1960s a lot of attention was focused around Mt. Colonel Foster. Its untrod summit was a lure for many and various parties tried their hand at different routes on the mountain. The Bitterlich brothers Ulf and Adolf attempted the Snow Band Route in 1955. Hugh and Ferris Neave along with Karl Ricker made a spirited climb to the south summit from the west side up the West Couloir amidst foul weather in July 1957. They believed at the time they may have made it to the main summit but clouds hid the higher summit from view and they descended none the wiser.[2]

Finally in 1968 Mike Walsh made an extraordinary solo ascent of Mt. Colonel Foster along the summit ridge from the north to the main summit and then on to the upper glacier from where he descended down the west side of the mountain. Walsh's achievement reaching the most challenging of the Island's major unclimbed summits will stand as one of the pivotal moments in alpine climbing on Vancouver Island. His ascent along with Ron Facer, Barrie McDowell and Steve Todd's first ascent of Rambler Peak in July 1964 heralded the start of a 'golden age' of Island alpine climbing. During the 1970s and 80s with all the major summits having been climbed, attention became focused on progressively more challenging routes.

Mike Walsh continued to be one of the driving forces behind this alpine revolution, climbing numerous fine lines all over the Island mountains during the early 1970s. Walsh's resumé includes the South Ridge of Elkhorn with Tom Volkers in 1970, the North Buttress and traverse of Rambler in 1975 and the South Face of the North Tower and the Snow Band route on Mt. Colonel Foster with Joe Bajan in 1973 and 1974 respectively.

Despite the activity of Island locals a true plum was poached by Coast Range legend Dick Culbert who along with Fred Douglas and Paul Starr climbed the now classic East Face on Mt. Colonel Foster (a.k.a. the Culbert Route) in 1972. Culbert's ascent of the East Face was a seminal event and the subsequent publication of Culbert's guide to South West BC began to shine light on the Island peaks.

Through the mid to late 70s Joe Bajan took the helm setting new standards for alpine routes on the island with bold lines on the higher peaks, climbing the North Ridge of Elkhorn in 1972 with Tom Muirhead, Dave Smith and Stuart Wazny. Bajan teamed up with Peter Busch in June 1977, climbing the North Face of Elkhorn.

In January 1978 Bajan along with Ross Nichol made the first winter ascent of Mt. Colonel Foster climbing the striking 1,000 metre Direttissima over three days., an epic climb which saw Nichol completing the route with a single crampon and a hair raising descent off the mountain.

Bajan also made a bold solo of the Grand Central Couloir on the Colonel and with Paul McEwan made the first ascent of the North Ridge of the Golden Hinde a route still unlikely to have been repeated.

Perry Beckham and Scott Flavelle made a rare appearance on Vancouver Island in August 1977 establishing one of the finer short routes on Mt. Colonel Foster, the North Buttress of the North Tower. This route takes in some of the best alpine rock on the island providing all the atmosphere of climbing on the Colonel without the commitment of the longer east face routes.

Sparked perhaps by the imminent publication of Bruce Fairley's 'Guide to Hiking and Climbing in Southwestern BC' John Gresham, Don Newman and Jim Sandford ascended the South Face of the Golden Hinde in 1983.

The extension of the Island Highway from Sayward to Port Hardy and the improvement of the Pacific Rim Highway 4 opened up much more of the Island alpine to exploration. Rick Eppler, Rob MacDonald, Wendy Richardson, Sandy Briggs and Don Berryman Victoria based mountaineers and Alpine Club of Canada

Ross Nichol on the first winter ascent of Mt. Colonel Foster, climbing Direttissima.   photo: Joe Bajan

6 Rambler Peak from above Elk Pass in winter.

Greg Child on the first winter ascent of the Grand Central Couloir, Mt. Colonel Foster.   photo: Doug Scott

members became key figures in a campaign of exploration. This very active group have made many first ascent forays all over Vancouver Island from the late 1970s to the present day.

A number of excellent, visionary routes were ascended by Campbell Riverites Chris Barner, Doug Lee and Paul Rydeen during the 1980s and 90s. Barner was pivotal to this development establishing a number of fine lines on Mt. Septimus-Rousseau, Mt. Haig-Brown, Victoria Peak and Mt. Albert Edward among others.

This was matched by a period of intense activity on Matchlee Mountain near Gold River, spearheaded by the Put brothers John and Fred. Taking advantage of the proximity of Matchlee to their new home town and the ever encroaching logging roads to its base the Put brothers turned the mountain into something of their own personal alpine playground. Their activity began with the East Ridge in 1983 and then in June and July of 1985 John and Fred Put established routes on both the North West Ridge and North Buttress of Matchlee Mountain.

The Put's activity on Matchlee did not go unnoticed and in July 1986 Rick Johnson and Don Newman made a foray to the massif establishing the Fickle of Pickle. In January the following year Johnson and Newman returned to put up the first of the mountain's winter lines up the North Couloir.

It was at this time that Mt. Colonel Foster saw one of its more celebrated climbs completed with Greg Child, Doug Scott and Rob Wood's winter ascent of the Grand Central Couloir in January 1985.[5]

To the north, Victoria Peak saw two excellent climbs with Rick Johnson's lead of the North Face in winter closely followed by Greg Foweraker and Don Newman's ascent of the North East Buttress the next summer.

One of the few comparable faces to Mt. Colonel Foster's East Face is the South West Face of Rugged Mountain. In June 1987 Sandy Briggs and Don Berryman, taking advantage of radically improved logging road access to the Haihte Range put up the first route on this striking face. Two years later in 1989 a variation was established by Rick Johnson and Don Newman.

In 1988 Greg Foweraker and Peter Croft made a speedy crossing of the complete Summit Traverse of Mt. Colonel Foster in a matter of hours as part of a larger attempt to enchain all the peaks of the Elk River.

Attention remained focused on the Colonel with the first new summer route on the east face in over a decade put up with Phil Stone and Sarah Homer's ascent of Cataract probably the longest face route on Vancouver Island. The following summer Stone along with Chris Lawrence and Corrie Wright climbed the twin buttress to right of the Culbert Route on the North East Summit calling the line Into the Mystic.[6] Stone continued

Phil Stone on the first ascent of 'Into the Mystic'.
photo: Chris Lawrence.

a period of intense new route development with a variety of partners establishing routes on King's Peak, Big Den Mountain, Elkhorn, Mt. Tom Taylor and Victoria Peak throughout the 1990s. In February 1993 Stone teamed up with Chris Barner and Robin Slieker making the coveted first winter ascent of the Golden Hinde, the island's highest peak. Almost a decade later in January 2003 Phil Stone, Cameron Powell and Ryan Stuart made the long overdue first winter ascent of Rambler Peak.

Other activity during this time included Chris Barner's ascent with longtime partner Paul Rydeen of the West Buttress of Rambler Peak in July 1990. The Put brothers made a first ascent on Colonel Foster's North Tower, Lost Boys in 1989.

Many of these characters were also responsible for establishing the sport climbing area at Crest Creek which now boasts over 200 excellent rock climbs along with other lesser known areas at Tennent Lake and Marblerock Canyon.

Route development has kept a steady pace throughout the late 1990s notably by the Waters twins Mike and John who waged a quiet, productive campaign on several Strathcona summits. At Mt. Cain Paul Kendrick and Tim Saukko's established several fine summer and winter routes on this sporty, accessible peak.

Sceptre on the north west face of Victoria Peak was climbed by Curtis Lyon and Phil Stone in August 1997 and Jan Neuspiel and Andrew Finlay made a ground breaking ascent of Finnegan's Buttress which finally confirmed that there is a major granite face on Mt. Tom Taylor.

In August 1998 Lindsay Elms and Keith Wakelin made a lightening fast approach and ascent of the Golden Hinde in just under 24 hours from Westmin-Boliden via Phillips Ridge. Elms' and Wakelin's feat opens up a tangent of mountaineering accomplishment, one where speed and endurance parallel and at times go hand in hand with technical achievement. Elms

Chris Barner and Robin Slieker on Phillips Ridge en route to winter ascent of the Golden Hinde.

has carried his brand of rapid fire climbs and traverses to numerous island peaks matching this energy only with his energy in compiling historical accounts of Vancouver Island exploration of which he is our premier authority.

The new millennium was heralded by Mike Norton and Scott Jackson who climbed a new line up the South Ridge of Victoria Peak. Mt. Colonel Foster returned to the forefront of Island alpinism in August 2001 with John & Mike Waters and Aaron Hamilton's bold and scary creation 'X-Rated' which climbs the grey scar left by the landslide on the Colonel's North Tower. The Waters twins returned to the Colonel the following year to put up a direct start to Cataract, calling the variation 'Expressway'. This start bypasses a particularly thrilling rappel on the original line and opens up Cataract, via Expressway as one of the Island's finest routes.

With the publication of this guidebook doubtless there will be a run on new route development in the coming years (the Vancouver Island Top Tens listed on pages 38-39 may become the most thumbed spread in this book!). There remains an almost infinite number of possible routes to be climbed in the Vancouver Island mountains and some Canadian classics still awaiting. There are even several large alpine faces that still don't have a single route gracing them and a number of bold lines that have been attempted but so far remain incomplete.

The coming years promise to continue to be an exciting period for alpine exploration on Vancouver Island.

Suggested Reading

The following books and periodicals offer a more in depth account of various aspects of Vancouver Island exploration and mountaineering.

• **Beyond Nootka** - A Historical Perspective of Vancouver Island Mountains by Lindsay Elms ISBN 0-9680159-0-5
A thoroughly researched book detailing the early history of European exploration on Vancouver Island. Profiles six of the more prominent peaks on the island. Excellent read complemented by a regularly updated web site: www.members.shaw.ca/beyondnootka

• **Strathcona: A History of British Columbia's First Provincial Park** by Wallace Baikie with Rosemary Phillips ISBN 0-919537-29-4

• **Towards the Unknown Mountains** by Rob Wood ISBN 0-919537-18-9
An autobiographical account of Island mountaineer Rob Wood's adventures with friends and family throughout the Coast Mountains and literally around Vancouver Island.

• **Pushing The Limits** by Chic Scott ISBN 0-921102593
The definitive story of Canadian mountaineering.

• **Island Bushwhacker** - journal of the Vancouver Island Section of the Alpine Club of Canada. Read as many back issues as you can find!

• **Canadian Alpine Journal** - annual of the Alpine Club of Canada.

Mike Waters on the wonderfully exposed arete of Cataract, after climbing Expressway.   photo: John Waters

10   Shea Wilson amongst Vancouver Island's highest alpine terrain, above Elk Pass, Strathcona Park.

About The Island Alpine

The Terrain

The topography of Strathcona Park and the mountain areas of Vancouver Island are characterized by steep forested valleys, high connecting ridges and craggy summits. Typically ascents into the alpine start with one of several scenarios. In Strathcona the park's network of trails aids access to the high country with trails either climbing in a series of switchbacks up a hillside to the treeline such as the Phillips Ridge trail, or following a river course up a valley to gain the alpine at the head of the watershed just like the Elk River Trail.

Elsewhere outside of parks and along the park boundaries, access is usually dictated by the route logging roads take in the vicinity of the desired objective. Recent initiatives by the Ministry of Forests have led, under the guise of 'environmental sensitivity', to the decommissioning or 'debuilding' of many roads that have historically been used for alpine access. It pays to obtain copies of logging road maps from the appropriate company in a given area and phone their engineering division for up to date information on current road conditions. Be aware that a road marked on a map is no indication of its drivability or even hikability!

In the absence of trail access be prepared for some dense vegetation in the zone between 3,000 and 4,000 ft. Thick undergrowth of blueberry, rhododendron and slide alder can try the will of all but the most determined climber as its downhill nap resists forward motion with every step.

However you begin your trip the approach will bring its rewards at treeline around 4,500 ft. Above here you enter the Mountain Hemlock zone and the sub-alpine. The lush rainforest of the valleys and lower slopes gives way to a stark but exquisitely beautiful landscape. Closer to the west coast, for example near Mt. Bate, or in particularly rugged terrain such as around Landslide Lake the treeline may be as low as 3,500 ft.

This is where the magic of the Island alpine is found. During the summer months the open ridges are carpeted with low heathers and dotted with small clumps of gnarled mountain hemlocks, and yellow cedars. Here and there, still ponds rimmed with wildflowers create the illusion of one having stepped into a Japanese garden. By fall the vegetation has ignited in a myriad of hues adding further to the magic. Of course during winter and spring much of this lies hidden under a thick carpet of snow.

Hiking higher through the sub-alpine the vegetation dwindles as you approach the glaciated and upper mountain alpine tundra zone. Generally above 5,000 ft expect to be travelling in mountainous terrain within this zone. The features you will find are listed below.

Typical Vancouver Island sub-alpine meadows on the approach to Crown Mountain, Strathcona Park.

About the Island Weather

Situated between the open Pacific Ocean and the vast BC Coast Range mountains, Vancouver Island's weather is influenced by moist air off the ocean and drier continental air from the mainland.

Winters are mild and wet with occasional periods of outflow conditions when cold dry air from the BC Interior surges down the mainland inlets bringing clear skies and freezing temperatures. Most of the annual precipitation that falls on the alpine falls as snow. The immense winter snowpack is the single biggest variable to be encountered in the Vancouver Island mountains. Snowpacks of 30 ft are normal and produce a mini ice age every six months. Winter temperatures in the alpine vary between 5°C and -10°C. In the alpine the best ice climbing conditions usually occur between December and February. Good low elevation ice climbing conditions are very rare with the last such winter being 1989.

Island creeks swell quickly after heavy rain.

Summers are warm with occasional rainy periods at any time. Temperatures rarely exceed 30°C and are often very comfortable for hiking and climbing. Lightning is rare on the west coast as a whole but when electrical storms do form they can be particularly violent lasting many hours, often at night. The best months for summer climbing are July to October.

The west coast of Vancouver Island receives over twice the annual precipitation of the eastern part. If a forecast predicts precipitation you would like to avoid then destinations in the Beaufort Range or East Strathcona may help your chances of staying dry.

Online check in at: **weatheroffice.ec.gc.ca**

Winter sees the Island alpine blanketed in snow, here the Elk River.

The Vegetation

If seasonal snow cover is the widest spanning variable for travel conditions in the alpine then the vegetation is the biggest variable encountered below treeline. The natural processes of forest growth and succession are greatly complicated on Vancouver Island by the removal of forest cover by logging activity. It is important to understand the types of natural vegetation zones and the cycles of logging activity to make off-trail travel as smooth as possible.

The ideal scenario for off-trail travel is mature old-growth forest of Douglas Fir, Western Hemlock and Red Cedar between an elevation of 1,000 and 3,000 ft. Very often within this zone undergrowth is limited because of the the shade cast by the tree canopy. Travel is fast and only hindered by some fallen branches and rotting logs.

On the other end of the spectrum are scenarios like avalanche paths and recent (3-10 year old) clearcuts. Here avalanches or logging remove the old-growth trees which are replaced by thick bushes like slide alder, salmonberry, devil's club and salal. Travel in this terrain can be extremely difficult, even dangerous and should be avoided if possible.

Between these two scenarios are many stages and types of forest growth. Regenerating forest may have piles of charred, rotting logs from slash fires lit after logging. An area where a forest fire burned may now be choked by six foot high fir saplings covered in dew like carwash rollers. Logging roads which were used by heavy machinery are now deactivated and covered in a porcupine's coat of alder trees.

The best general advice is to stick to the old-growth as much as you can and look for signs of animal travel to follow. Often bear, deer, elk and other large animals wear good paths through the forest, although they don't clip the branches! Avoid recent and regenerating clearcuts by looking for points where old-growth reaches any road. Stick to the ridges and keep out of the gullies. Anticipate creeks by reading the topo map carefully. Use creeks and gullies as references in the forest when wider views are restricted.

Lastly remember when bushwhacking in dense undergrowth stay in visual contact with everyone in your group but travel far enough apart to avoid getting bushwhipped. Consider eye protection and pack rain gear if expecting a thrash even if it is sunny. The dew'll soak ya!

The infamous Devil's Club. Ouch!!

New Route Information

New route information or corrections and updates for any access details are welcome for subsequent revisions and new editions of Island Alpine. Route information is best supplied using two photographs. One clean photo for scanning and inclusion in the book and a second picture or photocopy which may have the route marked on in ink. Don't write on the back of prints, use Postits™ or sticky labels instead. Pictures that work best are horizontally composed and of a sufficently wide enough angle to show the route's location on the mountain. A brief written description is also required giving route name, length, grade and any other pertinent information like access details.

Information can be submitted to Wild Isle Publications, PO Box 482 Heriot Bay BC V0P 1H0

For regular postings of new & updated route info log on to www.wildisle.ca/islandalpine

Winter Ascents

Winter ascents of summits are recorded between December 21st and March 21st. Some winter routes have been climbed outside of these dates which seems reasonable as the intent of the first ascentists was to 'winter climb'. However for an 'official' winter ascent of a peak it must take place during winter and the dates mentioned above.

Island Glaciers

Like most of British Columbia's mountains the island peaks have been shaped by successive ice ages. On Vancouver Island only remnants of these once vast ice sheets remain. They cling to only the shadiest of slopes and the bottoms of north facing cirques. There are a few exceptions where glaciers retain something of their former majesty. The largest icefields on the island are only a few square kilometres in area and found, in descending order of size, on Mariner Mountain, Rugged Mountain and the Haihte Range, Comox Glacier, Cliffe Glacier, Mt. Tom Taylor, Big Interior Mountain and Mt. Septimus/Rousseau. The order of this list is debatable.

Generally the immense winter snowpack, some years as deep as 30 ft (8 m), keeps crevasses well covered until late June or even July. As summer progresses the seasonal winter snow melts away exposing the glacial ice underneath. Snow bridges become perilously thin and crevasses start to yawn wide open. By September or October most island glaciers will be exposed ice requiring crampons to cross or climb safely. At any time of year be prepared for glacier travel if your objective includes one. A familiarity with route finding on glaciers and crevasse rescue techniques are essential tools of the mountaineers trade.

Typical late summer glacier conditions on Big Interior Mountain

The location of the larger icefields is due to their proximity to the west coast inlets which cleave their way inland from the open Pacific. In some cases the inlets almost cut right across Vancouver Island allowing moisture laden weather systems to reach the high peaks that then bar their way. The Comox Glacier is fed by Alberni Inlet, Mariner Mountain by Bedwell Sound and the Rugged Glacier by Tahsis Inlet.

Regardless of their size the island glaciers still hold all the potential hazards of glaciers the world over so don't treat crossing one lightly. Crevasses, serac fall, bergschrunds and moats are just some of the obstacles that may be encountered albeit at a smaller scale than elsewhere in BC.

Sadly there is little in the way of steep glacier ice for year round ice climbing. Most of the glaciers on the island are on moderate or low angle terrain in the base of deep cirques. Hidden in some of the glaciers are deep crevasses and sink holes. Some on the Rugged Glacier up to 60 ft deep have been climbed by rappelling into the bottom! If you do have a hankering for some summertime ice check out the terminal seracs of some of the larger glaciers. These are pretty hazardous features though. The best bets for late season ice are in the gullies and couloirs like the Grand Central Couloir on Colonel Foster.

Island Ice Climbing

Vancouver Island isn't known as a great water ice climbing destination. It is a rare winter indeed when freezing temperatures last long enough for any significant low-elevation ice to form. The last really significant freeze was in February 1989 when Upper Campbell Lake froze completely. When a deep freeze does arrive however, the quality of the ice produced is second to none.

It is the mild West Coast temperatures that helps high quality ice to form. Repeating cycles of freeze and thaw along with heavy wet snowfalls can mature Island ice into a sublime plastic nevé.

Some of the areas to look for good low elevation ice include: Comox Lake, Upper Campbell Lake, Buttle Lake, the White Rdige and Highway 28 right to the head of Muchalet Inlet. There are plenty of other places but these areas have good access.

In a more typical winter you will have to look at least as high as 3,000 ft (1,200 m) to find any ice in condition. The best locations all round for Island ice climbing are at: Mt. Arrowsmith along Pass Main, Boston Lake below Mt. Becher, Mt Washington, and at Tennent Lake. While these areas offer waterfall climbing the very best of Vancouver Island ice is found high on the north faces of the mountains.

Mt. Colonel Foster is home, by far and away, to the most challenging winter climbing on the Island. The 3,500 ft (1,000 m) north-east face of the Colonel is scored by several huge couloirs and numerous other more complex lines. Only a few routes have been established on this incredible peak with many new ones waiting to be done.

If you are looking for winter climbing of a less commiting nature try Mt Arrowsmith, Big Den Mountain, the Haihte Range, King's Peak. Each of these peaks have classic gully climbs of just a few hundred metres giving a great taste of Vancouver Island's winter alpine climbing.

There are a lot of great routes all over the Island waiting for discovery in the right conditions at all elevations. Some have almost obscene access difficulties but at the same time incredible climbing. Mt Cobb is one such peak where three parallel waterfalls have been seen formed as thick icefalls cascading off the north side of the mountain in a series of vertical steps. Victoria Peak is another mountain wating for more winter lines to be established. Wait for the next edition of Island Alpine for more news!

Curtis Lyon on Boston Falls, Mt Becher.

Island Geology

Vancouver Island has a fascinating geological make-up and is of great interest to geologists and climbers alike. It is thought that Vancouver Island, which sits on its own mini continental plate, once resided alongside the islands of the Indonesian archipelago. The distinct geology of the Island from the nearby mainland seems to bear this out. On the Island can be found sandstone, limestone, basalt and granite, a wider diversity of rock than is found across the Strait of Georgia on the coastal BC mainland.

It is the volcanic basalt that is the most prevalent rock type found in the mountains. This rock is characterized by excellent friction, a solid nature and few natural cracks (and thus protection). The higher mountains, Golden Hinde, Mt. Colonel Foster, Elkhorn and Victoria Peak are all basaltic. Pillow lava formations can be found on most Island peaks. These lava formations occur when magma rises up under the ocean and is cooled very rapidly by the ocean water. Victoria Peak is the basalt core of an extinct volcano and Warden Peak a secondary volcano. The older outer rock has long since eroded away leaving their sheer basalt walls behind.

Paul Rydeen sampling some typical Island basalt on Earthly Delights, Crest Creek Crags.

The irrepressible Sandy Briggs with the dramatic spires of Victoria and Warden peaks. photo: Peter Rothermel

In the south part of Strathcona Park the landscape is shaped by granite batholoiths which are domes of magma which form under the Earth's surface and cool slowly producing the larger crystals typical of granite. Mt.. Myra, Mt. Thelwood, Mt. Tom Taylor, Splendour Mountain and Moyeha Mountain are all classic examples of batholithic mountains. The alpine ridges throughout South Strathcona Park and in some other parts of the North Island are littered with thousands of granite bluffs for some awesome campside bouldering or cragging.

A treat for island climbers is the sedimentary limestone found around Mt. McBride, notably in Marblerock Canyon and Marble Meadows. The limestone is peppered with bands of flint-like chert which being harder wearing rock protrudes to form a climbing sports surface familiar to climbers at Horne Lake. Sandwiched between impervious layers of basalt the limestone here is riddled with caves and resurgent water tumbles out of the middle of sheer cliff faces, some almost 1,000 ft high.

Island Rock Climbing

The igneous basalt rock which dominates the geology of the majority of Island peaks is also the most frequently found rock type at Island crags. Comox Lake and Crest Creek are two of the more established cragging areas on the Island and the best places to get a taste for the alpine climbing on the high peaks.

The Island basalt offers excellent climbing both at the crags and on the alpine faces. Friction is superb and the rock is very solid with little loose rock on steeper ground- gravel and scree does of course collect on ledges in gullies and lower angle terrain. At the low elevation crags the basalt is prone to heavy moss and lichen growth and almost all the climbs now established were once coated in vegetation of one type or another. A great deal of work has gone into scrubbing and preparing these routes for general consumption. This makes the attraction of clean rock in the alpine all greater.

The main drawback with the basalt is the infrequency of natural protection placements. Many of the sport routes on basalt are bolt protected or at the least a mix of fixed and natural gear. There are very few sport climbs on basalt with purely natural pro.

In the alpine this trend is repeated, although on the whole the more intense forces of nature produce somewhat better natural protection than lower down at the crags. Nevertheless on the basalt faces like Mt. Colonel Foster, Elkhorn, Victoria Peak and Rugged Mountain be prepared for some run out leads albeit on solid positive holds.

Gear that seems to be indispensible includes: mid-size camming units (eg: #2-3 Friends), stoppers and a selection of pitons. To date no bolts have been placed on any alpine routes (although some have been used for rappel stations on descents) and this author would like to propose that this ethic is respected on mountain routes especially within the parks. Whatever your own choice please never add bolts to an existing climb. Among climbing faux pas this would rank as one of the more heinous crimes.

As far as descents go, many of the more technical alpine peaks require rappels. The more popular routes may have stations that are easy to locate but don't take that for granted, become familiar with creative anchor building. Of course always bring plenty of 'tat' to rig your own rappel stations.

Other rock types can be encountered in the Island alpine notably granite in the southern areas of Strathcona Park and to a lesser extent limestone which is scattered randomly at various places all over the Island.

The Island granite is superb but is a largely overlooked climbing resource despite the high quality. Much of the Island granite is found scattered along the alpine ridges of southern Strathcona in 1 to 3 pitch bluffs. Its zenith is the the impressive south face of Mt. Tom Taylor which has a series of 1,000 ft (300 m) buttresses. Any hiking trip by rock climbers to the Mt. Myra and Mt. Thelwood areas should see rock shoes thrown in the pack to at take advantage of the endless bouldering on the maze of granite crags. As to be expected with granite the protection here is superb and if you've climbed at Squamish you're primed for the Island granite experience.

As far as the limestone goes, the most impressive concentration of this climbers dream rock is around Marble Meadows and Marblerock Canyon. Many routes have been climbed here and the quality is second to none. However, in the intrests of preserving the wilderness nature of these areas no reporting of climbs has been done. If you go, enjoy it and keep it to yourself!

Phil Stone taking in some limestone steeps in Marblerock Canyon, Strathcona Park.   Photo: Greg Shea

Island Backpacking

It is the backcountry hiking that brings many visitors to Vancouver Island and in particular to: Strathcona Park, the West Coast Trail, Nootka Island and Cape Scott. The hiking experiences on the Island are among the finest adventures found anywhere.

The Strathcona Park-Clayquot Sound region is home to the largest tract of pristine wilderness on any of Canada's Pacific coast islands and a world-class destination for alpine hiking. The high alpine ridges that divide the deep river valleys found all throughout the Island's mountainous interior present ideal terrain for multi-day alpine treks.

There are a number of recommended traverses and circuits ranging in duration from weekend excursions to ten day expeditions. The ultimate in Island mountain travel is the Vancouver Island Backbone Hiking Route which connects 300 km of travel across alpine ridges, forested valleys, logging roads and river courses between Port Alberni and Port McNeill. More details can be found about the Backbone Hiking Route on page 459.

The rugged character of the mountain summits surrounding the high ridge routes is emulated in the rugged nature of the hiking terrain. Good route finding and navigation skills are essential to travel in the Island backcountry where, for some you may find yourself as much as 3 days travel from a road. However, with the right skills, equipment and physical fitness the wilderness experiences of the Vancouver Island mountains are worth every bit of effort to attain them.

Backcountry travel on the Island may range in experience from hiking clearly worn footpaths along the north ridge of Mt. Burman on a sunnt August morning, to battling with a soaking tangle of slide alder in an early winter sleet storm in the upper Salmon River. One thing all Island adventures share is a level of visual intensity in the surroundings that motivates people from all walks of life to seek more of it! To preserve these wilderness values practice strict no-trace camping.

Watching the great orange orb of the sun sink over the shimmering Pacific horizon looks very similar whether you are jugging granite chickenheads on the south face of Mt. Tom Taylor or returning from a short day hike up Crest Mountain.

The very best of the Island traverses are:

Nimpkish/Tolnay Creek to Tahsis: 6-12 days pg. 384
Elk River-Westmin/Boliden: 5-10 days pg. 248
Mt Albert Edward-Flower Ridge: 6-10 days pg. 160
Mt. Albert Edward-Comox Glacier: 3-6 days pg. 160
Phillips Watershed Traverse: 3-5 days pg. 268
Shepherd Ridge-Flower Ridge: 3-5 days pg. 168
Augerpoint Traverse: 2-4 days pg. 170

Additional Info:
- Hiking Trails III - Northern Vancouver Island & Strathcona Park - (9th ed. 2002 Richard K. Blier, ed.) VITIS

Lesia Kuzyk kickn' back on Mt Landale. photo: Chris Shepard

Island Ski Touring

Vancouver Island receives one of the world's deepest annual snowfalls. Some winters as much as 30 ft. / 8m of snow can accumulate! The abundant snow combined with a generally stable snowpack, mild temperatures and the superb high ridge traverse routes makes for excellent if hard won ski touring trips.

On the down side; Island ski touring means frequently strenuous approaches up steep trails or routes packing skis or snowboard to reach the high snowline, skins gummed up with conifer needles and bark bits, rain storms and incredibly deep dumps of fresh snow taking brutal effort to break trail through.

There are only a few cabins on the whole Island and they play a limited role in winter travel on Vancouver Island. The deep snowpack makes snowcaves a very viable accommodation option but if your route involves a trek up one of the valley trails like the Price Creek Trail then a tent is going to be a must.

While the Island snowpack is generally stable care is always required to keep informed of potential avalanche hazards. There are some notable areas where well used routes are exposed to huge potentail slides particularly during spring thaw when most of the Island avalanche activity occurs. Travel with care anywhere along the Elk River Trail and pay attention to cornices on the high ridges.

Chris Lawrence ski touring near Morrison Spire

But if all this sounds like heaven for you then the rewards are many. The winter snows completely bury the understory vegetation all but eliminating the presence of the dense Island bush, in addition the notoriously intricate and rugged micro-terrain becomes smoothed over with a full load of snow making travel fast and route finding arguably easier than in summer. In clear weather the views of the Island's ice encrusted peaks are dramatic. There are big powder ski/snowboard descents to be discovered and almost guarenteed solitude.

Ski touring should be expanded in this context to include touring with a split snowboard and snowshoeing. Each of these modes of travel have their strengths and times in the Island alpine.

Always check current avalanche forecasts with the Canadian Avalanche Association (www.avalanche.ca), carry self rescue equipment, an avalanche transceiver and get training and practice on their use.

Some of the best Island ski tours are:
Elk River-Westmin/Boliden: 5-10 days   pg. 248
Mt Albert Edward-Flower Ridge: 6-10 days   pg. 160
Mt. Albert Edward-Comox Glacier: 3-6 days   pg. 160
Phillips Watershed Traverse: 3-5 days   pg. 268
Shepherd Ridge-Flower Ridge: 3-5 days   pg. 168
Augerpoint Traverse: 2-4 days   pg. 170

Additional Info:

• Island Turns and Tours - Wild Isle Publications in print spring 2004

20 Phil Sera at a tranquil river bend in a pristine valley of old-growth forest.

Wilderness Travel

Climbers and other backcountry travellers have a special duty to familiarize themselves with, and practice strict no trace camping techniques. By leaving the wilderness untouched by our passage we ensure that the environment endures in as pristine a state as possible. By minimizing our impact on the wildlife, vegetation and terrain we preserve the wilderness integrity of wild places and ensure that others who follow will have an experience comparable to our own.

Please do not light fires, the presence of firepits is unsightly and the collection of firewood at higher elevations places undue pressure on the fragile alpine ecology. The continuing cycles of growth and decomposition are disrupted by burning wood that is destined to die and rot creating new soil for future generations of trees and other vegetation.

Fires are discouraged within Provincial Parks year round. If you do encounter firepits left by those unfamiliar with no-trace ethics, take the time to dismantle them. We must not only ensure our own passage leaves no trace but also take positive action in caring for our diminishing wilderness.

Buy a lightweight campstove and use it for cooking. Extreme care must be exercised when lighting stoves and smoking. A forest fire can be devastating, and many fires start each year through carelessness.

Pack out what you pack in and please take the time to remove any garbage left by others. At the crags please pay particular attention to disposing of tape, chalk spills and cigarette butts.

Dispose of all personal waste with due care to the water supply and do not leave toilet paper or other paper products lying around on the ground. Most trails and other high use areas within the Provincial Parks have outhouses and designated campsites that should be used. In the backcountry pack all soiled toilet paper out, or carry a small tin can which can be used to burn it in a safe manner. Fly in groups should consider flying out their shit. A lined plastic garbage can or bucket with a tight fitting lid works best.

Vancouver Island is one of the wettest places on Earth and water is rarely far away. The mountains of Strathcona are the headwaters of watersheds supplying drinking water for several island communities. The purity of the water supply can be preserved by following some simple measures.

Never wash dishes or yourself with soap, even with so called biodegradable soap, don't drop food scraps in fragile alpine lakes. Pack out food waste and learn to cook only what you need to eat.

Don't swim in lakes with your skin covered in insect repellent or sun tan lotions. Remember that the mountains are the source and headwaters for all the rivers on the Island and any pollutants left here will affect the entire watershed downstream. Toilet waste should be buried in cat holes far from any bodies of water. Human coliform bacteria in water is an increasing global problem. Please help stop the spread of water borne bacteria and disease by defecating responsibly.

Last but not least, please be sparing with flagging tape and cairns especially in the alpine. Many wilderness routes by nature do not require marking and if you found your way, then you can trust that other who follow will figure it out too. You may feel you are helping out those who come after you but remember that they may be seeking the pioneering experience too. Marking routes has its place but please note it is a form of impact and not everyone appreciates the sign of human presence it implies.

Roosevelt Elk browsing in lush sub alpine meadows.

22 Jonathon Bonk makes the final step onto the summit of Rambler Peak.

Using This Guide

How you start planning a trip into any mountain area is first determined by your familiarity with the mountain range in question. If you are familiar with the area, the chances are you have developed a keen interest in certain peaks and a curiosity about others. If you don't know the area then you'll first try to get a sense of what the options are by looking at photographs, chatting with other hikers and climbers or flipping through a guidebook such as this one. Either way at some point you and your group are going to settle on an objective and pick up your copy of Island Alpine.

The first thing to confirm is that the chosen objective is suitable for: the ambitions and technical abilities of your group, the time you have and the prevailing conditions at the time.

Locate your mountain objective from the index and read the peak description, approach details and the climbing route list. The photos and peak description will give a sense of the mountain and may provide a gauge of whether or not the peak appeals to your party. The approach and route descriptions will allow you to judge if there is a route of suitable difficulty within the abilities of everyone in your group. Check the approach details including driving distances to ensure you have enough time to complete the ascent. Pay particular attention to journal references listed under each peak's '**Additional Info**'. Last but not least, check that seasonal conditions are suitable for both the approach and the chosen climbing route.

To ascertain the conditions of the approach divide the approach into these sections. Highway driving, logging road driving, trail hiking, off-trail hiking and climbing route. Measure the distance and estimate the time it will take you from your departure point to the point you either park or leave the highway. Check current highway conditions from weather reports, radio traffic reports or directly from the Ministry of Highways and their contractors.

Next use logging road maps (see Additional Resources p37) and the approach description to plot your course. Call or email the Forest Service District office responsible for the area in question. Ask to speak to someone about current road conditions and closures and describe your route to them. Ask which logging company(s) built and/or maintains the roads you will use. Ask if the Forest Service have any current information about road conditions, logging activity in the area, snow levels and any possible road closures. Contact the relevant logging company offices (see Additional Resources p.39) and ask the same questions. Use the road names and branch numbers from the most recent logging road map you have to make sure you are finding out the right information.

If your approach uses a Forest Service or BC Parks trail, visit either ministry's web site or call their local office for details of current trail conditions. Pay particular attention to bridge conditions, snow levels and specific cautions for your trail.

If your approach does not use a trail then seek general information about current snow levels and pay particular attention to the topo map and approach descriptions to plot your route into the alpine.

During the winter and early spring check current avalanche forecasts and bulletins. Log on to the Canadian Avalanche Association website at: www.avalanche.ca

Check weather forecasts by your usual means. For detailed weather info log on to www.weatheroffice.ec.gc.ca

Read the climbing route information carefully and talk to any climbers you may know who are familiar with the route. Visit www.islandhikes.com and check the discussion forum for threads on your objective. Prepare your equipment accordingly.

Travel Modes

The variation in seasonal snow cover in the island mountains presents a number of options for travel throughout the year.

In high summer through fall expect moderate to little snow cover. Unless planning to travel across any glaciers good hiking boots are all that is required. Consider gaiters off-trail to keep needles and twigs out of your boots.

During the winter, frequent heavy snowfalls blanket the alpine. Travel is best by skis or snowshoes. Don't even consider travelling in the alpine without either between December and April.

As spring arrives the snowpack consolidates and by mid-May travel is usually okay with just boots but ski touring conditions may be good as late as the end of June.

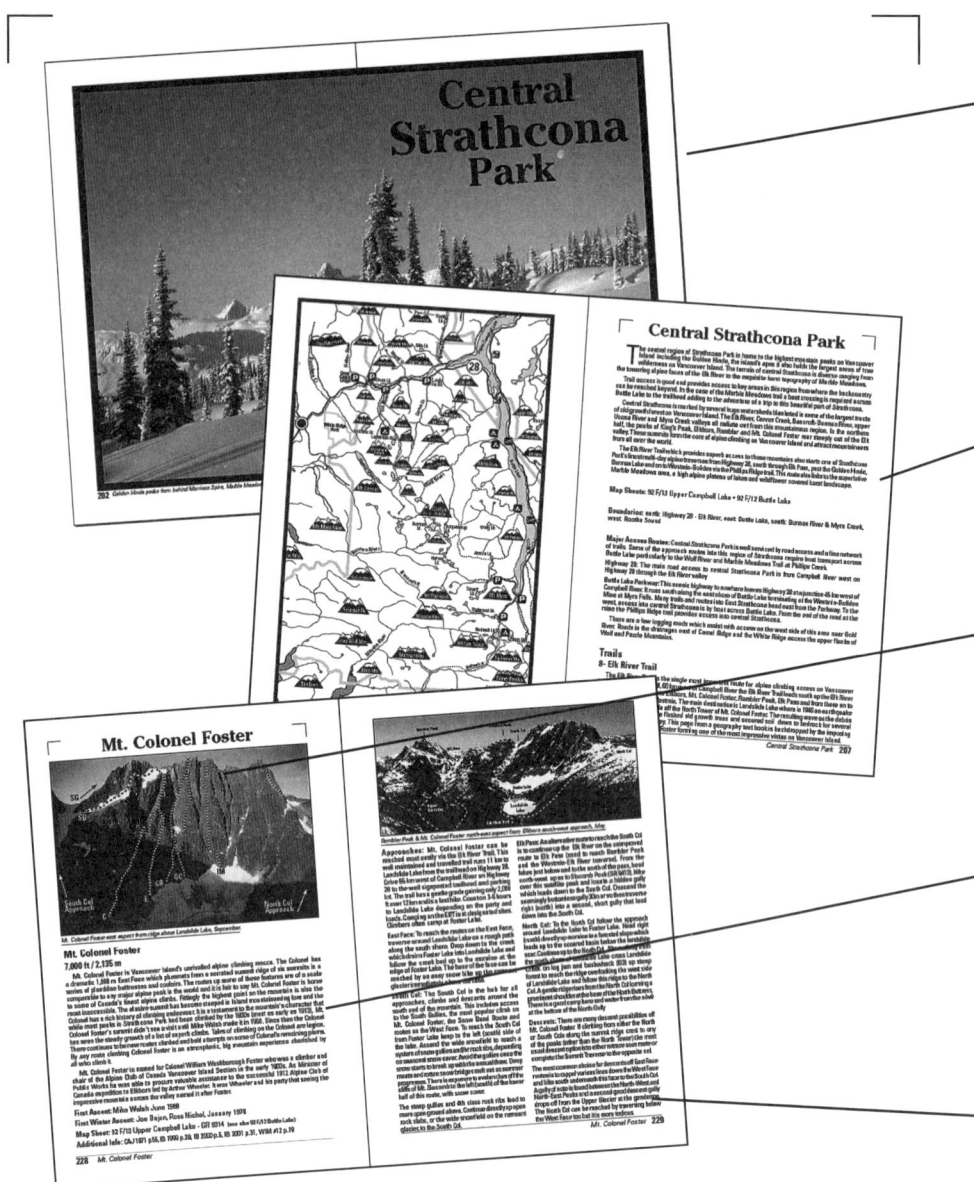

Travel Times

Because travel times vary so widely with season, the fitness level of each group and a whole range of other factors, the use of suggested travel times is minimal in Island Alpine. Instead it is recommended that you use personal experience and a few rules of thumb to gauge how long any particular trip may take you and your party.

Measure the distance of your route on the map with a piece of string and count contour lines to gauge elevation gain and loss. On average expect to travel 4-6 kilometres per hour on trails or open alpine, with an additional 1 hour for each 1,000 ft / 300 m of elevation gain. Descents may take as little as half the time of the approach.

Look for new route info, updates and additions: **wildisle.ca/islandalpine**

24 Using This Guide

Island Alpine is divided into 4 distinct regional sections covering Vancouver Island from south east to north west. These regions are: Southern Vancouver Island, Central Vancouver Island, Strathcona Park and Northern Vancouver Island.

Most of these sections are then further subdivided into chapters logically centred around the geography and transport logistics of the area.

Each section includes a map detailing the region followed by a simple list of the major access routes, applicable map sheets and additional resources.

In addition each chapter starts with a description of the area along with a list of the map sheets covering the region, major access routes and trail descriptions, contact details for local forestry offices and companies and additional resource suggestions.

The area chapters continue with detailed descriptions of each individual mountain within that area. Most peaks are described with one or more photographs showing the peak often from a variety of angles and seasons. Approaches and climbing routes are marked on many of the photographs with dashed or dotted lines (see below).

The details of each peak listed include its official or local name followed by basic facts such as elevation, map sheet and grid reference, a description of the location and character of the mountain along with occasional trivia.

Approach details refer to the major access routes and trail information listed in the relevant chapter introduction. Some approach routes may also refer to approach details of adjacent peaks especially when the mountain is climbed as part of an alpine traverse. The approach details will describe access to the base of any technical routes and in the case of non technical ascents, the route to the summit.

Some peak entries include references to journal articles that may provide valuable, additional information. Abbreviations used are: IB = Island Bushwhacker, CAJ = Canadian Alpine Journal & WIM= Wild Isle Magazine www.wildisle.ca. The value of such background reading can't be emphasized enough.

For the more technical climbing routes, routes are divided by season, either summer or winter and described individually with a reference to the line as illustrated on accompanying photographs, technical grades, length, quality rating, route details and first ascentionists when this information is available.

For more information on grading systems used see the following page.

Legend for Photographs

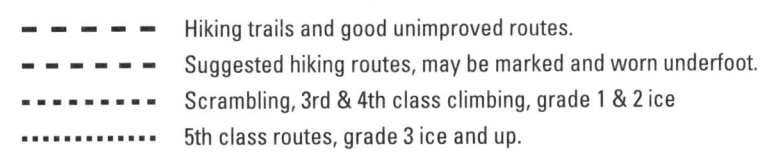

- − − − − − Hiking trails and good unimproved routes.
- − − − − − − Suggested hiking routes, may be marked and worn underfoot.
- · · · · · · · · · · Scrambling, 3rd & 4th class climbing, grade 1 & 2 ice
- · · · · · · · · · · · · 5th class routes, grade 3 ice and up.

Using This Guide

Grading Systems

Several well established grading systems are employed throughout this book to define the technical difficulties encountered on individual climbing routes. As with all descriptive information these grades are only a general guide arrived at most often from the first ascentionists' description. Parties following may encounter varied conditions and may even vary on the route climbed. Treat all grades supplied as subjective.

- **International Alpine Numeral Grade** Is used for all routes of a technical nature, giving an idea of overall commitment and time needed to complete and descend the route.

(I) a climb taking 1 or 2 hours

(II) involves half a day

(III) route requires most of a day to complete and descend

(IV) a long day climb requiring pre-dawn start.

(V) route requires at least one bivouac

(VI) serious multi-day route

- **Yosemite Decimal System** is used to define the technical difficulty of terrain encountered on alpine rock routes, in relation to other routes.

Class 1 - Hiking terrain

Class 2 - Steep hiking off trails often with use of vegetation or rock for handholds.

Class 3 - Rocky scrambling terrain, handholds required with short steep steps. May be exposed to drops below.

Class 4 - Exposed, steep terrain and some tricky moves with handholds. Some parties may use roped belays.

Class 5 - Vertical rock terrain requiring roped belays, protection anchors and running belays otherwise considered 'solo' climbing.

5.0-5.4 - Large foot and handholds akin to climbing a ladder on exposed terrain where a fall may have serious consequences.

5.5-5.8 - More serious terrain with strenuous climbing on positive holds. Ropes and protection required by all but the most confident climbers. The limit of difficulty that can be reliably climbed with full shank mountain boots.

5.9 up - Vertical rock terrain requiring a high level of fitness, climbing consists of small hand and foot holds or very strenuous moves on larger holds. Most parties will use rope belays, considerable protection and rock shoes.

Routes climbed in summer conditions as rock climbs are listed with a star rating, route name, Yosemite Decimal grade, route length in metres and an Alpine grade indicating time and commitment, like this example.

*** North Buttress: 5.8 400 m (III)

The following suffixes are used when applicable; R-runout, X-no protection, S-serious lead. The technical grade is given for the hardest single pitch and further pitch grades are given in the detailed route description if applicable.

- **Scottish Ice Climbing** grading system is to describe the difficulty of technical winter routes.

1 - Steep snow walking terrain. An ice axe is essential in summer conditions with crampons to be considered in late summer fall, especially if there is bare glacial ice exposed. Skiable terrain in winter. Akin to 3rd class in Yosemite system for summer conditions.

2 - Routes with short steep sections and minor pitches, two tools to be considered and crampons or step cutting required. Like 4th class in the Yosemite system for summer conditions.

3 - Routes with at least one steep ice pitch and several minor ones. Sustained ridge climbing, similar to 5th class in Yosemite system for summer conditions.

4 - Climbs with several long steep ice pitches with sustained climbing of a serious nature. Mixed ice and rock terrain to be expected.

5 - Long difficult routes with sustained vertical ice. Mixed terrain to be technical but well protected.

6 - Technically exacting routes. Multiple rope lengths of continuously vertical ice. Mixed terrain to be technically very hard and poorly protected and so on...

A distinction between pure waterfall climbs and those of an alpine or mixed character is made using the prefixes WI and AI respectively. e.g.:

*** Happy Warrior: WI4+ 90 m

** The Great Escape: AI3 400 m (III)

As to be expected alpine ice routes include an alpine numeral grade for commitment and time.

Ryan Stuart up close and personal with some fine Island bush on Merry Widow Mountain.

• **Island Bush Grade** helps define the unique experiences encountered while travelling through the vegetation of Vancouver Island.

B1 - Open old-growth, knee height or smaller vegetation. Travel remains at trail speed.

B2 - Light chest high vegetation, travel not impeded but slowed. No thorns, expect a dew bath.

B3 - Dense, thorn free, head height vegetation. Travel impeded and route finding becomes affected. Vegetation may assist progress at times.

B4 - Thick, entangled vegetation requiring constant negotiation. Travel constricted with frequent obstacles often on steep grades. Thorns, fallen logs and slash/burn debris to be expected.

B5 - A higher plane of existence, where the mind transcends the body trapped in the painful, primordial struggle for bio-global supremacy between plant and animal.

Star Quality Rating

To give a relative idea of a route's quality, 1 to 3 stars are allocated to routes where an opinion was available. Absence of a star is not necessarily an indication of its quality, no opinion may have been possible. The rating is given relative to other routes on the same mountain or neighbouring peaks.

Photographs In This Guide

The photographs used throughout this guidebook are chosen to show the hiking and climbing routes detailed as clearly as possible. Although in some cases photographs are selected just for inspiration because they show the peak from an interesting angle.

The huge variation in seasonal snow cover creates widely varying conditions in the alpine throughout the year. This should be taken into consideration when looking at the photographs. Many of the Vancouver Island mountains look far more impressive during the winter and spring with their mantle of snow than during the summer or fall. The month each picture was taken is mentioned in the caption to help put the picture in seasonal perspective.

In some cases, where space was limited or another photo was not available, a photo taken in one season (say winter) may be used to show routes climbed in an opposite season (summer). Often winter photos have been deliberately chosen to show summer routes beacuse the detail is clearer in black and white. All photos are by the author unless otherwise noted.

Grid References

Extensive use of grid references appears throughout this guidebook. Grid references relate to the blue grid overlaying the 1:50,000 government topo map sheets. Most references are simple four figure coordinates appear in the text as: GR 8941

The grid reference is split into two parts. So in our example 89 and 41. Grid references are read with eastings first and northings last. Reading across the top row of numbers look east to 89. Then cross reference that column with row 41 from the northings down the left edge of the map to find the square contained at 8941. The reference indicates Eena Lake.

In a six figure reference such as; GR 879378 the numbers are still split in half 879 and 378. The first two figures in each trio work as explained above. The third digit (9 and 8) refer to a further factor of ten division of the square at those coordinates. 879378 is the six figure grid reference for the summit of Horseshoe Mountain.

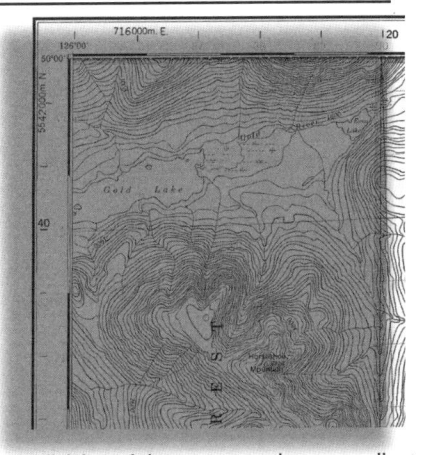

Using This Guide **27**

A Word on Ethics

To start with I didn't think a section on ethics was necessary in this guide. Who is to say what should and shouldn't happen and what is right and what is wrong? We are blessed with such an abundance of mountainous terrain and climbing possibilities that the question may be asked "does it really matter?". In the end I think it does matter. Climbers are proud people and we have much to be proud of. The accomplishments of climbers are respected by their peers and revered by the general public. Our heroes are people who have been bold and survived but what makes truly great climbers is that they are bold and survive with style. The culture that surrounds climbing is also something to be proud of and like it or not ethical debate has been a large part of climbing culture since its inception and should be passed on along with the bowline.

What is important about an ethical debate is that it takes place. By airing opinions, the wheat is separated from the chaff. Who could believe on Vancouver Island that on certain crags in Europe not only is bolting completely taboo but the use of chalk discouraged. In a contemporary North American context these issues seem almost laughable. Freedom of expression is the law. However, climbers are very privileged people, we often travel in remote areas where few if any have gone before. It is our duty to ensure our passage is light and in that, there is style.

So what are our Island ethics? What are the issues that face Island climbers? Well there are the obvious points about no-trace camping, leaving nothing but footprints and taking nothing but pictures. But what about air access, bolting and ?.

It is my own opinion that climbers' conduct should be appropriate to the area in question. For example it is difficult to argue that bolting is a form of environmental impact at Crest Creek where a major highway, logging road, two powerlines and a river diversion pipeline all pass below the crags. Similarly at Tennent Lake where a washed out cat track and concrete dam have completely altered the integrity of the surrounding landscape to make no mention of the ugly gash at the bottom of the hill! However on the backcountry peaks deep within Strathcona a no bolting ethic should prevail. It is worth mentioning that under no circumstances should bolts be added to any established routes thereby undermining the spirit of the first ascent.

As for air access I believe personally that there is no place for helicopters and other aircraft in Strathcona Park. The raison d'etre of the park is to protect wilderness and any mechanized activity in the park is at odds with this mandate. And why should there need to be aircraft flights through the park, there are plenty of places outside of parks for this kind of activity. Only 13% of British Columbia is parkland that leaves an awful lot of room for flying.

In short ethics amount to a discussion of what is and isn't appropriate. If a climber takes a particular action, the rest of us are going to talk about it!

Soaking in the view of Mt. Colonel Foster at Landslide Lake.

Backroad Mapbooks
the start of every adventure!

6 BC Titles

Fishing BC
an evolution in angling!

5 Titles

Available at leading book retailers
For more information call

604-438-FISH(3474) or 1-877-520-5670

or visit us at

www.backroadmapbooks.com

Hints & Cautions

Trails versus Routes

One of the most important distinctions to understand for backcountry travel on Vancouver Island is the colloquial difference between a 'trail' and a 'route'.

It is generally accepted that a 'trail' is a purpose-built hiking thoroughfare which is regularly cleared, maintained and well signposted and marked. Example are the loop trail at Cathedral Grove or the Elk River trail in Strathcona.

An 'un-improved trail' is one that is only maintained and cleared by users. Good examples are Jack's Augerpoint trail and the Elkhorn north west approach. Such trails are often clearly marked by ribbons of survey flagging tape or cairns.

An 'established route' is a backcountry path that may show clear signs of regular travel on the ground but sees no improvements beyond the impact of travelling hikers and wildlife. The Westmin - Elk River traverse is a great example of an established route. Flagging and cairns are sporadic but often prominent at route finding difficulties.

A 'route' is on the wilderness end of the hiking spectrum and is nothing more than a suggested or accepted line of travel. Flagging and cairns are unlikely or sparse and route finding is a constant act. For experienced backcountry travellers.

Wildlife

Vancouver Island has a unique blend of flora and fauna due to its size, isolation from and proximity to, mainland North America. The towering evergreen forests and swirling tidal oceans are home to a wide variety of fish, birds, reptiles, amphibians and mammals. The British Columbia coast is one of the richest ecosystems in the world.

When hiking on Vancouver Island encounters with some wildlife is certain. Eagles, jays and osprey are familiar sights. In the ocean salmon, dolphins, sea lions and orca whales are all visitors to the coast. Living in the forest and on the mountains are grouse, ptarmigan, deer, Roosevelt elk, cougar, black bear, pine marten, wolf, river otters and of course marmots. Many of these larger land mammals are distinct sub-species unique to Vancouver Island. Some of these animals such as the Vancouver Island Marmot are present in dwindling numbers and are listed endangered or at risk.

There are some notable absences among the animal life of the Island. There are no grizzly bears or moose on the Island and racoons were introduced and have a limited range.

For the most part the larger mammals are elusive and encounters with them while hiking are rare and to be treasured when they do occur. There is of course a possibility of an aggressive brush with cougar, bear or wolf. If you find yourself confronted by a predator remain calm and maintain a confident air. Retreat from the area with deliberate steps keeping a close watch of the animal(s). If you are surprised or attacked, scream aggressively and fight back with every ounce of strength.

Wildlife encounters may be reported to: 1-800-663-9453

Water

A huge annual precipitation delivers an abundance of fresh water to the mountains of Vancouver Island. The numerous rivers and torrents that tumble seaward shape the land and are the lifeblood of the rich island ecosystem. Island rivers must be both respected and cared for.

Crossing rivers should be undertaken with great caution. Slick rocks and cold, fast moving water can be a deadly combination. Always undo pack waist belts and loosen straps before wading a river. This way you can shed the pack if you stumble. Use a staff or ski poles for stability. In deeper water use a roped belay, pfd and keep boots on. Avoid crossing rivers close, upstream of large rapids or waterfalls. Read and practice roped technical river crossing techniques.

The Island water supply is generally pure and untainted in the alpine. In high use areas such as Paradise Meadows and Bedwell Lake however filtration or sterilization should be practiced to avoid water borne illness. There is a duty to preserve the purity of fresh water. Read the section on 'Wilderness Travel' and practice techniques to minimize contamination to bodies of water. Always camp in designated sites in high use areas and use the outhouses provided. If in doubt boil water to destroy any pathogens that may be present.

Avalanches

Avalanches are a serious threat to mountaineers and every year in British Columbia skiers and mountaineers are caught in snow slides sometimes with fatal consquences. with them. On the whole the deep Vancouver Island snowpack is considered fairly stable in comparison with say the Rocky Mountains. But snow stability is a complex and inexact science and nothing should ever be taken for granted when travelling in avalanche terrain.

Learn how to read the terrain and identify avalanche paths. Practice route finding avoiding terrain traps like open chutes, creek beds and areas where twisted and bent trees indicate signs of avalanche events.

Familiarize yourself and everyone in your group with safe travel techniques and carry and practice self rescue with avalanche transceivers, shovels and probes. Remember that in the backcountry survivors in your group are the first responders and only likely people able to conduct a successful rescue. Help may be sought but should never be counted on.

One of the most dangerous times of the year for avalanches is the spring thaw. As the thick winter snowpack warms it becomes lubricated by liquid water and comes crashing down gullies and creek beds in massive heavy wet slides. These slides may unexpectedly threaten low elevation areas below. A good example of this is the Elk River trail where avalanches from the mountain faces thousands of feet above the evergreen forest pour down long gullies in some cases right to the floor of the valley. Paying attention to what is going on high above you is a good rule of mountain travel.

Ticks

The most loathsome of insects, ticks, are arachnids which latch on to the skin causing a painful swelling while they fill their abdomens with your blood. Ticks may carry Lyme's disease which can cause fever, facial paralysis and eventually severe arthritis and heart problems. If a tick attaches itself to you use tweezers or proprietary tick pliers to gently and steadily tug the tick until it releases its grip.

Don't pull so hard as to leave mouth parts embedded in your skin and don't try to burn or pull too hard. If you suspect infection keep the tick in a ziploc™ and take it when you seek medical attention for testing. Tick season on the Island lasts from late March to late May.

Hornets

Every year Yellow Jacket and Black Headed hornets build paper hives from partially digested wood fibre they harvest from driftwood and fallen trees. As their nests grow so does the population of hornets inside until around August when the numbers of angry hornets presents a hazard to unwary hikers.

Hives may be built in holes in the ground (sometimes right in the middle of a trail) or in the branches of trees and shrubs. Passing hikers disturb the insects who swarm out and may inflict multiple stings. Some people may have or develop severe allergic reactions to hornet stings including life-threatening anaphylactic shock. Consider carrying an Epipen™ or AnaKit™ from late July to late September when hornets are most active. Travel in small groups and keep a brisk pace in the forest.

Private Property

Some of the more accessible mountain areas on Vancouver Island such as the Beaufort Range and Mt. Alexandra-Mt. Adrian are on private land. The larger land owners are most often private forestry companies whose prime interest is the harvesting of timber and the safety of their employees and the public. Access restrictions therefore usually centre around safety concerns to prevent the public encountering heavy machinery and trucks on the logging roads during working hours.

Our duty is to respect posted closures and seek permission before entering private lands. Keeping good relationships by demonstrating respect for the land owner is the best way to ensure continued public access.

Ecological Reserves

Ecological reserves protect sensitive ecosystems for scientific research and conservation. Reserves differ from Provincial Parks in that public access and recreation is discouraged and a permit is required for a legitimate visit.

There are a few Ecological Reserves that include alpine terrain, Haley Lake near Nanaimo Lakes and the Michael Bigg/Robson Bight reserves come to mind. Please respect the sensitivity and value of Ecological Reserves by avoiding travelling through them.

Logging roads, love 'em or hate 'em, you're gonna use them!

Logging Road Travel

Many of the alpine areas of Vancouver Island are only practically accessed by driving on gravel roads. Some gravel roads are major Forest Service roads open at all times and well maintained under contract from the BC Forest Service. These roads are 2 wheel drivable and ploughed during the winter. However, across Vancouver Island there are thousands of kilometres of private logging roads.

Logging roads whether on Crown Land or not are not required to be accessible by the public. Some roads are on private forest lands and often closed by locked gates. Current forestry practices require the regular deactivation or 'debuilding' of logging roads that have fallen out of use for current timber harvesting plans. Deactivated roads may still be drivable by high clearance vehicles but debuilt roads are completely impassable to vehicles and can become overgrown in a matter of just a couple of years.

Roads into areas of active logging are often closed during working hours while work commences. Great care must be taken while driving any logging roads. Road conditions may vary widely and great caution must be had around heavy machinery and the huge double wide logging trucks that may appear around any corner!

Nothing should be taken for granted when planning an approach that includes logging road travel. Any given logging road may be closed or otherwise impassable at any time. Consider throwing a chainsaw or, at the least, an axe in the back of your vehicle. One fallen tree could ruin your day especially if you are upstream of it! Check with local logging companies for current road conditions.

Logging Road Systems

The natural course of the many creeks and streams that run through the valleys into larger rivers and on to the ocean is emulated by the logging roads which weave across the island.

Typically a main line road leads inland from the tidewater along a major river. As this river forks into upper valleys so the road branches into ever higher spurs, eventually zigzagging across the mountain hillsides.

Logging roads are named sequentially starting often with parallel main lines e.g.: East and West Main, on each bank of the river. Branch roads off these main lines are then numbered e.g.: East 100 (E100). From the branches spur roads are further numbered e.g.: East 110 (E110)

Driving Safety Tips

The British Columbia Forest Service recommends these safety tips when travelling on Forest Service Roads:

• Drive with your lights on at all times - day and night.

• Drive at a safe speed. You should always use caution and expect the unexpected. You must be able to stop safely in any emergency or in encountering unforeseen obstructions.

• Use seat belts while travelling on Forest Service Roads

• Please give logging trucks and other industrial traffic the right-of-way. Loaded logging trucks definitely have the right-of-weight! When you see a logging truck coming - or any other heavy equipment - get to a turn-out and let it by.

• Obey all road signs but do not expect the same level of signing as on public highways

• Taking large travel trailers on steep, rough, isolated and infrequently used roads can be dangerous. Loaded logging rigs can not back up steep grades so it is best to avoid the use of trailers on these roads.

• Logging trucks take up a lot of room and Forest Service Roads are built for their use. It is essential that logging trucks and fire-fighting equipment be able to proceed without delay. Don't stop on the road surface for any reason. If you do stop, park well off the road.

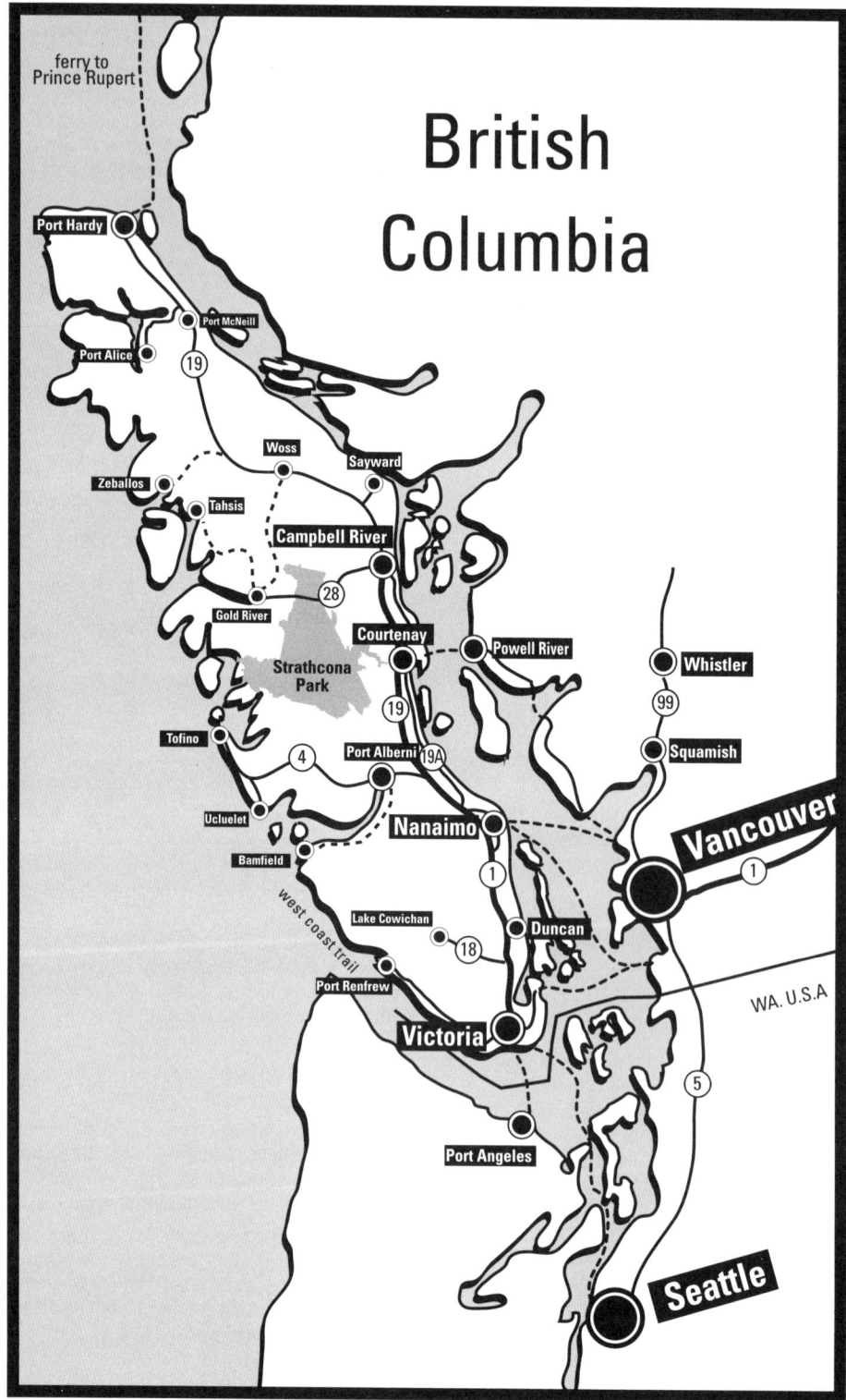

Vancouver Island and South West British Columbia map.

Island Logistics

How To Get Here

Vancouver Island is a large island, some 500 km long and 150 km wide, lying just off the south west coast of British Columbia, Canada. The population centres and major highway routes are concentrated along the south and east coasts of the Island and can be reached on a variety of scheduled ferry routes.

Horseshoe Bay BC—Departure Bay (Nanaimo)
Tsawwassen BC—Duke Point (Nanaimo)
Tsawwassen BC—Swartz Bay (near Victoria)
Seattle WA—Victoria
Port Angeles WA—Victoria

The major highways linking the north and south ends of the island are: the Trans Canada Highway Route 1 between Victoria and Nanaimo and the Inland Island Highway 19 which links all communities between Nanaimo and Port Hardy. A scenic route along the east coast of Vancouver Island is the Oceanside Highway 19A between Parksville and Campbell River.

Visitors should note that locally the various regions of Vancouver Island are referred to as 'South Island' 'North Island' etc. This may be confusing to some as it sounds as if there may be several islands. Vancouver Island is a single island and these designations just refer to regions at either end of the island.

Camping and Accommodation

Vancouver Island is a very popular vacation destination and accommodation facilities abound for every budget in every town. The best way to find roofed accommodation and private RV and tenting campgrounds is to consult local visitor guides or get a copy of the annual British Columbia Accommodation Guide which are all available at local Visitor Info Centres. For a list of online links to Vancouver Island towns, log on to www.wildisle.ca/communities

There are many Forest Service and Provincial campsites across the island. Some useful campsites are: provincial campsites at Elk Falls just outside Campbell River on Highway 28, Buttle Narrows also on 28 and, Ralph River on the Buttle Lake Parkway.

Reservation systems are in place during peak summer season and you'd be well advised to check for site availability at these campsites before showing up in the dark! Online visit www.discovercamping.com

Along the roadways in Strathcona Park and other Provincial Parks, camping is not permitted within 1 km of the road. Camping is permitted only at designated sites along many of the higher use trails. Check at each trailhead for the locations of the designated sites in the area you are headed. Once in the backcountry simply use discretion in choosing low impact sites and follow our Wilderness Travel guidelines.

Emergency Numbers

(no charge for 1-800 telephone numbers)

Marine and Air Search and Rescue: 1 800 567-5111

Rescue Coordination Centre: 250 363-2339

Air Ambulance BC: 250 952-0888

RCMP British Columbia: 604 264-3111

Forest Fire Reporting: 1 800 663-5555

Other Emergencies: 911

Vancouver Island Hiking Trails Volume 1
ISBN 0-9697667-2-6
www.hikingtrailsbooks.com

Vancouver Island Hiking Trails Volume 3
ISBN 0-9697667-4-2

Vancouver Island Hiking Trails Volume 2
ISBN 0-9697667-3-4

Backroad Mapbook Volume II
ISBN 1-894556-10-0
www.backroadmapbooks.com

Beyond Nootka
ISBN 0-9680159-0-5
www.members.shaw.ca/beyondnootka/

Towards the Unknown Mountains
ISBN 0-919537-18-9

36 Additional Resources

Additional Resources

Maps
The following National Topographic Series (NTS) maps cover the regions included in this guide. They can be bought locally or ordered from the Geological Survey of Canada: 604 666-0271.

South Island: C/16 Cowichan Lake • C/15 Little Nitinat River • F/1 Nanaimo Lakes • F/2 Alberni Inlet • F/3 Effingham River • F/6 Great Central Lake • F/7 Horne Lake

Strathcona Park: F/11 Forbidden Plateau • F/12 Buttle Lake • F/13 Upper Campbell Lake • F/5 Bedwell River • F/6 Great Central Lake

North Island: L/1 Schoen Lake • E/16 Gold River • L/1 Schoen Lake • L/8 Adam River • K/5 Sayward • L/7 Nimpkish • L/6 Alice Lake • L/3 Kyuquot • L/4 Brooks Peninsula • L/5 Mahatta River

Publications

- **Hiking Trails I - Victoria & Vicinity** - 12th Edition 1997 edited by Susan Lawrence, published by Vancouver Island Trails Information Society ISBN 0-9697667-2-6
Covers the Capital Regional District, Saltspring Island, Saanich Peninsula, the Juan de Fuca Marine trail. There is no overlap with this guide but it does offer some great Southern Island hiking ideas.

- **Hiking Trails II - South-Central Vancouver Island** - 8th Edition 2000 edited by Richard K. Blier published by Vancouver Island Trails Information Society ISBN 0-9697667-3-4
Covers Duncan, Cowichan Valley, Gulf Islands including Gabriola, Nanaimo, Parksville, Port Alberni Carmanah Walbran Provincial Park and the West Coast Trail. An essential compliment to Island Alpine.

- **Hiking Trails III - Northern Vancouver Island & Strathcona Park** - Ninth Edition 2002 edited by Richard K. Blier published by Vancouver Island Trails Information Society ISBN 0-9697667-4-2
Covers Strathcona Park, Schoen Lake Park, Cape Scott Park and Quadra Island among others. An essential complement to Island Alpine.

- **Backroad Mapbook Volume II Vancouver Island**, Mussio Ventures
ISBN 1-894556-10-0
If you're looking for a comprehensive overview of all the logging roads on Vancouver Island and some basic info on trails and other recreation opportunities this is a good bet. Any logging road information shouldn't be relied on as conditions and openings may change at any time.

- **Hiking and Climbing in South Western BC** - First Edition 1986 by Bruce Fairley
ISBN 0-919574-99-8
Has served the BC mountaineering community for many years. Information on Vancouver Island is sparse and will likely be absent from the second edition due in 2003.

- **Beyond Nootka** - A Historical Perspective of Vancouver Island Mountains by Lindsay Elms
ISBN 0-9680159-0-5
A thoroughly researched book detailing the early history of European exploration on Vancouver Island. Profiles six of the more prominent peaks on the island. Excellent read.

- **Strathcona: A History of British Columbia's First Provincial Park** by Wallace Baikie
ISBN 0-919537-29-4   with Rosemary Phillips

- **Towards the Unknown Mountains** by Rob Wood
ISBN 0-919537-18-9
An autobiographical account of Island mountaineer Rob Wood's adventures with friends and family throughout the Coast Mountains and literally around Vancouver Island.

- **Island Bushwhacker** - journal of the Vancouver Island Section of the Alpine Club of Canada
A mine of information, some editions are available online at: www.islandnet.com/~acc/

- **Canadian Alpine Club Journal** - annual publication from the Alpine Club of Canada

38 Snowshoeing up to Wolf Mountain.

Government of B.C.
online directory: www.dir.gov.bc.ca

Ministry of Parks
http://wlapwww.gov.bc.ca/bcparks/

Discover Camping
www.discovercamping.ca
1-800-689-9025

Ministry of Forests
www.gov.bc.ca/for

South Island Forest District
3819 Trans Canada Hwy, Cobble Hill, B.C., V0R 1L0 Ph: (250) 743-8933

Alberni Forest District
4885 Cherry Creek Road, Port Alberni, B.C., V9Y 8E9 Ph: (250) 731-3000

Campbell River Forest District -
370 South Dogwood Street, Campbell River, B.C. V9W 6Y7 Ph: (250) 286-9300

Port McNeill Forest District -
P.O. Box 7000, 2217 Mine Road Port McNeill, BC V0N 2R0 Ph: 250 956-5000 eMail: Forests.PortMcNeillDistricOffice@gems3.gov.bc.ca

Clubs

Alpine Club of Canada:
www.alpineclubofcanada.ca

Alpine Club of Canada Van. Island section:
www.alpineclubofcanada.ca/vi
direct url: www.islandnet.com/~acc/

Central Island Caving Club:
www.cave-men.com

Comox District Mountaineering Club:
Adele Routledge 250 336-2130

Federation of Mountain Clubs of BC
www.mountainclubs.bc.ca

Island Mountain Ramblers:
Box 691, Nanaimo V9R 5M2
Nicki Westarp 250 247-8868

Outdoor Club of Victoria
www.mountainclubs.bc.ca/ocv/

The Heathens:
c/o 830 Greenwood St Campbell River V9W 3B9
Chris Barner 250 287-4611

UVic Outdoor Club:
www.uvss.uvic.ca/clubs/outdoors/

Logging Companies

Timberwest
www.timberwest.com

Beaver Cove Operation
-P.O. Box 2500, 5705 North Island Highway, Campbell River, BC V9W 5C5 Ph: (250) 287-9181

Cowichan Woodlands
-P.O. Box 375, 9370 South Shore Road, Mesachie Lake, BC V0R 2N0 Ph: (250) 749-7700

Nanaimo Lakes
-5055 Nanaimo River Rd. Nanaimo, BC V9X 1H3 Ph: (250) 729-3770

Johnstone Strait Operation
-P.O. Box 2500, 5705 North Island Highway Campbell River, BC V9W 5C5 Ph: (250) 287-9181

Western Forest Products Limited
-#118 – 1334 Island Hwy. Campbell River, BC V9W 8C9 Ph: 250 286-3767
-1594 Beach, Port McNeill BC V0N 2R0 Ph: 250 956-4446

Weyerhaeuser -
South Island Timberlands
-1825 Timberlands Rd, P.O. Box 75, Cassidy, BC V0R 1H0 Ph: 250-245-6300

West Island Timberlands - Franklin Operations
-Bag 2001, Port Alberni, BC V9Y 7N3 Ph: 250-720-4200

West Island Timberlands - Sproat Lake Operations
-Port Alberni, BC V9Y 7N4 Ph: 250-720-4100

North Island Timberlands
-P.O. Box 6000, 8010 Island Highway, Campbell River, BC V9W 5E1 Ph: 250-287-5000

Port McNeill Timberlands -
-400 South West Main, P.O. Box 5000 Port McNeill, BC V0N 2R0 Ph: 250 956-5200

Black-tailed buck high in the alpine on Mt. Cobb

Online Resources

BC Government Map Place:
www.em.gov.bc.ca/Mining/Geolsurv/MapPlace
Online database of British Columbia topographical maps.

• Beyond Nootka: - A Historical Perspective of Vancouver Island Mountains by Lindsay Elms

www.members.shaw.ca/beyondnootka
The online companion to Elms' thoroughly researched book detailing the early history of European exploration on Vancouver Island. Web site is regularly updated with newly researched stories.

Canadian Avalanche Association:
www.avalanche.ca
The home page for the Canadian Avalanche Association. Lots of links to weather and avalanche resources including current avalanche conditions posted at:
www.avalanche.ca/weather/bulletins

Canadian Mountain Encyclopedia:
www.bivouac.com
The Canadian climber's yellow pages!

Centre for Topographical Information:
www.maps.nrcan.gc.ca
A complete database of Canadian topographical maps. Search for map sheets using terrain name searches, retrieve coordinates for thousands of Canadian places.

Climbers Access Society of BC (CASBC):
www.casbc.bivouac.com
Box 72013, 4479 West 10th,
Vancouver, B.C. V6R 4P2

CoastalBC.com: www.coastalbc.com
Another excellent comprehensive overview of adventure activities on Vancouver Island. Also see its associated sister web site SurfingVancouverIsland.com

Online Hiking Guide:
www.islandhikes.com
Features trip reports, peak route info and a bulletin board messaging system for research and online chats.

Spectrum Digital Imaging:
www.mapsdigital.com
Complete CD-ROM of all Vancouver Island maps and marine charts (and much of the rest of Canada too). Maps calibrated for use with GPS units through OziExplorer software also avaliable from Spectrum.

Vancouver Island Trails Information Society: www.hikingtrailsbooks.com
The Vancouver Island Trails Information Society is a non-profit society dedicated to providing accurate information to the public about parks and trails on Vancouver Island. VITIS achieves this goal by self-publishing hiking trail guides covering Vancouver Island.

Weather Office: weatheroffice.ec.gc.ca
Complete online weather forecasts, satellite imagery etc..

Wild Isle Magazine: www.wildisle.ca
A vast online resource of information, back issues, links and stories of adventure sports on Vancouver Island. Covers the whole gamut from sea kayaking to mountain biking but there is a bias with plenty about hiking, climbing and mountaineering all over the island.
Look for updates and new route information at: www.wildisle.ca/islandalpine

---

Disclaimer

Climbing is a dangerous activity. Route information should be treated as subjective and as published herein only represents what past climbers have encountered on their ascent. Every climb is a new experience for each party that attempts it.

This book in no way should be taken as instruction or advice in any climbing or rope techniques. This book does not advocate climbing and is published as a record of past climbing activity. The author and anyone else connected with this guidebook's compilation, publication and distribution take no responsibility whatsoever for anyone using its contents. You climb at your own risk.

Coast Mountains

OCEAN to ALPINE
Wilderness Adventures

Homestead lodging on Maurelle Island

1-866-285-2724
toll free

Nootka Island

www.oceantoalpine.com

Avalanche Awareness Training

Shred Safe

Don't Leave Home Without It!
- CAA Curriculum
- Certified Instructors
- Safety Gear Rentals
- Certificate Courses

Call for more info
250-897-3254
pepi@island.net
www.island.net/~hipski

NoZone
Sun Protective Funwear

NoZone Clothing Company
2001 Douglas St.
Victoria B.C. V8T 4K9

Tel: (250) 472-2247
Fax: (250) 382-2002
info@nozone.ca

www.nozone.ca

Wild Isle
The Islands' Adventure Magazine

WHISTLER-SQUAMISH REGIONAL PROFILE

Wild Isle
The Islands' Adventure Magazine
FREE

West Coast Ski Resorts

10 Island Backcountry Stashes You Should Know

www.wildisle.ca

STRATHCONA OUTFITTERS

HIKING · CLIMBING · RENTALS · TRAVEL
SALES

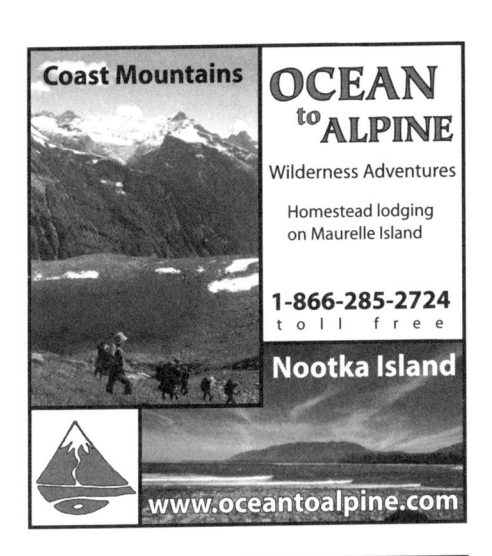

FOR MORE ROUTE INFO CALL US

campbell river
250.287.4453
nanaimo
250.390.0400

Van Isle Top Tens

Top Ten Highest Peaks

Golden Hinde - 7,219 ft / 2,201 m — pg 271
Elkhorn Mountain - 7200 ft / 2,195 m — pg 218
Victoria Peak - 7,095 ft / 2,193 m — pg 346
Mt. Colonel Foster - 7,000 ft / 2,134 m — pg 228
Rambler Peak - 6,900 ft / 2,104 m — pg 241
Mt. Albert Edward - 6,868 ft / 2,094 m — pg 150
Mt. McBride - 6,829 ft / 2,082 m — pg 263
King's Peak - 6,774 ft / 2,065 m — pg 214
Mt. Celeste - 6,696 ft / 2,041 m — pg 158
Mt. Filberg - 6,677 ft / 2,035 m — pg 257

Top Ten Alpine Summits

Triple Peak
Mariner Mountain
The Red Pillar
Golden Hinde
Mt. Colonel Foster
Crown Mountain
Victoria Peak
Mt. Bate
Rugged Mountain
Snowsaddle Mountain

Top Ten Summer Alpine Routes

The Nose Route - Mt. Arrowsmith
Into the Mystic - Mt. Colonel Foster
North East Buttress - Victoria Peak
South West Face - Rugged Mountain
Culbert Route - Mt. Colonel Foster
West Buttress - Rambler Peak
North Ridge - Elkhorn
North West Ridge - Golden Hinde
Summit Traverse - Nine Peaks
North West Ridge - Redwall

Top Ten Winter Alpine Routes

Dirrettissima - Mt. Colonel Foster
Grand Central Couloir - Mt. Colonel Foster
The Great Escape - Big Den Mountain
South East Couloir - Golden Hinde
Dan's Route - Rugged Mountain
North Face - Victoria Peak (incomplete)
The Snow Gully - Mt. Arrowsmith
North Face - Warden Peak
Lost Gully - Mt. Arrowsmith
West Face - Mt. Kitchener

Top Ten Day Ascents

King's Peak - North Spur
Elkhorn - North West Ridge
Mt. Albert Edward - Hiker's Route
Mt. Arrowsmith - Judge's Route
Redwall - North West Ridge
Steamboat Peak - Cavers' trail
Victoria Peak - South Face
Hkusam - Stowe Creek circuit
Pinder Peak - Standard Route
Mt. Cain West Peak - South Face & Gully

Top Ten Multi Day Treks

Elk River to Westmin traverse
Mt. Albert Edward to Flower Ridge
Mt. Tom Taylor - Mariner Mountain traverse
Mt. Rosseau circumnavigation
Mt. Thelwood Horseshoe
Beaufort Range Traverse
Augerpoint Traverse
Phillips Watershed Traverse
Shepherd Ridge - Flower Ridge Horseshoe
Woss Lake to Zeballos Peak

Top Ten Ski Tour Expeditions

Mt. Albert Edward to Flower Ridge
Forbidden Plateau to Mt. Washington
Elk River to Westmin traverse
Mt. Thelwood, Myra Creek Horseshoe
Haihte Range
Tlupana Range Traverse
Buttle Lake to Bedwell Sound valley route
Mt. Tom Taylor - Mariner Mountain traverse
Mt. McBride via Marble Meadows
Nine Peaks via Big Interior Mountain

Top Ten Ski/Snowboard Descents

Comox Glacier to Century Sam Lake
Rugged Glacier - Haihte Range
Mt. Arrowsmith - Super Gully
Victoria Glacier - Victoria Peak
South East Couloir - Golden Hinde
McBride Glacier - Mt. McBride
North Glacier - Mt. Septimus
Dream Chute - Mt. Cain
West Bowl - Mt. Cain
South Glacier - Mt. Colonel Foster

Top Ten Ski Tour Day Trips
Mt. Becher - Forbidden Plateau
Mt. Albert Edward
Mt. Myra
Mt. Beadnell - Rodger's Ridge
Elk Mountain
Crest Mountain to Idsardi Mountain
Green Mountain
Upper Abel Creek
Heather Mountain
Rosseau Chute circuit - Mt. Cokely

Top Ten Bushwhacks
Upper Thelwood Valley
Filberg Creek
Cathedral Creek - Wolf River
Perry Creek to Alava Lake
Cat's Ears approach
Splendour Mountain approach
Triple Peak from Marion Creek
Zeballos Peak west flank from Zeballos Rd.
Karmutzen Mountain from Tlakwa Creek
Lone Wolf Mountain approach

Top Ten Last Summer Problems
Super Arete - Mt. Colonel Foster
East Ridge - Elkhorn
North West Ridge - Mt. Bate
Traverse of Golden Hinde via Wolf River fork
Mt. Colwell East Face - any route
South East Face - Mt. McBride
Eric Creek headwall - north of Rees Ridge
East Face - Warden Peak
East Face Sutton Peak - any route
West Main Buttress - Mt. Colonel Foster

Top Ten Last Winter Problems
Super Couloir - Mt. Colonel Foster
North West Face - Mt. Albert Edward
South West Face - Rugged Mountain
Sceptre - Victoria Peak
North Face - Victoria Peak
North East Couloir- Elkhorn,
North West Buttress - Merlon Mountain
Della Falls
Mt. Colwell East Face - any route
Three Sisters Waterfalls - Mt. Cobb
North West Ridge - Redwall

Top Ten Views
Mt. Colonel Foster from Cervus-Wolf divide
Milla Lake from Iceberg Peak
Mt. Bate from Mt. Alava
Cream Lake from any angle
Landslide Lake from any angle!
Haihte Range from Pinder Peak
Mariner Mountain from Tofino (& vice versa)
Buttle Lake from Syd Watts Peak
Mt. Albert Edward from Mt. Washington
Victoria & Warden Peaks from Queen Peak

With the obvious exception of the top ten highest peaks these lists are in no particular order and are just for fun and purely a matter of opinion. Also note that what may be a day trip for some might require an overnight for others so plan carefully.

Island Qualifiers
Members of the Vancouver Island Section of the Alpine Club of Canada may qualify for a plaque by climbing the main summit of the following peaks.

Golden Hinde
Elkhorn Mountain
Victoria Peak
Mount Colonel Foster
Warden Peak
Rugged Mountain
Mount Septimus
Nine Peaks
Mount Harmston

Rob Wood on the crux traverse of the Grand Central Couloir, Mt. Colonel Foster.   photo: Doug Scott

Van Isle Top Tens **43**

Entrance Island lighthouse and Mt. Arrowsmith

Southern
Vancouver Island

46 Rick Johnson hiking up the South Ridge of Mt. Hooper   photo: Sasha Kubicek

Southern Vancouver Island Contents

Mt. Whymper	52
Mt. Landale	53
El Capitan Mountain	54
Mt. Service	55
Heather Mountain	56
Mt. Buttle	56
Mt. Grey	57
Mt. Hooper	57
Logan Peak	58
Mt. Olsen	58
Patlicant Mountain	58
Mt. Brenton	58
Mt. Spencer	59
Marmot Mt.	59
Gemini Mountain	60
Green Mt.	60
Mt. De Cosmos	61

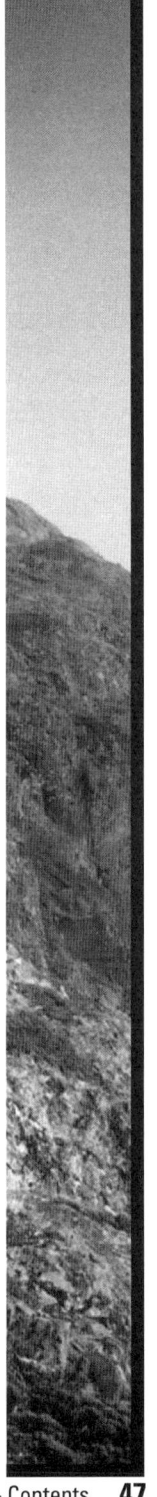

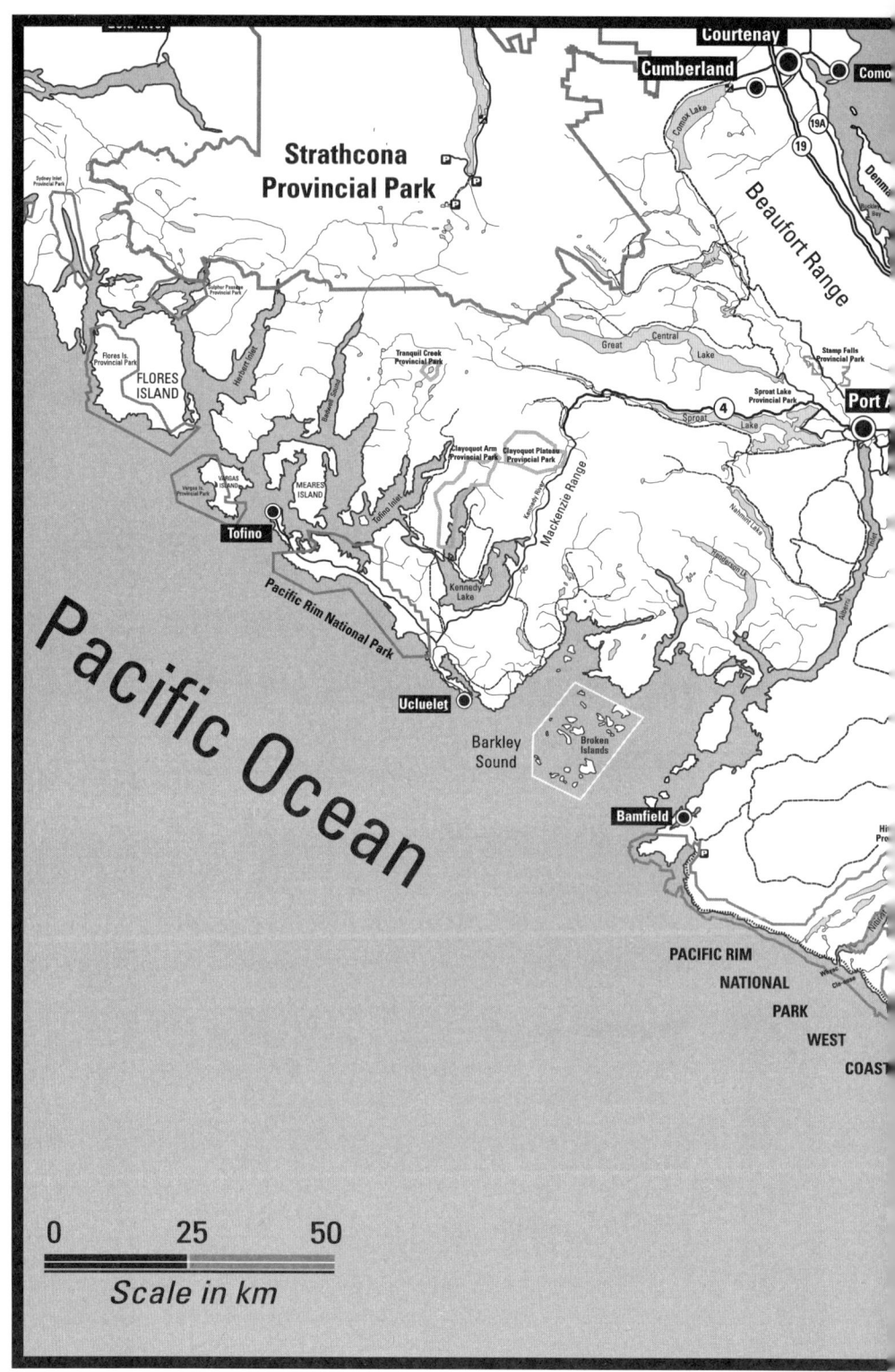

48 Southern Vancouver Island - Map

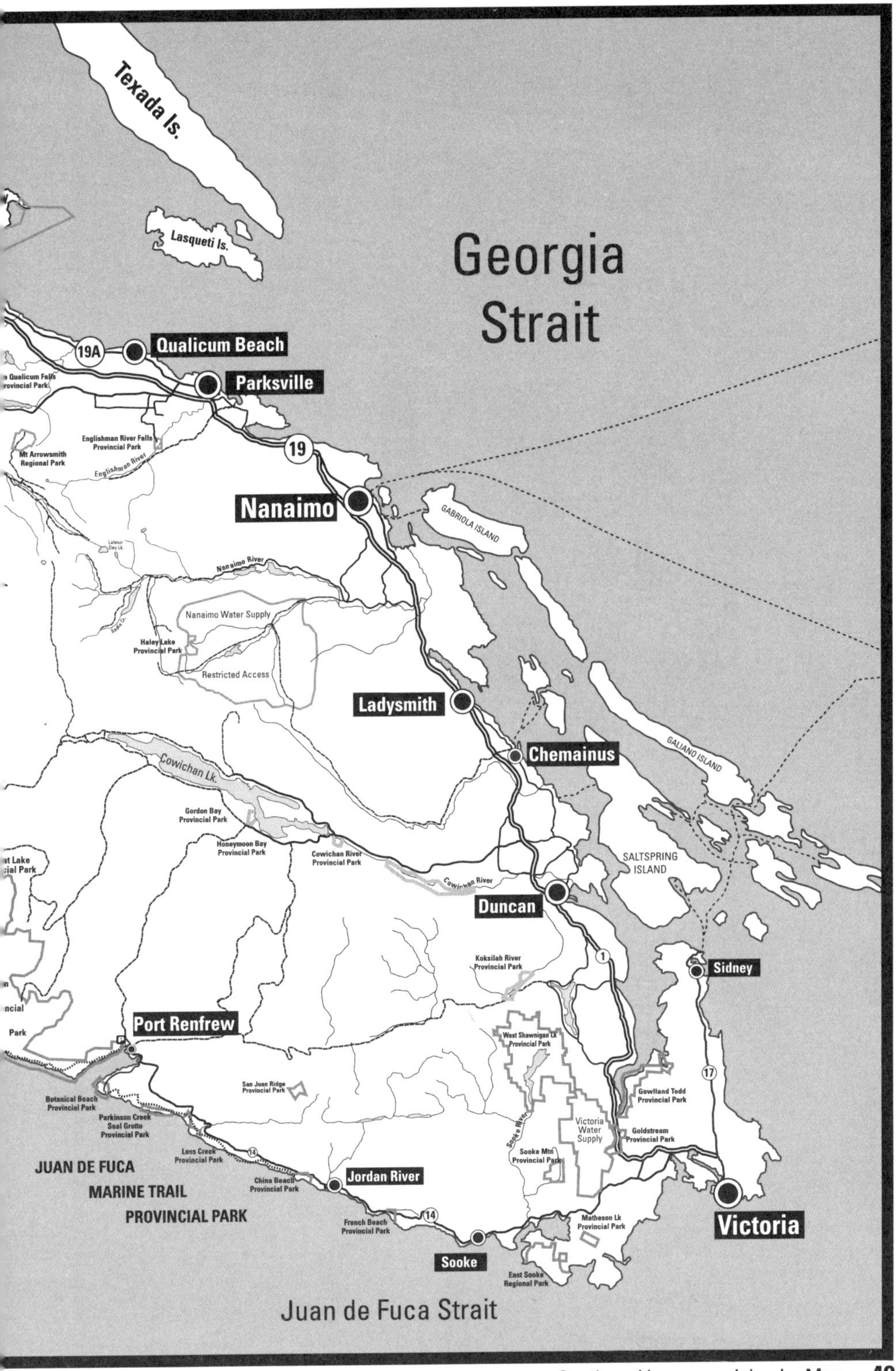
Texada Is.
Lasqueti Is.
Georgia Strait
19A
Qualicum Beach
Parksville
Qualicum Falls Provincial Park
Englishman River Falls Provincial Park
Mt Arrowsmith Regional Park
Englishman River
19
Nanaimo
Gabriola Island
Nanaimo River
Nanaimo Water Supply
Haley Lake Provincial Park
Restricted Access
Ladysmith
Chemainus
Galiano Island
Cowichan Lk.
Gordon Bay Provincial Park
Honeymoon Bay Provincial Park
Cowichan River Provincial Park
Cowichan River
Saltspring Island
Duncan
1
Sidney
Koksilah River Provincial Park
Port Renfrew
West Shawnigan Lk Provincial Park
17
San Juan Ridge Provincial Park
Botanical Beach Provincial Park
Parkinson Creek Seal Grotto Provincial Park
Gowlland Todd Provincial Park
Victoria Water Supply
Goldstream Provincial Park
Sooke River
Sooke Mtn Provincial Park
Loss Creek Provincial Park
14
JUAN DE FUCA MARINE TRAIL PROVINCIAL PARK
China Beach Provincial Park
Jordan River
French Beach Provincial Park
Matheson Lk Provincial Park
Victoria
Sooke
East Sooke Regional Park
Juan de Fuca Strait

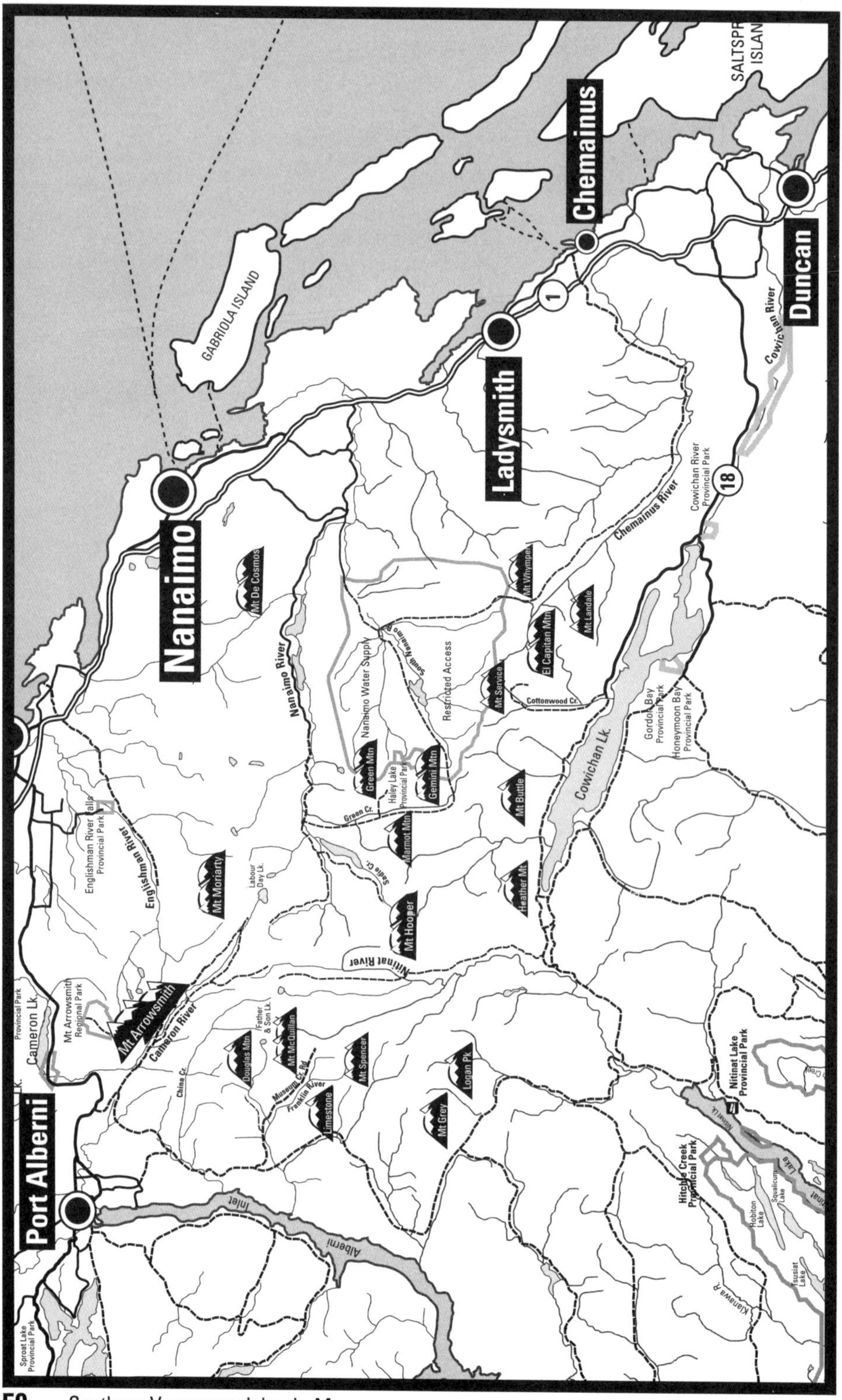
Port Alberni
Nanaimo
Ladysmith
Chemainus
Duncan
SALTSPR
ISLAN
GABRIOLA ISLAND
1
18
Mt De Cosmos
Nanaimo River
Nanaimo Water Supply
South Nanaimo R.
Restricted Access
Mt Whymper
Mt Landale
El Capitan Mtn
Mt Service
Cottonwood Cr.
Chemainus River
Cowichan River Provincial Park
Cowichan River
Gordon Bay Provincial Park
Honeymoon Bay Provincial Park
Cowichan Lk.
Green Mtn
Haley Lake Provincial Park
Gemini Mtn
Green Cr.
Mt Buttle
Marmot Mtn
Sadie Cr.
Heather Mt
Mt Hooper
Nitinat River
Englishman River Falls Provincial Park
Englishman River
Mt Moriarty
Labour Day Lk.
Mt Arrowsmith Regional Park
Mt Arrowsmith
Cameron Lk.
Provincial Park
Cameron River
China Cr.
Douglas Mtn
Father & Son Lk.
Mt McQuillan
Museum Cr. Rd
Franklin River
Mt Spencer
Limestone
Logan Pk
Mt Grey
Nitinat Lake Provincial Park
Nitinat Lk.
Hitchie Creek Provincial Park
Hobiton Lake
Tsusiat Lake
Klanawa R.
Alberni Inlet
Sproat Lake Provincial Park

Southern Vancouver Island

The southern half of Vancouver Island paints a quintessential west coast scene. Rolling evergreen hills, wide sunny valleys rich with soil and shaped in a pastoral mold. There are gorgeous beaches, the Gulf Islands, the provincial capital, Victoria, and of course the renowned West Coast Trail. Luckily this temperate slice of lotus land is also blessed with some fine alpine albeit at a more modest scale than the northern half of the island.

As with the rest of Vancouver Island the southern island landscape is dominated by the topography of river valleys and ridge lines. Typically river watersheds run out from a central backbone of higher ridge tops and mountain summits, to either the west or east coast of the island. Each river valley is separated by a lateral ridgeline of varying elevation and complexity. It is along this spine of the island that we look to find the higher alpine areas. In the southern half of Vancouver Island these alpine areas are concentrated at the headwaters of the Chemainus, Cowichan, Nitinat, Cameron, Nanaimo and Englishman Rivers.

Being closer to the larger Vancouver Island communities the South Island mountains are blessed with generally good access and there is an excellent network of hiking trails all over Southern Vancouver Island. On the flip side there is intensive forestry conducted in this region of the Island leaving a far from pristine landscape. Logging road access is no less complicated than anywhere else on the Island, with the additional complications of private logging company land, many gates, closures and deactivations to attend to.

Map Sheets: 92 B/13 Duncan • 92 C/16 Cowichan Lake • 92 F/1 Nanaimo Lakes • 92 C/15 Little Nitinat River

Boundaries: north: Englishman River, **east:** Strait of Georgia, **south:** Juan de Fuca Strait, **west:** Nitinat River.

Major Access Routes: The Trans Canada Highway 1 between Nanaimo and Victoria* provides the principal highway access along southern Vancouver Island. This major highway has several key tributary roads which branch off westward into the centre of the Island to reach the mountains including Highway 18 to Lake Cowichan. *(Note: north of Nanaimo the major highway changes designation to the Island Highway 19.) The major logging roads off Highway 1 & 18 are:

Cowichan Valley Forest Road: Leaves the town of Lake Cowichan and runs around the north shore of Cowichan Lake.

Cottonwood Main: Branches off the Cowichan Valley Forest Road north toward Mt. Service, El Capitan and the Lomas Lake trail.

Copper Canyon / Chemainus Main: Heads west from the village of Chemainus through a gated pass between Mt. Whymper and El Capitan Mountain which links to the Nanaimo River Road.

Nanaimo River Rd: From Cassidy south of Nanaimo the Nanaimo River Rd heads west to the chain of lakes in the Nanaimo River valley.

Englishman River Main: Heads south-west from Parksville to the lower flanks of Mt. Moriarty.

Forest Service & Logging Company Offices:

Duncan Forest District - 5825 York Rd, Duncan BC V9L 3S2 Ph: 250 746-5123

Port Alberni Forest District - 4227 Sixth Ave, Port Alberni BC V9Y 4N1 Ph: 250 724-5786

Weyerhaeuser - 1825 Timberlands Rd, P.O. Box 75, Cassidy, BC V0R 1H0 Ph: 250-245-6300

- Franklin Operations -Bag 2001, Port Alberni, BC V9Y 7N3 Ph: 250-720-4200

Other Information Sources:

• Hiking Trails I - Victoria & Vicinity (12th ed. 1997 Susan Lawrence, ed.) VITIS
• Hiking Trails II - South-Central Vancouver Island & Gulf Islands (8th ed. 2000 Richard K. Blier, ed.) VITIS

Special Thanks:

Thanks to Sandy Briggs, Chris Shepard, Craig Wagnell, Sasha Kubicek, Bill Readings and Don Cameron for assistance with this chapter.

Mt. Whymper

Mt. Whymper north-west ridge, December.   photo: Sandy Briggs

Mt. Whymper
5,055 ft / 1,541 m

Mt. Wymper lies on the divide between the Chemainus River to the south and the South Nanaimo River to the north. Mt. Whymper, along with the mountains to its west -Mount Landale, El Capitan and Mount Service- marks the southern end of significant alpine terrain on Vancouver Island. Mt. Whymper is the highest mountain in Canada south of the 49th Parallel.

Map Sheet: 92 C/16 Cowichan Lake - GR 1522

Approaches : Mt. Whymper is most easily reached from the Chemainus Main logging road. From Highway 19 in Chemainus turn west onto the Chemainus Main and drive for ~40 km to spur C-27. Gain about 200m elevation and then turn hard right on the upper section of C-29 (the two roads cross here.) At the time of writing, these roads are accessible by 2-wheel drives. Currently the top eastern end of spur C-29 is at about 870m on the South-East Ridge of Mt. Whymper. Eventually flagging indicates the clearcut will reach to about 1200m, within about 100m of the cliff band. From the end of C-29 drop very slightly rightward off the bank and follow flagging and metal tags marking a rough trail up the South-East Ridge. The cliff band is class 3 and the summit is easily reached in under two hours. No doubt there will be an awkward recovery period for this route after the now-imminent logging ceases.

Alternatively, the open forest of the west ridge makes a pleasant ascent in spite of there being no actual trail. Follow C-27 below recently logged slopes (fall '02) to a right bend before its end. Hike upward, tending slightly right, through nice forest. Eventually there is a relatively short section of thickish bush in the lower part of an old burned-off area, but this soon gives way to a pleasant ramble through rolling meadows. The final peak involves some steep scrambling or, in winter, steep snow.

North-West Ridge: Class 3/4
This route is best done as a west to east traverse of the mountain. From the El Cap-Whymper Pass hike up through logging slash and enter the forest to the left of a set of bluffs. Ascend the ridge eastward to reach the first summit (1360m). Head north-east down to a col. Scramble up ledges and gullies (up to class 4) to a 1440m summit. Continue north-east into a second col then south-east toward the main summit. Hike over a series of minor summits passing a deep notch by means of a gully descent and a ledge traverse on the right (west) side (If you don't find the ledge then you will have to rappel.) Scramble back to the ridge crest and continue along to the summit, which can be climbed directly if you like exposure, or more easily by spiraling around to the right. Descend the south-east ridge to C-29. This makes a very fine loop tour in spring snow conditions, and you can usually drive relatively close by mid-to-late April. It is advantageous to have two vehicles and position them to avoid the 7 km road walk back to the El Capitan-Whymper pass.

Additional Info: IB 1999 p.18

Mt. Landale

Aerial view of Mt. Landale west aspect — photo: Don Cameron

Mt. Landale
5,042 ft / 1,537m

Mt. Landale lies at the headwaters of the Chemainus River with the Nanaimo River draining to the north and a small tributary of Cowichan Lake, Cottonwood Creek, draining its west side. In many respects Mt. Landale can be considered to be the southern terminus of alpine on Vancouver Island. From Landale a connecting ridge runs north-west around the headwaters of the South Nanaimo River (Greater Nanaimo Watershed Area) across El Capitan Mountain and Mount Service.

Map Sheet: 92 C/16 Cowichan Lake - GR 1121

Approaches: Approach Mt. Landale on the Lomas Lake trail from Cottonwood Creek. From Youbou on Cowichan Lake drive up to the gate on Cottonwood Creek Main. It is ~7km from the gate to the trailhead. Take the trail up a tight-sided creek valley on the south-west side of Landale to reach Lomas Lake in a cirque under Landale's north-west side and the south-west of El Capitan Mountain. (See El Capitan approach details.)

Summer Route: Class 3

From the east end of Lomas Lake hike up eastward through forest and meadows to the base of a small blocky 1,420 m summit between El Capitan and Landale. Hike up the gully to an old mine site, then up a scree slope to a notch in the ridge. Drop back 10m below the notch traversing south on ledges across the west face of the ridge. Return to the crest of the ridge and hike south to an open slope west of the summit. A short final scramble leads to the summit. Descend same route.

Landale may be climbed from Sherk Lake up the South-West Ridge. Another possibility is to climb El Capitan Mountain and traverse the wide connecting ridge southward to Mt. Landale.

Winter Route

Climb the prominent gully from the south side of Lomas Lake to the top of the rock band. Keep left where the gully forks. From here Mt. Landale is straightforward on snow, or rock ledges in later season.

The El Capitan-Mt. Landale traverse is a fun outing on spring snow with at least one steep step in either direction. Parties not confident on steep snow may wish to carry a rope, or bypass difficulites off the ridge crest.

Another popular winter route starts by the high waterfall seen hiking up the East Cottonwood logging road across the valley at the edge of the clearcut. From the end of the road at the base of the falls cross the small creek and bypass the falls on the right (south) side. With good snow cover rejoin the creek gully above the high falls, but in low-snow conditions the creek should be avoided - one or two short steps which need to be taken seriously in icy conditions. Roughly 300m above the falls switch left into a wider gully and continue up to join the South-West ridge just below the summit.

El Capitan Mountain

El Capitan Mountain south-east aspect from Mt. Whymper. photo: Chris Shepard

El Capitan Mountain
4,895 ft / 1,492 m

El Capitan Mountain is a rocky summit north of Mt. Landale at the headwaters of the Chemainus River to the south and east, the South Nanaimo River to the north, and Cottonwood Creek, a tributary of the Cowichan River feeding Cowichan Lake to the west.

Map Sheet: 92 C/16 Cowichan Lake - GR 1022

Approaches: El Capitan may be reached from the Chemainus Main logging road. From Highway 19 in Chemainus turn west onto the Chemainus Main and drive for ~45 km to just before the gated pass between Mt. Whymper and El Capitan Mountain. A route runs up the forested slope on the Capitan's north-east flank.

Alternatively from Youbou on Cowichan Lake drive up the Cottonwood Creek Main. The road is gated, unstaffed, and seldom open. It is 5 km to the small bridge across Cottonwood Creek, which is at the bottom of a big hill and about as far as you will be able to drive. The Lomas Lake trail leads up a tight-sided creek valley on the south-west aspect of Landale and turns to reach Lomas Lake in a cirque under Landale's north-west side and the south-west flank of El Capitan Mountain. This was the site of a short-lived and small scale mining operation many years ago, and signs of this operation can be found high in the gullies behind Lomas Lake in summer. The miners' track is a rough trail which has deteriorated in recent years from avalanche activity and lack of maintenance. It leaves the deactivated Cottonwood East logging road, one section of which has been restored to grade, after a switchback at approximately GR 097222. A major avalanche about 1998 destroyed a fine forest grove behind Lomas Lake, so that the path now winds through a small area of downed trees.

South-East Ridge: Class 3
From the east end of Lomas Lake, climb up the forest and meadows heading east, toward a small blocky 1420m summit between El Capitan and Landale. Hike up the steep chute to some old mine workings below the blocky summit and turn left (north) on a faint trail. Continue north-west below a cliff a short distance to a rocky gully leading up into a band of trees. Scramble up this to the top of the ridge and continue north-west along the ridge to reach the summit.

West Ridge: Class 3
Approach on the Lomas Lake trail leaving it as it begins traversing east across the south slope of El Capitan, 50m before the stream crossing below the Service / El Capitan col. Head north into the col then hike east up the West Ridge. A few rock steps lead up to the summit. Descent is via the South-East Ridge.

In winter ascend the prominent gully from the south side of Lomas Lake to the top of the rock band. Keep left where the gully forks. From here Mt. Landale is mostly straightforward on snow, or rock ledges in later season. The El Capitan-Mt. Landale traverse is a fun outing on spring snow, but there is at least one steep step in either direction. Parties not confident on steep snow may wish to carry a rope, or drop off the side of the ridge for one or two short sections.

Mt. Service

Mt. Service taken from the El Capitan/Landale Ridge looking north-west   photos: Chris Shepard

Mt. Service
4,888 ft / 1,490 m

Mt. Service lies 3 km north-west of El Capitan Mountain on the divide between the Nanaimo River to the north-east and Cottonwood Creek, which feeds Cowichan Lake to the south-west.

Map Sheet: 92 C/16 Cowichan Lake - GR 0823

Approaches: The fastest approach to Mt. Service may be made from Youbou on Cowichan Lake up the Cottonwood Creek Main which leads right up onto the south-west flank of the mountain. From a high spur hike easy terrain to the top. Except for a short steep section on the upper mountain this is a fine Southern Island ski tour.

Mt. Service may also be reached from the Chemainus Main logging road. From Highway 19 in Chemainus turn west onto the Chemainus Main and drive for ~47 km to just after the pass between Mt. Whymper and El Capitan Mountain. A gate at the pass is often locked. Either climb El Capitan Mountain and follow the connecting ridge north-west to Mt. Service or gain the prominent north-east ridge from logging spurs on the Nanaimo side of the Chemainus - Nanaimo pass.

A third option is from logging roads in Jump Creek from the north-west, however access to this tributary of the Nanaimo River may be restricted as it is within the Greater Nanaimo Water Supply area.

El Capitan and the south ridge taken from near Mt. Landale looking north.

Heather Mountain taken from the meadows looking north. photo: Chris Shepard

Heather Mountain
4,413 ft / 1,345 m

Heather Mountain is located at the west end of Cowichan Lake above the north shore. It is a worthy destination for a visit in both summer and winter. The gentle terrain around the mountain is ideal for snowshoeing and ski touring.

Map Sheet: 92 C/16 Cowichan Lake - GR 9323

Approaches: Drive around either shore of Cowichan Lake to the sharp corner in the road by the Heather Forest Service Campsite at the far west end of the lake. A network of hiking and riding trails weave across the south flanks of Heather Mountain. Take the Heather Mountain trail which uses old roads to climb on to the subalpine ridge south of the mountain. Follow the height of land north through subalpine forest to a final steep hike up the south ridge to the summit and great views of Cowichan Lake.

Mt. Buttle east aspect from Mt. Service, May photo: Sasha Kubicek

Mt. Buttle
4,528 ft / 1,380 m

Mt. Buttle is a small steep-sided mountain on the divide between McKay Creek and Shaw Creek overlooking the north shore of Cowichan Lake.

Map Sheet: 92 C/16 Cowichan Lake - GR 0223

Approaches: Approach Mt. Buttle from the west using the East Shaw or Marguerite Main logging roads. Alternatively, logging roads above McKay Creek reach about 800m on the south-east spur of the south ridge.

Mt. Hooper south-east aspect from Heather Mountain, June.   photo: Sasha Kubicek

Mt. Hooper
4,891 ft / 1,491 m

A somewhat isolated summit on the Nanaimo Nitnat divide north-west of Heather Mountain.

Map Sheet: 92 F/2 Alberni Inlet - GR 8929

Approaches: This peak can be reached from a rough trail in the upper Shaw Creek valley which leads to the divide near Balmer Lake. Alternatively, bypassing the Heather mountain turnoff one can hike past a gate to roads in the valley directly south-east of Mt. Hooper. Expect some bushy scrambling either way. But for the problem of gates, access to the west side of Hooper from high roads in the upper Nitnat is likely quite good.

Mt. Grey west aspect from Logan Peak south ridge, June.   photo: Sasha Kubicek

Mt. Grey
4,570 ft / 1,393 m

Mt. Grey is little known and not often climbed but it is still quite impressive peak for the area. The mountain lies at the head of a high valley in the headwaters of Little Nitnat River.

Map Sheet: 92 C/15 Little Nitinat River - GR 7528

Approaches: Drive south out of Port Alberni, toward Bamfield on the Bamfield Road. At Franklin Camp turn left (east) on South Main heading to Nitinat Lake. Three kilometres east of Franklin turn left at Francis Lake at the recreation area.

From Corrigan Creek Main hike up to the saddle between Logan Peak and some 1200m false summits of Mt. Grey. Traverse these false summits to get to Grey.

Logan Peak south-west aspect from south ridge, June. photo: Sasha Kubicek

Logan Peak
4,396 ft / 1,340 m

Logan Peak is found at the head of Little Nitinat River with views east over the main Nitinat River valley. To the north are Corrigan Creek and Mt. Spencer.

Map Sheet: 92 F/2 Alberni Inlet - GR 8029

Approaches: Logan Peak may be climbed by the west ridge from Corrigan Main. Cut up to the saddle and then up the west ridge.

Mt. Olsen
4,265 ft / 1,300+ m

Mt. Olsen is at the head of Corrigan Creek between two forks of the creek.

Map Sheet: 92 F/2 Alberni Inlet - GR 7931

Approaches: May be approached from Corrigan Creek Main with some steep bluffs to negotiate.

Patlicant Mountain
4,055 ft / 1,236 m

Patlicant Mountain sits between Franklin River to the south and China Creek to the north.

Map Sheet: 92 F/2 Alberni Inlet - GR 7444

Approaches: From any of a number of spur roads off Thistle Mine Rd, Branch 328 climbs nearly to the summit, try it.

Mt. Brenton
3,937 ft / 1,200 m

A plateau-like mountain visible from the Island Highway just west of Chemainus. It gives splendid views over the Strait of Georgia. In spite of being also popular with snowmobilers this is a common ski-tour destination in good-snow years because of its relative proximity to Victoria.

Map Sheet: 92 B/13 Duncan - GR 3716

Approaches: After about 10 km on the Chemainus River Road (Copper Canyon Main) a right spur called Mt. Brenton Br 1 leads to the mountain, which has a rough 4wd track to the summit, the site of various communications installations. In winter it is uncommon to be able to drive past the first bridge, maybe 5km up the Mt. Brenton branch road.

Mt. Spencer north-east aspect from Mt. McQuillan. photo: Craig Wagnell

Mt. Spencer
4,790 ft / 1,460 m

A prominent peak with a rugged north face located south of Mt. McQuillan.

Map Sheet: 92 F/2 Alberni Inlet - GR 7935

Approaches: Access the east and west Ridges of Mt. Spencer from Museum Creek Main or approach the south ridge via branches off Corrigan Creek Main.

Mt. Hooker
4,143 ft / 1,263 m

A high hill south of Second Lake, site of a former fire lookout and there is an old antenna on the top.

Map Sheet: 92 F/1 Nanaimo Lakes - GR 1236

Approaches: There is a rough road to the top on the east side from Price Creek.

Marmot Mountain south aspect from Heather Mountain, June. photo: Sasha Kubicek

Marmot Mt.
4,541 ft / 1,384 m

A peak at the head of Shaw Creek north of Heather Mountain.

Map Sheet: 92 F/1 Nanaimo Lakes - GR 9329

Approaches: Access via West Shaw Main and then up the trail that leads to Balmer Lake where the west ridge takes you to the summit. The east ridge is also accessed from West Shaw Main.

Gemini Mt. east aspect from Stuart Channel west of Gabriola Island, May.

Gemini Mountain
South Peak 4,973 ft / 1,516 m North Peak 4,938 ft / 1,505 m

Gemini Mountain is the twin peaks visible behind Nanaimo from the Georgia Strait. The mountain lies on the divide between Green Creek and Dunsmuir Creek, both of which drain into the Nanaimo River. The higher south peak falls within the Haley Lake Ecological Reserve, which preserves one of the few natural habitats of the endangered Vancouver Island Marmot. Access to Ecological Reserves is restricted so visits to this mountain should be confined to the north peak, an excellent consolation.

Map Sheet: 92 F/1 Nanaimo Lakes - GR0331

Approaches: Best from the west out of logging roads in Bell Creek at the end of the Nanaimo Lakes Road to Green Mountain. Both peaks can be reached easily from here.

Green Mountain south aspect, aerial view   photo: Don Cameron

Green Mt.
4,806 ft / 1,465 m

Green Mountain was for a time a ski hill serving the Nanaimo community. Recent snowfalls have been insufficient to maintain the area and little of the original facility remains. The mountain and the abandoned pistes make fine ski-touring country, a recreation resource of great value to residents of the greater Nanaimo area, but this terrain is all locked behind a staffed gate. The posted (and bizarre) winter closing time of 2:30 pm makes it nearly impossible to do a sensible day-trip here.

Map Sheet: 92 F/1 Nanaimo Lakes - GR 0234

Approaches: The K branches of the Nanaimo Lakes Road will get you to the old ski area, and there are at least two useful options; however, the situation changes as new logging occurs and gates come and go. Good luck!

Mt. De Cosmos

Mt. De Cosmos north aspect from end of logging road. photo: Sasha Kubicek

Mt. De Cosmos
4,445 ft / 1,355 m

Mt. De Cosmos is close to Nanaimo and a quick objective from the city. Drive west. Named for Amor De Cosmos (born William Alexander Smith) BC's second premier between 1872-1874. Established 'The British Colonist' (now Victoria's Times-Colonist).[1]

Map Sheet: 92 F/1 Nanaimo Lakes - GR 1141

Approaches: Mt. De Cosmos is reached from Nanaimo River Road. Head west off the Trans Canada 1 at the Bungy Zone on the Nanaimo River Road. (Harewood and Extension offer two routes off the Nanaimo bypass to reach Nanaimo River Road). Take Branch A off Nanaimo River Rd. Go as far as your vehicle can and then keep on walking up the logging road that goes around and up the north side of De Cosmos. Once the road ends, hike through the slash and then look for the easiest gully to get up above the bluffs that guard the whole summit area.

Mt. DeCosmos has a number of one-pitch gendarmes east of the main summit along a fault line. Some of these were climbed by Noel Lax and Pat Guilbride in the 1960s.

The Pinch: 5.7 70m

An interesting route up one of many rock faces around the top of Mt. De Cosmos. Drive to the base on logging roads. Scramble up to a ledge and belay the first pitch from here or start directly below the corner/chimney for a challenge. Climb on the left of the chimney, reaching back into it for protection, and belay from the trees on a big ledge above. The second pitch goes up a pocketed face into a left-trending corner, past a horizontal crack and over a series of steps to the top of the hill. Walk down gully to the climber's left back to the vehicle.

FA: Bill Readings, Scott Mitrenga, September 2001

The Pinch. photo: Bill Readings

Mt. Arrowsmith

East Central
Vancouver Island

64 Central Vancouver Island - Map

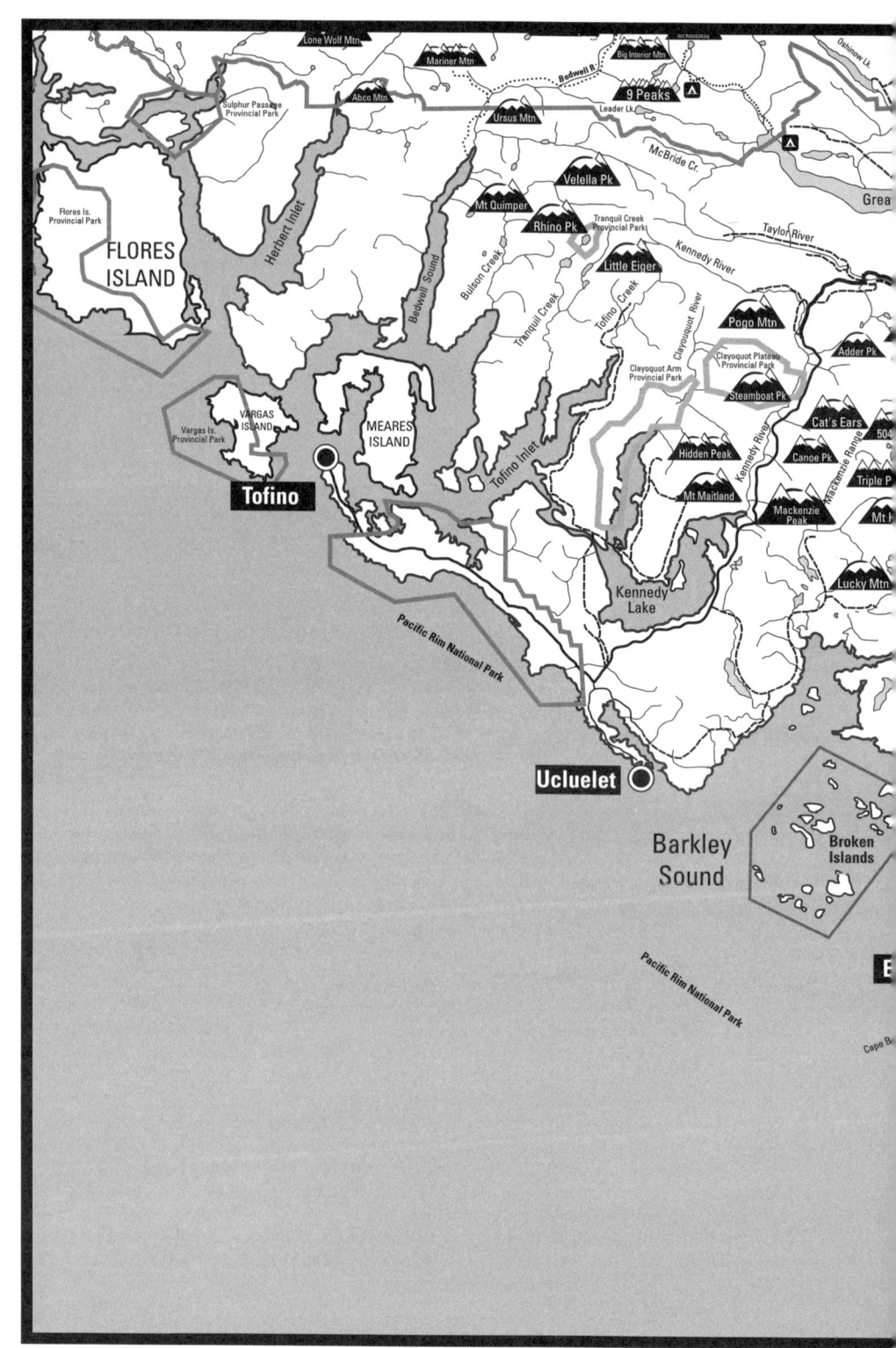

Central Vancouver Island - Map 65

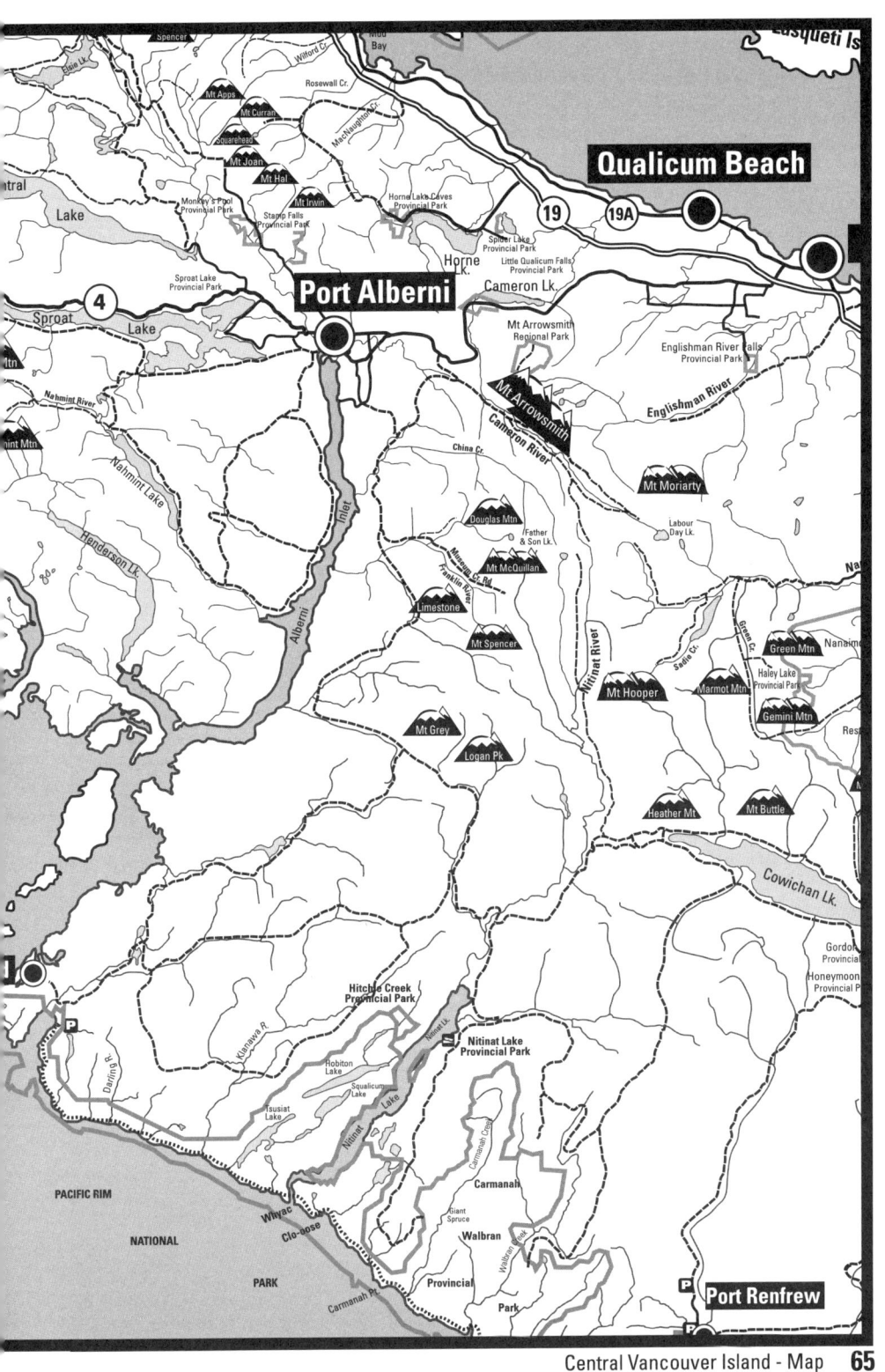

Waterfall ice above the Mt. Arrowsmith ski area road.

East Central Vancouver Island
Contents

Mt. Moriarty	**71**
Mt. Arrowsmith	**72**
Mt. Cokely	**77**
Mt. McQuillan	**78**
Douglas Peak	**80**
Limestone Mountain	**81**

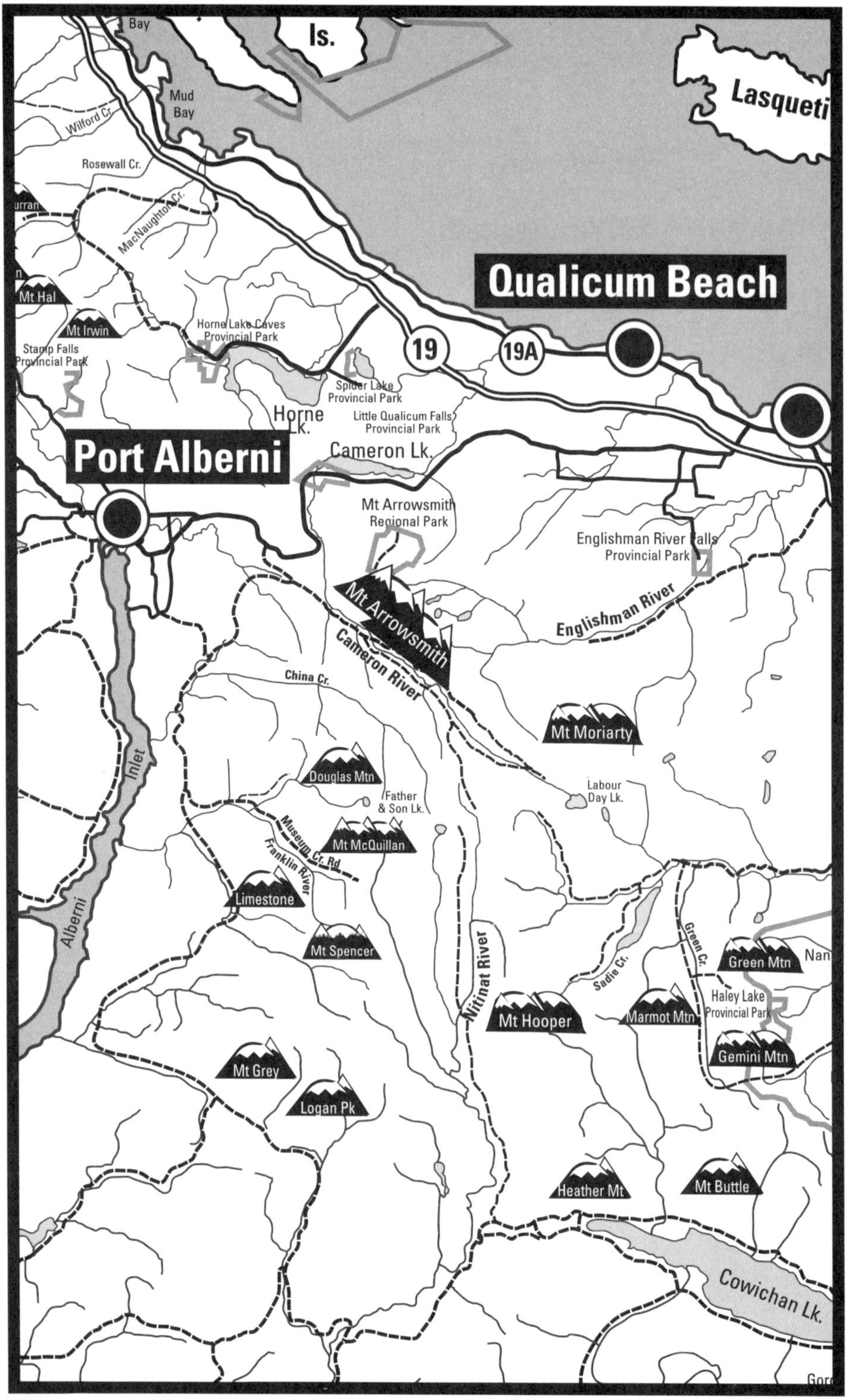

Bay
Is.
Lasqueti
Mud Bay
Wilford Cr.
Rosewall Cr.
MacNaughton Cr.
Qualicum Beach
Mt Hal
Mt Irwin
Horne Lake Caves Provincial Park
Stamp Falls Provincial Park
19
19A
Spider Lake Provincial Park
Horne Lk.
Little Qualicum Falls Provincial Park
Port Alberni
Cameron Lk.
Mt Arrowsmith Regional Park
Englishman River Falls Provincial Park
Mt Arrowsmith
Englishman River
Cameron River
China Cr.
Mt Moriarty
Douglas Mtn
Father & Son Lk.
Labour Day Lk.
Museum Cr. Rd
Franklin River
Mt McQuillan
Limestone
Inlet
Alberni
Mt Spencer
Nitinat River
Green Cr.
Sadie Cr.
Green Mtn
Haley Lake Provincial Park
Mt Hooper
Marmot Mtn
Gemini Mtn
Mt Grey
Logan Pk
Heather Mt
Mt Buttle
Cowichan Lk.

East Central Vancouver Island

From the innocuous foothills of southern Vancouver Island the topography changes around Mt. Arrowsmith and the Alberni Valley to a more mountainous landscape hinting at the progressively more rugged terrain further north. The Central Island is divided by the long reach of the Pacific Ocean through Alberni Inlet, which almost severs the island in two. At this point it is only 40 km from Port Alberni on the west coast of the island to Qualicum Beach on the east coast.

Alberni Inlet has a marked effect on the weather of this region, acting as a funnel for moisture-laden air coming inland off the open Pacific. This warm moist air keeps even the alpine zone milder and, as a result, the mountains of the Central Island have wide fluctuations in snow cover from year to year. However, further inland this precipitation pipeline feeds the icefields of Mt. Septimus and the Cliffe and Comox Glaciers in Strathcona Park. Ultimately the air from the Alberni Valley brings winter snow even as far as Mt. Washington.

A handful of peaks, including the Central Island's highest, Mt. Arrowsmith, are found to the east of Alberni Inlet. To the west of the inlet the Island's mountainous backbone fine-tunes its form and sweeps up from here 350 km to Quatsino Sound in northern Vancouver Island.

Map Sheets: 92 F/2 Alberni Inlet • 92 F/3 Effingham River • 92 F/6 Great Central Lake

Boundaries: north: Stamp & Cameron Rivers, **east:** Nitinat & Englishman Rivers, **south:** Pacific Ocean, **west:** Alberni Inlet

Major Access Routes: The main highway access through Central Vancouver Island is Highway 4, which crosses Vancouver Island east to west from Parksville to Port Alberni and from there to Tofino, Ucluelet and Pacific Rim National Park. Travelling north or south on the Island Highway 19 take the major junction west on Highway 4 following signs for Port Alberni and Tofino. The following logging roads provide access to the east central Island Peaks:

Nitinat River Road: A very useful road linking Cowichan Lake to the Cameron River valley and Port Alberni.

Cameron River Main: Leaves Highway 4 just west of Alberni Summit along the Cameron valley underneath the west flank of Mt. Arrowsmith. Gives access to Labour Day Lake and Mt. Moriarty also. Can be reached south of Port Alberni at the Weyerhaeuser Franklin operations marshalling yard.

China Creek Main: Runs south of McLaughlin Ridge from the Bamfield Road to King Solomon Basin and the north side of Mt. McQuillan.

Thistle Mine Rd. - Museum Creek Main: Leaves the Bamfield Road south or Port Alberni heading east to the Mt. McQuillan group.

Nanaimo River Road: From Cassidy south of Nanaimo the Nanaimo River Rd. heads west to the chain of lakes in the Nanaimo River valley.

Englishman River Main: Heads south-west from Parksville to the lower flanks of Mt. Moriarty.

Forest Service & Logging Company Offices:

Port Alberni Forest District - 4227 Sixth Ave, Port Alberni, BC V9Y 4N1 Ph: 250 724-5786

Timberwest - Nanaimo Lakes -5055 Nanaimo River Rd., Nanaimo, BC V9X 1H3 Ph: (250) 729-3770

Weyerhaeuser - West Island Timberlands - Franklin Operations -Bag 2001, Port Alberni, BC V9Y 7N3 Ph: 250-720-4200

Other Information Sources:
• Hiking Trails II - South-Central Vancouver Island & Gulf Islands (8th ed. 2000 Richard K. Blier, ed.) VITIS
• Island Hikes.com www.islandhikes.com

Special Thanks:
Thanks to Craig Wagnell, Peter Rothermel, Sasha Kubicek & Lindsay Elms for assistance in preparing this chapter.

70 Melissa Wagnell hiking up Moriarty above Labour Day Lake.   photo: Craig Wagnell

Mt. Moriarty

Mt. Moriarty
photo: Sasha Kubicek

Mt. Moriarty
5,282 ft / 1,610 m

Mt. Moriarty is a series of low domed summits. The mountain is situated at the head of the Cameron, Englishman and Nanaimo Rivers. Below its south-west side, Labour Day Lake is a popular day-trip destination at the headwaters of the Cameron River. Mt. Moriarty is named after Lt. William Moriarty R.N. 1832-1881 stationed on HM surveying vessel Plumper.[1]

Map Sheet: 92 F/1 Nanaimo Lakes - GR 9443

Approaches: Mt. Moriarty can be approached from Labour Day Lake which in turn can be reached from the Nanaimo River via Rockyrun Creek or from the Cameron River Main. From the latter follow a good trail from the logging road down to the east shore of the lake and part way along. Look for an indistinct trail and possible flagging tape leading rather directly up the open forest slope. This reaches the broad south ridge of Moriarty at about the elevation where there are natural meadows. Continuing north to the summit involves scrambling a couple of easy bluffs.

Additional Info: Island Bushwhacker 1996 p.21

North-East Ridge:
This would be a popular route but for the fact that the Englishman River Main from Northwest Bay is gated and the additional impediment that the roads in upper Moriarty Creek are becoming very overgrown with alders. Turn west off the Island Highway at the traffic light by the huge riding barn a few km north of Nanoose. The gate may be staffed. Follow Englishman Main and turn left at 17.2 km up Moriarty Creek. Go right at 20.2 km and right at 21.6 km. At about 23.2 km the road drops a little and crosses Moriarty Ck. There is a big area to park, but the road beyond here is likely undriveable and very overgrown. Traverse upward and find the highest (middle) spur road leading onto this north approach to the mountain and follow it to its end, all in clearcut on the ridge top. Skirt a bluff on the left and soon gain pleasant meadows on the narrowing crest of the North-East Ridge. After a small notch the ridge rises more steeply. In snow-free conditions avoid the apparently difficult rock move on the left. In spring snow the mid-ridge is a steep narrow arete. Traverse right where the ridge merges with the upper mountain and enter the saddle below the summit. A gully on the right leads to the top.

View off Mt. Moriarty over Labour Day Lake.
photo: Craig Wagnell

Mt. Cokely

Mt. Cokely & Mt. Arrowsmith, east aspect from Texada Island, May.

Mt. Cokely
5,301 ft / 1,616 m

Mt. Cokely is a satellite summit just north of Mt. Arrowsmith and is often climbed en route to Arrowsmith from the ski area parking lot. Cokely is the site of the 'Arrowsmith' ski area and remains a great winter destination for a few quick turns.

Map Sheet: 92 F/ 2 Alberni Inlet - GR 8455

Approaches: Mt. Cokely can be approached by the original CPR trail at the east end of Cameron Lake on Highway 4. Start at the trailhead at th east end of Cameron Lake off Hwy. 4. The well-graded trail gently switch backs up the north slopes of Mt. Cokely. About a third of the way up the trail divides with the left fork (Lookout Trail) and the right fork (CPR Trail) and join together again in the Regional Ski Park providing about a five hour loop hike or an all day round trip to Mt. Cokely.

Cokely may also be reached by driving up the old ski area access road. From the signposted junction on the south side of Highway 4 just west of the Alberni Summit turn south onto a gravel road and continue to a prominent junction on the far side of a bridge. Turn left and drive up the valley, cross back over the Cameron River and then take the left fork, up a steep road, under the west side of Arrowsmith onto Pass Main. Continue through switchbacks, to a hairpin turn where an access point leads up a narrow valley to the col between Mt. Cokely and Arrowsmith on the "Saddle Route" to Arrowsmith. Hike up this valley turning left (east) at the saddle to reach Mt. Cokely and right (west) toward Arrowsmith. Further up the road, if the gate is open, continue to the ski area and ascend Mt. Cokely from the runs which run right up its north-west ridge. Cokely is an easy hike/ski tour from either of these approaches.

Mt. Cokely (far L) & Mt. Arrowsmith west aspect, January.

Mt. Arrowsmith

Mt. Arrowsmith, north-west aspect from Loon Lake, February.　　　　photo: Denise Hook

Mt. Arrowsmith
5,962 ft / 1,817 m

Mt. Arrowsmith is arguably the most popular mountain on Vancouver Island and is the highest point on the southern half of the Island. Although not tall by comparison to other Island peaks, it does dominate the skyline from the east side of Vancouver Island and from Port Alberni to the west.

It is located along the Cameron River Valley and Cameron Lake which, from Port Alberni to Qualicum Beach nearly cleaves the island in two, and the Englishman River watershed to Parksville. It is a familiar landmark from these towns and has played a big role in their respective histories. The CPR saw Arrowsmith as a likely alpine destination at the turn of the 20th century and established a lodge and trail at Cameron Lake, bringing a taste of Rockies development to the West Coast.

More recently, in the 70's, logging roads have wound around the mountain along with the accompanying shaving of its forests. An ill fated ski resort adorned the ridge off Mt. Cokely and its recently failed expansion has subsequently seen more conservation minded planning fall into place. Named for English cartographers Aaron and John Arrowsmith renowned for their accurate maps.

First Ascent: Possibly John Mahoun (1887), James Fletcher (1901) or Edward Whymper (1901-05)

Map Sheet: 92 F/ 2 Alberni Inlet - GR 8353

Approaches: Mt. Arrowsmith can still be approached by the original CPR Trail from the east end of Cameron Lake on Highway 4. Start at the trailhead at th east end of Cameron Lake off Hwy. 4. The well graded trail gently switch backs up the north slopes of Mt. Cokely. About a third of the way up the trail divides with the left fork (Lookout Trail) and the right fork (CPR Trail) and join together again in the Regional Ski Park providing about a five hour loop hike or an all day round trip to Mt. Cokely. Most climbers now prefer to utilize the high logging roads in the Cameron River valley. From the well sign posted junction on the south side of Highway 4 just west of the Alberni Summit turn south onto a gravel road and continue to a prominent junction on the far side of a bridge. Turn left and drive up the valley, cross back over the Cameron River and then take the left fork, up a steep road, under the west side of Arrowsmith on to Pass Main. From here the Judge's Route and other routes on the west side can be reached or continue higher, through switch backs, to a hair pin turn where a second access point leads up a narrow valley to the col between Mt. Cokely and Arrowsmith on the "Saddle Route". Further up the road, if the gate is open, continue to the ski area and ascend Mt. Cokely from the runs which run right up its ridge.

Additional Info: IB 1998 p.10, IB 2000 p.16, WIM #6 p.8, WIM #10 p.17

Mt. Arrowsmith south aspect from Cameron Valley, August. photo: Peter Rothermel

LG- * Lost Gully Route:** 4th class
This unmarked route starts from the third spur along Pass Main found at km 12.8 on Summit Main. Park at the Judge's pullout, walk back down the road to the 2nd spur. From the end of the spur follow a broad forested ridge to the subalpine. Angle right on an open slope and up two steep gullies to the South summit and traverse to the Main summit. One of the finest winter/spring alpine routes on Mt. Arrowsmith requires an ice axe and only worthwhile with snow cover. Descend via Judge's Route. Again this route requires a full day.

Note: route descriptions are marked in kilometres from the turnoff at Alberni Hump on Highway 4 onto the logging road Summit (Loon) Main to their respective trailheads.

PR- Pete's Route: low 5th class 100m
Takes a line just left of Lost Gully Route. 4th class leads to a chimney and an exposed face of low 5th. The South Summit has great promise for hard routes.
FA: Peter Koughan and Peter Rothermel

RR- Rudy's Route: low 5th class 150m
One of the finest moderate rock climbs on the massif. Start off at km 12.8 on spur Pass 32, the third spur on the right. Cross the creek as for Un-Judge's then leave that approach heading farther right parallel to Lost Gully. Climbs the south-west end of the mountain to Arrowsmith's South Summit. Rudy's Route has about three pitches of 5th and lots of exposed 4th class.
FA: Rudy Brugger

Arrowsmith South Ridge south-east aspect from the air, February. photo: Peter Rothermel

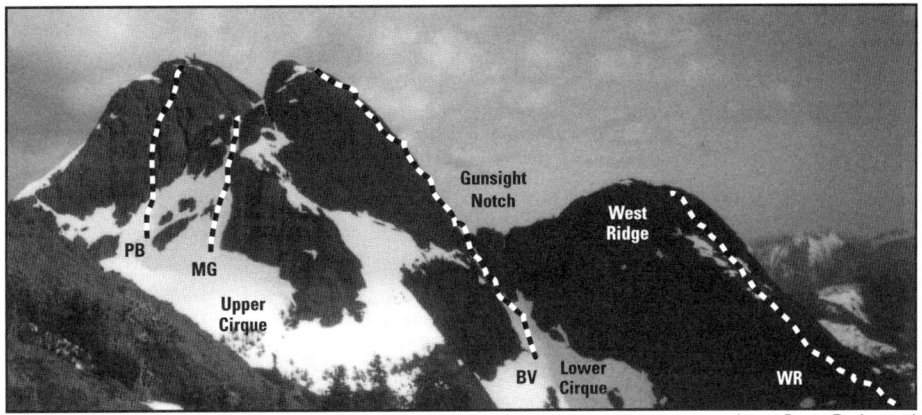

Mt. Arrowsmith, West Ridge north-west aspect from the Bumps, June.   photo: Peter Rothermel

UJ- *** Un-Judge's Route: 4th class
Start off at km 12.8 on spur Pass 32, the third spur on the right. The Un-Judge's heads up a ridge to the right of Judge's Route after crossing a creek bed. The upper ridge is bluffy and exposed in places with class 3 and 4 scrambling. It tops out to the west of the south summit and then follows a mostly 3rd class traverse to the main summit with a last step of class 4. Descend via Judge's. A great all-day trip in summer/fall.

JR- Judge's Route: 3rd class
Judge's is the shortest and easiest way to reach the summit of Arrowsmith. In the early 1970s Ralph Hutchinson, while pioneering this route, was pondering whether or not to accept an offered judgeship to the courts. He decided to take the "Judge's Route" and the name stuck. Start at the fourth logging road spur heading up Pass Main from km 13.3. Park at the pullout just past the start of the trail. Follow the well marked route with some 3rd class. Minimal exposure and difficulties are short lived. An excellent descent from other routes although some vehicle shuttling may be needed.
FA: Roger Neave, Bob Tustin, Ralph Hutchinson 1975

WR- **West Ridge: AI 2 (III)
Starts form the last switch back up Pass Main at Km 10.3. Start by hiking off the end of the switch back down into the creek draw. Instead of traversing along the creek (as for the Main Snow Gully), climb straight uphill through the mountain hemlock forest until you reach the subalpine. Climb the ridge along its crest, avoiding vertical rock bands by traversing south (right) and back to the crest. The ridge leads up and then down to the gunsight notch at the top of Brugger's. From here there are several variations possible to reach the summit; the easiest way is to traverse 100m across a shallow gully to the south (climbers' right) joining Judge's Route to the summit. or take the Newman-Foweraker gully to the top.

BV- Brugger's Variation: 4th class
A variation to the Judge's Route. Starts from the last switchback going up Pass Main at km 15.9. The start is unmarked but once underway flagging marks the route leading down into a draw and then up through the forest along side a creek. Eventually the route reaches the first of two cirques with a tarn and a couloir. From the first cirque the Brugger's Variation leads up a 35 degree gully, topping out to a traverse on to the Judge's Route.

MG- Main Snow Gully Route: 4th class
Starts from the last switch back going up Pass Main at km 15.9. The start is unmarked but once underway flagging marks the route leading down into a draw and then up through the forest alongside a creek. Eventually the route reaches the first of two cirques with a tarn and a couloir. Continue up the creek to a second Upper Cirque.
This Upper Cirque has numerous couloirs leading up to the "Bumps" and the "Nose". The most prominent of these gullies, the Main Snow Gully, a 45 degree couloir, goes to the right of the Nose topping out north-west of the summit. An excellent round trip can be made up the Main Snow Gully and descending partway down the Judge's, traversing to Brugger's Variation and down the same route to your vehicle. A great Winter/ Spring route area.

Mt. Arrowsmith Main Summit north aspect, January.

Mt. Arrowsmith Nose and Main Gully north aspect.
photo: Peter Rothermel

NF- **North Face:** (II)
Climbs the steep north-west face to the main summit. Approach on the Saddle Route and from the col below the Nose descend into the cirque on the west side of the mountain. Climb open corners and face left of an obvious gully that splits the middle of the face.
FA: Mike Walsh, 1975 or 1976

N- *** **The Nose via Saddle Route:** 4th class
This most popular hiking area starts at a hairpin turn on Pass Main at km 17.8 and leads to the col dividing Mt. Cokely and Mt. Arrowsmith. There are two flagged routes. To the right it is bluffier with views and to the left is an easier forest hike. From the col head left (east) to Mt. Cokely for a 3 hour return trip or head right (west) toward Mt. Arrowsmith. Keep to the ridge crest with some 3rd class over the "Bumps". Alternatively, from the col traverse out into the basin on the north-east side of the mountain. Ascend one of several gullies onto the summit ridge. The easternmost gully, the "Hourglass Couloir, is the easiest, at about 35 degrees. A final 45m pitch of exposed 4th class with bolted belays on the "Nose" gains the summit.

76 Mt. Arrowsmith

Mt. Arrowsmith, north-east aspect from Mt. Cokely, November. photo: Peter Rothermel

Direttissima:
The north side of Arrowsmith's main summit has a three-pitch mixed fifth class climb up a couloir that narrows to shoulder width in places.

Rosseau Trail: 3rd class
This old trail, built in the 1950s, is named after a Port Alberni mountaineer, Ralph Rosseau. Most climbers now access this route from Pass Main before the gate to the Regional Ski Park at km 18. It is an easy trail leading to a ridge hike and onto Mt. Cokely taking three hours round trip. A recommended loop hike is up the Saddle Route to Mt. Cokely and return via the Rosseau Trail, with a ten minute walk on the road back to your car.

Rambler's Route via Hidden & Fishtail Lakes:
There are a number of high alpine lakes and meadows on the east side of Mt. Arrowsmith. These routes go up the mountain from these lakes and are approached from the Island Hwy. at Weyerhaeuser's Northwest Bay Division on 155 Main. At about km 19 it crosses Englishman River, then left onto 143 A. Park at the gate if it's locked and hike up to the Arrowsmith Lake Dam site. The old route went clockwise around the lake but with possible rising levels of water from the dam, an alternative route might have to be found. Once on the north-west side of the lake a trail takes you to Hidden Lake. Further on is a tricky 3rd class route up and then down to Fishtail Lake or take an alternate route up a narrow draw.

Mt. Arrowsmith, north-east aspect from Mt. Cokely, March.

Mt. Arrowsmith **77**

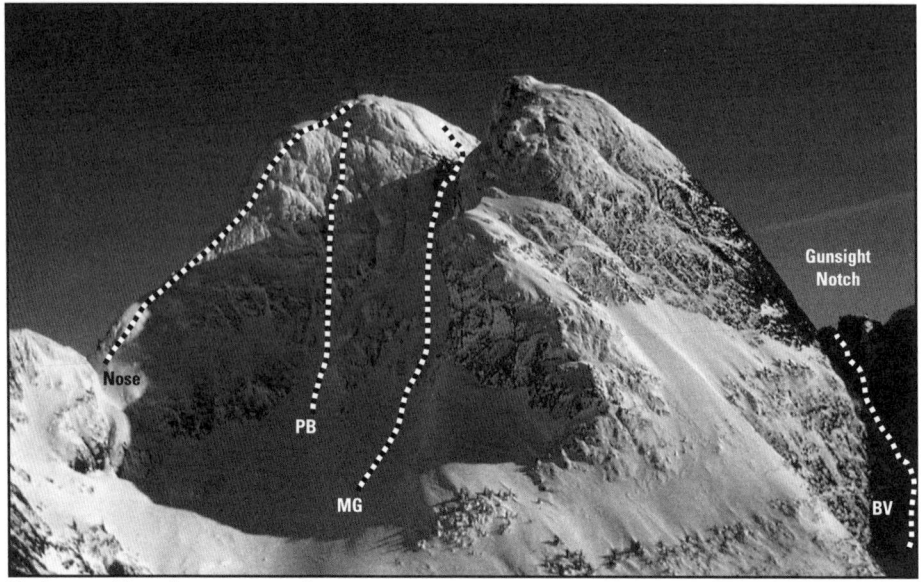

Mt. Arrowsmith north-west aspect, January.   photo: Sandy Briggs

Either route will lead to a ridge on the Rambler's Route to the "Dome", a prominent bump south of the south summit. This side of the massif is little visited, mostly due to access rather than the desirability of the terrain, which was a popular backcountry ski destinations, when the logging roads were in better shape.

Winter Routes

NF Newman - Foweraker Route: AI3 150m
Climbs a short steep gully on the West Ridge of the mountain. Approach from the top of "Brugger's" on the Main Snow Gully Route. Start up a short 15m section of 75° ice. Above the angle of the gully eases to 65°. Continue up some mixed ground to the top of the West Buttress.
FA: Don Newman, Greg Foweraker, spring 1987

Sunday Stroll: AI4 50m
Takes the buttress left of the main ridge from Cokely col. 1 pitch climb that has thin water ice in a narrow gully. Gully is so narrow at one point that you have to turn your shoulder sideways. Protection almost none existant.
FA: Mike Walsh, Joe Bajan, circa 1975

Too Thin: AI4/5 100m
Left of the Nose and exits directly onto the summit. 2 pitches on thin ice.
FA Don Cohen, Joe Bajan, 1986 or 1987

In a winter if conditions are right, there are several ice climbs which form up on the crags along the Pass Main road to the ski area. At the beginning of the Saddle route on the right is a 50m weepy wall.

About 1.5km past the park gate on the right is a very serious 120m wall with a creek trickling down its face, with route names like "Crystal Chandelier" and "Bloody Knuckles".

A beginner's area can be found along the creek on the Snow Gully route where the water cascades over some small drops in a small box canyon. Called "The Ice Box", it has a half-dozen climbs of about 15m.

Rock Climbs

Most notable wall for hard technical routes is the first cirque on the Snow Gully route. Greg Sorenson has established three routes on this wall, known as 'the Bee Hive'. Rappel/ belay bolts have been placed at the top of each pitch:

'When Nature Calls' a three-pitch crack at 5.10, 'Lift Me Up' a two-pitch crack at 5.9 and 'Hypnotizin' a two-pitch face climb at 5.11

Another climbing area of great potential is along the Rosseau Trail, just as it gains the ridge. There is a broad band of pillow lava that promises to hold many short, yet challenging rock climbs.

Mt. McQuillan

Mt. McQuillan west aspect from west summit, July. photo: Sasha Kubicek

Mt. McQuillan
5,167 ft / 1,575 m

Mt. McQuillan is found at the head of the Franklin River which drains into the east shore of Alberni Inlet halfway down the inlet. The surrounding area around Mt. McQuillan, Douglas Peak and Limestone Mountain is a popular recreation area for Alberni locals. Mining activity among these mountains has left a legacy of old trails many of which are still utilized by hikers and climbers.

Map Sheet: 92 F/2 Alberni Inlet - GR 8240

Approaches: Mt. McQuillan may be reached from Port Alberni via the Bamfield and China Creek roads. Or from Lake Cowichan via the Nitinat Main to Bamfield Road.

From Port Alberni follow signs for Bamfield. At Weyerhaeuser's yard 6 km south of town leave the Bamfield Road and take the China Creek Main heading left at a T junction. Drive south-east along China Creek Main to McQuillan Creek, park and hike in the trail southward to King Solomon Basin. From the east side of the basin locate an old miners trail and follow it up to a gully on the south side of the mountain. Continue up the gully to the west ridge of Mt. McQuillan. Scramble up the west ridge to the summit.

Alternatively approach from the west from Thistle Mine Rd. and the Mt. McQuillan trail. Drive south from Port Alberni following signs for Bamfield. Take a left up Thistle Mine Rd just north of the Franklin River bridge. Head east on Thistle Mine Road crossing the Franklin River on a bridge and continuing to the Mt. McQuillan trailhead. Hike the trail up the west ridge to the top.

A direct route up Mt. McQuillan is to scramble your way up the South Face from Panther Creek valley off Museum Creek Road. The route is steep bush with the odd rock bluff to climb up. Some route finding is required to avoid some cliffs and through the large bowl west of the South Face.

Driving in from Lake Cowichan on Nitinat Main; following signs for Bamfield is the best route to reach Thistle Mine and Museum Creek roads from the South Island.

Additional Info: IB 1996 p.17, IB 2001 p.17

Douglas Peak

Douglas Peak south aspect from Mt. McQuillan west summit, July. photo: Sasha Kubicek

Douglas Peak
4,888 ft / 1,490 m

Douglas Peak sits to the north-west of Mt. McQuillan on the north side of Father and Son Lake. The mountain is an easy day objective but can be combined with ascents of Mt. McQuillan or Limestone Mountain to make an overnight stay at Father and Son Lake worth the trip.

Map Sheet: 92 F/2 Alberni Inlet - GR 8043

Approaches: Douglas Peak is an easy climb from most aspects and is surrounded by logging roads offering access points all around the mountain.

A fine way to climb the mountain is from Father and Son Lake up the south ridge (see photo above). Follow approach description for Mt. McQuillan from Thistle Mine Road. Park at the end of Thistle Mine Road and start up the trail. Take the left (north) fork off the Mt. McQuillan trail toward Father and Son Lake. Hike around the west shore of the lake, leave the lake trail and head north to the summit of Douglas Peak.

Douglas Peak may also be approached from the west off Duck Main or from the north-east out of King Solomon Basin.

Unnamed peak south-east of Mt. McQuillan.
photo: Craig Wagnell

Limestone Mountain

Limestone Mountain summit. photo: Craig Wagnell

Limestone Mountain
4,856 ft / 1,480 m

A long high karst ridge between Franklin River, Father and Son Lake to the north and Museum Creek to the south.

Map Sheet: 92 F/2 Alberni Inlet - GR 7939

Approaches: Limestone Mountain is easily reached from spur roads off Thistle Mine Road. Follow approach description for Mt. McQuillan from Port Alberni on Thistle Mine Road. Just 1.5 km short of the end of the road turn right on BR 50. Keep right and follow the roads up the north-west flank of the mountain. Hike up the gentle terrain along the west ridge.

Museum Creek Main and then up road P100 and it's branches gives acces to the East Ridge of Limestone Mountain.

Additional Info: IB 1996 p.8

Looking down the west ridge of Limestone Mountain. photo: Craig Wagnell

Kennedy Lake from Mackenzie Range. photo: Francis Bruhwile

West Central
Vancouver Island

84   Kennedy River alongside Highway 4.

West Central Vancouver Island
Contents

Mt. Klitsa	89
Adder Peak	90
Mt. Gibson	90
Mt. Hannah	91
Nahmint Mountain	92
50-40 Peak	93
Mt. Hall	94
Triple Peak	95
Cat's Ears Peak	96
Canoe Peak	97
Mackenzie Range	99
Redwall	101
Pogo Mountain	102
Steamboat Peak	103
Mt. Maitland	104
Hidden Peak	105
Rhino Peak	106
Little Eiger	107
Velella Peak	108
Mt. Quimper	109

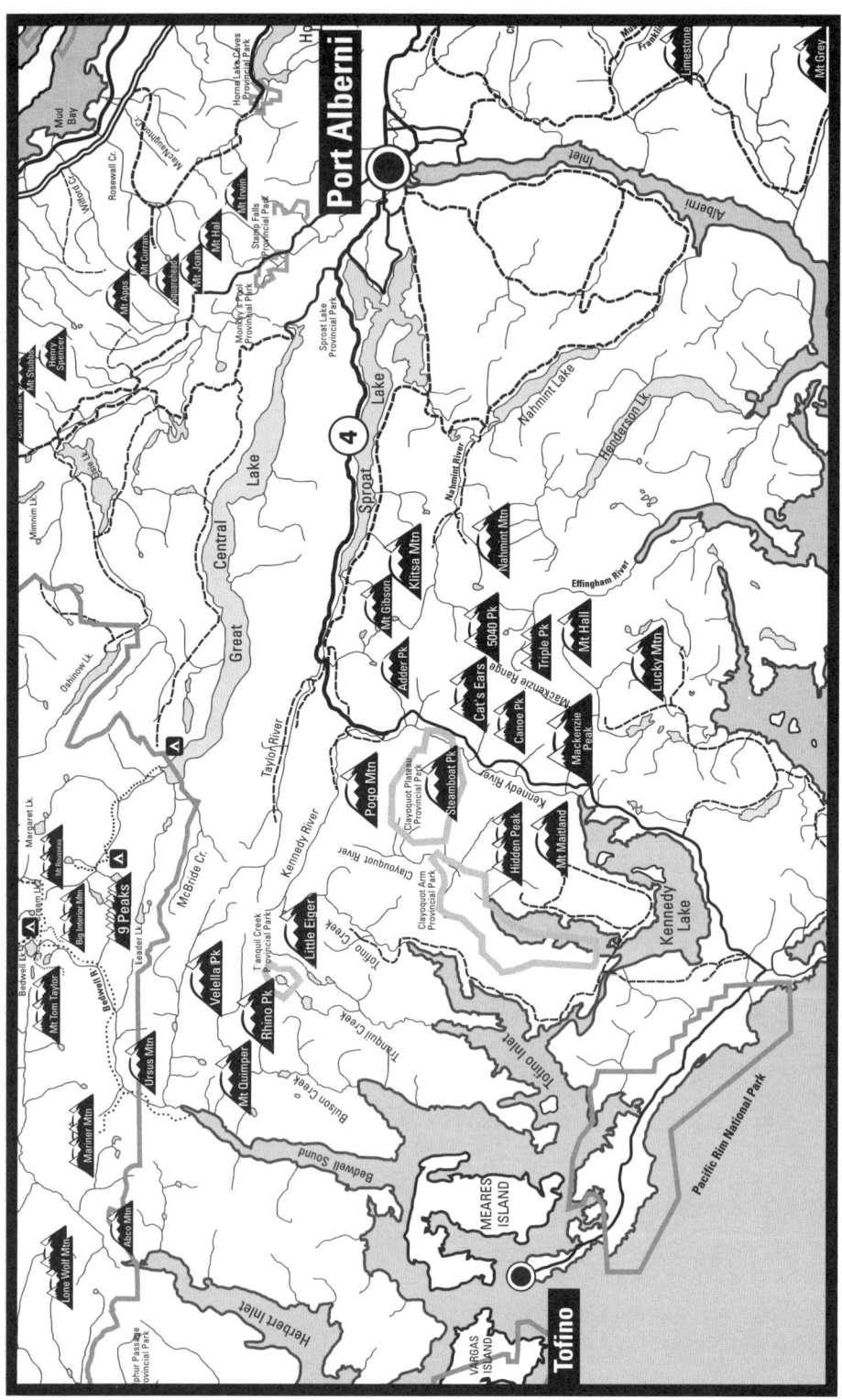

86 West Central Vancouver Island - Map

West Central Vancouver Island

To the west of Alberni Inlet the Island's mountainous backbone becomes more pronounced and from the west central Island this alpine spine makes an uninterrupted run 300+ km to Quatsino Sound in northern Vancouver Island. The west central Island peaks are small but very rugged and offer a taste of the character of their higher cousins to the north. The area offers both moderate hiking peaks and short but challenging alpine climbs, with superlative views of Barkely and Clayoquot Sounds.

Map Sheets: 92 F/3 Effingham River • 92 F/6 Great Central Lake • 92 F/4

Boundaries: north: Ursus & McBride Creeks, **east:** Alberni Inlet, **south:** Barkley Sound, **west:** Pacific Ocean

Major Access Routes: The main highway access through Central Vancouver Island is Highway 4 which crosses Vancouver Island east to west from Parksville to Port Alberni and from there to Tofino, Ucluelet and Pacific Rim National Park. Travelling north or south on the Island Highway 19 take the major junction west on Highway 4 following signs for Port Alberni and Tofino. Continue through Port Alberni on 4. Some of the peaks in the west central Island may be reached directly from this highway while others require a drive on some of the gravel logging roads listed below.

Two of the most important logging roads into the west central Island leave Highway 4 just west of Port Alberni. The Sterling Arm Road runs around the south shore of Sterling and Two Rivers arms of Sproat Lake, eventually linking to both the Nahmint Main, which heads south to Nahmint Lake and the South Taylor Main, which continues along the south side of Sproat Lake to rejoin Highway 4 at the west end of Sproat Lake. The second road system heads south from Port Alberni along the west side of Alberni Inlet. This road weaves in and out of a number of valleys and also provides access into the Nahmint River valley.

At the west end of Sproat Lake the Taylor Main crosses Highway 4 and continues west up the Taylor valley. Just a few kilometres before the Ucluelet-Tofino junction on Highway 4 the West Main Road crosses the highway. The north branch of this road leads around the west side of Kennedy Lake and to Clayoquot Arm and Tofino Inlet.

Forest Service & Logging Company Offices:
Port Alberni Forest District - 4227 Sixth Ave, Port Alberni BC V9Y 4N1 Ph: 250 724-5786

Weyerhaeuser - West Island Timberlands - Sproat Lake Operations
-Port Alberni, BC V9Y 7N4 Ph: 250-720-4100

Other Information Sources:
Island Bushwhacker
Island Hikes: www.islandhikes.com

Special Thanks:
Thanks to Craig Wagnell, Sandy Briggs and Francis Bruhwiler for assistance in preparing this chapter.

88 Jami Thompson just below summit of Steamboat Peak. photo: Craig Wagnell

Mt. Klitsa

Mt. Klitsa north-west aspect from approach route, May photo: Craig Wagnell

Mt. Klitsa
5,387 ft / 1,642m

Mt. Klitsa overlooks the west end of Sproat Lake on its south shore. The mountain's impressive north east face is clearly visible from Highway 4 west of Port Alberni overlooking Sproat Lake. Klitsa is derived from 'Kleet-sah' an aboriginal word meaning 'always white' or 'snow'.

First Ascent: Possibly surveyors in 1927

Map Sheet: 92 F/6 Great Central Lake GR 3757 (see also 92 F/3 Effingham River)

Approaches: Follow Highway 4 from Port Alberni west along the north shore of Sproat Lake. Just west of the Taylor River rest area take a left off the highway onto the South Taylor Main logging road. Take spur road 552E right to the Gibson-Klitsa trailhead which climbs the standard route up the north-west ridge of the mountain past a small lake.

Another route takes the long east ridge from Antler Creek Main. From South Taylor Main head south along Antler Creek Main. Drive to the end of the road and gain the east ridge by hiking up a fairly clean clearcut to the timber line. Once in the timber head south-west and stay on the crest of the ridge. Watch for sinkholes while crossing over a small limestone area. The ridge opens up to small rock bluffs that are easily passed, pleasant hiking in open meadows to the repeater that sits south of the summit.

In early season with good snow cover the Great Gully" (the snow gully in the back of the basin, east of the trail route), may be a better alternative and makes a good ski descent; however, the top of this gully is quite steep and is prone to avalanches. From this same basin one can turn left up a different gully and gain a spur ridge which joins the upper part of the east ridge making a pleasant loop, descending the normal trail.

Mt. Klitsa can also be reached from Brigade Lake. See Mt. Gibson approach details. From Brigade Lake make your way to north end of Richards Lake (lake furthest south), and then up west ridge of Klitsa. The fastest route is a flagged line from the Nahmint valley off Br 600 near the water survey tower.

Additional Info: IB 1998 p.23, IB 2001 p.13, WIM #12 p.21, www.islandhikes.com

Adder Peak

Adder Peak, July. photo: Craig Wagnell

Adder Peak
4,855 ft / 1,480 m

Adder Peak is a low, dome-shaped summit located at the headwaters of the Nahmint River which drains to its east. Adder Peak overlooks Highway 4, which curves around its north and west sides through Sutton Pass. To the west is Kennedy River. Adder Peak is at the north end of the mountain ridge system that includes the Mackenzie Range to the south.

First Ascent: Jackson-McCaw survey party 1941

Map Sheet: 92 F/3 Effingham River - GR 3157

Approaches: Adder Peak can be reached from logging roads in Marion Creek which leaves Highway 4 eight kilometres west of Sutton Pass. Hike up branch MC 30 which switchbacks up the west flank of the mountain. In winter or spring climb a long snow gully (the Adder's Tongue) to the ridge north of the summit. An alternative approach may be made from the south-east in the Nahmint valley by following spur road N-800 to the very end, or directly from logging roads above Sutton Pass.

The Louise Geotting Lake Trail is another good way to access Adder Peak. Follow Marion Creek Main to MC40. Follow MC40 to upper left clearcut near creek. Head up cut looking for flagging tape marking trail. Trail follows south side of creek to lake. Cut down to west side of lake crossing start of creek and then up slopes, staying left of rock bluffs to the east. Hike direct to the summit.

Mt. Gibson
4,370 ft / 1,332 m

A summit north-west of Mt. Klitsa overlooking the west end of Sproat Lake. A good destination for a day hike or an overnight trip with a cluster of alpine lakes to explore to the south-west of the peak.

Map Sheet: 92 F/6 Great Central Lake GR 3559

Approaches: Follow the approach details for Mt. Klitsa. From the pass between Mt. Klitsa and Gibson, ascend the east side of Mt. Gibson with an easy hike to the top. Alternatively, a trail to Brigade Lake leads to a subsequently bushy ascent from the west. This trail starts from the upper tier logging road above a large logging road intersection just off Highway 4 near South Sutton Creek. There has recently been logging near this trail.

Mt. Hannah

Mt. Hannah north aspect, May.　　　　　　　　　　　　　　　　　photo: Craig Wagnell

Mt. Hannah
4,101 ft / 1,250 m

Mt. Hannah is a low but surprisingly impressive peak located on the south side of the Nahmint River only a few kilometres from the ocean at Nahmint Bay, Alberni Inlet.

Map Sheet: 92 F/2 Alberni Inlet - GR 5636

Approaches: From Port Alberni, travel west down Alberni Inlet via logging roads to the McTush Campsite, a short distance farther the main line turns away from the Inlet and head towards Nahmint Lake. At 37 km start looking for a main road on your left. This will take you across the Nahmint River. Once across, take the next road to your left, drive up a small hill which starts to follow back downstream on the other side of the river. Stay on this road for about 4 km keeping to the right at all times. You will have to keep a watchful eye out for an old road on the left that has a sign posted warning about alder snags- this is the road to hike up. If you've gone too far you will come to an abandoned bridge. Hike 3 km up the old road to reach the old-growth forest. Once at the old-growth timber hike up the prominent north ridge and just below the rock face head left and climb the avalanche-prone snow bowl to the summit ridge.

Additional Info: www.islandhikes.com

Mt. Hannah north aspect, May.　　　　　　　　　　　　　　　　　photo: Craig Wagnell

Nahmint Mountain

Aerial view of Nahmint Mountain north-west aspect, May.   photo: Craig Wagnell

Nahmint Mountain
5,144 ft / 1,568 m

Nahmint Mountain lies just south of the Nahmint River valley, one of the most beautiful watersheds in the central Island. It is an impressive peak and overlooks Nahmint and Henderson lakes to the east, and Barkley Sound to the south.

Map Sheet: 92 F/3 Effingham River - GR 3852

Approaches: West ridge has been made possible as a day hike due to recent logging. Head up the N-600 Mainline to 68 km post- you get an excellent view of French Falls here. Turn left and left again, then drive over two bridges and follow the road up to its highest point. Hike up the slash and look for flagging tape that should take you up to the alpine. From here you can either cross over the north bowl and head up to the saddle, or stay on the ridge, climb a small peak and then back down to the saddle. Climb steep grassy knolls or stay in the juniper to reach the summit.

Nahmint Mt. can also be reached by hiking the high connecting ridge from 50-40 Peak (see photo below). Or alternatively from the Nahmint Main and its branch, the Beverly Main, to gain access up the east ridge.

Additional Info: IB 2001 p.39, www.islandhikes.com

50-40 Peak and the connecting ridge to Nahmint Mountain south-west aspect, August.

50-40 Peak

50-40 Peak south-west aspect — photo: Craig Wagnell

50-40 Peak
5,040 ft / 1,536 m

A round-topped peak at the head of the Effingham River. 50-40 Peak is a good day trip objective and provides access to Beverly Lake and Nahmint Mountain to the east for a longer outing.

First Ascent: Geological Survey of Canada 1910

Map Sheet: 92 F/3 Effingham River - GR 3351

Approaches: Approach 50-40 Peak from the Marion Creek Main which is found 8 km west of Sutton Pass off Highway 4. Drive ~10 km along the road to park at the foot of the broad north-west ridge of the mountain between the two bridges. Walk up the deactivated road "Marion 80" for only about 50m before heading up into the timber. Follow a rough flagged route through a band of cliffs just below treeline. Continue on easy hiking terrain along the ridge directly to the summit.

Another route takes the south ridge from Effingham Creek which gives faster access to the alpine. Drive past the pull-out to the north-west Ridge and follow the road up to the very end at its highest point. Hike into the timber up the steep bushy south ridge to the alpine. Hike around the rock buttress on the south side and head up to the col. Left takes you to the 50-40 summit, and straight takes you down towards the high alpine ridge that leads towards Nahmint Mountain and Beverly Lake (see photo below)

photo: Craig Wagnell

Mt. Hall

Mt. Hall north aspect, October.   photo: Craig Wagnell

Mt. Hall
4,724 ft / 1,440 m

Mt. Hall is an isolated mountain in an impressive situation overlooking the head of Effingham Inlet on the divide between the Effingham and Toquart rivers.

First Recorded Ascent: Russ Moir, Rick Johnson, Hinrich Schaefer, Sandy Briggs, June 24, 2002

Map Sheet: 92 F/3 Effingham River - GR 3444

Approaches: Mt. Hall may be approached with a long drive from logging roads in Toquart River. Logging roads in the upper Toquart River lead to the base of Mt. Hall on the northwest and southwest sides, though some bridges have been removed and the last few kilometres must be hiked.

Hike up the drainage northwest of the summit and then directly up the basin to the top. It's an easy snow ascent early in the season.

Additional Info: www.islandhikes.com

Peaks east of Kennedy River from Hidden Peak, September.   photo: Francis Bruhwiler

Triple Peak

Triple Peak north aspect from 50-40 Peak, August.   photo Craig Wagnell

Triple Peak
5,003 ft / 1,525 m

Triple Peak is south-east of Cat's Ears and to the west of Effingham Lake. It is a very impressive peak with several prominent rock buttresses offering some fine sport for technical lines.

First Ascent: Rick Eppler, Rob Macdonald, 1984

Map Sheet: 92 F/3 Effingham River - GR 3247

Approaches: Approach from the Cat's Ears Creek logging road which is reached 60 km west of Port Alberni on Highway 4. Continue up the valley to the end of the logging road and pick up an old miners' trail which leads up to the pass between Cat's Ears Creek and Effingham River.

Head south up very steep, timbered terrain to the treeline and the high lake perched at the north-west end of the Triple Peak massif. Hike up the ridge south from the lake and continue along the crest as it swings south-east to meet the foot of the north summit tower. Drop around on the north side of the north summit and traverse a snowfield to below the middle (highest) summit.

A better approach involves following the Marion Creek main through the Effingham pass and downhill until directly opposite the several waterfalls of the creek draining the lower of the two lakes north-west of Triple Peak. Leave the road and head for the right side of the bottom of the cascade. It is easy to cross the nascent Effingham River here but a small ravine shortly thereafter is more difficult. About an hour of bushwhacking gets you to the bottom of the cascade a little above its confluence with the Effingham River. Scramble upward on the right side (river left) of the creek, a sequence of open rock and short bush thickets. Cross the creek about 100m below the lake and scramble easily in open terrain to the lake outlet.

The normal route leaves the snowfield to gain the left of two minor gully systems slightly to the right of centre of the north-east face of the main (middle) peak. Climb rightward for about a pitch (low 5th class, rope may be required), then move left into a steep heather gully that leads up to a chimney topped with a chockstone. Climb behind the chockstone and ascend steep heather to reach the summit ridge. Follow the ridge to the summit.

From the col between the middle and north peaks the north peak may be climbed up the east ridge with class 4 difficulties.

Additional Info: IB 1996 p.27, IB 2001 p.38 www.islandhikes.com

Cat's Ears Peak

Cat's Ears Peak north aspect, May. photo: Craig Wagnell

Cat's Ears Peak
4,855 ft / 1,480 m

Cat's Ears is a long ridge of a mountain at the north end of the Mackenzie Range having an impressive twin-peaked-gendarme on its north side from which it takes its name.

First Ascent: R. Eppler, D. Hobil, K. Johnson, R. Macdonald - 1980

Map Sheet: 92 F/3 Effingham River - GR 2948

Approaches: Approach Cat's Ears from Highway 4 up the Cats Ears Creek logging road 60 km west of Port Alberni. Gain the west ridge of the mountain (steep, timbered). then follow the ridge to below the west 'ear' and continue up 5th class scrambling to the top- a rope may be required.

Alternatively take the same approach as you would to climb Triple Peak. Starting from the back end of Marion Creek walk up the "washed out" logging road that takes you to the headwaters of Cat's Ear Creek. Climb steep bush to be able to gain access to the upper ridge head west and scramble up the ridge (good exposure). In late spring you can climb up the North Face to the summit, making for and enjoyable snow route.

Additional Info: IB 1997 p.11, IB 2000 p.22, www.islandhikes.com

Triple Peak (L) Mackenzie Peak (C) & Cat's Ears Peak (R) north aspect from Peak 50-40, August.

Canoe Peak

Canoe Peak south aspect, October.　　　　　　　　　　　　　　　　photo: Craig Wagnell

Canoe Peak
4,724 ft / 1,440 m

Canoe Peak lies at the head of Canoe Creek between Cat's Ears Peak to the north and Mackenzie Peak to the south. The mountain is a superb vantage point from which to view the more dramatic peaks that surround it.

First Recorded Ascent: Lindsay Elms, August 23, 1996

Map Sheet: 92 F/3 Effingham River - GR 2847

Approaches: Follow approach details for Mackenzie Peak on the 'Climber's Trail' to the alpine. Drop down from the col on the west side of Redwall Peak. Contour under Redwall until you can descend to below the north side of the pinnacles. Traverse to the ridge that connects the Mackenzie Range Pinnacles to Canoe Peak. Hike up the West Ridge of Canoe Peak. A steep dark gully ascends through a rock band followed by an easy scramble to the summit. An alternate approach is from Canoe Creek.

photo: Craig Wagnell

Darcy MacGillvray rappelling off North-West Ridge of Redwall.   photo: Francis Bruhwiler

Mackenzie Range

Mackenzie Range north aspect from Cat's Ears Peak, April.   photo: Sandy Briggs

Mackenzie Range
4,450 ft / 1,360 m

The Mackenzie Range, as marked on the NTS map sheet, refers to the range of mountains betwen the headwaters of Toquart Creek to the east and Kennedy River to the west. This includes Cat's Ears and Canoe Peak at the north end of the range. Climbers, referring to the Mackenzie Range, usually mean the east-west line of rocky pinnacles concentrated near GR2747. Mackenzie Peak is the highest of these summits south of Canoe Creek, in the centre of the range as marked on the NTS topo. The Mackenzie pinnacles as a whole are home to the most concentrated group of technical routes in the Central Island with room for many more lines. The situation overlooking Kennedy Lake with Pacific Rim National Park beyond is superb which, combined with good trail access off Highway 4, makes the Mackenzie Range the southern Island's premier alpine climbing destination. It is always a good idea to take helmets when climbing here; water can be a problem in late summer and fall.

First Ascent: P. Guilbride, S. Watts 1968

First Winter Ascent: B. Perry, M. Walsh 1972

Map Sheet: 92 F/3 Effingham River - GR 2746

Approaches: About 2.5 km south-west of Canoe Creek on Highway 4, just before a wide gravel pull-out on the right, there is an overgrown logging road heading left toward the range. Park 50m up this road. Hike the road to where flagging leads left, crossing a small creek. The narrow trail ascends through the old clearcut to the forest edge where a sign marks the 'Climbers' Trail'. The rough, steep trail leads to some meadows with a cluster of very small ponds below the west end of Mackenzie Peak. To the north is 'Perez Lookout', a small promontory at 1280m. To reach Redwall, hike through the col between Mackenzie Peak and Perez Lookout.

Additional Info: IB 1997 p.26, IB 1996 p.5, IB 1993 p.13, www.islandhikes.com

Redwall from Flat Top.   photo: Francis Bruhwiler

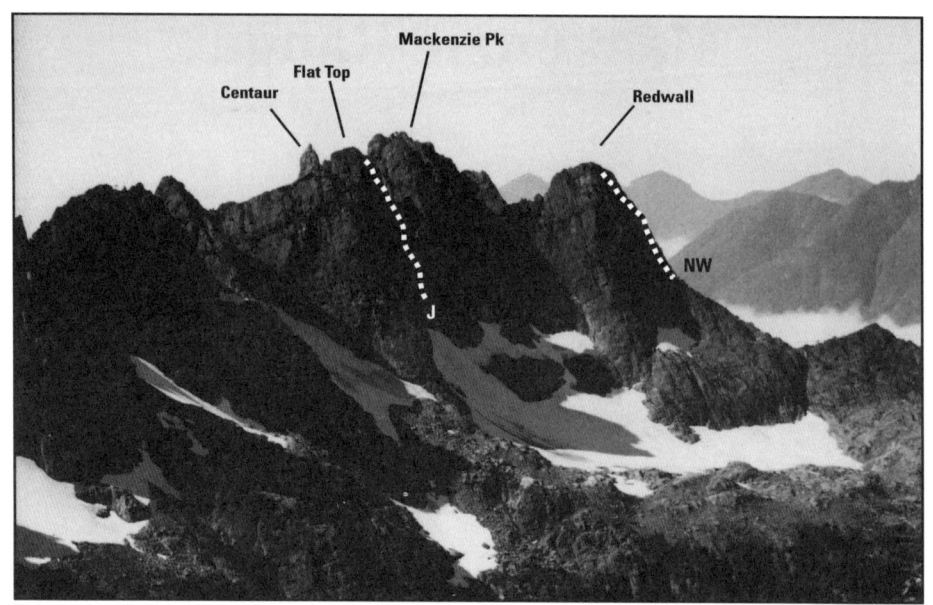

The Mackenzie Range summits, north-east aspect from Canoe Peak, September.   photo: Francis Bruhwiler

The Centaur

A double-topped spire toward the eastern end of the main group of pinnacles. From some viewpoints it has the approximate profile of this mythical beast, though from its south side approach it looks like a short tower.

Approaches: Climb the gully on the south side between the Centaur and the Witch Hat. After the snow goes, this involves climbing up behind a large chockstone, followed by a harder move to reach the friendly terrain at the base of Witch Hat. Traverse east around the base of Centaur to the North-East Ridge.

North-East Ridge: 5.6 (III)
Exit the gully below the col to gain the crest of the North-East Ridge. Great scrambling with a little 5.6
FA: Ron Facer, Mike Walsh, 1969

Witch Hat

Standard Route: Class 4
The is the next double peak west of the Centaur, and rather lower. Approach up the same gully as for the Centaur up the south side of the peaks to the col. From the col it is a class 3/4 scramble up the west side of the two pinnacles.
FA: Ron Facer, Mike Walsh, 1969

Flat Top

Standard Route: low 5th Class
Approach by climbing from the south, part way up the gully left (west) of Shadowblade. Traverse up and right, through bush around the base of Shadow Blade and then climb clean rock (at least class 4) to the gully between Shadow Blade and Flat Top. From the notch between Flat Top and Shadow Blade climb direct with a few 5th class moves leading to easier ground.
FA: Mike Walsh, Bill Perry, 1972

J - Jinx Removal: 5.9 300 m (II)
Starts up the easternmost chimney to climbers' left of the main gully between Flat Top and Witch's Hat. Climb three pitches to a ledge near the top of gully. Scramble up the gully to a treed ledge. Traverse right 40 m on the ledge. Climb up a crack past a small roof 5.9 to another ledge. Take a small chimney to the summit.
FA: John Kristian, Francis Bruhwiler, Sept 26, 1998

Mackenzie Peak

This is the highest summit in the Mackenzie Range. Mackenzie Peak is usually approached and climbed from the west with a bushy, stiff 4th class scramble to the summit- a rope may be required especially for the descent. Mackenzie may also be climbed from the col between it and Redwall Peak. The summit offers great views of Kennedy Lake to the west and the Broken Islands to the south.

100 Mackenzie Range

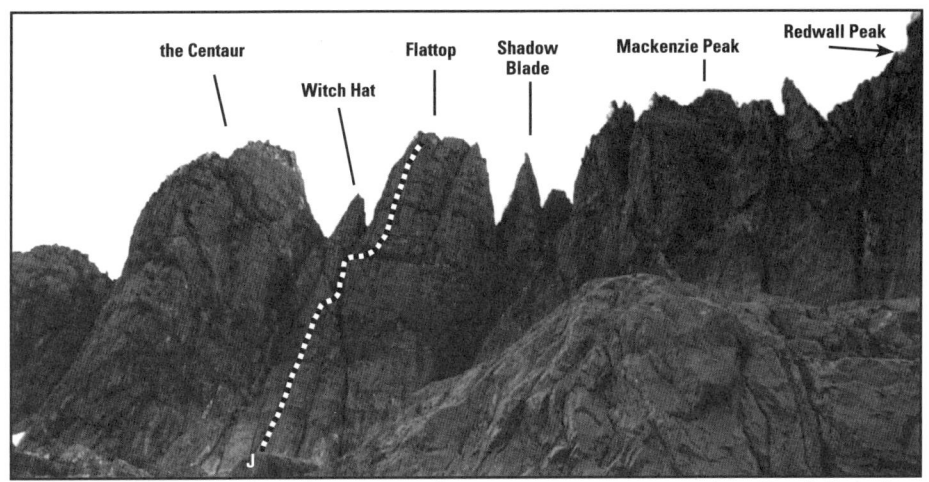

The Mackenzie Range summits north-west aspect, August. photo: Francis Bruhwiler

Shadowblade

Standard Route: 5.6 75m
Climb the slender pinnacle from the Flat Top - Shadow Blade col.
FA: Mike Walsh, Bill Perry 1972

Redwall

A dramatic basalt spire at the north-west end of the Mackenzie Range.

SR- ***Standard Route:** Low 5th Class
Approach directly to the col between Redwall and Mackenzie Peak by scrambling up a series of bushy, loose ledges and a grotty corner you may want to belay. Continue direct up the South-East Ridge after an awkward start. Two variations are possible 1) make a long traverse out right above the South Face on a narrowing ledge to steep 5.4 moves up to the summit or 2) climb the crest of the ridge with 5.6 moves leading to easier ground. Either route is runout on good rock. Descend by rappelling the route. (IB 1996)
FA: Richard Culbert, T. Stevens 1960

Looking up Redwall's North-West Ridge.
photo: Francis Bruhwiler

NW- ****North-West Ridge:** 5.6 225m (II)
A southern Island classic! A bit bushy but a fun route up fairly good rock and superb atmosphere. Start up a steep exposed ramp covered in small cedars. Five short pitches of steep 4th class and low 5th lead to the base of a 15m wall. Climb the wall direct, 5.6, to the summit. Descend by rappelling/downclimbing the Standard Route down the South-East Ridge or back down the North-West Ridge. (IB 1993)
FA: Rick Johnson, John Pratt, 24 May 1993

Redwall Peak.
photo: Francis Bruhwiler

Mackenzie Range

Pogo Mountain

Pogo Mountain south aspect from 50-40 Peak, October.　　　photo: Craig Wagnell

Pogo Mountain
4,888 ft / 1,490 m

Pogo Mountain is a familiar landmark from Highway 4 clearly visible overlooking the Kennedy River valley from just west of Sutton Pass. It was previously, unelegantly known as 'Tit Mountain'.

First Ascent: Jackson-McCaw survey party 1941

Map Sheet: 92 F/5 Great Central Lake GR 2459

Approaches: Leave Highway 4, 1.5 km west of Sutton Pass on the logging road that breaks off the highway westward just before Kennedy River joins the highway corridor. This road follows the upper Kennedy River. Leave it after only .8 km, turning left on BR 560. Drive south on BR 560 parking at the bridge over Kennedy River and continue on foot for a total of 2 km. Locate a spur road, which may help gaining some elevation on Pogo Mountain's east flank. Hike up the forested hillside east of the summit to the top. Bushy. and much better with snow.

Alternatively, Pogo Mountain can be climbed by its elegant north ridge. Follow Upper Kennedy River logging road (513) across the bridge over Kennedy River. Park about 100m farther in small pullout on right. Head south through short clearcut and then old-growth to alpine. Follow the open north ridge gaining the final summit ridge via a short scramble.

Pogo Mountain east aspect from Adder Peak note North Ridge on right skyline, May.　　photo: Craig Wagnell

Steamboat Peak

Steamboat Peak south-east aspect from 50-40 Peak, August.   photo: Craig Wagnell

Steamboat Peak
4,806 ft / 1,465 m

Steamboat Peak lies in the middle of the Maitland Range in Clayoquot Plateau Provincial Park. It overlooks Kennedy River and Highway 4, which run along its east side, while to the west is the open alpine terrain of the Clayoquot Plateau and the Clayoquot River valley beyond. Steamboat Peak and the surrounding alpine across the plateau offer some of the more expansive and readily accessible areas of alpine in the central Island. There is enough terrain to soak up a few days exploring on foot or on skis.

First Ascent: Jackson-McCaw survey party 1941
Map Sheet: 92 F/3 Effingham River - GR 2354

Approaches: Follow approach description for Pogo Mountain. Continue along Branch 560 to just before a bridge over an unnamed creek draining the north side of Steamboat Peak. Turn right onto this road to locate the 'Cavers' trail' at the end. Hike up the Cavers' trail onto the high open summits north-west of Steamboat Peak. Hike south-east to a col ("the lake district") below Steamboat then take the open ridge above the north side of the lakes over Peak 1113 and on to the ridge just north of the summit. There is a prominent eastern summit known as 'the Prow' of the Steamboat. It involves a little 5th class climbing from a loose notch.

A recent cavers' "Quaggers" trail has been built that makes it possible to hike up to the summit and back out in one day. Take a right off Highway 4 at km 55. Drive over the Kennedy River follow the road downstream and take the first right. Hike up or drive (4 x4) to the end of the road to almost the highest point. Cross over the creek and walk up an overgrown road for 100m, turn right and hike up a dry creek bed to the top of the slash. From here you can follow the flagging tape all the way up to the lower of the two lakes. Cross over the outlet stream then hike up the alpine for a ways, then cross over to the main draw on your left. Hike up the creek taking the obvious route to the summit. Steamboat Peak may also be climbed from the south off the Kenquot Main logging road. Hike the south ridge to the summit.

Unnamed Peaks north-west of Steamboat Peak   photo: Craig Wagnell

Mt. Maitland

Mt. Maitland (L) & Hidden Peak (R) north-east aspect from Adder Peak, June.   photo: Craig Wagnell

Mt. Maitland
3,937 ft / 1,200 m

Mt. Maitland is an unassuming peak at the south end of the Maitland Range with a superb situation overlooking Kennedy Lake. It is overshadowed by its much more attractive neighbour Hidden Peak to the north. Curiously the peak is not the highest peak in the Maitland Range. Likely this is because Mt. Maitland is the summit most visible from boats off Long Beach (or even on Kennedy Lake) and the higher top is.. well hidden. The mountain is named after Rear Admiral Sir Thomas Maitland 1803-1878.[3]

First Ascent: Jackson-McCaw survey party, 1941

Map Sheet: 92 F/3 Effingham River - GR 2045

Approaches: The Maitland Range and Hidden Peak have been approached from the south-west out of the Sand River valley via Mountain Woodfern Lake. See under approach details for Hidden Peak.

A newer bridge over the Kennedy River 2 km upstream of the river's outlet into Kennedy Lake can be used to approach Mt. Maitland from the north-east. Cross the Kennedy River bridge which is about 2 km upstream from Kennedy Lake. Go north about 1 km and turn left onto a spur that gains the hanging valley containing the small lake east of the summit. Continue to the back of this valley where further spur roads lead to nearly 1000ft. The slope is steep and a little bluffy above. Some 3rd class leads to the summit.

Additional Info: IB 1994 p.40

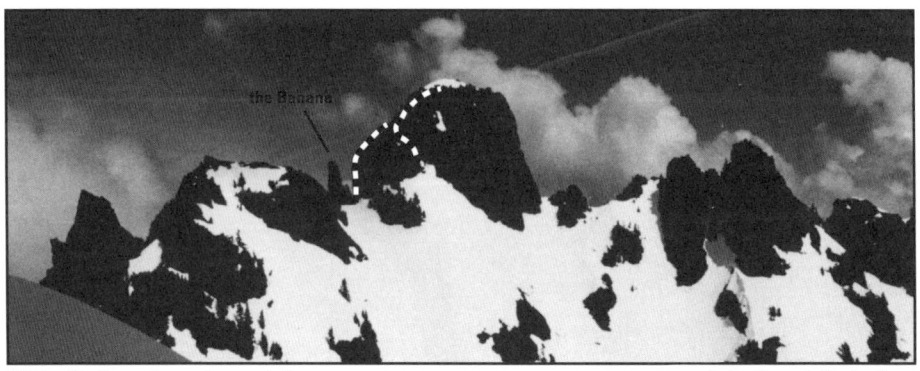

Hidden Peak south-west aspect, June.   photo: Francis Bruhwiler

Hidden Peak

Hidden Peak north aspect from ridge above Kennedy River, February.   photo: Craig Wagnell

Hidden Peak
4,799 ft / 1,463 m

Hidden Peak is the major peak of the Maitland Range overlooking the Kennedy River estuary where it empties into the huge Kennedy Lake basin. Hidden Peak is visible from a variety of points along Highway 4 between Sutton Pass and Kennedy Lake.

First Ascent: Island Mountain Ramblers 1975

Map Sheet: 92 F/3 Effingham River - GR 1949

Approaches: The Maitland Range and Hidden Peak have been approached from the southwest out of the Sand River valley via Mountain Woodfern Lake. Drive west along Highway 4 from Port Alberni to just a few kilometres before the Pacific Rim junction where the highway splits to Tofino and Ucluelet. Turn north on West Main 11.5 km to the Kennedy River bridge. Cross the bridge and then take the right fork on Sand River Road around the west shore of Kennedy Lake. The road leaves the lake shore after crossing a bridge over the river. It continues north into the Sand River valley under the south-west flank of Hidden Peak.

A newer bridge over the Kennedy River 2 km upstream of the river's outlet into Kennedy Lake can be used to approach Hidden Peak from the east. Leave Highway 4 to the west on H290 toward 'Jump-Off Bridge'. Cross the Kennedy River bridge and head north on H290. A little more than 1 km past the bridge there is a left spur leading high on the east slope of Hidden Pk. Ascend clearcut and steep forest to the ridge near horizontal control point 3690ft. Traverse the north side of the first peak and the south side of the middle peak to reach Hidden Pk. Go up to the notch between the Banana gendarme and the summit block. A very short rock face with low 5th class moves gives way to a short summit scramble. The Banana has also been climbed by Mike Walsh and Joe Bajan with two 5.10 pitches.

Roads further north may reach toward the lake in the north basin of Hidden Pk.

Hidden Pk has also been approached from the south, from the lowest saddle between it and Mt. Maitland. (Likely better on spring snow.) This saddle was gained from the east side.

W- West Ridge: low 5th class 150 m (I)
Start direct from the col between the summit block and 'the Banana'.

S- South Face: 3rd class 150 m (I)
Climb easy vegetated ledges directly up South Face to join the West Ridge up to the summit.

Rhino Peak

Aerial view of Rhino Peak north aspect, May.   photo: Craig Wagnell

Rhino Peak
4,698 ft / 1,432 m

Rhino Peak is the pyramid-shaped horn overlooking the north shore of Paradise Lake at the head of the west branch of Tranquil Creek. To the north of the mountain is Bulson Creek which flows into Warn Bay. The east branch of Tranquil Creek runs into Tranquil Creek Provincial Park. Velella Peak and Little Eiger are other worthwhile objectives to make the trip to this area worth the effort.

First Ascent: R. Eppler, A. Denman, A. Macdonald, R. Macdonald - July 1985
Map Sheet: 92 F/5 Bedwell River GR 0866

Approaches: Rhino Peak may be approached via Paradise (Kylma) Lake. How to reach the lake is the challenge. From Tofino travel by boat or air to the head of Tranquil Inlet. Hike up the Tranquil Creek Main road to the end and then continue up the rough trail following signs for Tranquil Creek Provincial Park. Leave the trail and head up the west branch of the creek, passing Synka Lake around the east shore. A steep climb at the back of the valley leads to Paradise Lake. Hike up to the pass north of the lake at the foot of the north-east ridge. Paradise Lake and Synka Lake are both large enough to fly in by floatplane, an attractive, if pricey, option.

Rhino Peak may also be reached from the Kennedy River. Follow the approach details for Little Eiger onto its south ridge. Either traverse up and over the Little Eiger's summit or make a wide traverse across its east side to the north ridge. Descend the north ridge to the high pass at GR 1166. From the pass hike due west up and over a small top and onto the foot of the north-east ridge of Little Eiger.

However you approach it, the mountain can be climbed up the north-east ridge. From the pass at the foot of the ridge, hike up the crest to a prominent gendarme. Traverse off the ridge across the north side of the mountain onto a snowfield. Continue up the steep snow and rock slabs to the summit.

Little Eiger

Little Eiger (L) & Velella Peak (R) south-east aspect from Pogo Mountain, August.   photo: Francis Bruhwiler

Little Eiger
4,990 ft / 1,521 m

Little Eiger overlooks the headwaters of Tranquil Creek in Tranquil Creek Provincial Park. This is a small but beautiful park encompassing a high forested valley encircled by a ring of alpine peaks including the Little Eiger.

First Ascent: Unknown

Map Sheet: 92 F/5 Bedwell River GR 1265

Approaches: Little Eiger can be reached from Tofino. Travel by boat or air to the head of Tranquil Inlet. Hike up the Tranquil Creek Main road to the end and then continue up the rough trail following signs for Tranquil Creek Provincial Park. Follow the creek right up the valley and into a high pass at GR 1166 at the foot of the north ridge. The pass may also be reached by flying into Paradise (Kylma) Lake and hiking across on the ridge from the pass north of the lake. From the pass at GR 1166 climb the mountain by hiking directly up the north ridge to the summit.

Alternatively you can try your hand approaching Little Eiger from the upper Kennedy River. Considering the logistics in reaching the mountain from Tofino, a little bush thrash may not prove a bad thing. Turn off Highway 4, 1.5 km west of Sutton Pass on the logging road that breaks off westward just before Kennedy River joins the highway corridor, BR 513. Drive up BR 513 crossing to the south side of Kennedy River on BR 513F 3 km from the highway. Park at the Clayoquot Valley Witness trailhead. Head west on the Witness trail to just before Solstice Lakes. Leave the Witness trail and continue up the main valley to a high pass at GR 1166. From this pass climb the mountain by hiking directly up the north ridge to the summit.

Another option is to gain the ridge west of Solstice Lakes and follow the alpine route north-west. A descent off this ridge leads to a ridge that connects to the south ridge of the Little Eiger around the south shore of a lake at GR 1465. Hike up the steep rock and snow onto the ridge crest south of the summit. Head north directly up the south ridge to the top.

Little Eiger (C) and the Ashwood - Ursus Creek divide north aspect from Mt. Tom Taylor, June.

Velella Peak

Velella Peak north aspect from Bedwell-Moyeha divide, June.

Velella Peak
5,288 ft / 1,612 m

Velella Peak is located on the divide between Bulson Creek to the south and Ursus Creek to the north. It is one of the more visible peaks in the central Island region from Strathcona Park being close to the southern boundary of the park. Velella Peak is an isolated mountain requiring some determination to reach.

First Ascent: R. Eppler, A. Denman, A. Macdonald, R. Macdonald - July 6, 1985

Map Sheet: 92 F/5 Bedwell River GR 0969

Approaches: The mountain can be approached from Paradise (Kylma) Lake. Follow the hiking approach details for Rhino Peak to Paradise Lake or fly in to the lake. From Paradise Lake hike up the back of the valley to the col at the foot of the north-east ridge of Rhino Peak. Head east onto the knoll at GR 1066. Turn north-east and follow the ridge system around the head of Bulson Creek to a pass at GR 1068 at the foot of Velella Peak's south-east ridge.

This same pass may also be reached from the Kennedy River valley. Follow the descriptions for Little Eiger to the high pass at GR 1166. From the pass, continue west to join the ridge system at the knoll at GR 1066 and follow it north around Bulson Creek. A more direct route may be forged by heading up the north fork of the upper Kennedy River to a pass at GR 1368. From this pass, hike south-west on the ridge crest to the top of a knoll on the Bulson - Kennedy divide and then continue west descending to the pass at the foot of Velella Peak's south-east ridge GR 1068.

Hike directly up the south-east ridge until it levels out at the south summit. Traverse a snowfield on the east flank to the base of a gully that leads up to the south side of the summit pinnacles. Tackle the final step up vegetated talus on the south-west side of the summit pinnacle.

Velella Peak east aspect from Mt. Porter, June. photo: Craig Wagnell

Mt. Quimper

Mt. Quimper north aspect from Mt. Tom Taylor, June.

Mt. Quimper
4,258 ft./ 1,299 m

Mt. Quimper is an isolated summit standing sentry over the east side of the head of Bedwell Sound. It is a perfect objective for a direct ocean-to-alpine trip, being close to Tofino and readily accessible by water from Tofino up Bedwell Sound. It gives an excellent perspective on the Maitland Range and the mountains in southern Strathcona Park. Named after Spanish Sub-Lt Manuel Quimper who surveyed the coast south of Nootka in 1790. He was responsible for naming many southern Island places.[3]

First Ascent: Jackson-McCaw survey party, 1943

Map Sheet: 92 F/5 Bedwell River - GR0067

Approaches: Mt. Quimper may be approached from the head of Bedwell Sound by floatplane or boat from Tofino. A variety of ridges run up from the inlet shore and the one to take may be determined more by where a suitable landing site may be found for the plane or boat bringing you up the sound. Try the ridge whose foot drops to the south edge of the tidal flats at the very head of the sound. Respect the First Nations reserve IR 14 Oinimitis by travelling around it. Consider hiking up the ridge to the west of the first creek west of the tidal flats to take advantage of water and possible camping at the lakes at GR 9869.

Continue up the ridge crest to a knoll just one kilometre north of the summit. Hike along the crest of the narrow ridge to a snowfield or rock slope which can be ascended directly to the summit.

If you really need something to do, Quimper could be approached from Buttle Lake over the Bedwell and Oinimitis Trail to Bedwell Sound. Cross the Bedwell River by swimming and reach the tidal flats as described above.

Looking down the Bedwell valley from Big Interior Mountain, September. Mt. Quimper is at the distant left.

110 Beaufort Range & Powell River-Comox ferry from near Harwood Island.

Beaufort Range

112   Hiking along the Beaufort Range on Mt. Clifton.

Beaufort Range
Contents

Mt. Hal	116
Mt. Irwin	116
Mt. Joan	117
Beaujest Peak	118
The Squarehead	118
Mt. Curran	119
Mt. Apps	121
Mt. Stubbs	122
Mt. Henry Spencer	122
Mt. Chief Frank	123
Tsable Mountain	123
Mt. Clifton	123

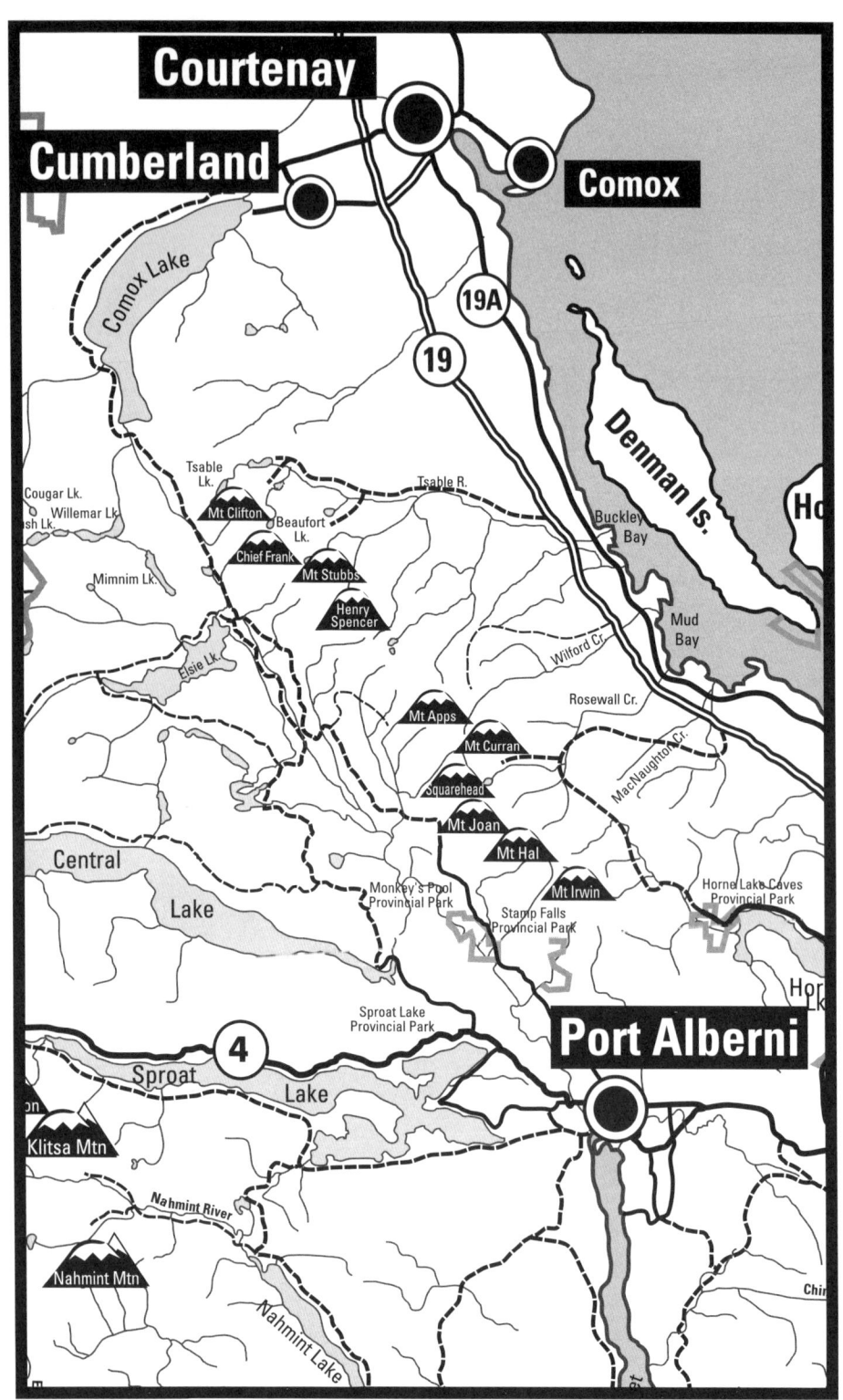

114　Beaufort Range - Map

Beaufort Range

View north-east over Kim Lake from Mt. Clifton, June.

The Beaufort Range is a distinct ridgeline of low subalpine and alpine running along a 25 km stretch of Vancouver Island's east coast between Port Alberni, in the Alberni Valley and Cumberland in the Comox Valley. The range is separated from the nearby Strathcona mountains by Comox Lake and the Puntledge and Ash River valleys.

While not particularly impressive as mountains and scarred by logging on all sides the Beauforts offer a unique alpine experience on Vancouver Island with stunning views of Strathcona Park and the Strait of Georgia. The long continuous nature of the ridge linking the summits of the Beaufort Range creates perfect hiking and ski touring terrain with little objective hazard. Most peaks are easy one day trips but access on the east side is severly restricted with numerous gated roads barring access to the private forest lands that include the range. The range is named for Sir Francis Beaufort hydrographer with the British Royal Navy succeeded by Rear Admiral John Washington in 1855.[1]

Map Sheets: 92 F/6 Great Central Lake • 92 F/11 Forbidden Plateau • 92 F/7 Horne Lake

Major Access Routes: The Beaufort Range is surrounded by roads both in the valleys around its base and logging roads that climb all over its flanks on every side. The easiest access to the peaks from the east is off the Inland Island Highway 19 between Qualicum Beach and Cumberland or from the west off Comox Lake Main a.k.a. 'the Valley Connector', a gravel road linking the Comox Valley to Port Alberni.

Logging roads enter almost every drainage off both of these major roads. From Qualicum and points south, access to the Valley Connector is off Highway 4 in Port Alberni. Most peaks can be reached from both sides, east or west, the only determinant being logging road openings which need to be researched beforehand to avoid disappointment!

Forest Service & Logging Company Offices:

Campbell River Forest District - 370 South Dogwood Street, Campbell River, B.C. V9W 6Y7 Ph: (250) 286-9300

Alberni Forest District - 4885 Cherry Creek Road, Port Alberni, B.C., V9Y 8E9 Ph: (250) 731-3000

Weyerhaeuser - West Island Timberlands - Franklin Operations -Bag 2001, Port Alberni, BC V9Y 7N3 Ph: 250-720-4200

• **Timberwest** -5705 North Island Highway Campbell River, BC V9W 5C5 Ph: (250) 287-9181

Other Information Sources:

• **Hiking Trails III** - Northern Vancouver Island & Strathcona Park - (9th ed. 2002 Richard K. Blier, ed.) VITIS

• **Island Bushwhacker** 1997 p.20, 2000 p.10 • **Wild Isle Magazine** #17 p.17

Mt. Hall

Ptarmigan on the Beaufort Range — photo: Craig Wagnell

Mt. Hal
4,885 ft / 1,489 m

The last (or first) vestige of alpine at the southern end of the Beaufort Range. Mt. Hal and Mt. Irwin to its south-east are separated from the main Beaufort Range ridge and Mt. Joan by a low pass at the head of Rosewall Creek.

Map Sheet: 92 F/7 Horne Lake GR 6370

Approaches: A trail leads up from the Port Alberni side of Mt. Hal along the north side of Hal creek. Either hike out of Port Alberni on the Log Train Trail or join the Log Train Trail just east of Stamp Falls Provincial Park by taking a road out of Beaver Creek northward to a signposted access point on the Log Train Trail. Cross Hal Creek on the Log Train Trail then follow the signposted junction for the Mt. Hal Trail. The trail leads up a forested ridge to the alpine on the south side of the mountain. Continue up the gentler upper ridge to the top.

Alternatively, Mt. Hal can be reached from the east off the Cook Creek/Horne Lake Forest Service Road. From logging roads high on the east ridge Hal is an easy summer hike or winter ski tour.

Mt. Irwin
4,265 ft / 1,300 m

Mt Irwin is an indistinct mountain easily reached from Mt Hal.

Map Sheet: 92 F/7 Horne Lake GR 6370

Approaches: Follow the approach details for Mt. Hal up the Mt. Hal Trail. Follow the ridge crest through the forest east and then south around the head of Hal Creek to the top of Mt. Irwin. A maze of logging roads also run up the south-east flank of Mt. Irwin from Cold Creek past Esary Lake. Roads also head up the south-west flank from Kitsucksus Creek which can be accessed off the gated road near McLean sawmill on Smith Rd., Port Alberni. Many of the old roads are now used as mountain bike trails and biking is a perfect way to reach Mt. Irwin.

An alternative approach may be made from the Qualicum River side of the mountain following a ridge system from the east.

Additional Info: Hiking Trails III 9th Edition

Mt. Joan

Mt. Joan from Mt. Apps trail, May. photo: Craig Wagnell

Mt. Joan
5,108 ft / 1,557 m

Mt. Joan is the southern-most summit along the main Beaufort Range ridge system. It is located south-west of Mt. Curran and The Squarehead between the head of Rosewall Creek to the east and the Alberni Valley to the west. Mt Joan is a superb day-trip destination especially when combined, as part of a cicuit around the head of Roaring Creek, with hiking over The Squarehead and Mt. Curran.

Map Sheet: 92 F/7 Horne Lake GR 6075

Approaches: Mt. Joan may be best reached from the east from the Bowser and Qualicum Forest Service Roads, which form a loop on the east side of the Beaufort Range. From the Cook Creek Road junction and traffic light on the Inland Island Highway 19, drive 14 km on the Bowser Forest Service Road. Turn right and cross Rosewall Creek, 2-wheel drive vehicles will need to park here. If you have a 4x4 drive, or otherwise continue on foot, up the washed out road up several switchbacks to a prominent junction. Keep left to reach the sign-posted trail junction where the left trail branch heads up to Mt. Joan and the right branch trail goes up to Mt. Curran.

After a slight descent the trail to Mt Joan climbs up through clearcut to a saddle above a cluster of tarns in a small bowl below Mt Joan's nort-east side. From the tarns the trail follows the bank of a small creek, through a high meadow and onto the crest of Mt. Joan's east ridge. Follow the gentle ridge with easy hiking to the top.

Alternatively, approach by hiking along the main Beaufort Range ridge from Mt. Apps, see the approach details for Mt Apps.

To complete a circuit around the head of Roaring Creek from Mt. Joan, hike down the north ridge keeping to the height of land through a col and onto The Squarehead. Hike north-east from The Squarehead remaining on the ridge crest to the top of Mt Curran. Read the Mt Curran approach details to follow the Mt Curran trail down Curran's south-east ridge to the tail junction and the parking area in the Roaring Creek valley.

Additional Info: Hiking Trails III 9th Edition

The Squarehead

Looking over to Mt. Curran from The Squarehead. photo: Craig Wagnell

The Squarehead
4,593 ft / 1,400 m

This unsurprisingly square topped mountain lies south-east of Mt. Apps at a point on the main Beaufort Range ridge that forms a 'T' with one branches heading north-east to Mt. Curran and second branch heading south-west to Mt. Joan. the Squarehead is best climbed as part of a circuit around Roaring Creek including Mt. Curran and Mt. Joan.

Map Sheet: 92 F/7 Horne Lake GR 6076

Approaches: Approach from Mt. Curran or Mt. Joan following either mountains' approach details from Roaring Creek. Or approach from Mt. Apps taking the approach details to Apps' summit then hiking south-east along the ridge crest to The Squarehead.

Additional Info: Hiking Trails III 9th Edition

Beaujest Peak
4,593 m / 15,069 ft

A reportedly difficult mountain to locate on a subsidiary ridge system to the main Beaufort Range. Consistently high winds on this heavily glaciated, friable sandstone spire gave their name to an archaic system of wind speed measurement.

First Ascent: Unknown but likely Mike Walsh on a grade 3 field trip.

Map Sheet: 92 F/7 Horne Lake GR 2345

Approaches: Approach from near the base of the mountain trending upwards toward the summit. Avoid impenetrable bush encircling the lower flanks with ungulatesque manoeuvres to reach a verglassed talus slope above. Continue up the talus to gain the foot of the upper North by North-West Ridge. Difficult boulder start on overhanging shale leads to easier mixed climbing above. Before tackling the final ice mushroom to the summit make a sustained and difficult negotiation with the elderly but obstinate foresty company employee staffing the gate. Descend an alternative undescribed route.

Additional Info: Comedians Guide to Mountaineering 12th Edition.

Mt. Curran

Mt. Curran from Mt. Apps, October.　　　　　　　　　　　　　　　　　　　　　photo: Craig Wagnell

Mt. Curran
4,849 ft / 1,478 m

Mt. Curran is situated on a spur off the main Beaufort Range ridge, north-east of The Squarehead between Wilfred Creek to the north and Rosewall creek to the south. It is a prominent feature on the skyline inland from Mud Bay. An excellent outing around Mt. Curran is to include the peak as part of a day-traverse around the head of Roaring Creek over Mt. Joan and The Squarehead.

Map Sheet: 92 F/7 Horne Lake GR 6277

Approaches: Mt. Curran may be reached from the Horne Lake Forest Service Road. Turn off the Inland Island Highway at the Horne Lake junction north of Qualicum Beach. Drive west to Horne Lake turning right (west) to follow the Horne Lake FSR around the north shore of the lake. Continue past Horne Lake Caves Provincial Park and along the Qualicum River. The road leads through a low pass between the Qualicum River and Rosewall Creek. Drive through the pass and around a tight righthand curve. Cross the bridge over Rosewall creek and then immediately left and then right onto the Roaring Creek Road. Branch roads in Roaring Creek run up the south-east flanks of the mountain.

A faster option, if coming south from the northern Island, to Roaring Creek is on the Bowser Forest Service Road which leaves the Inland Island Highway at an interchange at Cook Creek. From the Cook Creek Road junction and traffic light on the Inland Island Highway drive 14 km on the Bowser Forest Service Road. Turn right and cross Rosewall Creek. Drive up switchbacks to parking area.

Hike up the trail to a sign-posted junction indicating the routes and trails up to both Mt. Curran & Mt. Joan. Take the right branch at the junction and follow the trail up to the end of an old road. The trail continues through forest to an old forest fire burn on the south-east ridge of Mt. Curran. The faint trail continues up the south-east ridge to the top of Mt Curran.

Additional Info: Hiking Trails III 9th Edition

120 Beaufort Lake with Denman & Hornby Islands beyond in the Georgia Strait.

Mt. Apps

View from first summit of Mt. Apps toward East Summit. photos: Craig Wagnell

Mt. Apps
5,042 ft / 1,537 m

Mt. Apps is found at the head of Wilfred Creek which runs to the east and Wolf Creek which flows to the west. It is an easily reached mountain and a popular destination from Port Alberni. Mt. Apps is the highest summit in the Beauforts and is named after Don Apps a Courtenay mountaineer.

Map Sheet: 92 F/7 Horne Lake GR 5878

Approaches: May be reached from logging roads in Wilfred Creek but the best access is from Port Alberni on the west side up logging roads in Wolf Creek. From Port Alberni head north on Beaver Creek Road. This road parallels the Beaufort Range along its west side becoming Toma Main to Comox Lake and altogether referred to as the Valley Connector or Valley Link Highway.

Leave the Valley Connector before the bridge over Laternman Creek turning right through a gate onto BR 112. 1 km past the gate turn left on BR 113 and follow this road way up the hillside to the Mt. Apps trailhead. Hike the short haul into the alpine and on to the summit of Mt. Apps.

Mt. Apps may also be approached from logging roads in Cougar Smith Creek.

Summit cairn on Mt. Apps

Looking up North Gully, Mt. Apps.

Beaufort Range - Mt. Apps

Mt. Henry Spencer (L) & Mt. Stubbs east aspect from Georgia Strait, May.

Mt. Stubbs
4,852 ft / 1,479 m

To the south off Mt. Stubbs' summit is a large area of open subalpine meadows perfect for ski touring and enjoying summer flowers. Mt Stubbs also offers great views of the spectacular Beaufort Lake.

Map Sheet: 92 F/11 Forbidden Plateau - GR 5284 (see also 92 F/6 Great Central Lake)

Approaches: Best reached from the Mt. Cheif Frank Trail or Mt Clifton Trail, hiking south from Tsable Mountain along the flat ridge to the summit of Mt. Stubbs. Alternatively Mt. Stubbs can be reached heading north along the main Beaufort Range ridgeline from Mt Apps.

Mt. Henry Spencer
4,862 ft / 1,482 m

Probably the hardest of the Beaufort Range peaks to reach, Mt. Henry Spencer offers great access to Tumblewater Meadows, a large area of alpine meadows. Named for Henry Spencer, a Comox valley resident, politician and founder of Canada's health care system in the 1920s.

Map Sheet: 92 F/11 Forbidden Plateau - GR 5483

Approach: From the Valley Connector (Comox Lake Main) take BR 104 east of the bridge over Lanternman Creek. The road follows the Lanternman drainage to the north. Continue up the drainage to the end of the road.

The summit cairn on Mt. Stubbs looking south toward Mt. Curran, June.

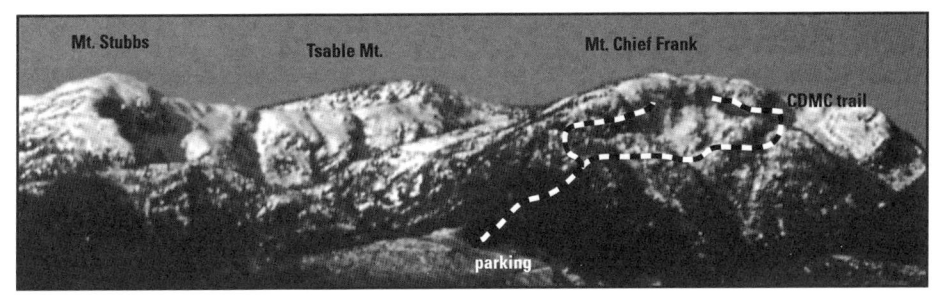

Mt. Stubbs (L) Tsable Mountain (C) & Mt. Stubbs (L) east aspect from Georgia Strait, May.

Mt. Chief Frank
4,822 ft / 1,470 m

Mt Chief Frank is distinct from Courtenay looking south. A Comox District Mountaineering Club trail provides great access to the mountain and the rest of the north end of the Beaufort Range. Named for Chief Andy Frank from the Comox area.

Map Sheet: 92 F/11 Forbidden Plateau - GR 5186

Approaches: Drive west up the Buckely Bay Main logging road from the Buckley Bay (Denman ferry) junction on the Island Highway. The gate just off the highway is closed during the week but staffed at weekends. After 16km turn left (south-west) onto Shelia Lake Main crossing a bridge over the Tsable River. Park and hike (or continue driving if you have a 4x4), following cairns on the road to the trailhead. The trail takes the north-east ridge to the top with another option leaving the trail to traverse south onto the crest of the south-east ridge. A circuit is possible around these two routes.

Alternatively, from Mt. Clifton, hike south along the main ridge crest through a pass and up some steep rock alongside a little waterfall. The scrambling is not difficult but can be wet and is exposed.

Tsable Mountain
4,888 ft / 1,490 m

A small summit sandwiched between Mt. Chief Frank and Mt. Stubbs on the main Beaufort Ridge.

Map Sheet: 92 F/11 Forbidden Plateau - GR 5085

Approaches: May be reached from Mt. Chief Frank following the main ridge crest south.

Mt. Clifton
4,724 ft / 1,440 m

A rock outcrop just above treeline marks the top of Mt Clifton, the most northerly summit in the range. Open forest and alpine meadows greet hikers or ski tourers that venture up to this end of the Beauforts.

Map sheet: 92 F/11 Forbidden Plateau – GR 5087

Approaches: If the two gates on Buckley Bay Main are open then access to Mt Clifton is a snap off the Inland Island Highway. The first gate may be staffed at weekends although Weyerhaeser charge a $2 entry fee! A second gate at 14km requires a key which may be obtained from Weyerhaeser's Northwest Bay division (a hassle if coming from the northern end of the Island). Turn left off Buckley Bay Main onto Lunchtime Lake Main. A 4x4 is required to get all the way to the trailhead so if your vehicle isn't up to the road conditions you may have to hike the last few kilometres to the trailhead. The flagged trail heads east around the north shore of Kim Lake then turns south, taking you up a steep ridge crest to the summit plateau. About half a kilometre short of the summit the route turns yet again to the west for the last stretch up to the summit.

Additional Info: Hiking Trails III 9th Edition

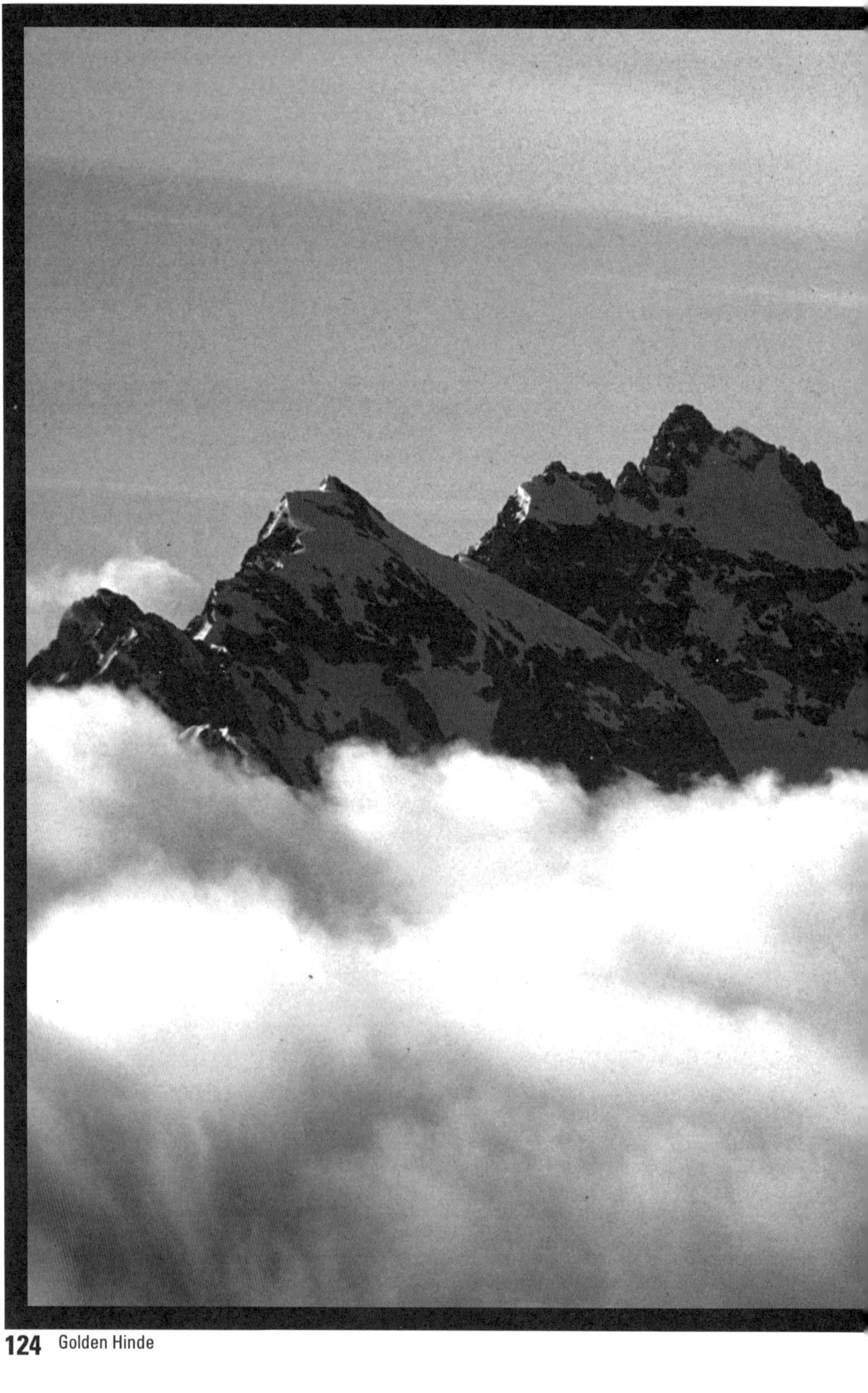

Strathcona Park

Buttle Lake from Syd Watts Peak.

Strathcona Park
Contents

Strathcona Park Trails Index   **128**

Strathcona Park History   **129**

Strathcona Park East   **136**

Strathcona Park North   **182**

Central Strathcona Park   **202**

Strathcona Park South   **278**

Strathcona Park West   **310**

Strathcona Park Trails

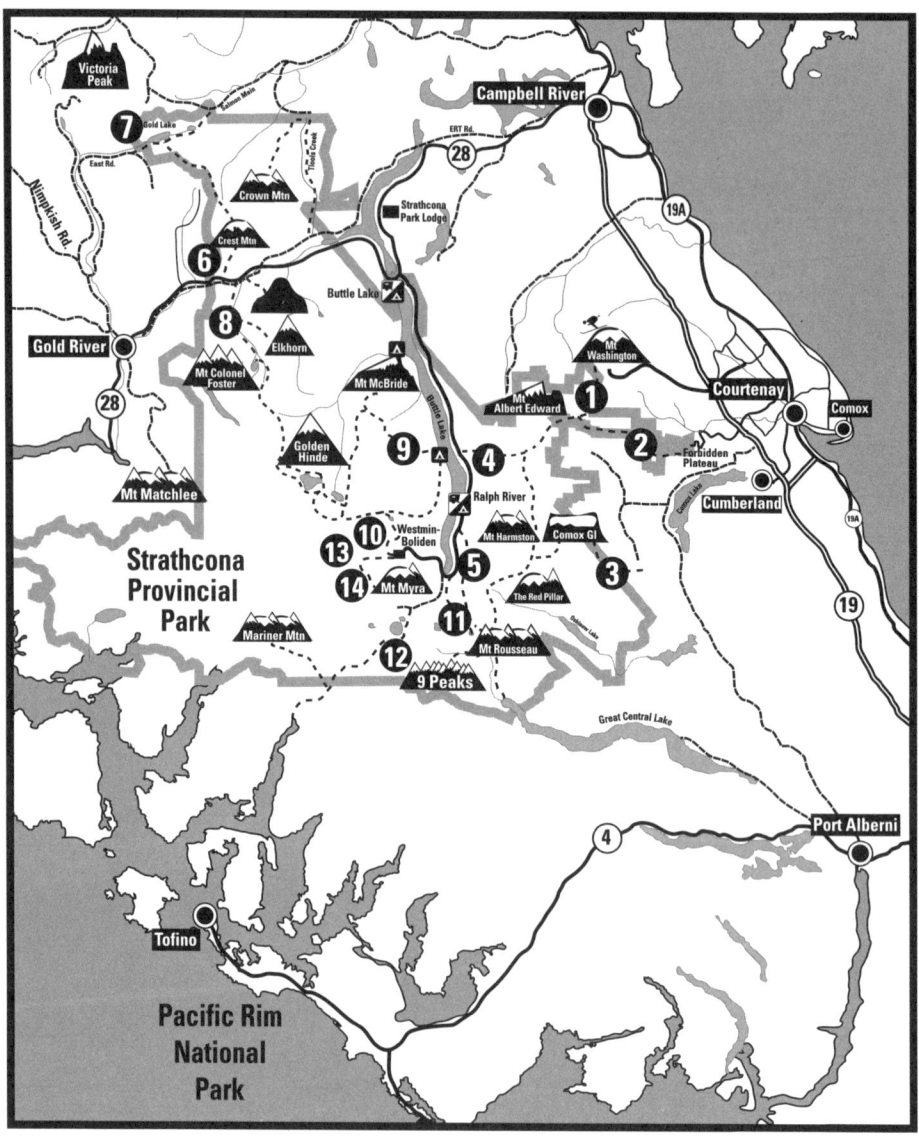

1- Paradise Meadows Trail	pg. 141	8- Elk River Trail	pg. 207
2- Becher Trail	pg. 142	9- Marble Meadows Trail	pg. 209
3- Glacier Trail	pg. 142	10- Phillips Ridge Trail	pg. 209
4- Jack's (Augerpoint) Trail	pg. 142	11- Price Creek Trail	pg. 283
5- Flower Ridge Trail	pg. 142	12- Bedwell Lake Trail	pg. 284
6- Crest Mountain Trail	pg. 187	13- Upper Myra Falls Trail	pg. 284
7- Gold Lake Trail	pg. 187	14- Mt Myra Trail	pg. 284

• **Hiking Trails III** - Northern Vancouver Island & Strathcona Park - (9th ed. 2002 Richard K. Blier, ed.) VITIS

128   Strathcona Park

Strathcona Park History

The welcoming Elk Portal at the Buttle Narrows entrance to Strathcona Park.

The forces of nature have shaped and transformed the land we now know as Strathcona Park for hundreds of millions of years, and what fine work these forces have wrought. Continental upheaval, plate tectonics, the accumulation of sedimentary limestone, the violent power of volcanic activity and the masterful strokes of glaciation have all played a role in shaping the mountains of Vancouver Island.

The First Nations people criss crossed the Island on well worn trading routes for untold millenia. Their legends and cultural ties to the mountains are rich and deep. European settlers arrived on the west coast of British Columbia in the late 1700's. But it took a full one hundred years of fur trading, coal mining and settling along the shorelines before any serious interest was paid to the rugged interior of Vancouver Island.

Several expeditions set out to explore this uncharted territory in the later half of the 19th century but it wasn't until 1890 that a pivotal endeavour embarked that would lay the foundation for the formation of Strathcona Park.

In that year, 1890, William Ralph was commissioned by the nascent British Columbia Government to survey a swath of land along the east coast of Vancouver Island to be ceded to the Nanaimo & Esquimalt Railway Company. The eastern boundary of this land grant was to be the east shoreline of the island and it was Ralph's task to survey the western boundary which was to parallel the coast some 50 miles inland. This line ran from Sooke Bay near Victoria to Crown Mountain west of Campbell River.

Unbelievable though it may sound Ralph and his party travelled in more or less a straight line placing survey posts at 5 mile intervals. It is this line that we see striking a prominent diagonal along the eastern boundary of Strathcona Park today.

A second key event in the formation of the park, and indeed the exploration of Vancouver Island as a whole, was the 1894 & 1896 expeditions led by the Reverend William W. Bolton. Bolton's forays were enviable affairs journeying from near Shushartie on the northern tip of the island via Quatsino Sound, Nimpkish Lake, Woss Lake, Nootka Sound, Muchalet Inlet, Burman River, Buttle Lake and thence through Price Pass to Great Central Lake and on to Victoria.

In the hundred years plus since Bolton's journey, industrial roads have carved through most of this territory stripping timber and leaving a greatly altered landscape. Bolton's experience will never be equalled as the wilderness that he and his party traversed has been diminished to a fraction of its former glory. (Note: In 2002 Peter Janes traversed the length of Vancouver Island in an incredible 500 km solo hike.)

Curtis Lyon climbing up to the South Summit of Mt. Colonel Foster.

William Bolton paved the way for a third expedition and one that was seminal in the establishment of a park preserve. Acting on the advice of the Governor General of Canada to create a National Park in British Columbia, and impressed by Bolton's account, the then Premier of B.C., Sir Richard McBride, reserved an area in the centre of Vancouver Island for a park in June 1910. The park was named Strathcona after Donald Alexander Smith - Lord Strathcona and Mount Royal, Alberta. Lord Strathcona was notable for having driven the last spike on the trans-continental railway.

To formalize the land to be set aside in the park the Minister of Lands, Price Ellison, set off to explore the area departing Campbell River on July 7, 1910 with a party of twenty three including his daughter, 20 year old Myra Ellison. Travelling up the Campbell River on the lake chain Ellison and his party spied Crown Mountain and settled on it to be their prime objective.

Climbing west over Mt. Evelyn and crossing the Tlools Creek valley the party reached the summit of Crown Mountain on July 29, 1910. Ellison and his entourage chose Crown Mountain on a whim but fate played them and the new park a fine hand. Crown Mountain's position on the north side of the Elk Valley looking south into the most impressive group of summits on Vancouver Island gave the Minister one of the most spectacular alpine views on the island, doubtlessly sealing it in his mind that this was to be the area of the new park.

After resupplying at Buttle Lake, Price Ellison and his party continued in Bolton's footsteps up the lake to Price Creek and followed the route over Price Pass to Port Alberni. Ellison submitted his report on the expedition to cabinet and on March 11, 1911 Strathcona Park was officially designated.

Work began almost immediately under the supervision of Col. Reginald Thomson to bring a road from Campbell River to Buttle Lake and to survey the boundaries of the new park. Thomson commissioned W.W. Urquhart to lead a survey party along with photographer W.R. Kent. Together Urquhart, Kent and Einar Anderson travelled over, through and to the top of almost every major feature in the park during the summers of 1913 and 1914. They named many of the rivers and peaks and their own names will forever be associated with the mountains of Strathcona Park.

The elaborate plans proposed for Strathcona Park in 1911, including a railway branch line and no less than two CP hotels, were quickly put on the shelf with the coming of the First World War. The huge spruce and cedars of the Elk Valley were sequestered for the war effort and this began a change of tide for Strathcona Park.

The ore conveyor and mill at Boliden-Westmin Myra Falls mine.

From that point until the present day the history of Strathcona Park has been one of dogged pursuit by industry for the rich resources within and all around the park. Logging and mining have insidiously chipped away at the original splendour of this great park. A large scale hydro electric project on the Campbell River saw Buttle Lake's rim logged and the valley flooded, raising Buttle Lake and swelling Upper Campbell Lake back into the Elk River. This disastrous act has affected local wind patterns, wildlife habitat and the seasonal fluctuation of the lake reservoirs creates an ongoing eyesore exposing the stumps of a once glorious forest. It is a sad fact that much of this industrial abuse has been perpetrated by Crown corporations and their offspring, overseen by the very provincial government that once had the foresight to declare the region parkland.

Strathcona Park faced its darkest hours in 1987-88 when then Environment Minister Stephen Rogers announced in January 1987 that the 'recommendations' of the Wilderness Advisory Committee would be implemented. This committee suggested deleting large areas from the park and turning them over to logging, mining and other resource interests. One area to be deleted was the entire Bedwell River valley. There was a public outcry and local activists united to form the Friends of Strathcona in order to organize their objections to the ill conceived government policies.[1]

A Vancouver Island Ptarmigan in summer plumage.

Matters came to a head in January 1988 when Cream Silver, a company who held mineral 'rights' around Cream Lake announced their plans to begin exploratory drilling. The Friends of Strathcona, the public and media descended on the area around Price Creek. A blockade was formed and for two months a tense standoff ensued. Kel Kelly became the first Canadian to be arrested for defending a park when the RCMP took him into custody. Fortunately the uproar caused the government to back down and instead they commissioned

Myra Falls, a popular place to visit with a short hike from the Buttle Lake Parkway.

132 Strathcona Park History

Rainbow Pass just east of Morrison Spire, Marble Meadows.

Peter Larkin to conduct an independent review on the future of Strathcona Park. The result was a report 'Restoring the Balance' which paved the way for the subsequent Master Plan which came from a series of extensive public hearings. When the dust settled, the Strathcona Park Master Plan saw park boundaries legislated making it far harder for ministers with shares in mining companies to remove parkland by a simple 'Order in Council'. Most of the park became designated as Wilderness Conservation land recognizing the true value of wilderness to British Columbians.

Strathcona is still not immune to the whims of political office and recent cutbacks in the Park's Department does not bode well for a smooth ride ahead. Those who love and cherish Strathcona Park should remain vigilant to ensure that it remains part of our children's heritage.

Old growth forest above Buttle Lake on Jack's (Augerpoint) Trail.

Strathcona Provincial Park

Established: 1911

Size: Approx. 250,000 hectares

Map Sheets: 92 F/6 Great Central Lake • 92 F/11 Forbidden Plateau • 92 F/12 Buttle Lake • 92 F/13 Upper Campbell Lake

Major Access Routes: Strathcona Park is well serviced by paved highway access while retaining a great deal of wilderness value. Along the east boundary the Island Highway 19 links the communities of Cumberland, Courtenay and Campbell River. The Strathcona Parkway is a paved road servicing the ski resort and growing village at Mt. Washington and provides the best alpine access on the island into Paradise Meadows and Mt. Albert Edward.

Highway 4: To the south Highway 4 runs west from Parksville on the Island Highway 19 through Port Alberni on to the Pacific Rim National Park and the communities of Ucluelet and Tofino. Highway 4 by way of gravel logging roads which branch off it accesses Great Central Lake, Oshinow Lake and the south boundary of the park. From Tofino much of the south west corner of Strathcona may be reached by boat or air.

Highway 28: The only paved road system to actually run through the park is Highway 28 which runs 90 km east to west between Campbell River and Gold River. This road provides access to the interior of Strathcona and most of its trails. A long spur road, the Buttle Lake Parkway a.k.a. Western Mines Road leaves Highway 28 45 km west of Campbell River and runs south down the east shore of Buttle Lake. The Buttle Lake Parkway also provides access to many trails and access routes into the park's mountains.

Menzies Main: To reach the north boundary of Strathcona two unlinked logging road systems must be used. On the north east corner the Menzies Main and Salmon Main branch off Highway 19 north of Campbell River at Menzies Bay. In the north west corner of Strathcona Park, the East and West Main roads (which can be reached off Nimpkish Road which links Gold River and Woss) give access to Gold Lake and the mountains in the north area of the park.

Camping: Buttle Lake campground has vehicle accessible campsites. Campsite reservations are accepted and there are first-come, first-served sites. Driftwood Bay group site on Buttle Lake is serviced by disabled access toilets and covered picnic shelter. This site is available by reservation only. Ralph River also offers vehicle accessible campsites on a first-come, first-served basis - campsite no reservations accepted.

Backcountry users are permitted to camp one km from main roads or, at designated sites where established such as: Bedwell Lake trail, Elk River trail, Della Falls trail and Forbidden Plateau area. Check notices at trailheads for site locations and any special cautions.

Forest Service & Logging Company Offices:

Port Alberni Forest District -4885 Cherry Creek Road, Port Alberni, B.C., V9Y 8E9 Ph: (250) 731-3000

Campbell River Forest District - 231 Dogwood Ave Campbell River BC V9W 2Y1 Ph: 287-2194

Weyerhaeuser - West Island Timberlands - Sproat Lake Operations
-Port Alberni, BC V9Y 7N4 Ph: 250-720-4100

Timberwest Johnstone Strait Operation
-P.O. Box 2500, 5705 North Island Highway Campbell River, BC V9W 5C5 Ph: (250) 287-9181

Weyerhaeuser - North Island Timberlands
-P.O. Box 6000, 8010 Island Highway, Campbell River, BC V9W 5E1 Ph: 250-287-5000

Western Forest Products -#118 – 1334 Island Hwy. Campbell River, BC V9W 8C9 Ph: 250 286-3767

Other Information Sources:
- **Hiking Trails III** - Northern Vancouver Island & Strathcona Park - (9th ed. 2002 Richard K. Blier, ed.) VITIS
- **Beyond Nootka** - A Historical Perspective of Vancouver Island Mountains by Lindsay Elms, www.members.shaw.ca/beyondnootka
- **Wild Isle Magazine:** www.wildisle.ca
- **BC Parks web site:** http://wlapwww.gov.bc.ca/bcparks/explore/parkpgs/strathco.htm

Della Falls upper cataract in full flow from Cream Lake, June.

Comox Glacier from Mt. Ginger Goodwin

Strathcona Park East

138 A familiar Strathcona sight!

Strathcona Park East
Contents

Forbidden Plateau	143
Mt. Becher	144
Mt. Drabble	145
Paradise Meadows	146
Mt. Washington	147
Mt. Brooks	148
Strata Mountain	148
Jutland Mountain	149
Mt. Albert Edward	150
Mt. Regan	152
Castlecrag Mountain	153
Mt. Frink	154
Mt. George V	155
Peak 1920	156
Peak 1909	156
Siokum Mountain	157
Mt. Celeste	158
Iceberg Peak	159
Kookjai Mountain	161
Black Cat Mountain	161
Comox Glacier	162
Argus Mountain	163
Mt. Harmston	164
The Red Pillar	165
Tzela Mountain	167
Shepherd Ridge	168
Central Crags - Flower Ridge	169
Augerpoint Mountain	171
Jack's Fell	173
Sid Williams Peak	174
Syd Watts Peak	175
Mt. Mitchell	176
Pearl Peak	177
Alexandra Peak	178
Mt. Adrian	179
Mt. Beadnell - Rodger's Ridge	180
Lupin Mountain	181

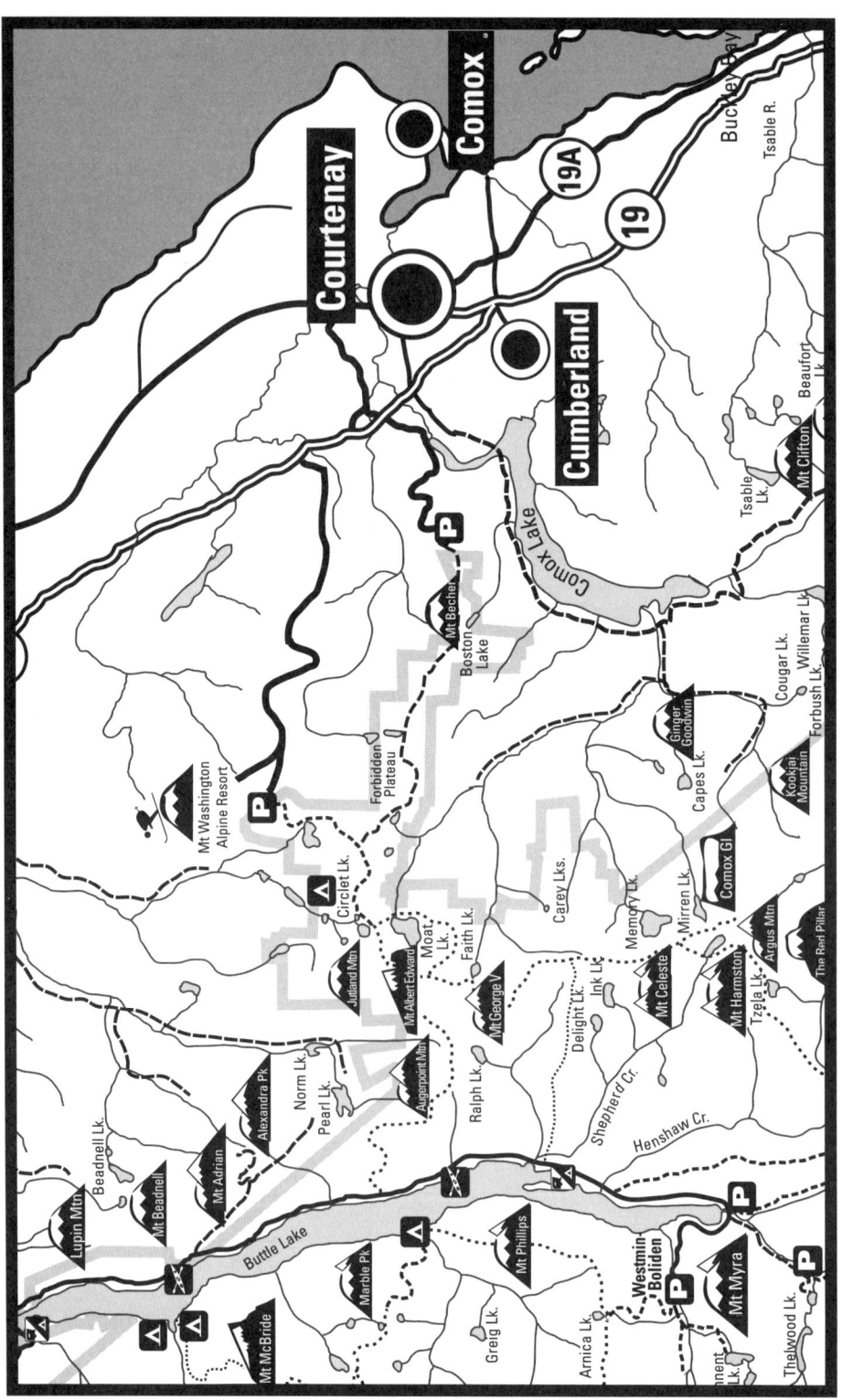

140   Strathcona Park East - Map

Strathcona Park East

The eastern region of Strathcona Park is characterized by high domed summits, rocky alpine ridges with superb hiking terrain and some of the largest glaciers on Vancouver Island. The rock is predominantly a red basalt in pillow lava formations. Bare exposed rock and steep cliff faces abound all over this area but do little to obstruct travel on the maze of interconnecting ridges that weave above the deep valleys. As to be expected bordering some of the major population centres and transportation routes of Vancouver Island, access into east Strathcona Park is fast with more options than the other Strathcona Park regions.

Mt. Albert Edward is a familiar landmark from Mt. Washington Alpine Resort and forms the north end of a long continuous ridge system which extends south to the Comox Glacier and the Red Pillar. This ridge constitutes the major feature of East Strathcona and traversing it from Mt. Washington - Paradise Meadows south to Comox Glacier or Flower Ridge is one of the finest multi-day alpine hiking traverses on Vancouver Island.

Another classic alpine traverse also departs from Mt. Washington - Paradise Meadows westward over Mt. Albert Edward to Buttle Lake via Ruth Masters Lake and Jack's (Augerpoint) Trail. This second route is less committing but still takes in some of the finest hiking and scenery in the park.

The most significant area for climbing in this region is on the peaks surrounding the Cliffe Glacier: the Red Pillar, Mt. Argus and Mt. Harmston. The rock quality especially on the Pillar is superb but the peaks lack the classic lines that draw climbers and so route development has been sporadic.

Map Sheets: 92 F/13 Upper Campbell Lake • 92 F/12 Buttle Lake • 92 F/11 Forbidden Plateau

Boundaries: north: Oyster & Quinsam Rivers, **east:** Strait of Georgia, **south:** Price Creek & Ash River, **west:** Buttle Lake

Major Access Routes: Eastern Strathcona is reached by paved highways and an extensive network of gravel logging roads. Highway access includes the **Strathcona Parkway** from the Inland Island Highway 19 to Mt. Washington Alpine Resort and **Forbidden Plateau Rd.** which services the now defunct skihill at Wood Mountain and still gives access to Mt. Becher and the south-east corner of the plateau. Buttle Lake Parkway which leaves Highway 28 to Gold River at Buttle Narrows runs down the east shore of Buttle Lake providing access to the whole west boundary of this area.

Valley Connector: links Courtenay to Port Alberni by way of the Puntledge River valley and Comox Lake to the Alberni Valley. From this mainline branches enter the Cruickshank River and Ash River to Oshinow Lake. Willemar and Forbush Lakes can also be reached from the Valley Connector. The north-east section of the Valley Connector is also called Comox Lake Main.

Trails

1- Paradise Meadows Trail

The Strathcona Parkway to Mt. Washington Resort provides superb high level paved highway access to Paradise Meadows, Mt. Albert Edward and points beyond including traverses to Augerpoint, Comox Glacier and Flower Ridge. From the Inland Island Highway 19 take the Strathcona Parkway junction east. After a 20 minute drive take a left turn following signs for Paradise Meadows or the Raven Lodge, Mt. Washington's Nordic Centre. Park your vehicle at the well signposted trailhead.

The Paradise Meadows trail begins at an elevation of 3800 ft and gives a great head start on reaching the alpine. It still takes some effort to hike across the meadows and above the treeline past Circlet Lake. This is a high use area and overnight stays must be at the designated campsites at Circlet and Kwai Lakes.

2- Becher Trail

The Becher Trail crosses Forbidden Plateau from the old ski area to Paradise Meadows and Mt Washington. To reach the trailhead exit the Inland Island Highway at Piercy Road and turn west onto Forbidden Plateau Road. Drive up to the parking lot at the old Forbidden Plateau skihill. Hike up the overgrowing ski runs to just north and below the top of the old Orange Chair and locate the trail heading across the plateau to Mt. Becher, Mackenzie Meadows, Paradise Meadows and linking with trails from Mt. Washington.

3- Glacier Trail

The Comox Glacier Trail is a popular 'mountain' trail offering an excellent hike to one of the West Coast's most famous mountain landmarks. Drive west from Courtenay on Laketrail Rd. to Comox Lake and cross the causeway over the Puntledge River by the BC Hydro dam. Continue south on the Comox Main a.k.a. the Valley Connector around the west shore of the lake. 15 km south of the causeway cross a high bridge over the Cruickshank River and immediately turn right and down a steep grade on the Cruickshank Main. Follow the newly reopened road 3 km to a T junction. Turn left (south) and drive for 5.5 km to another junction where you make a righthand turn and drive a further 5 km to the trailhead. (Much of the land east of Strathcona Park is private forest company land and active logging in this area may restrict access to the roads.) From the trailhead the trail switchbacks up a steep forested hillside to a campsite at the 'Frog Ponds'. The trail continues along a narrow ridge that is exposed in a few places over Black Cat Mountain and on to Lone Tree Pass immediately below the Comox Glacier. From the pass a straightforward hike leads up to the glacier.

4- Jack's (Augerpoint) Trail

Jack's Trail is an unimproved trail that rises from the Buttle Lake Parkway, 19 km south of Buttle Narrows and 1km north of the Augerpoint Day use area. The trail climbs up a steep forested hillside on gorgeous moss covered bluffs and open scree to the alpine north-west of Augerpoint Mountain. No sign marks the trailhead but for many years a large blue arrow has remained spraypainted on the asphalt on the Buttle Lake Parkway showing the start. There are several superb viewpoints overlooking Buttle Lake and a small lake at 800m. Jack's Trail is not a Park's sanctioned trail and takes a steeper line than would be normally expected on a Park's trail. The steep grade notwithstanding Jack's is an excellent trail providing access to some of the finest alpine hiking terrain in Strathcona Park.

5- Flower Ridge

Flower Ridge is one of Strathcona's most popular trails. This trail is a Park's trail and rises up gentle switchbacks from Buttle Lake to the alpine on the Price Creek - Henshaw Creek divide. Park at the signposted trailhead 30 km south of Buttle Narrows on the Buttle Lake Parkway. Hike up the well maintained trail to the treeline and continue on the unimproved route along the height of land to the top of Central Crags. From here longer traverses may be made via Tzela Lake east to the Comox Glacier and north to Mt Albert Edward, Paradise Meadows and Mt Washington.

Forest Service & Logging Company Offices:

Campbell River Forest District - 370 South Dogwood Street, Campbell River, B.C. V9W 6Y7 Ph: (250) 286-9300

Timberwest -5705 North Island Highway Campbell River, BC V9W 5C5 Ph: (250) 287-9181

Other Information Sources:

- **Hiking Trails III** - Northern Vancouver Island & Strathcona Park - (9th ed. 2002 Richard K. Blier, ed.) VITIS
- **Beyond Nootka** - A Historical Perspective of Vancouver Island Mountains by Lindsay Elms,
- **Wild Isle Magazine:** www.wildisle.ca
- **BC Parks web site:** http://wlapwww.gov.bc.ca/bcparks/explore/parkpgs/strathco.htm

Forbidden Plateau

Looking east across Moat Lake, Cruickshank Canyon and Forbidden Plateau from Mt. Albert Edward, March.

Forbidden Plateau

Forbidden Plateau is an extensive area of subalpine terrain east of the high mountain divide between Mt. Albert Edward and Comox Glacier. The plateau is drained by the Cruickshank River on its south side, the Browns and Tsolum Rivers to the east and the Oyster River on the north side. The topography of the Plateau is characterized by low rounded mountains rising above an extensive network of lakes dotted across the sparsely forested, subalpine terrain.

A trail network criss-crosses Forbidden Plateau linking the trailhead at the old Forbidden Plateau skihill to the trailhead in Paradise Meadows at Mt. Washington alpine village. Spur routes lead off the main trails up to the tops of the low mountains and to some of the many lakes on the plateau. Midway across the plateau there is a lookout above the Cruickshank Canyon. From Paradise Meadows trails head farther west to Mt. Albert Edward and the high mountains on the Puntledge-Campbell divide.

Forbidden Plateau is a perfect destination for day hikes and overnight camping trips out to Mt. Becher, Mt. Drabble, Mckenzie Meadows and the Cruickshank lookout. The Plateau is a relatively high use area and overnight camps must be made at one of the designated sites.

In the winter Mt. Washington Alpine Resort grooms cross country trails across the lower part of Paradise Meadows up as far as Lake Helen Mckenzie. Beyond there is awesome ski touring higher up on the Plateau and around Mt. Albert Edward and Castlecrag Mountain.

Map Sheet: 92 F/11 Forbidden Plateau

Approaches: The main point of access to Forbidden Plateau is from Forbidden Plateau Road which heads uphill west of Courtenay to the remaining facilities at the defunct Forbidden Plateau ski area. From Courtenay, (on the Inland Island Highway exit at Piercy Road on the north side of the town) drive north on Headquarters Road and then turn west onto Piercy Road. From Piercy Road turn south-west on Forbidden Plateau Road and follow it uphill around 15 km to the old ski area parking lots.

Hike up the overgrown ski runs keeping to the most obviously travelled trail. Head to the right (north) side of the runs near the top passing the base of the high T-Bar. The trail then turns south up a run toward the top of the old Orange Chair. Look for the well signposted trail on your right (south-west) which heads off into the subalpine forest.

The Becher trail has a rich history of use as a mountain recreation area and several cabins and lodges have popped up and rotted away over the years. Many years of travel by hikers, pack animals and skiers has shaped a wide and well used trail. 2 km west of the ski area the trail forks with branches going off to Mckenzie Meadows and Mt. Becher.

Mt. Becher

Mt. Becher south-east aspect from top of ski runs at Forbidden Plateau skihill, February.

Mt. Becher
4,544 ft / 1,385 m

Mt. Becher is a low mountain just west of the old Forbidden Plateau skihill at Wood Mountain. It is the first highpoint on the south-east corner of the plateau which stretches off for many kilometres to the north and west. Mt. Becher is a quick day trip in either summer or winter making a superb ski tour in the snowy months.

The small but steep cirque on the south-east aspect of the mountain that overlooks Boston Lake is a popular ice climbing destination in the winter providing some of the most accessible water ice on the island. There are only a handful of routes but in good conditions they form thick solid icefalls.

Map Sheet: 92 F/11 Forbidden Plateau - GR 3901

Approaches: Follow the approach details for Forbidden Plateau on the Becher trail. Follow the trail to the well signposted junction between the Mckenzie Meadows (Paradise Meadows) trail and the Mt. Becher trail. Take the left (south) fork uphill towards Mt. Becher. The trail climbs up a short ridge above Boston Lake with ever improving views to the summit.

Ski touring above Boston Lake, Mt. Becher.

Climbs above Boston Lake, Mt. Becher, January.

Winter Routes

Approach towards Mt. Becher from the old Forbidden Plateau ski area. At the base of the ridge that the trail takes up on to the summit there is a clearing and lookout. From here, traverse leftward (south-west) across the flank of the ridge in to a cirque. Boston Lake lies in the base of the cirque, a scant 3 km trek from the top of the ski runs.

A ** Strangler's Tea Party: WI3 100m
Climbs a gully on the left side of the basin. Climb the gully direct with two short steep sections.

B ** Unnamed: WI3 75m
A variety of lines are possible up this wide sweep of steep ice. Trend right toward the top.

C *** Boston Falls: WI4 125m
The finest line at Boston Lake. Starts in the chimney to the right of the main icefall. Head left up a steep bulge to a belay behind the impressive if short upper curtain. Climb the steep curtain to finish.

D * Shrapnel Chute: WI3 150m
Climb directly up the chimney as for Boston Falls then continue direct up the gully above and to the right of the main falls. Sketchy finishing on vegetated rock and precarious snow.

E * Waterboys: WI2/3 75m
Takes a ice smear right of Shrapnel Chute.

Mt. Drabble
4,472 ft / 1,363 m

Mt. Drabble is a small mountain north of Mt. Becher on the edge of Forbidden Plateau overlooking the Browns River valley. Named after George Drabble a surveyor and Comox Valley pioneer.

Map Sheet: 92 F/11 Forbidden Plateau - GR 3805

Approaches: Follow the approach details for Mt. Becher from Forbidden Plateau ski area. Continue past the turn off for Mt. Becher on the Becher trail following signs for Mckenzie Meadows. From Ash Pond a flagged route heads north past Drabble Lakes and up the south-east ridge to the top of Mt. Drabble.

Paradise Meadows

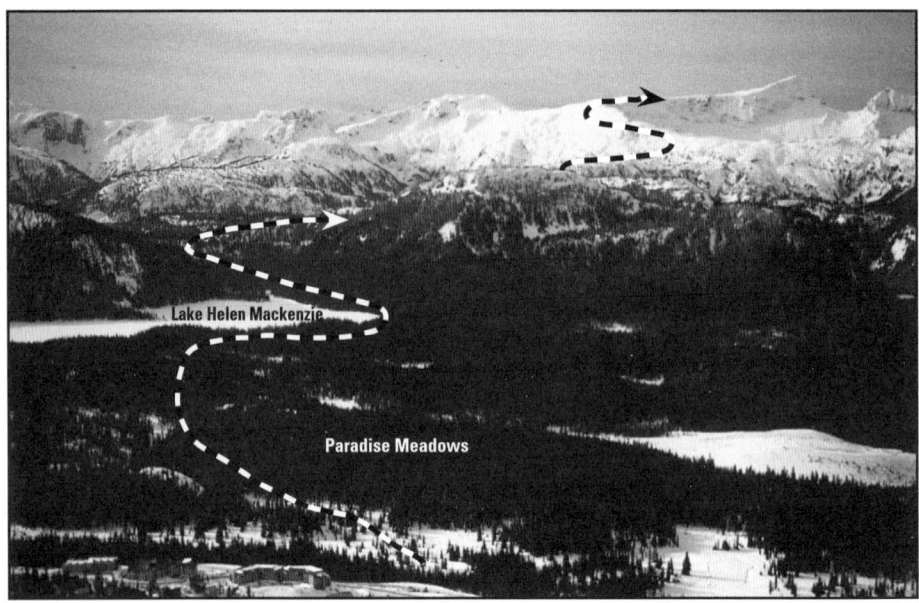

Paradise Meadows and approaches to Mt. Albert Edward north-east aspect from Mt. Washington, February.

Paradise Meadows

Paradise Meadows is the northern part of Forbidden Plateau at the base of the south side of Mt. Washington. The road access to Mt. Washington and the Paradise Meadows trailhead is the finest alpine access on Vancouver Island. The summer hiking trails are superb and groomed ski trails weave across the lower part of the meadows maintained by Mt. Washington through the winter months. Access to these cross country trails requires a pass available from the ski resort in the winter.

Map Sheet: 92 F/11 Forbidden Plateau

Approaches: Paradise Meadows is reached from the adjacent Mt. Washington resort and village. From the Inland Island Highway north of Courtenay take the Strathcona Parkway west. The paved road leads up past a lower parking lot for the Sunrise Quad and after a switchback and long hill climb a road breaks to the left (south) to the Raven's Lodge Nordic Centre and Paradise Meadows trailhead.

Alternative access to Paradise Meadows includes logging roads from the north-west in the Oyster River and from there up the Gem Lake route to the Albert Edward-Jutland col. Also from the Cruickshank Canyon although there is often logging activity in this valley restricting access on the roads.

Paradise Meadows and Mt. Washington south-west aspect from Mt. Albert Edward, March.

Mt. Washington

Mt. Washington south-west aspect from Mt. Albert Edward, March.

Mt. Washington
5,279 ft / 1,609 m

Mt. Washington is an isolated mountain at the very north-east corner of Forbidden Plateau. It stands somewhat removed from any surrounding high alpine. Its situation in the path of air masses rising up from Alberni Inlet, cooled as they pass the Comox & Cliffe Glaciers and high mountains to the south brings legendary winter snowfalls for skiing and snowboarding. A thriving resort community is centred around the base of the south side of the mountain with lift access alpine terrain, cross country trails and hiking and mountain biking in the summer. Information about current trail conditions is available at the resort. Outstanding features of Mt. Washington include the huge fresh snowfalls, unrivalled views of Strathcona Park, the islands below in the Strait of Georgia, the Coast Range and the sublime alpine access afforded by the Strathcona Parkway road that serves the resort, village and trails.

The mountain is named after Rear Admiral John Washington 1800-1863, a hydrographer of the British Navy and founding secretary of the Royal Geographic Society. He served under Sir Francis Beaufort eventually succeeding him in 1855.[1]

Map Sheet: 92 F/14 Oyster River - GR 3413 (see also 92 F/11 Forbidden Plateau)

Approaches: Mt. Washington is serviced by an excellent paved road the Strathcona Parkway reached off the Island Highway at Exit 130 between Courtenay and Campbell River. Drive up the parkway to the village and resort facilities centred around the base of the south side of the mountain.

Detailed trail information for downhill skiing, cross-country skiing, hiking and mountain biking is available from the resort.

Mt. Washington south-east aspect from Forbidden Plateau, January.

Mt. Washington north-east aspect from Black Creek, March.

Alternative access routes around Mt. Washington include logging roads from the Tsolum River on the north-east side of the mountain and the Oyster River from the north-west around Harris Lake.

Winter Routes

A number of icefalls form on the north facing bluffs in the east bowl on the opposing side of the mountain to the Sunrise Quad Chair in the lift service area.

Approaches: Fastest from ski area. Take the Sunrise Quad or Whiskey Jack (Yellow) chair descend Linton's Loop to the saddle overlooking the north-east cirque at the ski area boundary. Leave the ski area and drop down the steep slope traversing right staying close to the cliff base.

Alternatively approach from Micro wave station via a gated gravel access road that heads north from Strathcona Parkway, often snowmobiles have broken trails around here.

Around seventeen routes have been climbed along the cliff varying from grade 2/3 to 5 and between 1 and 2 pitches. The formation of this ice requires a combination of weather conditions and the ice quality varies widely from week to week and season to season.

Mt. Brooks
4,921 ft / 1,500 m

Mt. Brooks overlooks the south-west side of Lake Helen Mackenzie. Mt. Brooks and Mount Elma stand sentry either side of Lake Helen Mackenzie guarding the route into Paradise Meadows.

Map Sheet: 92 F/11 Forbidden Plateau - GR 3109

Approaches: From the Paradise Meadows trailhead at the base of Mt. Washington follow the trail to Lake Helen Mackenzie. Continue on the trail (or in winter cross the lake) past the lake and up into the low pass between Mt. Brooks and Mount Elma. Leave the main trail and hike up Mt. Brooks up the south ridge.

Strata Mountain
3,937 ft / 1,200 m

Strata Mountain lies between Circlet Lake and Divers Lake. It has a commanding view of Paradise Meadows and the many large alpine lakes that surround it.

Map Sheet: 92 F/11 Forbidden Plateau - GR 2908

Approaches: Follow the Paradise Meadows trail from Mt. Washington to just east of McPhee Lake. Leave the trail and head north up the south ridge to the top of Strata Mountain.

Jutland Mountain

Mt. Albert Edward (L) Mt. Regan (C) & Jutland Mountain (R) north-east aspect from Mt. Washington, February.

Jutland Mountain
6,003 ft / 1,830 m

Jutland Mountain is the summit to the north-east of Mt. Albert Edward overlooking Divers, Rossiter and Circlet lakes. It may be climbed as a long day trip from Mt. Washington or more leisurely from the campsite at Circlet Lake. Watch for snowmobilers!

First Ascent: Unknown

Map Sheet: 92 F/11 Forbidden Plateau -GR 2405

Approaches: Follow the Paradise Meadows trail from Mt. Washington to Circlet Lake. From here two options lead up on to Jutland Mountain. Firstly, you can continue on the main route to Mt. Albert Edward which passes the south side of Circlet Lake between Circlet and Moat Lake. Hike up a steep climb to gain the ridge connecting Jutland to Mt. Albert Edward. Turn right (north) leaving the route to Albert Edward and hike along the ridge top to the summit of Jutland Mountain.

Alternatively, from the north end of Circlet Lake, follow a trail north-west to Amphitheatre Lake. Hike around the lake to the toe of a ridge which heads up the north-east side of Jutland Mountain.

Jutland may also be reached from the Oyster River up to Gem Lake and from there up the west flanks onto the summit ridge.

Pearl Lake showing lower route on to Alexandra Peak and Jutland Mountain (C), west aspect, May.

Mt. Albert Edward

Mt. Albert Edward north-east aspect from Mt. Washington, February.

Mt. Albert Edward
6,868 ft / 2,093 m

Its namesake was king of Great Britain and Mt. Albert Edward is certainly the monarch of the Strathcona Park mountains east of Buttle Lake. The commanding summit is a familiar landmark to visitors to Mt. Washington Alpine Resort and a very popular destination for hikers and backcountry skiers. The hikers' route to the summit is an easy if long hike from Mt. Washington through the picturesque Paradise Meadows. Those that make the trip are rewarded with panoramic views of the Georgia Strait, the Coast Range mountains and Strathcona Park.

First Ascent: Possibly William Ralph et al 1892

First Winter Ascent: Possibly Phyllis and Don Munday, Len Rossiter et al February 1925

Map Sheet: 92 F/11 Forbidden Plateau - GR 2405

Approaches: Quickest access to Mt. Albert Edward is from Mt. Washington Resort on the Paradise Meadows trail, via Lake Helen Mackenzie, Circlet Lake and the North-East Ridge.

Can also be reached from Buttle Lake via Jack's Augerpoint Trail and Ruth Masters Lake along the West Ridge. The Augerpoint traverse is an excellent 3-4 day trek from Mt. Washington to Buttle Lake linking these routes. Access is also possible from Oyster River logging roads via Gem Lake, Moat Lake, Cruickshank Canyon or the Becher trail across Forbidden Plateau (1-2 days).

Mt. Albert Edward south aspect from Mt. Frink, August.

Mt. Regan (L) & Mt. Albert Edward (R) west aspect from Jack's Fell, August.

North-East Ridge - Hiker's Route: Class 2.
A strenuous hike from Circlet Lake which can be reached on the Paradise Meadows trail from Mt. Washington (see photo page 146). Continue from Circlet Lake up the steep trail which climbs a ridge which joins a major ridge running north south between Jutland Mountain to the north and Mt. Albert Edward to the south. Head south making a right angle turn as the ridge climbs up to the summit. Easy hiking terrain with a little scree in places.

WR - **West Ridge:** Class 2.
A long ascent from the foot of the ridge near Ruth Masters Lake. Climbed from Buttle Lake via Jack's Trail and the Augerpoint traverse to Ruth Masters Lake. Conversely used as descent route for parties travelling to Buttle Lake from Paradise Meadows.

NW - ****North-West Areté:** 5.8 A1 500m (IV)
Approach from Norm Creek via the Oyster River Main to Pearl Lake. Climb the fine areté on its crest to join the West Ridge below the summit.
FA: Chris Barner et al September 1976

South-East Ridge: Class 2.
This ridge joins Mt. Frink to Albert Edward and is used as a route south to Frink and the peaks to the south or as part of the Castlecrag Horseshoe a circuit from Paradise Meadows over Albert Edward by way of Moat Lake, Castlecrag Mountain, Mt. Frink and the North-East Ridge down to Circlet Lake and back to the Meadows.

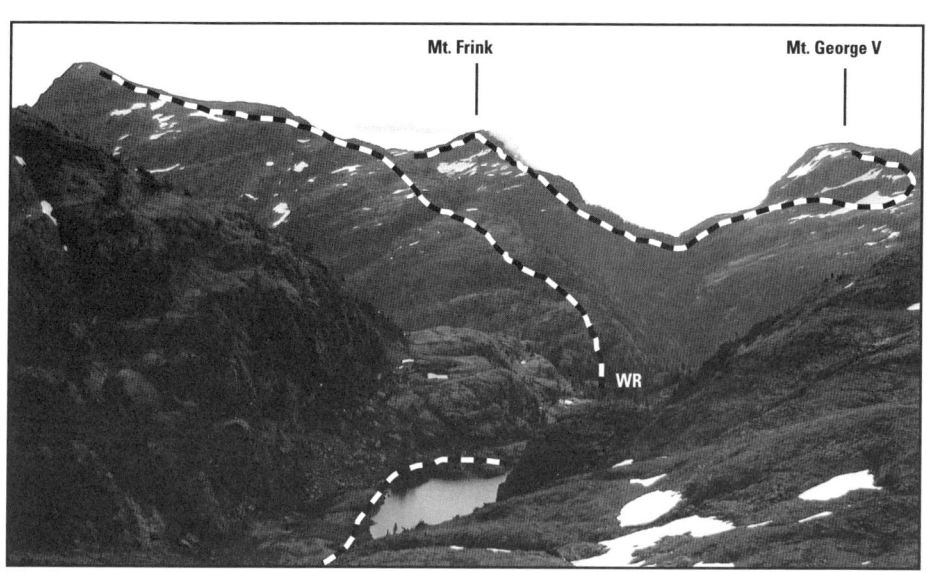

Mt. Albert Edward (L) and Ruth Masters Lake west aspect from near Syd Watts Peak, August.

Mt. Albert Edward

Mt. Regan

Mt. Regan north-east aspect from Mt. Washington, February.

Mt. Regan
6,496 ft./ 1,980 m

Mt. Regan is a satellite peak of Mt. Albert Edward perched on the latter mountain's north ridge. It forms part of the familiar landmark outline of these peaks from Mt. Washington. There are breathtaking views from the summit down to the north-east and west as the flanks of the mountain drop off steeply into the Oyster River valley.

Map Sheet: 92 F/11 Forbidden Plateau - GR 2406

Approaches: Mt. Regan may be reached easily from Mt. Albert Edward by making a descending traverse off Albert Edward's north-east face 100 m below the summit and in to the col separating the two summits. From the col Regan is a short scramble up reputedly rotten rock on the South Ridge to the summit.

Mt. Regan may also be reached from the Oyster River on the Gem Lake trail. Drive up the Oyster Main to an old spur which heads into Norm Creek. The Gem Lake trail leaves this spur climbing up the steep sided valley to Gem Lake below Mt. Albert Edward. Continue past the end of the trail up the head of the cirque to reach the icefield. Cross the icefield to the col between Mt. Albert Edward and Mt. Regan.

NR- **North Ridge:** AI1
Approach from the Gem Lake trail direct up the lower flanks of the North Ridge. Continue on the ridge crest on 50° snow or rock to the summit.

Mt. Regan (R) and Mt. Albert Edward (L) east aspect, March.

Castlecrag Mountain

Castlecrag Mountain north aspect from near Jutland Mountain, March.

Castlecrag Mountain
5,708 ft./ 1,740 m

A dramatic craggy offshoot of Mt. Albert Edward's south-east ridge overlooking Moat Lake and the upper Cruickshank Canyon, Castlecrag forms part of a short but spectacular horseshoe traverse around Moat Lake including Mt. Frink and Mt. Albert Edward. This trip makes an excellent weekend hike or ski tour.

First Ascent: Ben Hughes & ACC July 1928

Map Sheet: 92 F/11 Forbidden Plateau - GR 2703

Approaches: Castlecrag may be reached from Mt. Washington via the Paradise Meadows trail to Moat Lake. From Moat Lake leave the main trail and head along the east shore of the lake and up to the shoulder overlooking the south shore of Moat Lake. Continue south through the open basin on the east flank of Castlecrag and around to the south side of the mountain. The summit can be easily reached up the south side. The horseshoe route continues to the col between Castlecrag and Mt. Frink then up the east ridge of Mt. Frink to its summit. Head north to Mt. Albert Edward joining the trail from Paradise Meadows on the east ridge of Mt. Albert Edward.

Castlecrag may also be climbed on the north-east side up a gully to the right of the summit block.

Looking from Mt. Washington across Paradise Meadows at Castlecrag Mountain, Mt. Frink and Mt. Albert Edward.

Mt. Frink

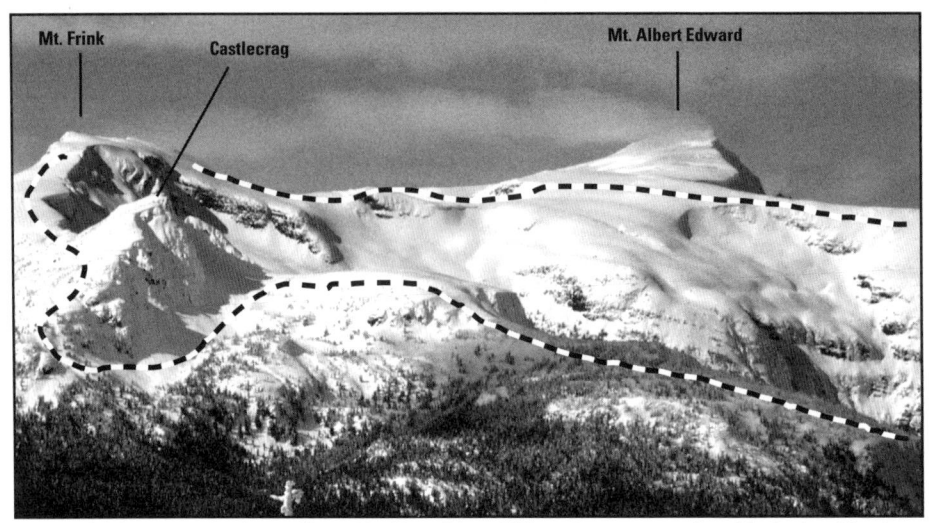

Mt. Frink (L) Castlecrag Mt. (lower L) and Mt. Albert Edward (R) south-east aspect from Mt. Becher, March.

Mt. Frink
6,332 ft./ 1,930 m

Mt. Frink lies just south of Mt. Albert Edward and to all intents and purposes can be considered a high point at the end of the higher mountain's south ridge. Along with Albert Edward and Castlecrag Mt. Frink forms part of a the superb hike or ski tour around Moat Lake on the Castlecrag Horseshoe shown clearly in the photo above. Named for a Miss Frink, girlfriend of a survey party assistant.

First Ascent: Possibly William Ralph 1892

Map Sheet: 92 F/11 Forbidden Plateau - GR 2603

Approaches: Follow the Paradise Meadows trail from Mt. Washington to Circlet Lake. Continue up the main route toward Mt. Albert Edward to the ridge crest east of Albert Edward. Take in the summit of Albert Edward as a side trip and/or head south along the connecting ridge to the easy summit of Mt. Frink.

Alternatively, climb Mt. Frink as part of the Castlecrag Horseshoe. Follow the description for this spectacular day traverse on the previous page.

Mt. George V (R) and the high Eric-Ralph pass with Mt. Frink east aspect from Syd Watts Peak, August.

Mt. George V

Mt. George V north aspect from Mt. Albert Edward, August.

Mt. George V
6,177 ft./ 1,883 m

Mt. George V is a bare rocky dome on the Cruickshank-Ralph River divide south of Mt. Albert Edward. Like most of the peaks along this divide it is most commonly climbed as part of a complete hiking or ski traverse from Paradise Meadows to Flower Ridge/Comox Glacier and points in between.

First Ascent: Possibly surveyors 1930s

Map Sheet: 92 F/11 Forbidden Plateau - GR 2402

Approaches: Mt. George V is reached from Mt. Albert Edward via Mt. Frink and the Ralph River - Eric Creek Pass. Follow the approach details for Mt. Albert Edward or Mt. Frink on the Paradise Meadows trail. From the summit of Mt. Frink head west down a boulder strewn ridge and descend into the high pass between Frink and George V (see photo bottom left on opposite page). Trend right (south-west) out of the pass on a gentle open snow/scree slope until a turn may be made in the route to head east on to the summit of George V. May also be reached directly out of the Eric Creek valley, a tributary of the Cruickshank River past Faith Lake and into the Eric-Ralph pass.

Mt. George V (L) & Peak 1920 (R) north-west aspect from near Augerpoint Mt., August.

Peaks 1920 & 1909

Peak 1909 north-west aspect from near Augerpoint Mountain, August.

Peak 1920
6,299 ft./ 1,920 m

Peak 1920 is a high dome shaped plateau on the Cruickshank-Ralph River divide south of Mt. George V. Its interest lies in the large area of very high terrain, by island standards, across the summit and the easy hiking passage and superb views it provides.

Map Sheet: 92 F/11 Forbidden Plateau - GR 2501

Approaches: Peak 1920 is usually reached as part of a traverse from Paradise Meadows- Mt. Albert Edward to the Comox Glacier or Flower Ridge. From Mt. George V both peaks are an easy hike along the crest of the main ridgeline.

Peak 1909
6,263 ft./ 1,909 m

Peak 1909 is the next summit on the Cruickshank-Ralph River divide south of Peak 1920.

Map Sheet: 92 F/11 Forbidden Plateau - GR 2599

Approaches: Peaks 1909 is easily reached on the height of land along the Cruickshank-Ralph divide.

Mt. George V & Peak 1909 west aspect from Syd Watts Peak, August.

Siokum Mountain

Siokum Mountain & Mt. Celeste north aspect from Peak 1909, August.

Siokum Mountain
6,036 ft./ 1,840 m

Siokum Mountain is located along the Cruickshank-Campbell divide at the head of Siokum Creek which is a tributary of Ralph River. It is a key point in this mountain group as ridges run in each direction of the compass from it. The surrounding alpine is some of the most spectacular in Strathcona particularly the meadows around Delight and Ink lakes, and the high open alpine terrain around the Aureole Snowfield. Siokum is a native word meaning 'in the sun'[2]

First Ascent: Possibly surveyors 1930s

Map Sheet: 92 F/11 Forbidden Plateau - GR 2597

Approaches: Siokum may be reached from a variety of directions as ridges run from it in all directions. If traversing south to Flower Ridge or the Comox Glacier from Paradise Meadows approach Siokum Mountain from Peak 1909. Head south-east from the summit of Peak 1909 along the ridge crest. Leave the ridge before it terminates in a steep bluff, making a hard right turn south-westward through a short snow/scree gully into a lower basin and a lake at GR 2499 in the head of the Siokum Creek valley. Continue south up open rock slabs and snow slopes to the north glacier and the summit.

From the east a spur ridge between Eric and Rees creeks connects to the main Campbell divide from the Cruickshank River. Hike up the Carey Lakes route from the Cruickshank and follow the flagged route west and south over Peak 1795 and then up the south-east ridge of Siokum Mountain.

The south side of Siokum Mountain is reached along the main divide from Mt. Celeste, Rees Ridge, hiking northward over easy, high terrain. The fastest direct route to Siokum is from Buttle Lake along Ralph Ridge. A steep hike up the bushy slopes on the south side of Ralph River leads to a superb high ridge line which forms the west ridge of Siokum Mountain. A great route!

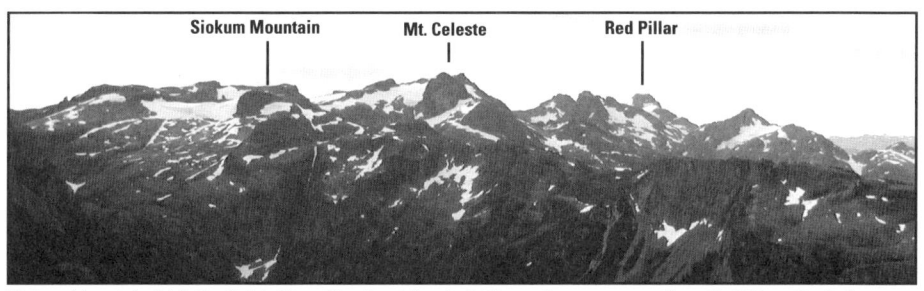

Siokum Mountain (L) & the Ralph River-Shepherd Creek divide north-west aspect from Syd Watts Peak, August.

Mt. Celeste

Mt. Celeste north-west aspect from Syd Watts Peak, August.

Mt. Celeste - Rees Ridge North
6,696 ft./ 2,041 m

Mt. Celeste is the summit at the north end of Rees Ridge. Its east flanks are adorned with the ever shrinking Aureole Snowfield and Memory Lake, one of the largest high alpine lakes on the island. To the west is Shepherd Creek a long trailless valley which drains from Milla Lake into Buttle Lake.

First Ascent: Jack Horbury, Jock Sutherland August 18, 1934

Map Sheet: 92 F/11 Forbidden Plateau - GR 2594

Approaches: Access to Rees Ridge is possible as part of the traverse from Paradise Meadows-Mt. Albert Edward south to the Comox Glacier or Flower Ridge. Follow the preceding approach descriptions from Paradise Meadows to Siokum Mountain or from the Comox Glacier.

From Siokum Mountain simply keep heading south along the height of land. Hike over some small domes to reach the north edge of the Aureole Snowfield. Mt. Celeste is easily climbed up the north-east side on the snowfield.

Mt. Celeste may be reached from the Comox Glacier or the Cliffe Glacier via Iceberg Peak and Rees Ridge. See Iceberg Peak approach details.

A superb horseshoe circuit is possible around Rees Creek from logging roads in the Cruickshank valley. From the Valley Connector turn on to the Cruickshank Main. Drive 3 km west to the T junction and take the righthand road. Drive north for 4 km to the Rees Creek Main and locate the route up to Carey Lakes. Follow the ridge system west and south-west from Carey Lakes to reach the north edge of the Aureole Snowfield. Mt. Celeste is easily climbed up the north-east side on the snowfield. Continue south along Rees Ridge to Iceberg Peak then swing east along the the Rees Creek-Kweishun divide back down to the Cruickshank.

Looking south from Peak 1909, August.

Iceberg Peak

Iceberg Peak and Milla Lake south aspect from Argus Mountain, September.

Iceberg Peak - Rees Ridge South
6,486 ft./ 1,977 m

Iceberg Peak is the summit on the south end of Rees Ridge. As with most of the mountains along the Campbell-Cruickshank divide between Mt. Albert Edward and the Comox Glacier it is relatively high for an Island peak but has a very rounded unimpressive shape. What Iceberg Peak does have is some amazing views overlooking Mirren and Milla Lakes both of which are ringed with several small glaciers.

First Ascent: Bill Bell & survey party 1930s

Map Sheet: 92 F/11 Forbidden Plateau - GR 2793

Approaches: From the Comox Glacier a steep mountaineers' route off the north-west side of the main glacier leads down on to a smaller glacier and a ridge west of Mirren Lake. Descend this glacier and ridge to a pass between Mirren and Milla Lakes. This route may vary with seasonal snow cover and is likely better in spring conditions. Keep to the ridge crest and onto the south end of Rees Ridge. Climb or bypass Iceberg Peak en route across Rees Ridge to Mt. Celeste.

A more reliable alternative to this route goes from the Comox Glacier around Argus Mountain on to the Cliffe Glacier (see approach details for Comox Glacier and Argus Mountain). At the foot of the south-east ridge of Mt. Harmston a gully leads down to the shore of Milla Lake and the toe of the Moving Glacier. Cross the lake if frozen or hike around on the Moving Glacier to a wide gully that leads back up to the col between Milla and Mirren Lakes. Continue north-west up on to Rees Ridge.

A superb horseshoe circuit is possible around the headwaters of Rees Creek from the Cruickshank valley. This route can be travelled in either direction via Carey Lakes, the Aureole Snowfield, Rees Ridge and the Rees Creek-Kweishun divide back down to the Cruickshank. Iceberg Peak is easily climbed en route.

Richard Dugas (R) & youth from Strathcona Park Lodge watch sunset from the summit of Mt. Albert Edward.

Mt. Albert Edward-Flower Ridge Traverse:

The high ridges of the Campbell River-Puntledge River divide offer the finest alpine hiking on Vancouver Island. Access is sublime with well-maintained roads giving way to clear trails into the high, open alpine. The true beauty of the terrain here are the uninterrupted ridgelines which run for many kilometres without dropping below treeline. From the Paradise Meadows parking lot to the Flower Ridge trailhead for example, the route courts the timber only once at Tzela Lake (and for a visit to such a lake it can be forgiven!).

There are a variety of options for planning an extended hiking or climbing trip along or across the main eastern Strathcona divide. The main ridge runs from Jutland Mountain due south, 22 km as the crow flies, to the Red Pillar. On both sides of this main divide, spur ridges branch off toward Buttle Lake to the west and the Cruickshank River valley to the east. Trips are possible entering or exiting at any of these spurs between 2 and 5 days or the entire traverse from Paradise Meadows to either Flower Ridge or Comox Glacier can be taken on in 5-10 days.

One of the considerations in planning any of the traverses through this range is the transportation logistics. If you have lots of time and the inclination to leave a second vehicle, or are able to arrange a drop-off or pick-up then it is feasible to hike across the range from the Comox Valley side to the Buttle Lake side. It is less complicated however to enter and exit on the same side of the range.

Rather than describe all the hiking routes possible here, the various entry/exit options are simply listed. Theoretically a trip may be planned starting and finishing on any of the routes below. For more detail refer to the individual mountain entries in this chapter and get a copy of Hiking Trails III.

Comox Valley Access:
(east side of the range) Paradise Meadows, Forbidden Plateau, Carey Lakes, Glacier Trail, Kookjai Mountain, Upper Puntledge River.

Oyster River Access:
(north end of the range) Gem Lake Trail.

Buttle Lake Access:
(west side of the range) Jack's Augerpoint Trail. Ralph River-Shepherd Creek divide, Shepherd Ridge, Flower Ridge, Price Creek Trail.

Ash River Access:
(south end of the range) Oshinow Lake.

While these routes are much more commonly tackled as summer hikes they offer equally excellent ski tours too.

Note that there are many names involved here but the connection between the following is crucial to understand. The Paradise Meadows trailhead is at the base area of Mt. Washington Alpine Resort and the trail crosses the meadows which are on Forbidden Plateau to Mt. Albert Edward at the north end of this range. Got it?

Comox Lake Area

Mt. Ginger Goodwin
3,806 ft / 1,160 m

Mt. Ginger Goodwin is a low mountain on the west divide of Cruickshank River. A C.D.M.C. trail up Mt. Ginger Goodwin provides excellent alpine access to Capes & Idiens lakes and the ridges around them- Lee Plateau and Capes Ridge. A circuit is possible around Capes Creek back to Cruickshank South Main. This mountain is named for Ginger Goodwin a Comox valley labour activist at the Cumberland coal mines who was martyred in the late 1800s, likely on the slopes of this mountain.

Map Sheet: 92 F/11 Forbidden Plateau - GR 3694

Approaches: Leave the Comox Main (the Valley Connector) and head west on Cruickshank Main. After 3 km the road reaches a T junction. Turn left on South Main and drive just ~400 m to park on the west (right) side of the logging road. Locate the trailhead and follow it up old roads to the old-growth forest and the summit beyond.

Kookjai Mountain
4,196 ft / 1,279 m

Kookjai Mountain is a long alpine ridge running east-west on the divide north of the upper Puntledge River valley. Named by Norman Stewart with a native word 'to see', in this case, the Comox Glacier.

Map Sheet: 92 F/11 Forbidden Plateau - GR 3487

Approaches: A longer approach to the Comox Glacier than the Glacier Trail with the attractions of easier hiking and beautiful meadows. Drive up the Cruickshank South Main, (see Mt Ginger Goodwin approaches). At a second junction go left for 2.5 km into Comox Gap. From Comox Gap hike west up a long forested ridge on to Kookjai Mountain. Keep to the ridge crest past Tatsno Lake. To reach the Comox Glacier continue north-west to Black Cat Mountain and Lone Tree Pass.

Black Cat Mountain
5,118 ft / 1,560 m

Black Cat Mountain is at the head of Datsio Creek just to the south of the Comox Glacier. The peak is easily by-passed on the Glacier Trail route but the Kookjai Mountain route from Comox Gap goes right over it en route to the Comox Glacier. It was named by a hiking group in the 1920s who after seeing a black cat cross the path of their car as they drove through a torrential rainstorm had fine weather and a successful trip which they attributed to the cat's good luck.

Map Sheet: 92 F/11 Forbidden Plateau - GR 3089

Approaches: Black Cat Mountain is reached from either of the main approaches to the Comox Glacier: the Glacier Trail and the Kookjai Mountain route. Follow the approach details for the Comox Glacier on the Glacier Trail to Lone Tree Pass. From the pass it is an easy hike up the north ridge.

Mt. Bueby
4,550 ft / 1,387 m

The gentle slopes of Mt. Bueby have been ravaged by intensive logging which has greatly reduced the attractiveness of this superbly situated mountain. Located due south of the Red Pillar between the Ash River and Drinkwater Creek, Mt. Bueby boasts incredible views into the south-east corner of Strathcona.

Map Sheet: 92 F/11 Forbidden Plateau - GR 3487

Approaches: Depending on current road conditions and logging activity Mt. Bueby can be approached by 4x4 to with in a few hundred metres of the summit from spurs out of Gretchen Creek.

Comox Glacier

Comox Glacier & Mt. Harmston (R) east aspect from Ryan Rd., Courtenay, January.

Comox Glacier
6,430 ft / 1,960 m

The Comox Glacier is not so much a landmark on Vancouver Island as a phenomenon. Its image adorns everything in the Comox Valley from music festival promos to vinyl siding. Understandably so as it dominates the skyline from Courtenay, Comox and even Powell River. It is often referred to as the last remaining glacier on Vancouver Island but of course a casual skim through this book will show that to be a wee inaccurate. It is certainly one of the larger glaciers on Vancouver Island only being surpassed by the Mariner Glacier and those found in the Haihte Range. The name originates from the Yuculta word for abundance, referring to the plentiful land in the district. [3]

First Ascent: Rev. G Kinney, A MacNivern, Mr.Tramlett, H Banks

Map Sheet: 92 F/11 Forbidden Plateau - GR 2890

Approaches: Approach on the Glacier Trail from Comox Creek. Reach the trailhead from Cruickshank River logging roads off the Valley Connector 15 km south of the Puntledge bridge. Drive 3 km west to the T junction and take the lefthand road, South Main. Drive a further 5.5 km to a second junction. Take the right for another 5 km to the trailhead. Hike up the Glacier Trail to the alpine at the Frog Ponds and then continue west over an exposed rock rib to Lone Tree Pass. From the pass the glacier is easily reached by hiking up the south-east ridge.

Another route comes over Kookjai Mountain from Comox Gap and Cougar Lake. To begin this route drive up the Cruickshank South Main, following the description for the Glacier Trail. At the second junction go left for 2.5 km into Comox Gap or from Forbush Lake locate an old trail up the hillside to the gap. From Comox Gap hike west up a long forested ridge on to Kookjai Mountain. Keep to the ridge crest past Tatsno Lake and then swing north-west to Black Cat Mountain and Lone Tree Pass.

From the Glacier trail trailhead a second trail heads up to Century Sam Lake from where the Comox Glacier may be reached up a long snow gully. This gully is not advised in winter or spring due to extreme exposure to avalanches but in summer provides a direct alternative to the Glacier trail. Climb the gully trending left (east) about 2/3 of the way up.

Active logging in the Cruickshank valley may change road conditions, locations and access may be restricted to the Glacier Trail , Century Sam Trail and routes from Comox Gap.

The Comox Glacier may also be reached from the Cliffe Glacier by either bypassing or climbing over Argus Mountain. See approach details for Argus Mountain. A route is also possible from Rees Ridge. See approach details for Mt. Celeste.

Additional Info: IB 2001 p.30

Argus Mountain

Argus Mountain north-east aspect from Comox Glacier, September.

Argus Mountain
6,500 ft / 1,980 m

Argus Mountain along with Mt. Harmston and the Red Pillar ring the Cliffe Glacier in a scene unlike any other on Vancouver Island and not completely dissimilar to a mini version of the Bugaboos. The rock on these peaks is of excellent quality but with the exception of the Red Pillar there is a notable lack of aesthetic climbing lines to draw the eye. However the atmosphere of the setting more than compensates for this quirk and the ability to bag three peaks in a weekend outing adds to the attraction of the area. Named for the Comox Argus newspaper in the 1930s.

First Recorded Ascent: W Bell. A Bell July 2, 1949 possibly G. Kinney 1922

Map Sheet: 92 F/11 Forbidden Plateau - GR 2789

Approaches: Argus Mountain and the Cliffe Glacier area are geographically central to this area of Strathcona and can be reached by a variety of routes. Most commonly it is approached from the Comox Valley via the Comox Glacier (see Comox Glacier approach details) in a long day. From Buttle Lake approach via Flower Ridge (see Central Crags approach details) or Shepherd Ridge (see Shepherd Ridge approach details) via Tzela Lake. The Cliffe Glacier can also be reached via Milla Lake and Rees Ridge from the ridge system heading south from Mt. Albert Edward.

Argus Mountain is notable for blocking easy access to the Cliffe Glacier from the Comox Glacier. The peak must be negotiated either by climbing up the North-West Ridge and descending the Southwest ridge to the Cliffe Glacier or making an exposed traverse around its east flank (see photo above).

NW- **North-West Ridge:** AI1 or low 5th Class 120 m
An easy scramble up from the ridge connecting to the Comox Glacier. A variety of lines are possible with great exposure.

South-West Ridge: 3rd Class 200m
A classic ridge scramble up from the Cliffe Glacier. Approach the toe of the ridge and keep to the crest to the summit savouring the views of the Cliffe Glacier.

Mt. Harmston

Argus Mt. (L), Mt. Harmston (C) and the Red Pillar (R) north-west aspect from Syd Watts Peak, August.

Mt. Harmston
6,500 ft / 1,980 m

Mt. Harmston is a somewhat remote peak requiring for most parties at least one overnight camp to reach. It is situated between the Ash River and Tzela Lake to the south Cliffe Glacier to the east and Shepherd Creek valley to the north. Milla Lake which sits in the bottom of a cirque on the north-east side of the mountain is one of the more dramatic places in Strathcona Park with the impressive Moving Glacier dropping steeply down under Argus Mountain toward the lake. Named for William Harmston an early Comox Valley settler.

First Ascent: Unknown

Map Sheet: 92 F/11 Forbidden Plateau - GR 2690

Approaches: Harmston may be reached via the Comox Glacier Trail from Cruickshank River. From the Comox Glacier continue across the glacier's south side to a connecting ridge that links to Argus Mountain. Climb up and over Argus or bypass it around the steep toe of Argus's east ridge to reach the Cliffe Glacier. Descend the Cliffe Glacier and swing around to the north below Argus Mountain's west side. Hike up steep moraine to the base of Mt. Harmston's South-East Ridge.

From Buttle Lake, 2 days may be needed to hike in via the Flower Ridge trail or Shepherd Ridge to Tzela Lake. A route is possible up Shepherd Creek to Tzela Lake & the west side of the mountain. The Cliffe Glacier is also often visited as part of a complete traverse of this range from Paradise Meadows to the Comox Glacier or Flower Ridge.

Additional Info: IB 1996 p.23

Mt. Harmston (L), Milla Lake & Rees Ridge (R) south-east aspect from Argus Mountain, September.

SE - South-East Ridge: Class 2-3
From the Cliffe Glacier hike up steep moraine on to the crest of the broad South-East Ridge. Follow the ridge up to the summit ridge.

WG - West Glacier: AI1 low 5th Class
From the pass between Tzela Mt. and Harmston, hike up the glacier on steepening snow or glacial ice in late season, on Mt. Harmston's west side.

WR - West Ridge: 5.5 800m (III)
Gain the crest of the West Ridge from the tongue of the Cliffe Glacier. Scramble up crest to top of the first dome. Rappel into the notch above. Leave the notch up a wide, steep chimney to a second dome. Rappel into the next notch and join the South-East Ridge to the summit.
FA: Chris Barner, Paul Rydeen August 1988

The Red Pillar

The Red Pillar west aspect from Flower Ridge, May.

The Red Pillar
6,665 ft / 2,031 m

The Red Pillar is an impressive summit rising out of the south side of the expansive Cliffe Glacier. The extremely high quality of the rock and imposing character of the mountain has great climbing appeal. The Pillar is located between the Puntledge River to the east and the Ash River to the south & west. The mountain is a landmark from the upper Alberni Valley which it overlooks. Watch from points west of the Red Pillar for a chicken shaped rock intrusion on the bluffs below the mountain!

First Ascent: Ben Hughes, Jack Gregson, Arthur Leighton, Adrian Paul, July 1931

Map Sheet: 92 F/11 Forbidden Plateau -GR 2788 (see also 92 F/6 Great Central Lake)

Approaches: The Red Pillar is usually reached from the north side via the Cliffe Glacier, approaching from either the Comox Glacier Trail, Flower Ridge Trail or the Shepherd Ridge route (see Comox Glacier, Central Crags and Shepherd Ridge approach details).

Alternatively the Red Pillar can be reached from the south from logging roads in the Ash River and canoeing up Oshinow Lake. Thrash through low elevation forest to Puntledge Lake at the toe of a long ridge which leads northward to the south side of the Red Pillar.

Additional Info: IB Fall 1987 (15:4) p.10

The Red Pillar south aspect from Mt. Porter, May.   photo: Craig Wagnell

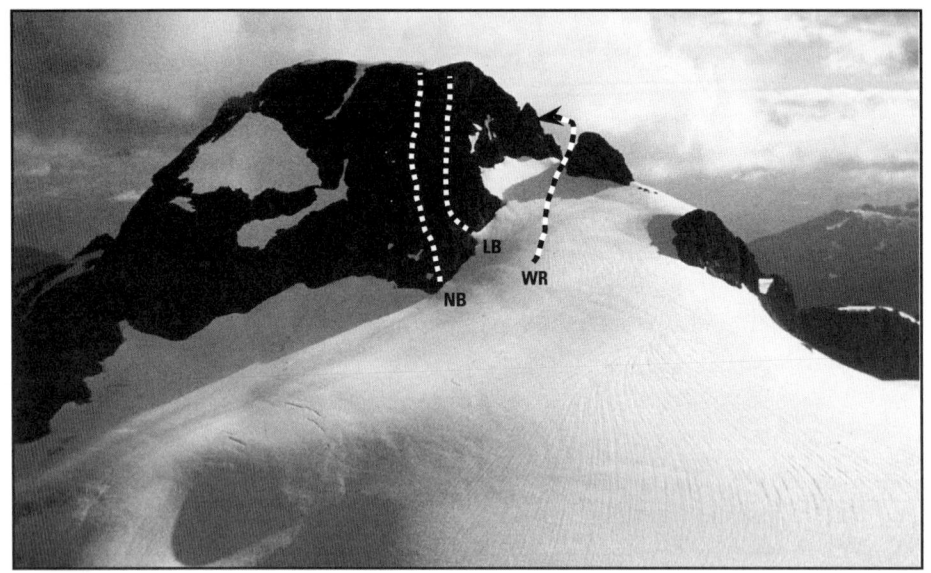

The Red Pillar north aspect from Argus Mountain, September.

WR - West Ridge: low 5th Class 120 m (II)
Approach from the Cliffe Glacier or from the Ash River. From the Cliffe Glacier ascend the wide snow chute on the north-west side of the mountain into a gap which leads through to the foot of the West Ridge. Scramble up a gully system on superb rock up the ridge to the summit.
FA: Ben Hughes, Jack Gregson, Arthur Leighton, Adrian Paul, July 1931

SR - South Ridge: 4th Class 250m (II)
Best approached from the south via Oshinow and Puntledge Lakes. Gain the crest of the ridge just north of Peak 1712 and follow it with some 4th class scrambling to the summit.
FA: Sandy Briggs, Ignaz Fluer, Wendy Richardson, Don Berryman, Aug '87

NB - **North Buttress: 5.6 300m (II)
Takes the righthand (western-most) of the two twin buttresses on the Red Pillar's north face. Approach up the Cliffe Glacier to the toe of the buttress. Climb three pitches on the crest of the buttress following a series of ramps and corners. Two harder pitches continue up the buttress with increasing exposure to the summit.
FA: Lyle Fast, Chris Lawrence, Fraser Koruluk, August 1987

LB - Lee Barner Route: 5.8 250m (II)
Climbs a series of gullies and corners to the right of the North Buttress.
FA: Doug Lee, Chris Barner, August 1978

The Red Pillar (L) and Argus Mountain (R) east aspect from the Beaufort Range, June.

Tzela Mountain

Tzela Mountain north-west aspect from Syd Watts Peak, August.

Tzela Mountain
6,167 ft / 1,880 m

Tzela Mountain sits above the north side of Tzela Lake. To the north of it, Shepherd Creek runs from Milla Lake north-west to Buttle Lake. It is an isolated summit requiring at least 2 days by most parties to reach.

First Ascent: Possibly surveyors 1930s

Map Sheet: 92 F/11 Forbidden Plateau -GR 2788

Mt. Harmston (L), Argus Mountain (C) and the Red Pillar (R) west aspect from Mt. Tom Taylor, September.

Approaches: Tzela Mountain may be approached from the south or west to reach the south ridge by which the mountain may be easily climbed. From Tzela Lake to the south, hike directly into the col between Mt. Harmston and Tzela Mountain. Continue directly up the south ridge with increasing exposure to the summit.

From the pass to the west between Tzela Mountain and Shepherd Ridge, hike up the north-west ridge to the pocket glacier on the west side of the summit. Hike up and across the glacier heading south to join the south ridge route which is followed along the crest to the top.

Shepherd Ridge south-west aspect from Flower Ridge, August.

Shepherd Ridge

Shepherd Ridge north aspect from Syd Watts Peak, August.

Shepherd Ridge
6,299 ft / 1,920 m

Shepherd Ridge lies to the north of the more famous Flower Ridge forming the divide between Shepherd and Henshaw Creeks. It provides excellent access into Mt. Harmston and the Cliffe Glacier. An overlooked option is the classic horseshoe hiking route it forms around Henshaw Creek with Flower Ridge. Both ridges drop to Buttle Lake within just a couple of kilometres of one another making vehicle logistics a park and hike affair. The Ralph River campground makes an ideal base from which to tackle this multi day trek.

First Ascent: Unknown

Map Sheet: 92 F/11 Forbidden Plateau -GR 2390

Approaches: Shepherd Ridge may be started from Buttle Lake just 500 m north of the Flower Ridge trailhead on the north side of the Henshaw Creek bridge on the Buttle Lake Parkway just 3 km south of the Ralph River campground. Leave Buttle Lake Parkway heading east into the forest and cross the wide, low elevation valley flats to the foot of the ridge. Hike up a steep forested hillside to gain the alpine at the north-west end of the ridge. Water may be an issue in summer. Continue along the ridge crest to Shepherd Peak with the option of descending a line to the pass between Shepherd Peak and Tzela Mountain through a beautiful cirque ringed with waterfalls.

Alternatively, Shepherd Ridge may be reached from the north or east via Tzela Lake traversing to Buttle Lake from Comox Glacier or Mt. Washington - Paradise Meadows.

Shepherd Ridge north aspect from Syd Watts Peak, August.

Central Crags

Central Crags (L) and Mt. Rousseau (R) from Ralph River, June.

Central Crags - Flower Ridge
5,387 ft / 1,642 m

Central Crags are the high point along the well known and well travelled Flower Ridge. They are an impressive sight on Buttle Lake with their craggy north face overlooking the Henshaw Creek valley and the south-east end of the lake. Flower Ridge has held historic importance as a route from the Comox Valley into Buttle Lake and still retains much popularity for hikers making this journey today. Long multi day traverses can be made from Buttle Lake via Flower Ridge across the high ridge systems east and north to Comox Glacier and Mt. Albert Edward - Paradise Meadows. These are some of the finest such treks on Vancouver Island with almost the entire routes well above treeline.

First Ascent: Rev. William Bolton & party 1896

Map Sheet: 92 F/11 Forbidden Plateau -GR 1986

Approaches: Drive up Buttle Lake Parkway along the east shore of Buttle Lake park at the signposted trailhead for Flower Ridge. Follow the Flower Ridge trail up a series of forgiving switchbacks into the alpine. Continue along the long, arcing ridge on an unimproved route onto the north-west ridge of Central Crags. Beyond the summit of the Crags the ridge can be followed further east to the Cliffe and Comox Glaciers and points beyond. From Tzela Lake gain the ridge and follow it to Central Crags.

Flower Ridge may also be approached as part of the traverse from Mt. Washington-Paradise Meadows. Follow details for this traverse in the peak descriptions from Mt. Albert Edward over Mt. George V to the Cliffe Glacier.

Another possibility is reaching Central Crags from Price Pass. Hike either up the Price Creek Trail from Buttle Lake and continue past the creek crossing- bushwacking up to Green Lake and from there up to the pass. Or hike to Cream Lake on the Bedwell Trail and traverse from the west shoulder of Mt. Septimus around the south end of the massif to Price Pass, lots of glacier travel on the latter route.

Flower Ridge south aspect from Cream Lake, June.

Looking south east near the top of Jack's Trail toward Augerpoint mt. (L) and Syd Watts Peak (R), August.

Augerpoint Traverse: The most accessible and one of the most popular (relatively) of the Strathcona Park backcountry traverses. The Augerpoint traverse crosses the Campbell-Puntledge divide from the Paradise Meadows trailhead at Mt. Washington Alpine Resort over Mt. Albert Edward to Ruth Masters Lake and on to join Jack's Trail down to Buttle Lake. For a sample of what the longer traverses entail the Augerpoint route is an excellent introduction.

Typically this route is traveled from east to west taking advantage of the paved road access to the alpine at the Paradise Meadows trailhead. From the Inland Island Highway drive up to Mt. Washington Alpine Resort and follow signs for Paradise Meadows.

A well maintained trail with bridges and boardwalks leaves the resort area and weaves around Lake Helen Mackenzie and up onto Forbidden Plateau. Continue past the Park Ranger's cabin and on to a mandatory first camp at either Kwai or Circlet lakes.

Continue up to the summit of Mt. Albert Edward (see page 150) and then descend the west ridge to Ruth Masters Lake. Keep to the north shore of the lake and hike up a steep route to the west col of Augerpoint Mountain. Augerpoint may be climbed as a side trip and the traverse continues west then north on a well trodden path toward Jack's Fell. Just below the fell the route traverses down the west side of this little peak to join the top of Jack's Trail at a bench of alpine lakes overlooking Buttle Lake.

Descend the steep trail taking care with route finding through a number of small talus slopes. There is a good campsite at a small pond perched on a bench at 800m. Continue down to the Buttle Lake Parkway.

Note: Although this route is fairly short and accessible it does cover some very rugged and high mountain terrain. Count on 1-5 days. Camping on Forbidden Plateau must be at one of the designated sites at Kwai and Cirlet lakes.

Ruth Masters Lake and Augerpoint Mountain south-east aspect from Mt. Frink, August.

Augerpoint Mountain

Augerpoint Mountain north-west aspect from alpine ridge at top of Jack's Trail, August.

Augerpoint Mountain
5,905 ft./ 1,800 m

Augerpoint stands guard over the headwaters of the Oyster River and lies on the divide between the Oyster and Ralph rivers. The mountain is a straightforward hike to the summit and is a popular side trip for hikers crossing on the 'Augerpoint Traverse' from Mt. Washington-Paradise Meadows over Mt. Albert Edward to Jack's Trail which is followed down to Buttle Lake.

First Ascent: William Ralph 1892

Map Sheet: 92 F/11 Forbidden Plateau - GR 2104

Approaches: Most commonly reached from the col immediately southwest of the summit. This col may be reached from Mt. Albert Edward via Albert Edward's west ridge and Ruth Masters Lake or from the west from Jack's Trail along the connecting ridge (see Jack's Fell). The routes around Augerpoint are very well travelled with ample flagging and cairns to mark the way.

Augerpoint may also be climbed from Ruth Masters Lake with a steep hike up the south ridge.

If heading west from the col south-west of Augerpoint, toward Jack's Trail, continue west on the height of land. Considerable time may be saved alternatively by descending and traversing on the exposed snow patches above Shark Lake to rejoin the usual route at the low point on the ridge south of Peak 1586.

Augerpoint Mountain south-west aspect from near Syd Watts Peak, August.

172 Taking a dip in an alpine lake at the head of Siokum Creek.

Jack's Fell

Jack's Fell south aspect from Syd Watts Peak, August.

Jack's Fell
5,643 ft./ 1,720 m

Jack's Fell is a rounded knoll overlooking Pearl Lake and Buttle Lake. It sits above Jack's Trail which provides a superb route from Buttle Lake into the alpine around Augerpoint Mountain and on over Mt. Albert Edward to Paradise Meadows. Jack's Fell is a strenuous day-trip return from Buttle Lake.

Map Sheet: 92 F/12 Buttle Lake - GR 1906

Approaches: This low alpine peak is easily reached from Buttle Lake via Jack's Trail to Augerpoint. Jack's Trail is an unimproved trail maintained sporadically but in generally good condition due in large part to the regular traffic it receives. 1km north of the Augerpoint Day Area on Buttle Lake Parkway, along Buttle Lake a large blue arrow spraypainted on the road asphalt marks the trailhead. There is a good pullout opposite, or park at the Augerpoint Day Area and hike back along the road.

Jack's Trail climbs steeply up the forested hillside across beautiful moss covered bluffs and some scree higher up. The route crests onto an alpine bench below the west side of Jack's Fell. A number of small lakes here make an ideal campsite. Follow the well flagged and well trodden route south-east as it traverses around to the south side of Jack's Fell. From here the main route strikes off across a wide open alpine basin to the connecting ridge with Augerpoint Mountain and points beyond.

To reach the top of Jack's Fell leave the Augerpoint Traverse route and head up the slope northward on open heather and rocky ledges to the summit.

Jack's Fell (L) and Augerpoint Mountain (R) south aspect from Syd Watts Peak, August.

Sid Williams Peak

Sid Williams Peak north aspect from Syd Watts Peak, August.

Sid Williams Peak
5,905 ft / 1,800 m

Sid Williams Peak is the steep and imposing pinnacle south of Syd Watts Peak, overlooking Karst Creek and Ralph River. Has been described as Augerpoint South Peak in Bruce Fairley's guidebook.

First Ascent: Ron Facer, Mike Walsh 1968

Map Sheet: 92 F/11 Forbidden Plateau - GR 2102

Approaches: May be reached from Syd Watts Peak, with some labour, by descending steep snow - scree gullies to the west and traversing to the South Ridge. Alternatively, bushwhack directly up Karst Creek or the ridge to the south of Karst Creek which winds round and up on to the South Ridge.

Sid Williams Peak north aspect from Syd Watts Peak, August.

Syd Watts Peak

Syd Watts Peak north aspect from the Augerpoint traverse, August.

Syd Watts Peak
6,036 ft./ 1,840 m

Syd Watts Peak overlooks the southern half of Buttle Lake forming the southern terminus of the ridge system which runs north as far as Lupin Mountain. Like many of the peaks on this side of Buttle Lake the views across the lake are excellent and well worth the hike to see. Syd Watts Peak may be climbed as a side trip if you are en route along the Augerpoint Traverse. The mountain is named for Syd Watts a prolific Island mountaineer.

First Ascent: Unknown

Map Sheet: 92 F/11 Forbidden Plateau - GR 2103

Approaches: Best reached from the Augerpoint traverse from Mt. Albert Edward via Ruth Masters Lake or Jack's Trail from Buttle Lake. Follow the descriptions for Jack's Fell and Mt. Albert Edward depending on direction of approach. From the ridge crest north of Ruth Masters Lake, and west of Augerpoint Mountain, head south along a sharp gravel covered ridge to a col and then hike up rock slabs and snow patches along the north-east ridge directly to the summit. Some 3rd class near the top.

May also be reached directly by bushwacking up Karst Creek from Buttle Lake into the basin on the south side of the mountain. Climb out of the basin up a gully and wrap around the east side of the mountain to join the route up the north-east ridge.

Syd Watts (C) & Sid Williams Peak (R) north aspect from Jack's Fell, August.

Mt. Mitchell

Mt. Mitchell south-west aspect from Augerpoint Mountain, August.

Mt. Mitchell
6,036 ft./ 1,840 m

Mt. Mitchell is a craggy summit standing sentry over Pearl Lake and Norm Creek at the head of the Oyster River. It is a popular destination with several excellent scrambling routes.

First Ascent: R. Martin, M. Walsh 1968

Map Sheet: 92 F/11 Forbidden Plateau - GR 2206

Approaches: Approach Mt. Mitchell from Augerpoint Mountain via Mt. Albert Edward or Jack's Trail. From the summit of Augerpoint head north-east to descend the connecting ridge which joins Mitchell's distinctive South Ridge. Alternatively Mt. Mitchell can be reached from the Oyster River between Norm Lake & Pearl Lake off logging roads.

North Ridge: 3rd Class
Mt. Mitchell's north ridge rises right from the valley floor. Hike up the toe of the ridge to a Class 3 scramble near the top.

North Gully: AI1
A steep prominent gully that forms a cleft in the rock band on the north face. With winter/spring snow cover it is a fast ascent to the top. FA: Lindsay Elms, Peter Ravensbergen May 26, 2002

North-West Ridge: low 5th Class
Hike south from Pearl Lake gaining the arcing north-west ridge. Follow along ridge crest with a few moves in a steep gully (low 5th) and a short slab above leads to the summit plateau.

Mt. Mitchell west aspect from ridge at the top of Jack's trail, August.

Pearl Peak

Pearl Peak & Mt. Mitchell (R) south aspect from Augerpoint Mountain, August.

Pearl Peak
5,511 ft./ 1,680 m

Pearl Peak is a low satellite of Augerpoint Mountain warranting distinction for its remarkable situation overlooking Pearl Lake and the Oyster River headwaters along with Augerpoint and Mt. Mitchell which surround it like a pearl.

Map Sheet: 92 F/11 Forbidden Plateau - GR 2105

Approaches: Follow approach details for Augerpoint Mountain and from the summit of Augerpoint descend directly down the snowfields on Augerpoint's north side to gain the ridge which sweeps back up onto Pearl Peak. May also be reached as an easy day trip by bushwacking up the upper Oyster River from Pearl Lake to gain the north ridge which is an easy hike to the top.

Mt. Mitchell (L) & Mt. Alexandra (R) above Campbell River & Discovery Passage, May.

Alexandra Peak

Alexandra Peak north-east aspect as seen from Quadra Island, August.

Alexandra Peak
6,506 ft./ 1,982 m

Alexandra Peak is an impressive, sprawling peak that presides over the Campbell River skyline. It is situated at the head of the Oyster River above Pearl Lake on private forest company land. The mountain is an ideal day trip destination and also holds some interest for backcountry skiing & snowboarding.

First Ascent: Adrian Paul, David Guthrie, Henry Ellis, August 1930

Map Sheet: 92 F/11 Forbidden Plateau - GR 2012

Approaches: Alexandra Peak may be climbed from logging roads in the Oyster River valley. The mountain and all the surrounding lands are privately owned by Timberwest and access on to the Oyster Main is restricted during working hours. Turn west on Cranberry Road off the Inland Island Highway 19 to the gate on the Oyster Main. Drive up the Oyster River Main to the south end of Norm Lake. A flagged route heads up from Pearl Lake parking but is tricky to locate. The route leads up the south-east ridge to the alpine and on to the summit. May also be reached from Buttle Lake Parkway.

North-East Ridge: NTD
Climbs the long ridge which divides the Oyster River from the Adrian Creek headwaters. Pass a high lake and on to the upper snowfields and the summit.
FA: S. Haigh, G Braithwaite, Chris Barner early 1980s

Alexandra Peak & Pearl Lake south aspect from Jack's Fell, August

Mt. Adrian

Mt. Adrian (C) and Alexandra Peak south aspect from ridge above Pearl Lake, June

Mt. Adrian
6,135 ft./ 1,869 m

Mount Adrian is an inconspicuous peak forming the southern end of the ridge system that runs north along the east side of Buttle Lake to Lupin Mountain and Hawkins Creek. The mountain resides outside of the Strathcona Park boundary on private forest company land and access to the mountain is determined by current logging activity in the area. Mt. Adrian's interest lies as a day hike destination or as part of a longer traverse north to Lupin Mountain. The Vancouver Island Backbone hiking route passes across Adrian's summit en route from Forbidden Plateau to Buttle Narrows.

First Ascent: Unknown

Map Sheet: 92 F/13 Upper Campbell Lake - GR 1714

Approaches: Access to Mt. Adrian is best from Buttle Lake via the new logging roads that climb up from the Buttle Lake Parkway on Adrian's west flank around into the high valley near Pearl Lake on the south side of the mountain. At the time of writing logging activity is ongoing around Mt. Adrian and access is restricted as a result. Adrian is a great day trip from Beadnell Lake/Rodger's Ridge.

Mt. Adrian may also be reached from the Oyster River. Follow approach details for Mt. Alexandra, turn right from the Oyster Main on OR 300 into the Adrian Creek valley to the north-east of the summit.

Mt. Adrian west aspect from Marblerock Canyon prior to recent logging, June.

Mt. Beadnell

Looking south across Rodger's Ridge from Mt. Beadnell, note Alexandra Peak (L) & Mt. Adrian (C), August.

Mt. Beadnell - Rodger's Ridge
5,728 ft./ 1,746 m

Mt. Beadnell, or Rodger's Ridge as it is more commonly known as, is an open area of high alpine on the east divide above Buttle Lake. It is a popular destination for hikers, ski touring and even snowmobilers. There are several large subalpine lakes in the base of cirques around the mountain. These cirques make for some excellent ski terrain and plans were hatched in the 1970s to establish a ski hill on Rodger's Ridge. More recently the area has been aggressively logged with roads rising high from Buttle Lake and the Quinsam Lake area. Luckily the carnage on its own flanks does little to diminish the superlative views to the west and south into Strathcona Park and to the east looking over the Georgia Strait, Discovery Islands and mainland Coast Range mountains.

Map Sheet: 92 F/13 Upper Campbell Lake - GR 1617

Approaches: Rodger's Ridge may be reached from a variety of approaches. The fastest access is from the high logging roads in the Sihun Creek drainage specifically Granite Main. To reach Granite Main turn south off Highway 28 at the Quinsam Coal Road west of Campbell River. Leave the road to the mine on the Argonaut Main and follow it around the shore of Quinsam Lake then up into a high valley on Granite Main. From the back of the Sihun Creek valley a short hike through clearcut and subalpine timber leads on to the crest of the ridge north of Mt. Beadnell. Hike south through beautiful meadows up the gentle north ridge to the top of Mt. Beadnell.

The area may also be reached from the Oyster Main to the east. Turn west on Cranberry Road from Highway 19 south of Campbell River to the gate on the Oyster Main. Drive up the Oyster River Main then turn right on to Eden Main. At the end of the road trails head west to Beadnell Lake. From the lake hike up the gentle ridge around the lake's north shore to the top.

Alexandra Peak (L) Mt. Adrian (C) & Mt. Albert Edward (R) north-west aspect as seen from Crown Mountain, July.

Lupin Mountain

Lupin Mountain south-east aspect from sub alpine meadows in upper Sihun Creek, August.

Lupin Mountain
4,898 ft./ 1,493 m

Lupin Mountain is a low knoll situated at the north end of the divide to the east of Buttle Lake. As the terminus of a lengthy ridge system running to the south and including Rodger's Ridge and Mt. Adrian, Lupin Mountain acts as the alpine start or finish of a hike or ski tour along that divide. Lupin Mt. is just outside the Strathcona Park boundary on private forest land. This should be borne in mind for any activity in the area as road access may be restricted at any time.

Map Sheet: 92 F/13 Upper Campbell Lake - GR 1620

Approaches: Lupin Mountain may be reached from a variety of approaches. The fastest access is from the high logging roads in the Sihun Creek drainage specifically Granite Main. To reach Granite Main turn south off Highway 28 at the Quinsam Coal Road west of Campbell River. Leave the road to the mine on the Argonaut Main and follow it around the shore of Quinsam Lake then up into a high valley on Granite Main. From the back of the Sihun Creek valley a short hike through clearcut and subalpine timber leads on to the crest of the ridge south of Lupin Mountain.

Lupin Mountain may also be reached by bushwacking up from Buttle Lake Parkway near Buttle Narrows to logging roads in the Hawkins Creek valley. Follow the Hawkins Creek Main high up on the north-west flank of Lupin Mountain then continue through remaining forest to the top.

Hawkins Peak (L) and Lupin Mt. (R) west aspect from Buttle Lake, July.

Crown Mountain

Strathcona Park North

184 Mia Falls and Big Den Mountain from Mt. Flannigan.

Strathcona Park North
Contents

Big Den Mountain	189
Mt. Flannigan	191
Crest Mountain	192
Idsardi Mountain	193
Mt. Heber	194
Trio Mountain	195
Crown Mountain	197
Mt. Judson	199
Tyee Mountain	200
Horseshoe Mountain	201

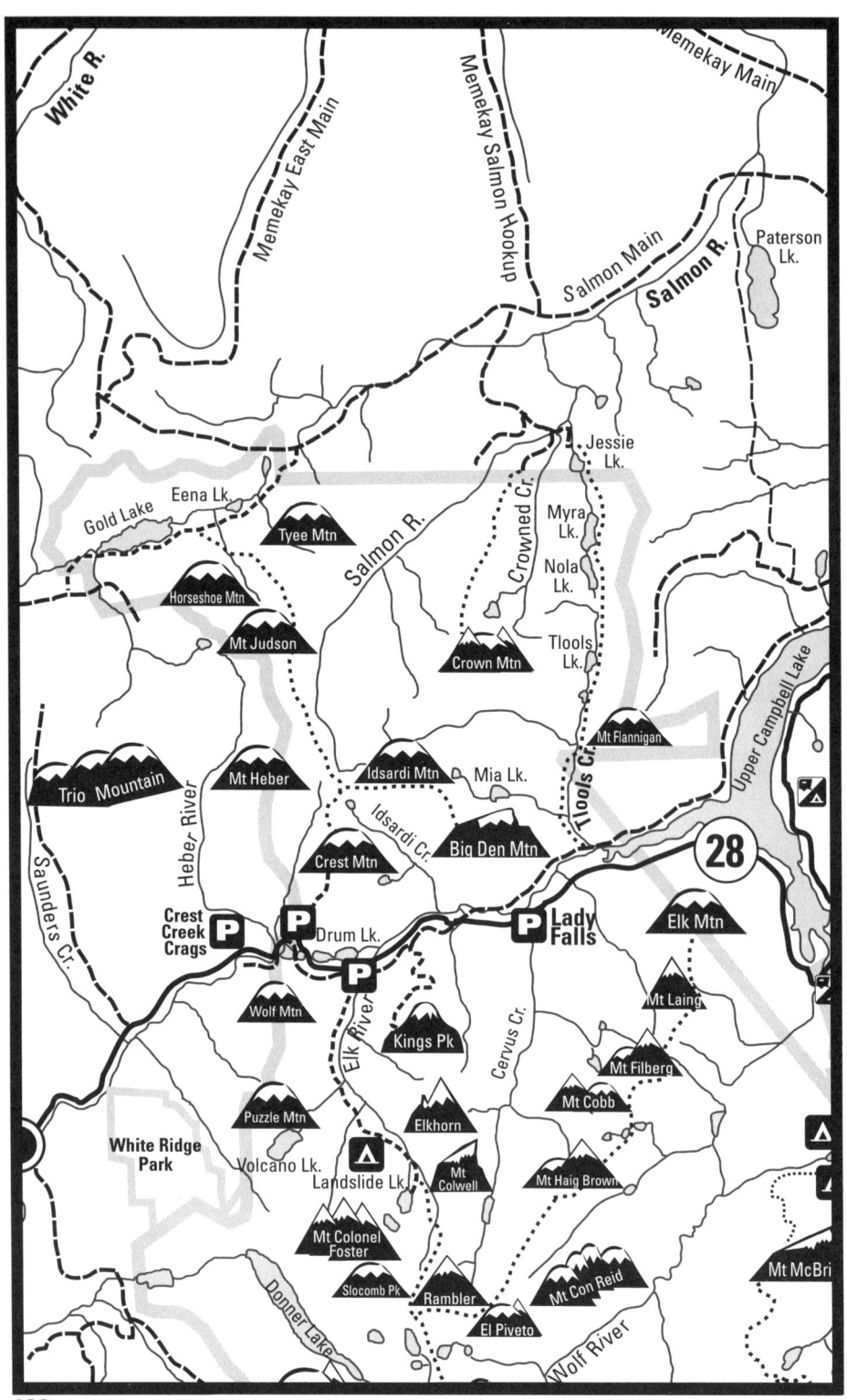

186 Strathcona Park North - Map

Strathcona Park North

North Strathcona Park consists of the area of Strathcona north of the Gold River Highway 28. This area is notable for its large tracts of old growth forest bordered by intensive logging around the park boundary. The mountains of this area are, for the most part, gentle, rounded peaks which only just break the 6,000 ft mark. A couple of exceptions are the craggy twin summits Crown Mountain and Big Den Mountain which offers some excellent alpine climbs. There are some longer hiking trips possible through this area of the park and a few gems waiting to be discovered too.

Map Sheets: 92 F/13 Upper Campbell Lake • 92 E/16 Gold River

Boundaries: north: Gold Lake & Salmon River, **east:** Upper Campbell Lake, **south:** Elk River, **west:** Gold River

Major Access Routes: Highway 28 between Campbell River and Gold River provides the main access to the northern region of Strathcona Park. An important compliment to the highway access is the adjacent gravel Elk River Timber Company Road which parallels the highway and also links Gold River to Campbell River. The ERT Road takes the north shore around Upper Campbell Lake before eventually crossing Highway 28 just west of Lady Falls. Sections of this road have already been closed and its future is likely to include further closures as it is for the most part on private land.

Nimpkish Road: From Gold River the East Main off Nimpkish Road (Woss-Gold River) provides gravel road access to Gold Lake and the north-west corner of Strathcona.

Menzies Main: From 14 km north of Campbell River on the Island Highway 19 the Menzies Main and North and South Forks of the Salmon River Main give access to the north boundary of the park and the east side of Gold Lake. Between them these logging roads almost completely encircle North Strathcona.

Trails

6- Crest Mountain: The Crest Mountain Trail is the most popular trail in North Strathcona and an excellent route into the alpine. From the trailhead on Highway 28, 60 km west of Campbell River head down to the bridge across Drum Lakes and then up a long series of switchbacks past a creek crossing in the lower third and two openings in the forest, where trees were cut for snowpack measurements. Continue up the trail through a steep gully to the alpine at a small lake at the south end of the summit plateau.

7- Gold Lake: The Gold Lake Trail is a through route connecting the Salmon Main from Campbell River to the east and East Main from Gold River on the west side. The trail leads through the park in a forest of huge cedar trees past Eena Lake, open bogs and around the south shore of Gold Lake.

Forest Service & Logging Company Offices:

Campbell River Forest District - 370 South Dogwood Street, Campbell River, B.C. V9W 6Y7 Ph: (250) 286-9300

Timberwest -5705 North Island Highway Campbell River, BC V9W 5C5 Ph: (250) 287-9181

Weyerhaeuser - North Island Timberlands -P.O. Box 6000, 8010 Island Highway, Campbell River, BC V9W 5E1 Ph: 250-287-5000

Other Information Sources:

• **Hiking Trails III** - Northern Vancouver Island & Strathcona Park - (9th ed. 2002 Richard K. Blier, ed.) VITIS

• **Beyond Nootka** - A Historical Perspective of Vancouver Island Mountains by Lindsay Elms,

• **BC Parks web site:** http://wlapwww.gov.bc.ca/bcparks/explore/parkpgs/strathco.htm

Special Thanks:
Thanks to Lindsay Elms and Chris Barner for assistance in preparing this chapter.

188 Phil Stone high above Mia Lake on Big Den's Great Escape. Photo: Chris Lawrence.

Big Den Mountain

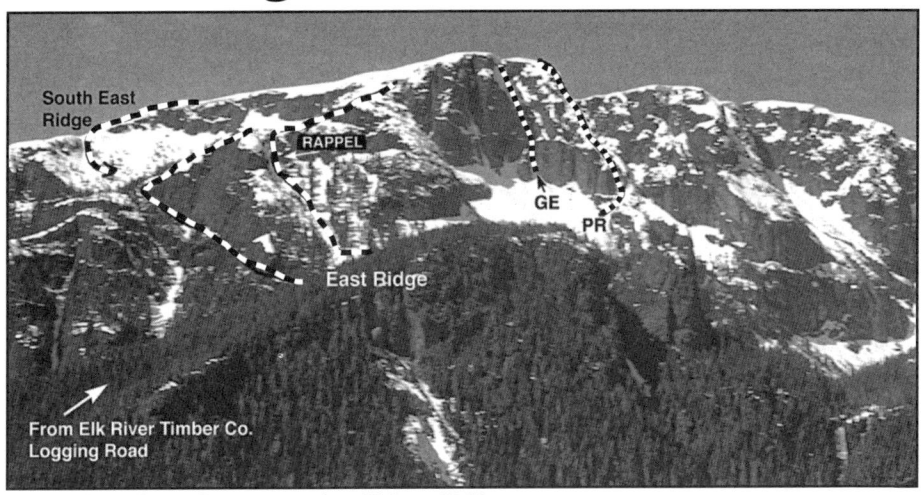

Big Den Mountain, south-east aspect from Highway 28, May.

Big Den Mountain
5,827 ft / 1,776 m

Big Den is an often overlooked peak standing alone with its steep north-east face turned shyly away from view as seen by passing climbers on Highway 28. However it makes a great day trip and is highly recommended as a climbing destination with great potential as both a summer and a winter venue. Numerous gullies and buttresses run the length of the north-east face with good rock climbing in summer and superb ice in winter.

Big Den bears more than a passing resemblance to Ben Nevis in Scotland, home of some classic winter climbs, right down to the flat plateau summit which is a dream come true for finishing a route on.

First Ascent: Unknown

Map Sheet: 92 F/13 Upper Campbell Lake - GR 9829

Approaches: Most easily approached by hiking from the Elk River Timber Company logging road up to a shoulder on the east ridge of the mountain and from there by the listed routes to the summit. In dry summer weather the fastest access to the shoulder is up a creek bed draining the south-east flank of the mountain. Identifying the creek while on the ERT Road can be tricky as the forest is very dense, but once the culverts are located the route right up the creek is straightforward. With water flow in the creek, a route parallel to it some 500m right (east) works best. By scouting from Highway 28 where a view across the Elk River gives a good look at the lower flanks of the mountain, a line avoiding as much of the nasty, burn/2nd growth bush as possible can be figured out.

Another possibility is to gain the shoulder by hiking the ridge line from a short way up Tlools Creek. However you reach it, the east ridge shoulder has water and a camp site which makes an excellent base to reach the climbs.

Big Den can also be reached as part of a hike from Crest Mountain via Idsardi Mountain. Park at the Crest Mountain parking lot and hike up the Crest Mountain Trail to the alpine lake on the summit plateau. Continue north across Crest Mountain and descend a treed ridge between Idsardi and Crest creeks. Trend south-east above a small lake in Idsardi Creek to gain the south-west ridge of Idsardi Mountain. Head east dropping to a pass just north-west of Big Den and climb out and gain the long north ridge which can be followed to the top.

Additional Info: WIM #9 p.20

Big Den Mountain, south-east aspect from east shoulder, December.

Routes

East Ridge: 4th class
From the shoulder on the east ridge, turn south and make a leftward (south) traverse up through subalpine timber to reach the base of a vegetated gully which leads up to the crest of the East Ridge. Some parties may require a rappel or handline on the descent in this gully. Scramble up the gully (exposed) onto the ridge crest which can be followed to the summit plateau with occasional 4th class steps on good rock.

PR ** **Perimeter Ridge:** low 5th Class 500m (II)
The most prominent of the buttresses on Big Den's nort-east face. Approach by traversing in to the north-east cirque from the east shoulder. Scramble up a short gully with a little loose rock to gain the crest of the ridge. Easy scrambling along the crest with a choice of short 5th class steps near the top.
FA: Philip Stone, Jacki Klancher, 19 September 1991

Winter Routes

GE ** **The Great Escape:** AI3 400m (III)
Climbs the longest and most prominent of the gullies on the north-east face. Access is on the same traverse as Perimeter Ridge from the east shoulder. Take caution crossing the cirque to the base of the climb as it is very exposed with a ski jump lip over Mia Lake. Start the gully direct at the base. 3 easy pitches of steep snow with short difficulties lead to the crux on pitch 4. Climb the steep chimney with good protection and a few awkward moves. The remainder of pitch 4 and pitch 5 is mainly steep snow. A huge cornice caps this gully which may need tunnelling. Luckily a large snow cavern can form under the cornice giving ample room from which to work! Easy descent on benign terrain down the south west ridge and back to the east shoulder.
FA: Philip Stone, Chris Lawrence 11-12 December 1990

Big Den Mountain, north aspect from Crown Mountain, July.

190   Big Den Mountain

Mt. Flannigan

Shea Wilson ski touring along the Mt. Flannigan ridge.

Mt. Flannigan
5,087 ft / 1,550 m

Mt. Flannigan sits on the north shore of the west arm of Upper Campbell Lake. The summit overlooks the Tlools Creek valley to the west, Upper Campbell Lake to the south and east, and the lowlands of Ranald and Greenstone Creeks to the north. The area is a popular destination for snowmobilers although the summit itself is within Strathcona Park's boundaries and off limits to mechanised vehicles.

The access to Mt. Flannigan is excellent on high logging roads making the summit a casual day trip perfect in any season. The views into Cervus Creek and of Elkhorn and King's Peak are salient Strathcona scenes.

Map Sheet: 92 F/13 Upper Campbell Lake - GR 0332

Approaches: The notorious 'Flannigan triangle' is just south of the summit of Mt. Flannigan. This area is named for the triangular shaped piece of land defined by the park boundary and the shore of Upper Campbell Lake. The unfortunate path of the park boundary admits private lands within the Tlools valley west of Flannigan where logging occurs in an otherwise fairly intact valley system.

The logging roads that facilitate the harvesting on the south and south-west slopes of Flannigan provide great alpine access to Mt. Flannigan and the alpine ridge which runs several kilometres to the north.

Crest Mountain

Crest Mountain, north-west aspect from Victoria Peak, August.

Crest Mountain
5,196 ft / 1,584 m

Crest Mountain is a high alpine knoll situated on the Island divide between Idsardi Creek and Heber River north of Highway 28. With Park's trail access Crest Mountain is a popular hike with rewards of wide open alpine meadows, a beautiful alpine lake and 360° views notably to the south down the Elk River toward King's Peak and Mt. Colonel Foster.

Longer hikes are possible from Crest Mountain including an excellent horseshoe round the Idsardi Valley to Big Den Mountain and also north via Mt. Judson to Gold Lake. The latter forming one leg of the Vancouver Island Backbone hiking route.

Map Sheet: 92 F/13 Upper Campbell Lake - GR 9393

Approaches: Straightforward up a well maintained Park's trail from Highway 28. Park at Drum Lakes, 60 km west of Campbell River on the north side of the highway just past the Elk River trail trailhead. Hike up the trail on a series of switchbacks with views at several clearings made by meteorologists studying snow depths for BC Hydro at the time of the damming of the Campbell River. Water is available at a year round stream in the lower third of the trail but then not again until reaching the lake at the top. This is a high use area so please follow the trail and use no-trace practices.

If approaching from Gold Lake and Mt. Judson or Big Den Mountain via Idsardi Mountain follow approach descriptions for these peaks.

Lindsay Elms on Crest Mountain.

Idsardi Mountain

Idsardi Mountain, north-east aspect from Crown Mountain, July.

Idsardi Mountain
5,449 ft / 1,661 m

Idsardi Mountain is an unremarkable summit viewed from the south but has not only some excellent hiking terrain but a secreted wall which drops into the west branch of Tlools Creek on its north face. This wall, at the time of writing, has nary a route on it but great potential considering the superb access winter and summer via the Crest Mountain trail.

As detailed under Big Den Mountain, Idsardi Mountain forms part of a hiking route around the Idsardi Valley between Crest and Big Den Mountains. Idsardi Mountain is named after Harold Idsardi who conducted a timber survey of the Idsardi valley in 1912.

First Ascent: Unknown

Map Sheet: 92 F/13 Upper Campbell Lake - GR 9431

Approaches: Best reached from Crest Mountain via the Park's trail from Highway 28 into the alpine (see Crest Mountain approaches). From the summit plateau of Crest, descend a north running ridge down into a col with a small knoll at GR 9330. Water from this knoll flows into three watersheds: the Salmon River, Idsardi Creek and the Heber River. Bypass the knoll on the right (south-east) and from a second pass, to its east, gain the treed south-east ridge of Idsardi Mountain which leads up easy hiking terrain to the summit.

From Big Den Mountain follow approach details to the summit of Big Den then hike north-west along Big Den's north-west ridge to a col just south of a small knoll overlooking a small alpine lake to the east. Descend westward into the pass between the west branch of Tlools Creek and Idsardi Creek. Hike up forested slopes onto the east end of Idsardi Mountain and continue west along the height of land to the top. Continue southward to crest Mountain and take the Crest Mountain Trail back down to Highway 28.

Mt. Heber

Mt. Heber, south aspect from Elkhorn approach, August.

Mt. Heber
5,468 ft / 1,666 m

Mt. Heber is a collection of low rocky summits north-west of Crest Mountain. Geographically it is interesting as the rivers draining its flanks run in to the Salmon, Campbell and Heber Rivers. There are likely some possibilities for shorter alpine rock routes on its east side. The mountain makes an excellent destination for climbers visiting Crest Creek Crags which are found at the base of the mountain along Highway 28. Mt. Heber is named for Heber G. DeVoe older brother of William Fowler DeVoe a young surveyor who made the first ascent of the peak and tragically drowned shortly after in the Campbell River in 1913.

First Ascent: William Fowler DeVoe, September 11, 1913

Map Sheet: 92 F/13 Upper Campbell Lake - GR 9030

Approaches: A straightforward approach from Highway 28 at Crest Creek Crags. At the Heber diversion pipeline bridge just west of the Projects Rock locate an old logging road which is used now as a trail to reach Black Crag and Crag X. Park at the highway or use the main Crest Creek Crags parking lot clearly signposted by BC Parks. Hike up the old road ignoring the trails to the crags in the surrounding forest.

The road quickly enters open regenerating forest on the lower flanks of Mt. Heber's south ridge. Strike up through the second growth forest to reach the remaining old growth and continue up the crest of the ridge to a triangulation point 4397 ft. From here the angle of the ridge eases and continues north over several knolls with easy hiking terrain to the top. Note that the north summit is actually higher than the official mapped summit so if you want to be sure of bagging this peak run north across the summit plateau to take in the higher top.

Mt. Heber may also be reached in a horseshoe traverse from Crest Mountain around the Crest Creek valley. Hike up the Crest Mountain trail and continue north across the summit plateau. Descend the north ridge of Crest Mountain to a knoll at GR 9330. From here head north-west to a small lake at the head of Crest Creek and on to the foot of the north-east ridge of Mt. Heber. Ascend the north-east ridge to the higher north summit and then continue south across Mt. Heber's summit plateau to the official summit of the mountain. Descend southward straight down the south ridge to logging roads in Crest Creek and on to Highway 28 and a short hitch hike or walk east along the highway to your vehicle at the Crest Mountain parking lot.

Additional Info: IB 1993 p.23

Trio Mountain

Trio Mountain, south-east aspect from Elkhorn approach, August.

Trio Mountain
5,683 ft / 1,732 m

Trio Mountain forms the steep sided divide between Saunders Creek to its west and the Heber River to the east. It is an expansive mountain with plenty of room to explore the alpine terrain across the complex summit ridge.

First Ascent: Unknown

Map Sheet: 92 E/16 Gold River - GR 1529 (see also 92 F/13 Upper Campbell Lake)

Approaches: From Highway 28 turn north on to the Heber River Main logging road just west of Crest Creek Crags. Drive up the Heber Main ~3 km to BR 32 which leads up a small tight valley on the south-east end of the mountain. From near the end of the road continue on foot up this valley heading for a col at GR 1528 due south of the summit. Head north up the south ridge with a little low 4th class scrambling near the top.

Mt. Heber (far L) and Idsardi Mountain (R) east aspect from Big Den Mountain, September.

Paul Agnew on the North Ridge of Crown Mountain, Winnifred Lake below.

Crown Mountain

Crown Mountain, north aspect from Peak 5412, July.

Crown Mountain
6,057 ft./ 1,846 m

A rarely visited but historically important peak. Crown Mountain's first ascent by the Hon. Price Ellison and his party in 1910 was pivotal in the formation of Strathcona Park. It was likely chance that elected Crown Mountain to be tackled by Ellison as he and his group approached the interior of Vancouver Island to survey the region for the purpose of creating a park. However fate played a Royal Flush of a hand as the views from Crown Mountain of the high peaks of the Elk River area were the impressive vistas Ellison sought and upon his return to Victoria the first boundaries of Strathcona Park were drawn up. Crown Mountain was for a time known as Ellison Peak.

Crown Mountain is worthy of far more attention than it currently receives (5 ascents recorded in the register between 1986 and 2002!). Its close proximity to Campbell River, superlative views of northern Strathcona Park, the strikingly beautiful alpine approach ridges and easy climbing terrain contrive to make Crown Mountain a desirable hiking destination.

First Ascent: Price Ellison, Myra Ellison, Col. William Holmes, J. Twaddle, A.L. Hudson, Harry Johnson, Charles Haslam, James Hasworth, Frank Ward July 29th 1910

Map Sheet: 92 F/13 Upper Campbell Lake - GR 9836

Approaches: Drive north on Island Highway 19 from Campbell River for 14.5 km to the Menzies Bay Main. Turn left (west) on Menzies Bay Main and follow it to just past 36 km where a there is a lefthand junction on to South Fork Main. Take this road to SF 900 and drive as far as you can up SF 900. Park and then continue on foot up SF 900. As the road rounds the toe of the ridge and enters the Crowned Creek valley it has been debuilt and a path along the old road bed continues until ending in a clearcut. From this point head uphill to reach the old growth and pick up a flagged route on to the crest of the north ridge. From here the flagging and indeed any sign of an established route ends. Continue on the height of land watching the map and keeping an eye on the compass to avoid any one of a number of 'sucker spurs'. Eventually, near Peak 5412, the trees open up and a clear view to the mountain can be seen ahead.

Alternative approaches might include the parallel ridge on the east side of Crowned Creek from the South Fork Main or the lower east ridge from the west fork of Tlools Creek from Highway 28.

Additional Info: IB 1992 p.10

Crown Mountain, east aspect from Quadra Island, July.

Crown Mountain, west aspect from west summit, July.

Routes

WG- North Glacier & West Gullies: 3rd class 100m
Approach from Peak 5412 along the ridge until a wide obvious ramp leads down on to the north glacier. Walk up the glacier to the col between the Main and West Summits. An easy gully leads up on the left (east) side of the col to the south side of the mountain. A short but exposed walk leads to the summit. Descend same route.

ER- East Ridge: 3rd class 300m
The original route up Crown Mt.. Approach from east divide of Crowned Creek or Tlools Creek. Ascend ridge crest until forced on to a small snowfield on the north side of the mountain to reach summit.
FA: Price Ellison et al 1910

NR- North Ridge: 4th class 150m
Approach from Peak 5412 on to north glacier then traverse straight across below the mountain to a snowfield at the base of the North Ridge. Alternatively, reach the same location directly from approaches on east side of mountain. Walk up snow/scree on left side of ridge until a break allows an easy scramble on to the ridge crest which is followed to the summit. Watch for aircraft wreckage on the upper part of the ridge and around the summit.

C- The Cleft: AI1 75 m
Steep snow climbing up the gully that splits the main summit just below the col between the main and west summits.
FA: Sandy Briggs, Don Berryman, Greta Smythe, Roseanne Van Schie, Dennis Manke 1992

Crown Mountain, south aspect from Big Den Mt., September.

Mt. Judson

Mt. Judson (L) & Horseshoe Mountain (R) east aspect from Crown Mountain, July.

Mt. Judson
5,732 ft / 1,747 m

Mt. Judson is one of the higher mountains in North Strathcona. It sits on the divide between the South Fork of the Salmon River to the east and the Heber-Gold Pass to the west. It is named for William Judson DeVoe father of William Fowler DeVoe a young surveyor who made the first ascent of Mt. Judson and Mt. Heber and tragically drowned in the Campbell River.

First Ascent: William Fowler DeVoe, August 30 1913

Map Sheet: 92 F/13 Upper Campbell Lake - GR 9035

Approaches: Mt. Judson can be approached from logging roads in the Heber valley. From Highway 28 head north on the Heber Main just west of Crest Creek Crags. Drive as far as road conditions and/or your vehicle allow, then continue on foot to the head of the valley to a pass between Judson and Horseshoe Mountain. Weave up the west ridge of the mountain avoiding some rock bluffs en route and make an easy scramble to the summit.

Judson may also be reached from the south via the Crest Mountain Trail from Highway 28. Hike across the summit plateau of Crest Mountain and descend a north running ridge down into a col with a small knoll from which water flows into three watersheds: the Salmon River, Idsardi Creek and the Heber River. Head north-west past the knoll to reach the forested south ridge of Mt. Judson which can be followed with no technical difficulty to the summit.

Mt. Judson and the upper Salmon River valley, south aspect from Crest Mountain, September.

Tyee Mountain

Tyee Mountain south-east aspect from Crown Mountain, July.

Tyee Mountain
5,486 ft / 1,672 m

Tyee Mountain is a beautifully forested knoll located east of Gold Lake on the Salmon - Gold River divide. The forest cloaking Tyee Mountain is striking when juxtaposed against the intensive logging that surrounds this end of Strathcona Park. Rewards from this unassuming summit are views of the Salmon River and Crown Mountain which sits just across the south fork of the Salmon from Tyee Mountain.

First Ascent: Unknown

Map Sheet: 92 F/13 Upper Campbell Lake - GR 9240

Approaches: Best reached from the north-east off the Salmon River Main logging road. From Campbell River drive 14.5 km north on the Island Highway. Turn west on to Menzies Bay Main this road becomes Salmon River Main at Mohun Lake. Continue driving west to the junction with Grisle Creek Main. Turn left across a bridge over Grisle Creek and locate branch road SR-15. Drive or walk up this road which weaves across the lower flanks of the north-east ridge of Tyee Mountain.

Hike up the broad, timbered ridge to a low summit at GR 9340. From here the ridge to Tyee Mountain becomes more distinct. Continue south-west from this summit to the upper north-east ridge which is an easy hike on to the summit plateau and on to the top.

Horseshoe Mountain north aspect from Elbow-Consort Creek divide, June. (Note: Crown Mt. far L.)

Horseshoe Mountain

Horseshoe Mountain north aspect from Victoria Peak, August.

Horseshoe Mountain
5,710 ft / 1,740 m

Horseshoe Mountain is found to the south of Gold Lake on the divide between Horseshoe Creek to the west and the upper Gold River to the east. It has spectacular views of Gold Lake.

First Ascent: Unknown

Map Sheet: 92 F/13 Upper Campbell Lake - GR 8737

Approaches: Approach Horseshoe Mountain from logging roads in the Heber River valley. From Highway 28 head north on the Heber Main just west of Crest Creek Crags. Drive as far as road conditions and vehicle allow then continue on foot to the head of the valley to a pass between Judson and Horseshoe Mountain. Head north-west up the steep south-east ridge of Horseshoe Mountain over Peak 5327. Continue along the easy ridge to the summit.

Horseshoe Mountain may also be approached from Gold Lake. Follow either east or west approach on the Gold Lake Trail. From 1 km east of the west end of the lake head south-east to gain a forested ridge which leads up to a flat topped summit north-west of Horseshoe Mountain at GR 8638. Continue south-east climbing up the west ridge to the summit.

Horseshoe Mountain east aspect from Crown Mountain, July.

202 Golden Hinde peaks from behind Morrison Spire, Marble Meadows.

Central Strathcona Park

204 Elkhorn reflected in Foster Lake.

Central Strathcona Park
Contents

Wolf Mountain	210
Puzzle Mountain	211
Volcano Peak	213
King's Peak	214
Elkhorn Mountain	218
Mt. Colwell	225
Mt. Colonel Foster	228
Slocomb Peak	240
Rambler Peak	241
Mt. DeVoe	247
El Piveto Mountain	249
Cervus -Wolf Divide	251
Ptarmigan Pinnacles	252
Mt. Haig-Brown	253
Mt. Cobb	255
Mt. Filberg	257
Mt. Laing	258
Elk Mountain	259
Mt. Titus	260
Mt. Con Reid	261
Marble Peak	262
Mt. McBride	263
Morrison Spire	266
Phillips Ridge	267
Mt. Phillips	269
Mt. Burman	270
Golden Hinde	271
The Behinde	277

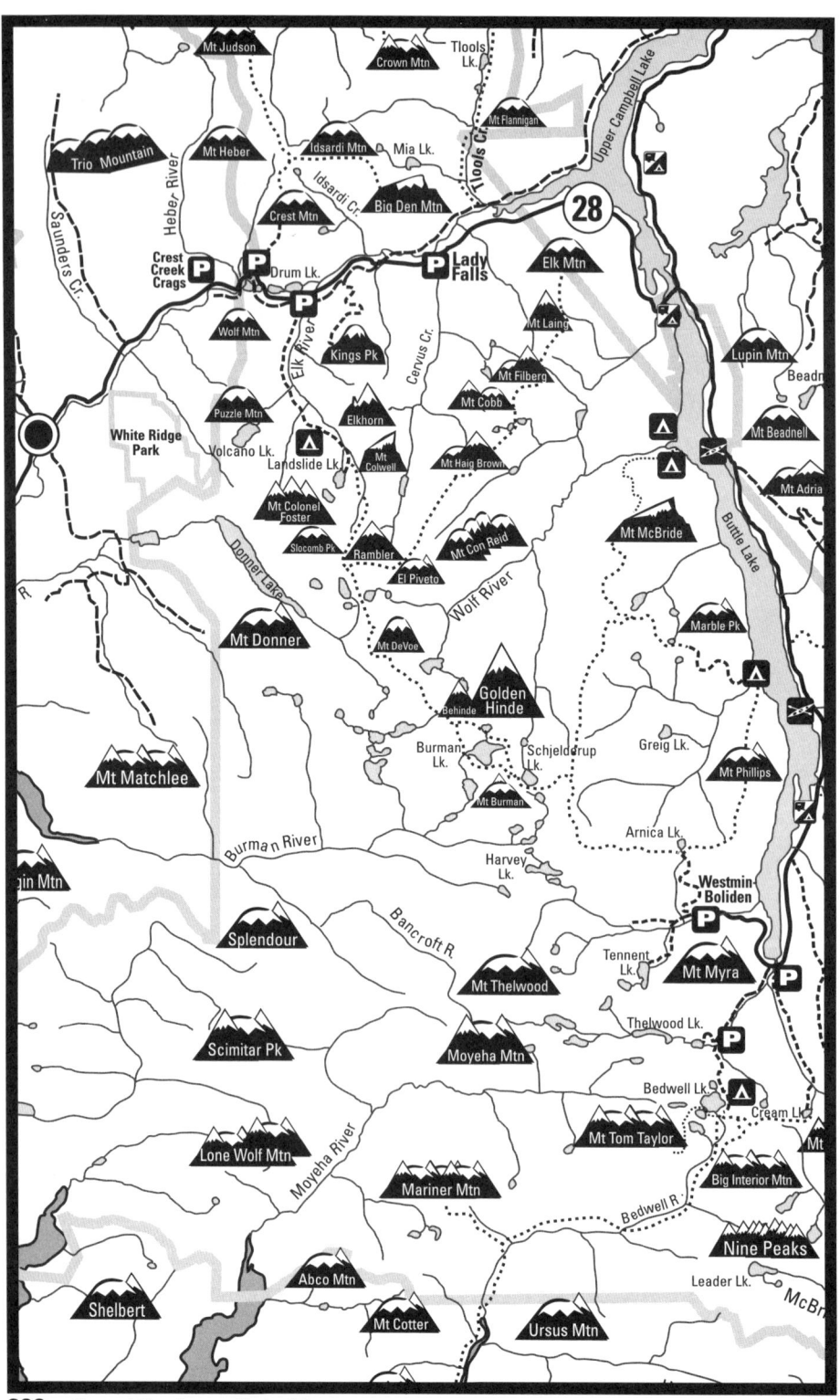

206 Central Strathcona Park - Map

Central Strathcona Park

The central region of Strathcona Park is home to the highest mountain peaks on Vancouver Island including the Golden Hinde, the island's apex it also holds the largest areas of true wilderness on Vancouver Island. The terrain of central Strathcona is diverse ranging from the towering alpine faces of the Elk River to the exquisite karst topography of Marble Meadows.

Trail access is good and provides access to key areas in this region from where the backcountry can be reached beyond. In the case of the Marble Meadows trail, a boat crossing is required across Buttle Lake to the trailhead adding to the adventure of a trip to this beautiful part of Strathcona.

Central Strathcona is marked by several huge watersheds blanketed in some of the largest tracts of old growth forest on Vancouver Island. The Elk River, Cervus Creek, Bancroft-Burman River, upper Ucona River and Myra Creek valleys all radiate out from this mountainous region. In the northern half, the peaks of King's Peak, Elkhorn, Rambler and Mt. Colonel Foster rear steeply out of the Elk valley. These summits form the core of alpine climbing on Vancouver Island and attract mountaineers from all over the world.

The Elk River Trail which provides superb access to these mountains also starts one of Strathcona Park's finest multi-day alpine traverses from Highway 28, south through Elk Pass, past the Golden Hinde, Burman Lake and on to Westmin-Boliden via the Phillips Ridge trail. This route also links to the superlative Marble Meadows area, a high alpine plateau of lakes and wildflower covered karst landscape.

Map Sheets: 92 F/13 Upper Campbell Lake • 92 F/12 Buttle Lake

Boundaries: north: Highway 28 - Elk River, **east:** Buttle Lake, **south:** Burman River & Myra Creek, **west:** Nootka Sound

Major Access Routes: Central Strathcona Park is well serviced by road access and a fine network of trails. Some of the approach routes into this region of Strathcona require boat transport across Buttle Lake, particularly to the Wolf River and Marble Meadows Trail at Phillips Creek.

Highway 28: The main road access to central Strathcona Park is from Campbell River west on Highway 28 through the Elk River valley

Buttle Lake Parkway: This scenic highway to nowhere leaves Highway 28 at a junction 45 km west of Campbell River. It runs south along the east shore of Buttle Lake terminating at the Westmin-Boliden Mine at Myra Falls. Many trails and routes into East Strathcona head east from the Parkway. To the west, access into central Strathcona is by boat across Buttle Lake. From the end of the road at the mine the Phillips Ridge trail provides access into central Strathcona.

There are a few logging roads which assist with access on the west side of this area near Gold River. Roads in the drainages east of Camel Ridge and the White Ridge access the upper flanks of Wolf and Puzzle Mountains.

Trails
8- Elk River Trail

The Elk River Trail is the single most important route for alpine climbing access on Vancouver Island. From Highway 28, 60 km west of Campbell River the Elk River Trail leads south up the Elk River valley providing access to Elkhorn, Mt. Colonel Foster, Rambler Peak, Elk Pass and from there on to the Golden Hinde and Westmin. The main destination is Landslide Lake where in 1946 an earthquake triggered a huge landslide off the North Tower of Mt. Colonel Foster. The resulting wave as the debris swept down into the lake flushed old growth trees and scoured soil down to bedrock for several kilometres down the valley. This page from a geography text book is backdropped by the imposing East Face of Mt. Colonel Foster forming one of the most impressive vistas on Vancouver Island.

208 Shea Wilson hiking up to Elk Pass with Elkhorn behind.

Usual times from the trailhead, 10 km to Landslide Lake, are 2-6 hours. Count on an additional 1-2 hours to get around Landslide Lake to the base of climbs on Mt. Colonel Foster. The length of the trail lends itself equally well to a day trip or an overnighter. This is a high use area and overnight stays must be at the designated campsites at Butterwort Creek and the Gravel Flats. No camping is permitted at Landslide Lake and climbers could respect the rational behind this regulation and avoid camping at Foster Lake too. Instead use the Gravel Flats as a base camp and the south or north cols for high camps. To continue onto Elk Pass, locate the unimproved trail which branches off just 200m up the open rock slab from the bridge over Landslide Creek and follow it into the upper Elk valley.

9- Marble Meadows Trail

Reaching Marble Meadows from Buttle Lake Parkway requires a boat to cross Buttle Lake from either the Augerpoint Day Area parking lot or the Karst Creek boat ramp to the north side of the outlet of Phillips Creek on the west shore of Buttle Lake. After securing your boat (keeping in mind that the level of Buttle Lake can vary widely even over just a few days) hike the well maintained trail up past a small swampy pond on to the alpine plateau above.

10- Phillips Ridge Trail

The Phillips Ridge trail leads up from Westmin-Boliden in the Myra Creek valley to the alpine at Arnica Lake. To reach the trailhead leave Highway 28 at Buttle Narrows and drive up the Buttle Lake Parkway to Westmin-Boliden. Continue right through the mine site to the signposted parking lot on the far (west) side. The trail begins on the righthand side of a gated gravel road a short way past the gate. The Upper Myra Falls and Tenent Lake trail to Mt. Myra also begin from the end of this gravel road which leads to a hydro electric powerhouse serving the mine.

Forest Service & Logging Company Offices:

Campbell River Forest District - 370 South Dogwood Street, Campbell River, B.C. V9W 6Y7 Ph: (250) 286-9300

Timberwest -5705 North Island Highway Campbell River, BC V9W 5C5 Ph: (250) 287-9181

Weyerhaeuser - North Island Timberlands -P.O. Box 6000, 8010 Island Highway, Campbell River, BC V9W 5E1 Ph: 250-287-5000

Other Information Sources:

- **Vancouver Island Hiking Trails Volume 3** - Ninth Edition 2002 by Richard Blier
- **Beyond Nootka** - A Historical Perspective of Vancouver Island Mountains by Lindsay Elms,
- **BC Parks web site:** http://wlapwww.gov.bc.ca/bcparks/explore/parkpgs/strathco.htm

Special Thanks:

Thanks to Sandy Briggs, Joe Bajan, Mike Walsh, Lindsay Elms and Chris Barner for assistance in preparing this chapter.

Wolf Mountain

Wolf Mountain north-east aspect from Highway 28, June.

Wolf Mountain
5,680 ft. / 1,731 m

Wolf Mountain overlooks the main Elk River valley and the west arm of Upper Campbell Lake. Along with Puzzle Mountain to the south, Wolf Mountain forms the west divide of the Elk River. It is clearly visible at the King's Peak lookout pullout on Highway 28 above the Elk River.

First Ascent: W.R. Kent, W.W. Urquhart, Einar Anderson 1913 or 1914

Map Sheet: 92 F/13 Upper Campbell Lake - GR 9021

Approaches: A flagged route from Crest Lake on Highway 28 is the best approach to Wolf Mountain up its north flank. This route is a great choice to combine with some cragging at the sport climbing area at Crest Creek Crags.

Wolf Mountain may also be climbed from the east side out of the Elk River. Hike 3 km up the Elk River Trail from the trailhead on Highway 28 to a creek in a slide path. Leave the trail heading up timbered slopes on the right (north) side of the slide path. The terrain narrows into a thin ridge before leading into the cirque with a small tarn at the foot of the north-east ridge of Wolf Mountain.

Logging roads high on the western flanks of Wolf Mountain in the drainage between Wolf and Camel Ridge provide good access as well. As these deactivated roads age and become more and more overgrown their attractiveness diminishes.

Puzzle Mountain (L) & Wolf Mountain (R) east aspect from Elkhorn approaches, August.

Puzzle Mountain

Puzzle Mountain east aspect from Elkhorn approaches, August.

Puzzle Mountain
5,997 ft. / 1,828 m

Puzzle Mountain is the next summit to the south of Wolf Mountain on the divide west of the upper Elk Valley. It is an interesting peak being granite in a region of basalt peaks and limestone ridges. Volcano Lake, a large alpine lake to the south, is a misnamed as the surrounding topography is clearly the result of glaciation. The lake and ridge that encircles it makes an excellent ski tour around to Volcano Peak.

First Ascent: W.R. Kent, W.W. Urquhart, Einar Anderson 1913 or 1914

Map Sheet: 92 F/13 Upper Campbell Lake - GR 9019

Approaches: Puzzle Mountain may be reached from Highway 28 up the Wolf Mountain route. From the summit of Wolf Mountain hike along the connecting ridge southward to the summit of Puzzle Mountain.

Logging roads in the valley between Puzzle Mountain and the White Ridge climb high on to the western flanks of Puzzle Mountain and provide a fast route to the alpine around Volcano Lake.

Puzzle Mountain south aspect from south of Volcano Lake, June.

212 Julie Micksch approaching the start of Pauper's Buttress, Queen's Face.

Volcano Peak

Looking across Volcano Lake at Volcano Peak with Elkhorn (R), west aspect, June.

Volcano Peak
5,500 ft. / 1,676 m

Volcano Peak is an impressive sentry overlooking the Elk River Trail. You can't help but notice it as you come and go along the ERT. The sharp cone makes a good destination from Puzzle Mountain making it worth a night or two to explore the rim of Volcano Lake on foot and on skis.

Map Sheet: 92 F/13 Upper Campbell Lake - GR 9118

Approaches: Volcano Peak is most easily reached by approaching from old (and prehaps new) logging roads in Camel Creek, the valley west of Camel Ridge. Leave Highway 28 a few kilometres past Saunders Creek heading south on a rough gravel road. Take Br 80 south across the Heber River and up the floor of the Camel Creek valley. Locate the highest open spur road or head for any remaining old growth and climb the hillside eastward to gain the crest of the rim around Volcano Lake, south of Puzzle Mountain. Make an incredible, circular hike counter-clockwise around the high lake rim and climb the south-west ridge to the surprisingly exposed summit of Volcano Peak overlooking the Elk River.

The cone may also be reached by traversing from the north from as far up the ridge as Wolf Mountain.

If your penchant for a true Island approach cannot be quenched then hike up the Elk River Trail to the Volcano Creek bridge and strike a direct line up to Volcano Lake. Keep as close to the creek as possible while keeping to the mature forest to avoid the worst of the bush. The best time to use this approach is after the spring thaw while some snow remains to smooth the route and cover the bush. Climb the cone by the north ridge.

Volcano Peak (C) & Puzzle Mountain (R) east aspect from Elkhorn approaches, August.

King's Peak

King's Peak (L) and the Queen's Face (R) north aspect from Highway 28, April.

King's Peak
6,774 ft / 2,065 m

King's Peak is one of the most frequented summits on Vancouver Island. Dramatic views, alpine atmosphere, close proximity to Highway 28 and an excellent trail all combine to make King's Peak an ideal destination for a day hike or as part of a longer, more serious outing. For climbing the rock is the best of the basalt characteristic of the area- solid, protectable and abrasive enough to effectively glue feet. There are a number of shorter alpine routes to be found on King's Peak and the adjacent Queen's Face. The benign terrain on the summit and especially on the top of the Queen's Face makes for excellent alpine 'cragging' with quick, trouble free descents allowing several routes to be climbed in a day.

King's Peak is typically ascended as a weekend trip with a camp either in the lower meadow (tread lightly if camping here), along the ridge leading to the Queen's Face or in the upper cirque on flat rock off the edge of the glacier (the best choice for climbing on Queen's or the Ramparts).

First Ascent: W.R. Kent, W.W. Urquhart, Einar Anderson 1913 or 1914

Map Sheet: 92 F/13 Upper Campbell Lake - GR 9521

Approaches: Leave Highway 28, 3 km west of Lady Falls, turning left (south) on to the Elk River Timber Co. Rd. Look for the signposted trail next to a bridge over the Elk River, 1 km off the highway, and follow it up under the powerlines and into the forest. The trail winds up a steep forested slope to enter a flat bottomed hanging valley just below the treeline. The trail continues along the left side of the creek entering a steep walled creek canyon just past a fork in the creek. Take care on the trail as it makes an exposed traverse along the canyon's left wall and into the lower meadow.

In winter and spring, exposure to avalanches in the canyon may be avoided by taking a steep gully up the right side of the hanging valley before the fork in the creek. From the top of the gully hike across a forested bench and into the meadow. From the lower meadow three options lead up higher on the mountain.

1) The creek, followed up the canyon, continues up a gully on the left (east) side of the meadow through a cliff band directly to the north glacier. This gully is very seductive because of the quick line it provides when full of snow but it is exposed to avalanches through winter and spring and the snow breaks up by June forming hazardous moats. Nevertheless in good conditions it is a fast line.

2) A better route to the glacier when the gully is unsafe, is to cross the meadow halfway, keeping close to the base of the cliff band to find an angled ramp, that with a little 4th class scrambling, leads up to the north glacier below the Queen's Face. Hike up the north glacier to the King's-Queen's col.

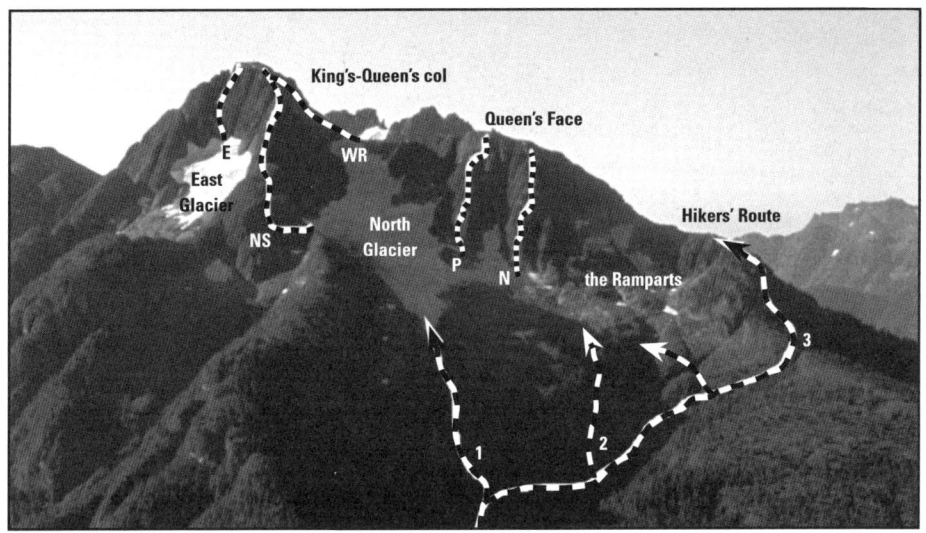

King's Peak north-east aspect from Big Den Mountain, September.

3) Alternatively, take the hikers' route right (west) across the lower meadow and into a smaller upper meadow. Find an obvious well travelled, flagged gully through the trees to the crest of Queen's Ridge, at the same elevation as the toe of the glacier. Just before topping out of this gully it is possible to traverse left to reach the north glacier below the Ramparts. A number of excellent campsites can be found on the ridge crest. Follow the ridge crest to the King's-Queen's col.

King's Peak can also be reached from Elkhorn via the connecting ridge or the basin between the two peaks.

Routes

WR- **West Ridge:** class 2, 175 m
From the King's-Queen's col the summit is easily reached by hiking up the rocky slopes of the west ridge. A well-trodden path leads up the ridge. before weaving through a small cliff band to the summit. Another route farther right rises up on less exposed ground but has a short 5th class step near the top.

*** **King's - Elkhorn Arete:** AI 1 2000 m+ (III)
A classic mountaineering traverse. Ideally completed by first ascending King's Peak by the North Spur to the summit.
From the Kings-Queens col head south-east on a descending traverse to join the crest of King's Peak's south ridge. Continue descending to a low point on the ridge and then carry on the crest. 3rd class scrambling with some 4th class negotiating a series of notches and pinnacles. At the last and largest pinnacle, drop down a rotten gully on the west side and traverse under the pinnacle and regain the crest at the foot of Elkhorn's North Ridge which may then be climbed to the summit.

NS- *** **North Spur:** low 5th class 700m (II)
Start from the north glacier by hiking up lateral moraine to gain the ridge crest at a low point. An initial steep 4th class section onto a knoll leads to easy ground. Pass a notch with 5.4 moves getting in and out of the notch and more 4th class on the upper ridge. Excellent scramble with lots of exposure.

Elkhorn (L) & King's Peak (R) east aspect showing the traverse route on the skyline, from Quadra Island, September.

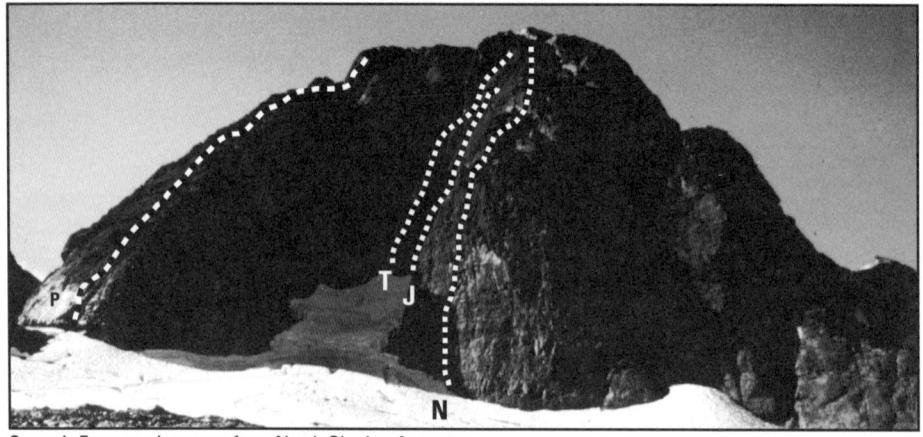

Queen's Face north aspect from North Glacier, August.

E- *East Gully: AI 1 200m (II)
Reach by crossing the north glacier to below a low point on the North Spur. Climb on to the crest of the North Spur and drop off the other side onto the East Glacier. Hike up the glacier to the base of the gully. Climb moderately angled snow up the gully to a short 4th class rock step onto the top.
FA: Tim Rippell, Chris Barner et al 1978 or 79

Queen's Face

T- * Tea With Her Majesty:** 5.8 300m (I)
In the centre of the large wall to the left of Jester is an obvious chimney and crack system with two "forks" in it. Climb this system keeping left at each of the two junctions to reach easier ground on the top of the buttress.
FA: Jan Neuspiel, Amanda Howe, 1992

P- * Pauper's Buttress: 5.7 300m (I)
An easy but fun route with short difficulties at the start. Approach up the North Glacier to the foot of the lefthand of the twin buttresses on the Queen's Face. Negotiate the glacial moat to reach the rock. Depending on seasonal snow cover start up over a small roof (5.7). With deep early season snow cover this roof may be banked out with snow. Climb direct up steep rock to a tiny belay perch on the buttress crest. A 2nd pitch of 5.7 leads to easier ground. Scramble up a long 4th/low 5th class stretch to the top. Join the Hikers' route which passes over the top of the Queen's Face making for an easy descent in either direction back to the North Glacier. Variations are possible taking in more of the steeper ground on this buttress.
FA: Phil Stone, Julie Micksch July 1992

King's Peak south-west aspect from Elkhorn approach, July.

216   King's Peak

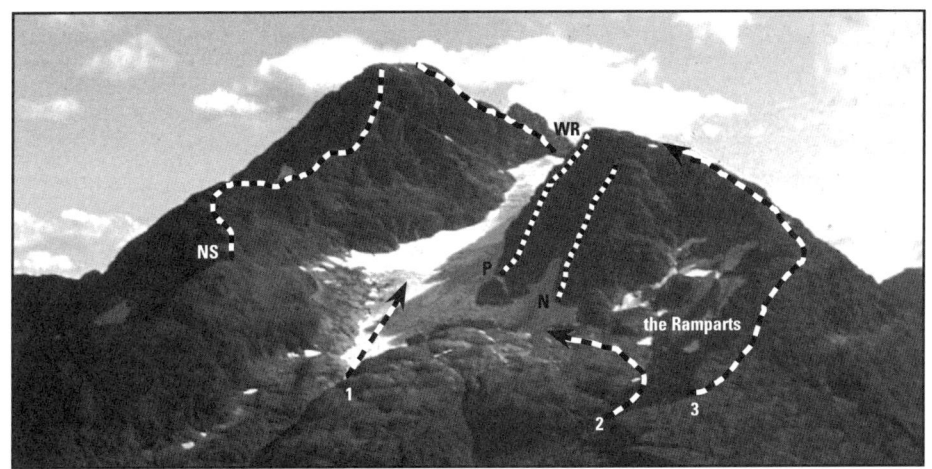

King's Peak north-west aspect from Crest Mountain, September

J- ** **Jester:** 5.8 100m (I)
A beautiful corner hidden on the right side of the glacial tongue that runs in to the amphitheatre between the two main buttresses. Approach from the North Glacier into the amphitheatre, care with crevasses in late season. Climb the obvious corner direct to the crest of the buttress. A 4th class scramble leads to the top of the face and the Hiker's Route to King's Peak.
FA: Lyle Fast, Corrie Wright, Melissa DeHaan June 1988

N- *** **Northern Lights:** 5.10c, 350m (II)
Climbs the prow of the righthand and steeper of the two twin buttresses of the Queen's Face. Approach from the north glacier starting just left of the buttress crest. Climb direct up a steep arete to meet a gully. Cross the gully and continue up a steep pinnacle, 5 pitches to easier ground. Scramble up 4th class past the top of Jester to the top of the Queen's Face and join the Hikers' route up to King's-Queen's col or back down the ridge.
FA: Phil Stone, Robin Slieker August 1990.

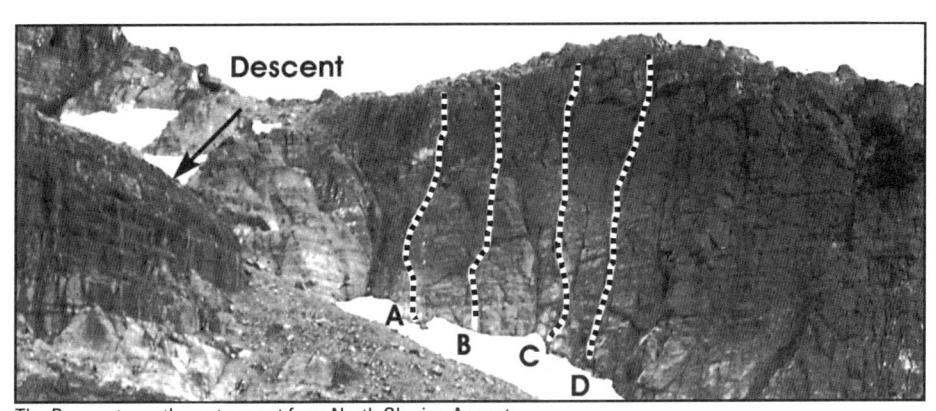

The Ramparts north-east aspect from North Glacier, August.

The Ramparts

The Ramparts are reached on the west side of the north glacier below the shoulder north of the Queen's Face. The summer hiking route runs over the top of the cliff and a short gully joins this route to the north glacier and the Ramparts. There are a number of crags all with excellent, short, and well protected routes in an alpine setting, many possibilities including potential for some hard lines.

A- **Two Degrees:** 5.10b 50m crack
B- **Squadron 51:** 5.9 50m crack
FA: Philip Stone, Robin Slieker, August 1990
C- **Route 3:** 5.9 50m crack
D- **Route 4:** 5.8 50m crack
FA: Phil Stone, Sheahan Wilson, August 1994

Elkhorn Mountain

Elkhorn Mountain north-east aspect from Mt. Flannigan, April.

Elkhorn Mountain
7,119 ft. / 2,195 m

Elkhorn is the second highest peak on Vancouver Island and pretender to the Golden Hinde's crown. It is one of the Island's most aesthetic summits, with a classic Matterhorn shape. Elkhorn can be climbed as a long day trip by fit parties although the mountain is worthy of a longer stay to savour its climbing options and stunning relief. Elkhorn has a reputation for loose rock which is unfounded. There in undeniably some loose gravel on the easier routes and a field of blocky boulders near the summit but the steeper ground is solid and provides some of the island's best alpine climbing on very high quality rock. The climbing potential on Elkhorn is vast, particularly on the south-west and east faces with plenty of scope for some sporty rock and ice routes.

First Ascent: A.O. Wheeler, Oliver Wheeler, Albert MacCarthy, D.A. Gillies, A.R. Hart, J.R. Robertson, H.O. Frind, L.C. Wilson and F.A. Robertson 1912

First Winter Ascent: P. Busch, A. Watts February 1968

Map Sheet: 92 F/13 Upper Campbell Lake - GR 9618

Approaches: Several well established approaches lead to the various sides of Elkhorn.

North-West approach - The most common approach to routes on the north and west sides of the mountain is via the Elk River Trail (ERT). From the trailhead on Highway 28 hike south up the ERT. At a point 2 km up, the ERT runs briefly alongside a wide gravel bar in the Elk River (not to be confused with the Gravel Bar camp which is much further up the valley). Across the Elk River, on the east side, the steep canyon of Elkhorn Creek can be seen rising up. Make sure you see an obvious steep sided valley on the other side of the river before crossing the river. Cross the Elk River by ford or logjam and pick up a well worn and recently re-flagged route that leads high above the right (south) side of Elkhorn Creek into a hanging valley of huge hemlocks. The route takes a steep gully right of the waterfall to a forested col on the north-west ridge. There is a view, water and a campsite 200m to the right (north) of this col on a little rocky knoll.

From the col head south-east along the ridge, eventually breaking out above the treeline. A number of options are possible from here. Either stay on the crest of the ridge as much as possible with several steep scrambling sections, to reach the base of the North-West Ridge. Alternatively make a wide traverse rightward (south) and traverse into the bottom of the West Basin and hike up on snow or scree to the base of the North-West Ridge or West Couloir.

King's Peak (L) & Elkhorn Mountain (R) south-west aspect from Mt. Colonel Foster south col, July.

To reach the North Face and North Ridge routes simply descend on the north side of the North-West Ridge down a steep snow/scree gully to the Elkhorn Glacier.

South-West approach - A direct approach to reach routes on the south and east sides of Elkhorn leads up from the Gravel Bar camp 10 km up the ERT. Cross the Elk River just south of the campsite and locate a flagged route following the right (south) side of a steep creek. Near treeline the route trends left into the boulder strewn creek bed. Head up the creek to a fork below the south-west face of the mountain.

For routes on the west and north sides, make a long traverse left (north) up a scree/snow slope Keep close to the bottom of a cliff band to reach the West Basin. To reach the South Ridge and routes on the East Face head up the right fork direct to the base of the South Ridge. This route is much more pleasant in spring snow cover than later when the boulders become exposed in the creek bed. The north-west and south-west approaches can be combined to climb Elkhorn en route either up or down the Elk River Trail.

from King's Peak - Elkhorn can also be approached from King's Peak by two main routes. The easier hiking route drops down the south-west side of King's Peak into the wide basin on Elkhorn's north-west side climbing back up on to the Elkhorn Glacier and joining the North-West Ridge at the toe of the upper ridge. A more difficult traverse may be made along the rocky ridge linking the South Ridge of King's Peak's with Elkhorn's North Ridge. 4th class and low 5th class scrambling with a couple of possible rappels. Conditions will vary with seasonal snow cover. See King's -Elkhorn Arete on page 215.

Elkhorn Mountain from north-west approach, August.

Elkhorn Mountain

Elkhorn Mountain north aspect from King's Peak, September.

Routes

N- *** **North Ridge:** 5.8 400m (III)
A classic arete. Reach by traversing the Elkhorn Glacier from the north-west approach or from King's Peak along the King's-Elkhorn Arete to a shoulder at the base of the prominent North Ridge. Start up 3rd class ground for 250m to below steeper rock.

Climb a steep face to a groove. Follow the groove to a large detached flake. Stem up a corner and over loose rock to a crack system. Follow the righthand crack and bypass a roof on the right to reach the base of a chimney. Climb the chimney to a boulder choke then head right around an arete to a short face and another chimney to easier ground near the top.
FA: Joe Bajan, Tom Muirhead, Dave Smith, Stuart Wazny 1972

NF- ** **North Face:** ~5.8 300m (III/IV)
A serious but excellent route. Approach on the north-west approach. From the toe of the upper North-West Ridge descend left (north) down a gully to the Elkhorn Glacier. Cross the glacier to below the middle of the North Face. Start to the left of the centre of the face up a rib between two parallel gullies. Steep climbing leads to the snowpatch. Climb direct up the snow/ice to finish up several steep rock pitches to the summit. (CAJ 1979 p.73)
FA: Joe Bajan, Peter Busch 18 June 1977

M- ** **Mitrenga Variation:** low 5th Class 100m
An alternative start to the North-West Ridge from the West Basin joining the ridge above the gendarme though an entertaining chimney.

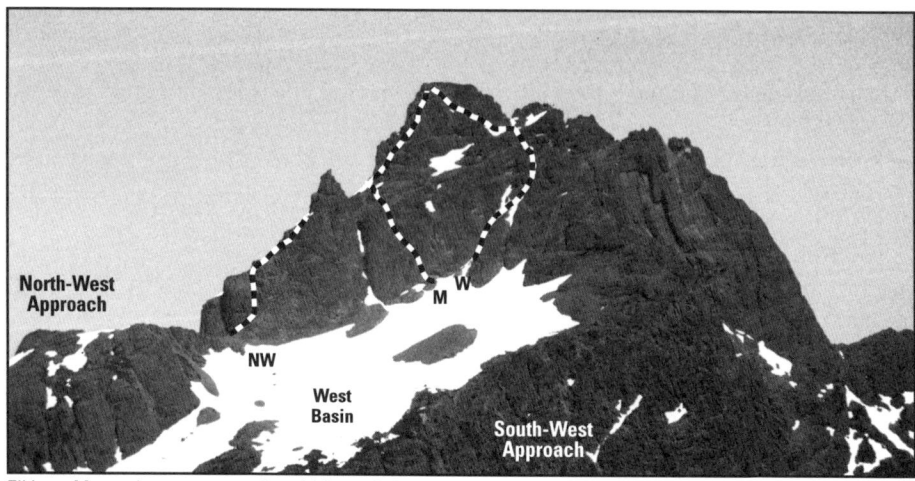

Elkhorn Mountain west aspect from Volcano Lake, June.

Elkhorn Mountain south aspect from Mt Colwell, August.

NW- * North-West Ridge:** low 5th class 400m (II)
The original route on the mountain and a classic. Start on the crest of the ridge approached from the West Basin by either the north or south-west approaches. Scramble up 4th class ledges and low 5th class rock steps below gendarme. Bypass the gendarme on the left (north) side on the Upper glacier then regain the crest over 5th class steps to reach a right trending ledge on the west side which is followed to a boulder field toward the top. The gendarme may also be bypassed on the right (south) side. Great exposure and care with route finding required. Descend same route or West Couloir.
FA: A.O. Wheeler et al 1912

W- ** West Couloir: low 5th Class 250m (II)
The standard and easiest route up Elkhorn and main descent from other routes. Approach the West Basin by either north-west or south-west routes to the top centre of the West Basin. Enter the bottom of a wide gully capped with a huge chockstone. Take a tiny ramp on the right side of the gully in to a little cave and chimney up, above the chockstone.

Continue scrambling direct up the gully system with short steep low 5th class rock steps and snow/scree sections. Head left to a boulder field and clamber up this to the summit. Take care to note the route on the way up for the descent.
FA: Unknown

S- ** South Ridge: low 5th class 600m (III)
Infrequently climbed but a very aesthetic feature of Elkhorn with great climbing and atmosphere. The South Ridge is key to access and descent for many of the possible routes on the East Face. Approach the south-west route from the gravel flats on the ERT or traverse below the west face from the north-west approach to the crux of a Y-shaped gully below the south-west face. Hike directly up the right (south) branch of the Y to a col at toe of the South Ridge between Elkhorn & Mt Colwell. (see page 225). Start directly on the ridge crest with easy ground to start. Follow steepening gullies and chimneys remaining on the crest to South Summit.
FA: Joe Bajan, Ron Facer 1971

King's Peak - Elkhorn Mountain Areté west aspect from north-west approach, August.

Elkhorn Mountain **221**

Elkhorn Mountain east aspect from Mt. Cobb, August.

I ** Into The Sadistic: 5.10b 500m (III)

A sporty route on an impressive alpine wall. Approach as for the South Ridge from the Elk River gravel flats campsite. From the narrow col between Elkhorn & Mt. Colwell, at foot of the South Ridge, traverse on a narrow, exposed ledge to the pocket East Glacier. Start up well protected, parallel cracks (5.10b) on a prominent buttress just left (south) of the East Ridge which bounds the far right side of the glacial cirque. Continue direct up an incredible black chimney/dyke (5.9) with wild exposure and excellent protection.

Make an easy 3rd Class traverse left to some run-out face climbing on friable rock. A series of steep aretes and corners follow leading on to the east ridge at the notch that has so far barred completion of the east ridge route. Descend gully on climber's left (Harrison Route) with 5 raps back to glacier or finish up the east ridge to the south summit.
FA: Philip Stone, Greg Shea, 18 September. 1993

H ** Harrison Route: 5.5 600m (III)

A bold and infrequently repeated route. Originally approached from Cervus Creek up a 3rd class rib adjacent to lower east face. From east glacier climb the righthand side of a gully system to the crest of east ridge. Exposed low 5th class scrambling on superb rock leads to the south summit.
FA: Alan Harrison, June 1975

NE ** North-East Face: 5.7 400m (III)

An atmospheric line originally soloed. Approach up Cervus Creek to an obvious kink in the line of the creek below the North-East Face of Elkhorn. Hike up a wide open creek bed below the face. Take care with avalanche hazard with any amount of snow cover in this gully. From an upper basin below the face head left up snowfields to the base of a long J shaped gully. Start up slabs to the right of the base of the gully. Keep right eventually joining an arete. Join the gully to your left near the top. Descend West Couloir to the ERT.
FA: Tim Rippel, June 1985

Elkhorn Mountain north aspect from King's Peak, January.

Winter Routes

W ** **West Couloir:** AI2 250m (III)
Climbs the obvious wide gully system just to climber's right of the North-West Ridge. A huge chockstone caps the gully and must be avoided on the righthand side by squeezing through a tight ice filled chimney. Depending on current conditions this chimney may be clogged with snow. Above continue up the gully system with several short steep pitches and easier climbing in between. Large belay stances with rock anchors make this an enjoyable winter route.
FA: Peter Busch, A. Watts February 1968

WN * **Winter Needle:** 5.7 AI4 200m (III)
Follow the North-West Ridge to just past the gendarme. Make a wide traverse across the Upper glacier to reach the bottom of a gully through the upper rock pyramid. Climb this gully on steep ice and snow to the summit.
FA: Randy Pearce, Rod Walker February 1996

Additional Info: IB 1996 p.10, WIM #5 p.12, WIM #21 p.9

Elkhorn Mountain north-east aspect from Mt. Flannigan, March.

Elkhorn Mountain 223

224 Greg Shea topping out from the chimney pitch on Into the Sadistic with Mt. Colwell behind.

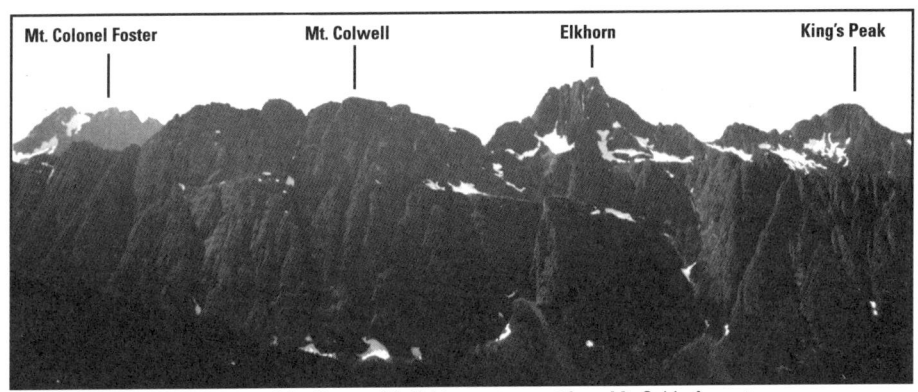

Mt. Colwell

Mt. Colwell and the mountains of the Cervus-Elk divide, east aspect from Mt. Cobb, August.

Mt. Colwell
6,526 ft./ 1,989 m

Sometimes referred to as 'Elkhorn South' Mt. Colwell is overshadowed by the bigger peaks of the Elk valley. This peak is nevertheless worthy of its place alongside them. The summit lies south of Elkhorn on the Elk River - Cervus Creek divide. Its sweeping ramp shape is a familiar landmark from Landslide Lake. Hidden from view on the Cervus Creek side of Mt. Colwell are some of, if not the highest alpine walls on Vancouver Island. From the base of the Cervus valley at 2,300 ft the buttresses of Mt. Colwell rise an astounding 4,200 ft to the top surpassing even Mt. Colonel Foster's East Face. What is more astounding is that this collection of contours has escaped the attention of climbers. The face presents vast climbing potential for both summer and winter routes. To date there isn't a single route recorded on this face. Mt. Colwell is named for George Colwell one of the early surveyors' assistants who visited this peak to take readings of the surrounding mountains in the 1930s.

First Ascent: Unknown
Map Sheet: 92 F/13 Upper Campbell Lake - GR 9717

King's Peak (L) Elkhorn Mountain (C) & Mt. Colwell (R) south aspect from Rambler Peak, September.

Mt. Colwell south-east aspect from head of Cervus Creek, November.

Approaches: Most easily climbed from the Elkhorn south col. Follow the south-west approach details for Elkhorn to the col at the base of Elkhorn's South Ridge. The terrain on Mt. Colwell's west slopes is very open with few route restrictions. Simply head south at any point just below the col up the open rock slabs and snowfields to the summit. Watch your step near the top!

To reach the base of the unclimbed east face hike up the Elk River Trail from Highway 28 and continue up the upper valley route toward Elk Pass. Just above the last camp leave the Elk Pass route and strike up for the col between Mt. Colwell and Rambler Peak at the toe of Rambler's North Buttress. Descend through the col into Cervus Creek and head south along the valley floor to the base of the face.

Mt. Colwell (L) Elkhorn (C) and King's Peak (R) north-east aspect from Mt. Flannigan, May.

Lake in Cervus Creek at the base of Mt. Colwell's east face, October

Looking across the top of the central couloir on Mt. Colwell's East Face, October

Mt. Colwell

Mt. Colonel Foster

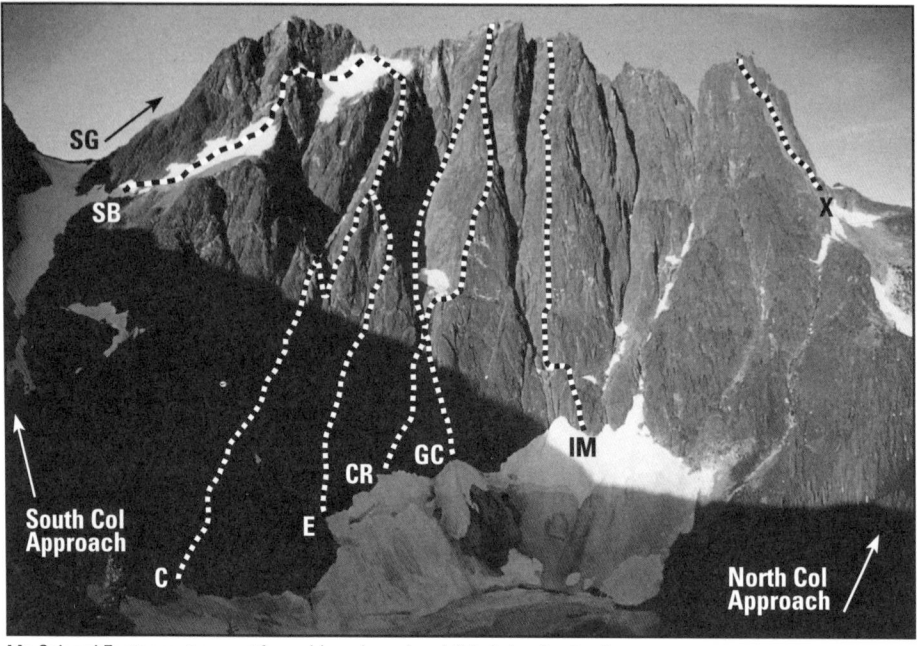

Mt. Colonel Foster east aspect from ridge above Landslide Lake, September.

Mt. Colonel Foster
7,000 ft / 2,135 m

Mt. Colonel Foster is Vancouver Island's unrivalled alpine climbing mecca. The Colonel has a dramatic 1,000 m East Face which plummets from a serrated summit ridge of six summits in a series of plumbline buttresses and couloirs. The routes up some of these features are of a scale comparable to any major alpine peak in the world and it is fair to say Mt. Colonel Foster is home to some of Canada's finest alpine climbs. Fittingly the highest point on the mountain is also the most inaccessible. The elusive summit has become steeped in Island mountaineering lore and the Colonel has a rich history of climbing endeavour. It is a testament to the mountain's character that while most peaks in Strathcona Park had been climbed by the 1930s (most as early as 1913), Mt. Colonel Foster's summit didn't see a visit until Mike Walsh made it in 1968. Since then the Colonel has seen the steady growth of a list of superb climbs. Tales of climbing on the Colonel are legion. There continues to be new routes climbed and bold attempts on some of Colonel's remaining plums. By any route climbing Colonel Foster is an atmospheric, big mountain experience cherished by all who climb it.

Mt. Colonel Foster is named for Colonel William Washborough Foster who was a climber and chair of the Alpine Club of Canada Vancouver Island Section in the early 1900s. As Minister of Public Works he was able to procure valuable assistance to the successful 1912 Alpine Club of Canada expedition to Elkhorn led by Arthur Wheeler. It was Wheeler and his party that seeing the impressive mountain across the valley named it after Foster.

First Ascent: Mike Walsh June 1968

First Winter Ascent: Joe Bajan, Ross Nichol, January 1978

Map Sheet: 92 F/13 Upper Campbell Lake - GR 9314 (see also 92 F/12 Buttle Lake)

Additional Info: CAJ 1971 p.55, IB 1999 p.29, IB 2000 p.5, IB 2001 p.31, WIM #12 p.19

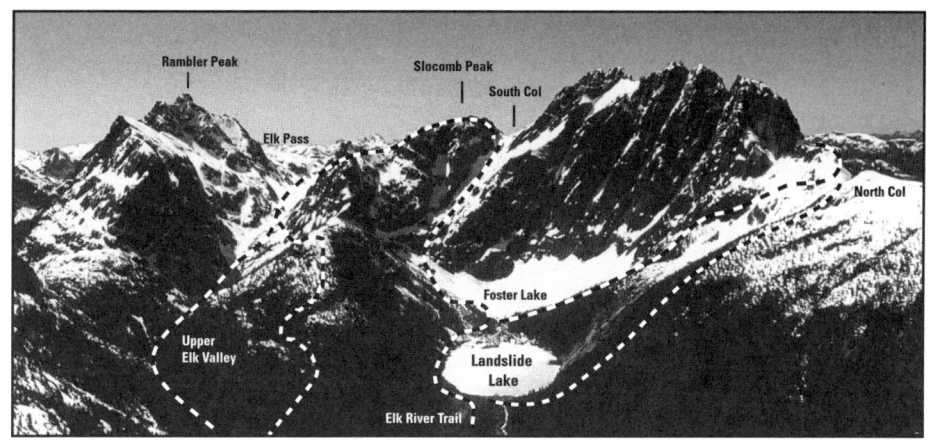

Rambler Peak & Mt. Colonel Foster north-east aspect from Elkhorn south-west approach, May.

Approaches: Mt. Colonel Foster can be reached most easily via the Elk River Trail. This well maintained and travelled trail runs 11 km to Landslide Lake from the trailhead on Highway 28. Drive 65 km west of Campbell River on Highway 28 to the well signposted trailhead and parking lot. The trail has a gentle grade gaining only 2,000 ft over 12 km and is a fast hike. Count on 2-6 hours to Landslide Lake depending on the party and loads. Camping on the ERT is at designated sites. Climbers often camp at Foster Lake.

East Face: To reach the routes on the East Face, traverse around Landslide Lake on a rough path along the south shore. Drop down to the creek which drains Foster Lake into Landslide Lake and follow the creek bed up to the moraine at the edge of Foster Lake. The base of the face can be reached by an easy snow hike up the remnant glacier immediately above the lake.

South Col: The South Col is the hub for all approaches, climbs and descents around the south end of the mountain. This includes access to the South Gullies, the most popular climb on Mt. Colonel Foster, the Snow Band Route and routes on the West Face. To reach the South Col from Foster Lake keep to the left (south) side of the lake. Ascend the wide snowfield to reach a system of snow gullies and/or rock ribs, depending on seasonal snow cover. Avoid the gullies once the snow starts to break up with the annual thaw. Deep moats and rotten snow bridges melt out as summer progresses. There is exposure to avalanches off the cliffs of Mt. Slocomb to the left (south) of the lower half of this route, with snow cover.

The steep gullies and 4th class rock ribs lead to more open ground above. Continue directly up open rock slabs, or the wide snowfield on the remnant glacier, to the South Col.

Elk Pass: An alternative route to reach the South Col is to continue up the Elk River on the unimproved route to Elk Pass (used to reach Rambler Peak and the Westmin-Elk River traverse). From the lakes just below and to the north of the pass, head north-west up on to Slocomb Peak (GR 9413). Hike over this satellite peak and locate a hidden gully which leads down to the South Col. Descend the seemingly bottomless gully 30m or so then traverse right (north) into a second, short gully that lead down into the South Col.

North Col: To the North Col follow the approach around Landslide Lake to Foster Lake. Head right (north) directly up moraine to a forested slope which leads up to the scoured basin below the landslide scar. Continue up to the North Col. Alternatively from the north shore of Landslide Lake cross Landslide Creek on log jam and bushwhack (B3) up steep forest to reach the ridge overlooking the west side of Landslide Lake and follow this ridge to the North Col. A gentle ridge rises from the North Col forming a prominent shoulder at the base of the North Buttress. There is a good camp here and water from the névé at the bottom of the North Gully

Descents: There are many descent possibilities off Mt. Colonel Foster. If climbing from either the North or South Cols along the summit ridge crest to any of the peaks (other than the North Tower) the most usual descent option is to either retrace ones route or complete the Summit Traverse to the opposite col.

The most common choice for descents off East Face routes is to rappel various lines down the West Face and hike south underneath this face to the South Col. A gully of note is found between the North-West and North-East Peaks and a second good descent gully drops off from the Upper Glacier at the gendarme. The North Col can be reached by traversing below the West Face too but it is more tedious.

Mt. Colonel Foster

Mt. Colonel Foster north-west aspect from near Volcano Lake, June.

*** Walsh's Foray: AI1- low 5th class 1100m

Superb climb, least technical line to Main Summit and the original first ascent route. Approach from the North Col over the shoulder below the North Tower to the base of the notorious 'Evacuation Gully'. Either climb the gully directly in winter/spring or keep to the rock on the right to avoid leg snapping bergschrunds in later summer.

Leave the gully two thirds of the way up working a series of ledges across to the crest of the North Ridge. Scramble up the ridge to a shallow gully which leads up to the North-West Peak. Make a steep descent southward down a loose gully to a deep col. Steep low 5th class steps and open gravel stewn ledges lead up 250m to the North-East Peak. Exposed climbing weaves through precariously perched boulders along the ridge crest, aross another col and up to the Main Summit.
FA: Mike Walsh, June 1968

South Gullies above the South Col, May

SG ** South Gullies: AI2-3rd to low 5th class 600m from South Col to South-West Peak

A straightforward, atmospheric climb and the most popular route to the South-West Peak. Difficulty depends on season and choice of route. Taking the easiest line is 3rd class. Approach from Landslide Lake to the South Col. From the col there are a number of options.

One route heads directly up from the col up a small scree/snow slope to the base of two parallel gullies (see photo below left). When full of snow either of these gullies are straightforward climbs. As the snow thaws out during summer they become more difficult with exposed rock steps and lots of loose gravel. Ascend either gully to easier ground on the ridge crest.

Another, easier gully arcs up from the left (west) of the centre of the South Col, joining the more direct lines just before the ridge crest.

Continue up the ridge crest watching for cornices and the precipice to the (right) east. Trend left (west) with some fun and airy 3rd class scrambling leading to the South-East Summit. A cairn and summit register may be found on this high point.

Downclimb or short rap the exposed and awkward chimney and cross the precarious blocks that choke the notch between the South-East and South-West Peaks. Drop to the left (west) side and follow an exposed but easy ledge leftward until a short easy scramble in a gully leads up onto the South-West Summit, the top of the South Peak.
FA: Alfred Slocomb, Jack Horbury 1936 to SE Peak

Mt. Colonel Foster east aspect from Elkhorn south-west approach route, October.

*** Summit Traverse: 5.8 2200m (III/IV)

A superb alpine traverse with huge exposure, varied and interesting climbing and one of Vancouver Island's finest summits as a reward. Can be tackled in either direction. Described here south to north. Follow the description for the South-West Peak via the South Gullies. From the summit of the South-West Peak scramble northward along, then down the ridge crest keeping to the right (east) side. At a point above the glacier the ridge drops away in a shattered band of granite. Rappel or down climb along the granite dyke/gully onto the glacier. Walk north across the snow to the base of a short steep wall.

Scramble up the easiest line at the left end of the wall (4th/low 5th class) to regain the ridge crest. Walk north along the top of the ridge as it narrows. Rappel or down climb a slab to a tight col. Climb loose and exposed ground on the right (east) side looking for a weakness on the left (west) side that leads onto a wide ledge system where there is an excellent bivvy site. An exposed line also leads up on the right (east) side above the Grand Central Couloir with sickening exposure and plenty of loose rock!! Gain the Main Summit to locate or drop off beer!

From the summit drop onto a ledge system on the left (west) side or continue down along the crest with one short rappel to the col between the Main and North-East Peaks. A short steep scramble leads up to the North-East Peak.

Descend north down scree covered ledges with up to three rappels to the col below the North-West Peak. An obvious wide and quite loose gully leads up onto the North-West Peak.

Keep on the left (now north) flank of the North-West Peak and regain the ridge crest north of the summit. Locate rappel anchors and descent with 3-5 rappels to the dramatic col at the top of Evacuation Gully. Descend the snow down the gully. Take extreme care to avoid the dangerous moats and bergshrunds that form during summer. Further rappels on the North Tower side of the gully may be needed to reach the North Col. From the North Col descend to Landslide Lake avoiding the landslide path through the bushy forest. CAJ 1971 p.55
FA: Mike Walsh, Bill Perry July 1971
FA with North Tower: Mike Walsh, Joe Bajan 1973

SB * Snow Band Route: AI2 5.10 800m (III)

Approach as for the South Col but leave the South Glacier on a spur glacier that rises under the South Summit. A couple of rock pitches (5.10) lead on to the Summit Glacier and joins the Summit Traverse near the gendarme. Can also be used as a descent route off the mountain with a couple of rappels over the rock step. Exposed!!
FA: Joe Bajan, Mike Walsh June 1974

Mt. Colonel Foster Summit Traverse east aspect from Mt. McBride, June.

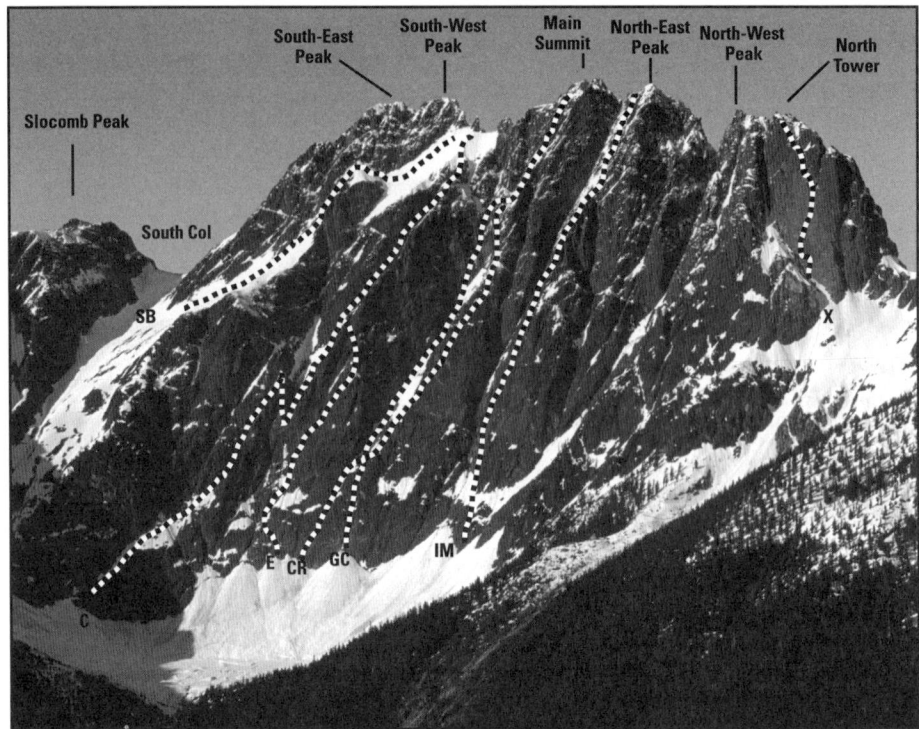

Mt. Colonel Foster north-east aspect from Elkhorn south-west approach, May.

SB * Snow Band Var.: AI2 5.10 800m (III)
Approach up the diagonal snowfield from the south glacier as for the Snow Band Route. At the base of the rock band climb up the gully above to near the crest of the south ridge. Descend by rappell an adjoining gully system back to the upper glacier. IB 1999 p.29
FA: Lindsay Elms, Pete Ravensbergen Aug 28,1999

C ** Cataract: 5.8 1350m (IV)
A very long route up a beautiful knife-edge arete above the waterfall that cascades down the left side of the face. Start far to the left of the waterfall that pours out of a cleft below the Snow Band Route. Climb 400m of 4th/low 5th class up lower of two parallel gullies leading to an incredible and committing 55m+ free hanging rappel down to the lip of the waterfall.

Cross the falls carefully and start direct up a steep bulge on the other side (~5.7). 20 pitches of 4th class up to 5.8 follow the knife-edge arete to a beautiful heather ledge below the Upper Glacier. A dramatic glacial arete leads up to the summit ridge near the gendarme. Take in the main summit and descend to the south.
FA: Philip Stone, Sarah Homer 6-7 August 1988

E * Expressway:** 5.8 1200m (IV)
A direct start to the awesome Cataract arete. Start right of the waterfall and weave up easy ground 200m to a right trending ramp. Follow the ramp up and right for 300m avoiding a rusty brown chimney. At the end of the ramp is a notch from where the rock steepens. Make an exposed unprotected traverse left and then up to join the easier ground on the Cataract arete. Continue up Cataract to the upper glacier and the summit ridge.
FA: Mike Waters, John Waters, August 17, 2002

CR ** Culbert Route: 5.8 1100m (IV)
The first route climbed on the Colonel's East Face and an established Island classic taking in some of the finest climbing on Mt. Colonel Foster.

Start up a triangular rock formation bounded by gullies, into lower basin of the Grand Central Couloir, 4th/low 5th class. Traverse right, out toward buttress crest under a snowpatch and continue to the Main Summit with a variety of possible finishes near the top, 4th class-5.7.

CAJ 1973 p.34, CAJ 1979 p.37

FA: Richard Culbert, Paul Starr, Fred Douglas August 1972

GC *** Grand Central Couloir: AI2 1200m (IV)

An awesome outing into the deeper reaches of the Colonel. Takes the main gully system below the Main Summit to climber's left of the Culbert Route. Start up a narrow gully to a large snowpatch in the main couloir above. Continue directly in the back of the couloir until you are forced to make an exposed traverse rightward on open rock slabs to finish.
FA: Joe Bajan August 1974

IM *** Into The Mystic: 5.9 1200m (V)

One of the finest alpine rock routes on Vancouver Island! Takes an imposing line direct up the buttress of the North-East Summit on steep and solid rock. Start with two 5.7 pitches, depending on snow cover, to a long ledge across the buttress toe. Walk to the left end of the ledge close to the couloir of the Dirrettissima to find a line of weaknesses in the overhangs above. Weave 13 pitches of 5.8-5.9 past roofs and steep ribs to 10 easier pitches up to the North-East Summit.

Fast descent down gully on west side from col between NE Summit and the NW Summit or head south along Summit Traverse to Main Summit and descend via South Col. CAJ 1990 p.51
FA: Chris Lawrence, Philip Stone, Corrie Wright 10-11 June 1989

Mt. Colonel Foster east aspect from Elkhorn's south col, October.

Chris Lawrence & Corrie Wright greeting the dawn from bivouac on 'Into the Mystic'.

The twin central buttresses of Mt. Colonel Foster.

234 Mt. Colonel Foster

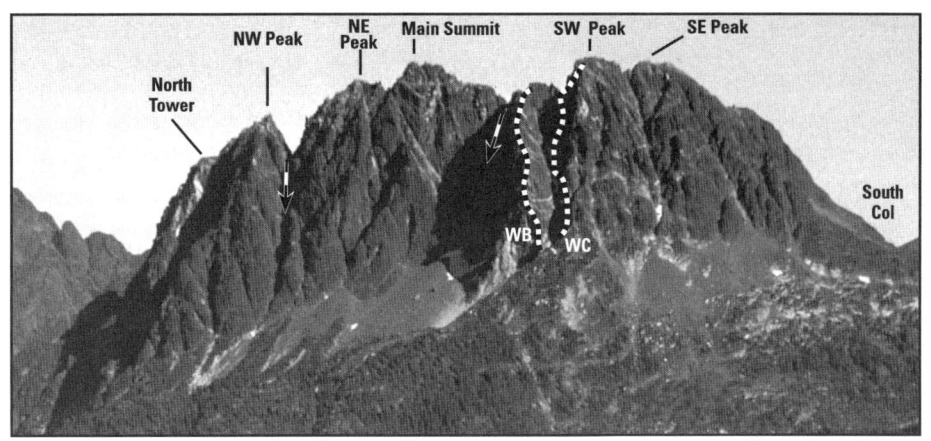

Mt. Colonel Foster west aspect from Matchlee Mountain, September. Photo: Sandy Briggs

WC- **West Couloir:** 5.8 S 450m (III)
Originally approached from Butterwort Creek in a spirited attempt to make the first ascent of the mountain when the South-West Summit was thought to be the highest summit. Now best approached from the South Col via a traverse under the West Face. The route takes an imposingly steep gully and chimney system up the West Face to a notch just north of the South Summit. Climb steep snow and/or scree to a chimney. Tackle the chimney to a large chockstone. Finish up chimneys to summit ridge crest. Head south to South Summit (South-West Peak). CAJ 1958 p.35
FA: Ferris & Hugh Neave, Karl Ricker July 30, 1957

WB- ** **West Central Buttress:** 4th class up to 5.8 450m (III)
Approach by traversing under the West Face from the South Col. Start up the easier and shorter right side of a triangular face to the buttress crest. Easy climbing leads soon to a fine steep dihedral of white rock (5.8). Mostly easier climbing above, with a little loose rock, leads onto the summit traverse route between the Main Summit and the Gendarme.
FA: Sandy Briggs, Ignaz Fluri 5 July 1991

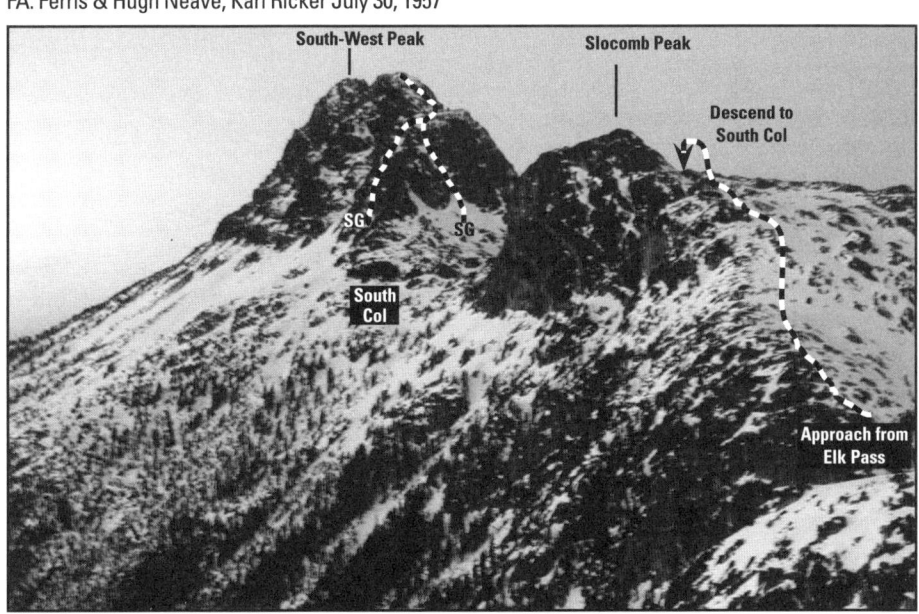

Mt. Colonel Foster & Slocomb Peak south aspect from above Elk Pass, January.

Mt. Colonel Foster

236 Greg Shea & Jan Nuspiel on the Summit Traverse, Mt. Colonel Foster.

North Tower

The North Tower can be approached from either end of Landslide Lake. From the the outflow of Landslide Creek, cross the log jam and head up through steep very bushy (B3) timber to gain the north col. Alternatively, follow the rough path around the south shore of Landslide Lake to the moraine by Foster Lake,. Head up timbered slopes to a boulder field of landslide debris. Gain the north col. Hike left west from the col onto the shoulder below the North Buttress. There is an excellent bivouac spot here.

SW- **South West Face:** low 5th class 100m (I)
The shortest & original route on to the North Tower and the usual rappel descent from other routes. Climb up the long snow gully to the upper north col. Two steep rock pitches lead to the maze of broken blocks on the summit. Descend with 2 rappels.
FA: Mike Walsh 1968

WF- **West Face:** low 5th class 175m (I)
Climb a gully system above a wide ledge left of the to an awesome chimney to finish.
FA: Mike Walsh, Joe Bajan, 1973

X- **X-Rated:** 5.9 S, 550m (III)
Climbs an X-shaped crack system up the grey landslide scar on the east side of the North Tower with very bad rock fall, poor belays, poor gear and loose rock. From the base of the scar climb a right facing corner to reach the left side of the "X". Four scary, low 5th- 5.9 pitches including a unprotected 5.8 chimney lead to the centre of the "X". Head left on loose flakes & blocks to a good belay. The remaining pitches are on good solid rock. Scramble the last 100 meters to the top. descend the West Face to the Upper north col.
FA: John & Mike Waters, Aaron Hamilton, August 11, 2001

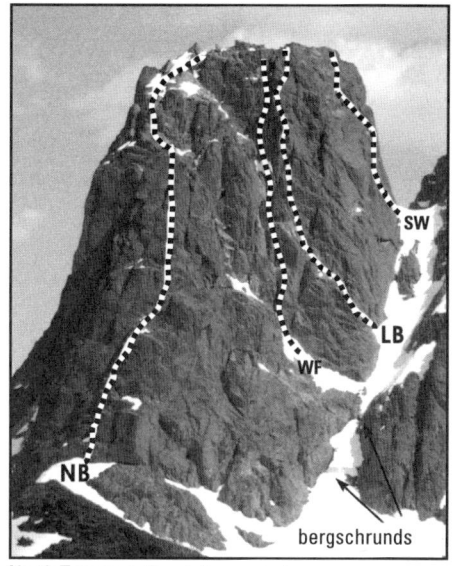

North Tower north-west aspect, June.

NB- *** **North Buttress:** 5.8 400m (III)
One of the finest alpine climbs on Vancouver Island. Takes in the great atmosphere of Colonel Foster without the commitment of the big East Face routes. Approach north col from Landslide Lake. Start at the foot of the buttress. Excellent steep rock and great protection for 6 pitches of 5.6-8, lead to a ledge. There are several options up a short, steep wall ~5.9-8 leading to a summit boulder garden. 2 rappels down West Face.
FA: Scott Flavelle, Perry Beckham, August 1977

LB- ** **Lost Boys:** 5.9 175m (II)
Climb an easy ramp and ledge system out of the couloir to the base of a steep chimney. Climb cracks up right wall ~5.6-7, to reach a 5.9 arete.
FA: John & Fred Put, September 1989

Mt. Colonel Foster north-east aspect from King's Peak, January.

Doug Scott descending the west face of Mt. Colonel Foster.   photo: Greg Child

Mt. Colonel Foster east aspect from ridge above Landslide Lake, January. photo: Geoff Peake

NE- ** **North-East Couloir:** AI 2, 5.9 700m (III)
Takes the gully between the North-West Summit and the North Tower on the East Face. Approach to the base up snowfield from Iceberg Lake. Climb moderate angled snow for 300m to a chockstone. Pull the chockstone and continue up with four steeper mixed pitches. Moderate angle snow leads to the upper North Col. Some exposure and meltwater depending on season. CAJ 2000
FA: Chris Lawrence, Chad Rigby 30, May 1999

Winter Routes

The winter climbing on Mt. Colonel Foster is some of the finest in Canada. Frequent freeeze-thaw weather cycles create some of the finest alpine nevé in the world. During periods of 'outflow', high pressure brings clear skies and cold winds from the Interior. This is when deep winter arrives on the island and climbing conditions are at their best. Descents off the Colonel in winter are serious, requiring multiple raps down the West Face on a variety of possible lines.

GC- *** **Grand Central Couloir:** AI 5 1000m (VI)
Ascends the major couloir left of the Direttissima and the Culbert Route. Begin right of the start to the Culbert Route on moderate angled snow and ice. Climb into the back of the huge couloir crossing the Culbert Route below a prominent round snowpatch at 1,000 ft / 330 m, possible bivouac on top of snowpatch. Continue direct up the steepening gully to cracks and ice bulge. Make a difficult traverse right on open slabs out of the gully. Climb trending right on open terrain to a second possible bivouac. Continue up meeting the top of the 'SuperCouloir' and on to the summit. Reference: Toward the Unknown Mountains p.83
FA: Rob Wood, Doug Scott, Greg Child, January 1985

D- *** **Direttissima:** AI 5 1000m (VI)
One of Canada's finest climbs and the first winter route established on the mountain. The first ascent took two bivouacs and became an epic ascent when Ross Nichol lost a crampon en route. The climb follows the plumbline couloir between the Main and North-East Summits. Start direct on 60-70° nevé for 400ft. The first crux is 600ft of 80° ice leading to easier angled climbing. A second 500ft crux of steep water ice follows. The angle eases near the top to 60° but the climbing may be precarious on unconsolidated snow. Usually now climbed in a single day. CAJ 1979 p.37
FA: Joe Bajan, Ross Nichol, 28-31 January 1978

Left- Mt. Colonel Foster north-east aspect from King's Peak, January

Mt. Colonel Foster **239**

Slocomb Peak

Slocomb Peak north-east aspect from Elk River, January.

Slocomb Peak
6,036 ft / 1,840 m

Slocomb Peak is the low satellite peak to the south of Mt. Colonel Foster between the South Col of Foster and Elk Pass. Named for Alfred Slocomb a surveyor who made the first significant ascent of Mt. Colonel Foster to the South-East Peak in the 1930s.

First Ascent: Likely W.R. Kent, W.W. Urquhart, Einar Anderson 1913 or 1914

Map Sheet: 92 F/12 Buttle Lake - GR 9413

Approaches: May be reached from Elk Pass by hiking up the easy south-east flank. Alternatively from the South Col of Mt. Colonel Foster up a gully system right out of the col. A direct line leaves the upper Elk River Trail just a few hundred metres past the turn off from the main Elk River Trail to Landslide Lake. Find an excellent elk trail right up the crest of the ridge. A good route to Elk Pass.

Slocomb Peak & Mt. Colonel Foster south-east aspect from Rambler Junior, September.

Rambler Peak

Rambler Peak east aspect from Mt. Beadnell, August.

Rambler Peak
6,906 ft / 2,105 m

Rambler Peak is an impressive peak rising at the head of the Elk River. Its flanks form the headwaters of the Wolf River, Cervus Creek, Ucona and Elk rivers. The lengthy approach and difficulties on the final summit tower helped put Rambler in a rare category of Strathcona Park summits in that it escaped the advances of the 1913-1914 Kent-Urquhart survey and other climbing parties until as late as 1964. Since then a variety of climbing routes have been established but the potential of Rambler is far from exhausted. Rambler Peak was originally named El Piveto Mountain after the pivotal summit tower but the name didn't stick. After the first ascent by three of its members the peak was officially named for the Island Mountain Ramblers mountaineering club.

First Ascent: Ron Facer, Barrie McDowell, Steve Todd, 19 July, 1964

First Winter Ascent: Cameron Powell, Philip Stone, Ryan Stuart, 11 January, 2003

Map Sheet: 92 F/12 Buttle Lake - GR 9212 (see also 92 F/13 Upper Campbell Lake)

Approaches: On the Elk River Trail from Highway 28. Follow the ERT to the bridge over Landslide Creek. Hike 200m up the open rock slab and leave the ERT to the left (south) on a flagged route up the Upper Elk Valley. The trail eventually comes to the bank of the Elk River and several piles of recent avalanche debris which clog the river bed. Make your way through the debris on the new route the trail takes. Cross the Elk River to the east bank and hike through a patch of old growth where there is a good campsite, the last before Elk Pass. Continue through an avalanche path and then underneath the huge walls of Rambler to Elk Pass. The North Col can be seen above the route and the foot of the North Buttress. Continue under the west flanks of Rambler to a couple of small lakes in the basin below the West Buttress and on to Elk Pass. CARE! There can be an extreme hazard from avalanches pouring off the cliffs on Rambler with any amount of snow cover.

Rambler may also be climbed as a side trip on the popular traverse route from Westmin through to the Elk River (see page 248).

Additional Info: IB 1997 p.9, IB 2001 p.19

242 The Needle a.k.a. Rambler Junior summer with Jonathon Bonk and winter with Ryan Stuart & Cam Powell

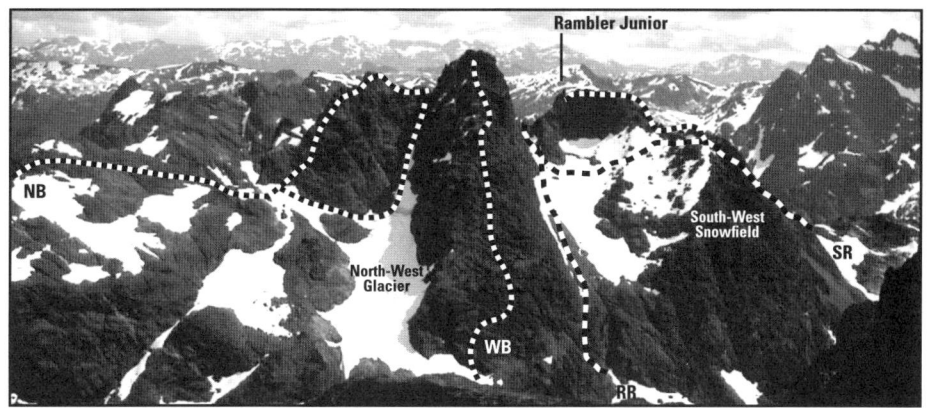

Rambler Peak west aspect as seen from Mt. Colonel Foster, August.

Routes

NB- ** **North Buttress and Ridge:** 5.5 400m (III)
Approach from the upper Elk River Trail which leaves the main ERT on the rock slabs just above the bridge across Landslide Creek. Hike up the trail into the upper valley past the river crossing and campsite before the slide alder path. Cross the slide path back into old growth timber. From here, leave the trail striking directly uphill keeping out of the bush as much as possible to gain the col between Mt. Colwell and Rambler Peak.

Start up to the left of the toe of the North Buttress climbing 300m on excellent rock with several low 5th class pitches to gain easier ground. Continue along ridge crest heading south to a second buttress. Climb buttress on crest or alternatively climb the snow gully to the right. From the pinnacle and col just north of the summit tower drop onto the high Rambler Glacier and join the Standard Route up to the summit.
FA: Mike Walsh 1975 as part of a complete north to south traverse of Rambler.

Rambler summit tower from South Ridge, September.

WB- *** **West Buttress:** 5.6 650m (III)
The finest technical route on Rambler Peak and an island classic. Start up between two waterfalls on 3rd class terrain. Climb gullies, cracks and chimneys along ridge crest until forced to make an exposed traverse rightwards on some loose rock to a chimney. The chimney leads up to a band of white rock climbed in two pitches to the top. Descend Standard Route to Elk Pass or rappel back down the route.
FA: Chris Barner, Paul Rydeen, 26 July 1990

EB- ** **East Buttress:** low 5th class 100m (II)
Two variations on the upper Main Summit Tower from the Rambler Glacier directly up the east side of the tower.
1-FA: Sandy Briggs, John Pratt, Rex Brown
2-FA: Sandy Briggs, Rick Reeve et al, Aug 1985

Rambler north-east aspect from Mt. Cobb looking across Cervus Creek, August.

Rambler Peak 243

Rambler Peak, north aspect from King's Peak, February.

RR- *** **Ramblers' Route:** low 5th class AI1 750m (III)
The original first ascent route on Rambler and a classic mountaineering climb. The Ramblers' Route takes a direct line up from the high hanging valley below Ramblers west side parallel to the prominent West Buttress.
Approach from the upper Elk River to the toe of the West Buttress near the small tarns at the base of the cwm. Depending on prevailing snow conditions, take one of a number of options up a band of rock to the right (south) of the buttress toe. Either steep snow or 3rd class rock scrambling leads through the rock band to the wide open and fairly steep South-West Snowfield. Keep to the left edge of the snowfield climbing directly to the col between Rambler and Rambler Junior (see photo right).
From the col easier ground leads across the Rambler Glacier heading left (north to north-west) around the main summit tower, keeping the tower to your left. The glacier leads up to the base of the steep but welcome upper North Gully. Climb the gully directly with some low 5th class moves and steep snow in early season to an exposed shoulder against the final summit block. Some parties may require a rope. Scramble up the narrow, airy shoulder and make some exposed low 5th class moves on to the top. Descend same route or Spiral Staircase route down the east side to Elk Pass.
FA: Ron Facer, Barrie McDowell, Steve Todd June 19, 1964

SR- * **South Ridge:** 4th class 220m (II)
To the south of the Main Summit are a series of jagged pinnacles. The northernmost and highest of these is known as Rambler Junior a.k.a. 'The Needle' and is an impressive sight from the Rambler Glacier. An exposed 4th class traverse may be made over the pinnacles including Rambler Junior by climbing directly up the South Ridge from the South Col. Join Ramblers' route at the Rambler Glacier.
FA: Mike Henry, Ron Facer 1966.

Rambler Peak, west aspect from Slocomb Peak, August.

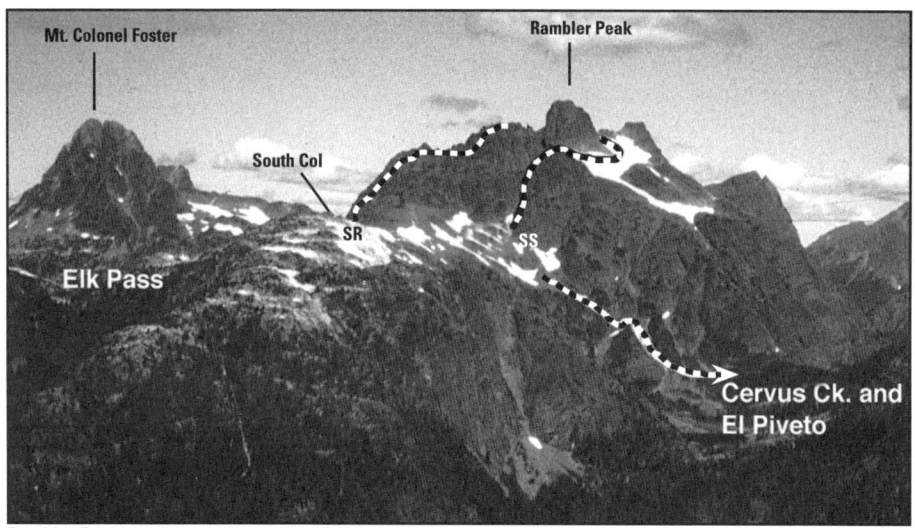

Rambler Peak, south-east aspect from Mt. De Voe, August.

SS- * **Spiral Staircase:** low 5th class AI1 400m (III)

Now the standard route to climb Rambler although not as atmospheric or direct as the Ramblers' Route. Follow the approach along the ERT to the upper Elk River valley and on to Elk Pass. From just below the pass at a collection of small tarns: either hike right into Elk Pass and follow the ridge to the left or climb rock steps and snowfields to gain the South Col at the toe of the South Ridge of Rambler. Make a slightly descending traverse across a scree/snow slope to reach the bottom of the prominent Lower East Gully (see photo below).

Scramble up the gully with low 5th class and/or steep snow to reach the Rambler Glacier. Hike north across the glacier keeping the summit tower to your left. Gradually ascend to the base of the steep, narrow upper North Gully on the north side of the Main Summit tower. Climb directly up the gully with some low 5th class to a slender arete. Some final exposed low 5th class moves lead onto the summit. Some parties may appreciate roped belays here and in the lower gully. Descend same route.

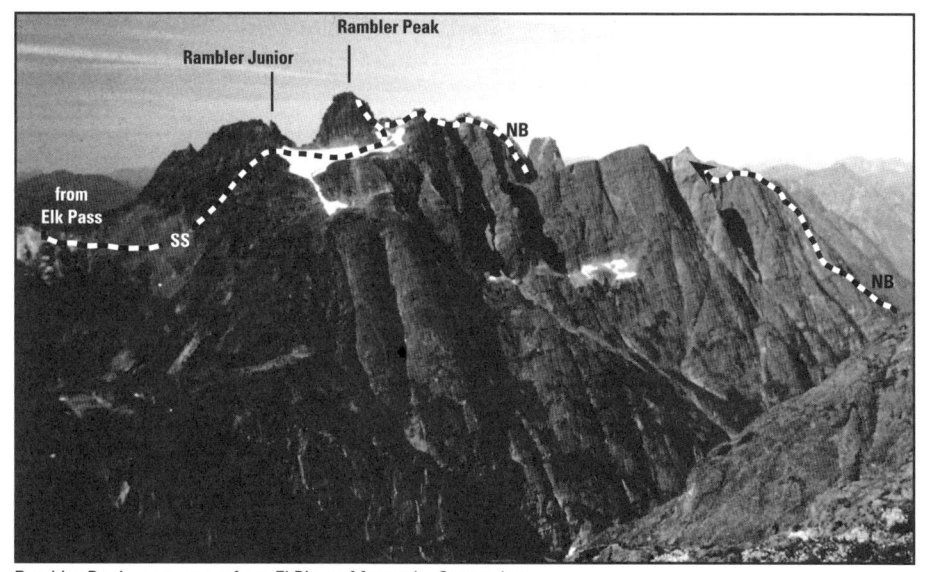

Rambler Peak east aspect from El Piveto Mountain, September.

Rambler Peak **245**

Rambler Peak (L) & Rambler Jr. (R) south-west aspect from above Elk Pass, January.

Winter Routes

SS- *** Spiral Staircase: AI3 400m (III)

With good winter climbing conditions Rambler Peak is an excellent climb despite the arduous march up the Elk valley. The route to Rambler through the upper Elk valley is extremely exposed to avalanches from the high cliffs on Rambler's western flanks and snow stability must be unquestionable to make a safe approach. Count on 2-3 days to Elk Pass via the Elk River Trail and upper Elk River.

From Elk Pass hike up the gentle lower south ridge to the South Col. From the col traverse an exposed snowfield on the south-east flank of Rambler (below Rambler Jr.) to the base of the lower East Gully. Climb moderate angled (55°) snow/ice up to the Rambler Glacier. Cross the Rambler Glacier climbing up and around to the base of the upper North Gully. Climb the 75m gully (AI3) to an exposed shoulder. Follow the shoulder to several final very exposed mixed moves onto the summit. Conditions on the summit may vary from bare rock/ice to heavily corniced. Descend same route with one rappel down upper North Gully.

FA: Philip Stone, Cameron Powell, Ryan Stuart 11 January, 2003

Ryan Stuart and Cam Powell at the top of the upper North Gully in a nasty winter storm on Rambler Peak.

Mt. DeVoe

Mt. DeVoe (R) and the Behinde (L) north aspect from Rambler Peak, August.

Mt. DeVoe
5,610 ft./ 1,710 m

Mt. DeVoe is a cluster of three knolls located on the divide between the Ucona and Wolf Rivers. It is a remote peak and is surrounded by some of the Island's highest peaks, including the Golden Hinde which is just a few kilometres to the south-east, Rambler Peak and the other high Elk River peaks to the north. It is a key feature along the popular Elk River to Westmin hiking traverse (see page 248). This superb multi day traverse passes across the knoll immediatly west of DeVoe from where it is easily climbed as a short side trip. The peak is named for William Fowler DeVoe a young surveyor who took part in the original survey of Strathcona Park but drowned in October 1913 in the Campbell River.

First Ascent: W.R. Kent, W.W. Urquhart, Einar Anderson 1913 or 1914

Map Sheet: 92 F/12 Buttle Lake - GR 9707

Approaches: Mt. DeVoe is usually approached along the backcountry traverse between Westmin and the Elk River travelling in either direction, (see page 248). From the col at the toe of Mt. DeVoe's West Ridge hike the West Ridge to the summit.

Golden Hinde (far L), Mt. DeVoe, and the Behinde north aspect from Elk Pass, January.

Looking south from Elk Pass along the Burman-Ucona divide (L), January.

Elk River - Westmin Traverse: This route is a journey through the wilderness heart of Strathcona Park between Highway 28 in the Elk River valley and the Boliden mine at the south end of Buttle Lake. The route can be traversed in either direction and is described here from north to south ie: Elk River to Westmin.

Follow approaches for Rambler Peak from Highway 28 to Elk Pass. From Elk Pass descend southward to the north end of the large alpine lake below the pass. Keep to the north side of the knoll on the lake's east shore and continue descending to the round lake at GR 9610. Keep to the west shore of this lake and hike up the hillside south-eastward, to gain the ridge north-west of Mt. DeVoe. Follow this ridge southward and skirt the west peak of DeVoe as you drop into a col on the west side of the summit of Mt. DeVoe.

Descend south into a high pass at GR 9707. Take a gentle climb onto an isolated section of alpine ridge. Hike down the crest of this ridge among some striking granite crags and pools. At the south end of the ridge descend south east to the Wolf-Burman-Ucona Pass at GR 9904.

From this three watershed divide either hike around the west shore of Burman Lake to gain the north ridge of Mt Burman, or climb up a boulderfield to a ridge crest alongside a steep creek. Hike up along the creek's west side to a shoulder below the south side of the Behinde.

From this shoulder the Golden Hinde may be climbed by any of a number of routes.

To continue south to Westmin-Boliden descend the well travelled route down to Burman Lake and up onto Mt. Burman's north ridge. From here follow approach details for Mt. Burman and Phillips Ridge.

Looking south from the Golden Hinde across Schjelderup Lake to Phillips Ridge, February.

248 Elk River - Westmin Traverse

El Piveto Mountain

El Piveto Mountain east aspect from Mt. Beadnell, August.

El Piveto Mountain
6,460ft. / 1,969m

El Piveto Mountain is a rounded dome of basalt on the Wolf River-Cervus Creek divide. It is a relatively inaccessible peak and is infrequently climbed. The standard route is straightforward but there are some harder climbing possibility including the North Ridge which looks entertaining.

First Ascent: Mike Walsh, Pat & Elizabeth Guilbride, Bob Tustin, Ray Paine, Syd Watts, John & Doreen Cowlin Aug 3, 1966

Map Sheet: 92 F/12 Buttle Lake - GR 9911

Approaches: Follow approach details as for Rambler Peak to Elk Pass. From the point after dropping down the east flank of Rambler to reach the base of Rambler's East Gully simply continue down the talus descending past the base of Ramblers East Gully to a narrow pass between Cervus Creek and Wolf River. A small knoll (Cervus Mountain) sits between this pass and the main Cervus Creek-Wolf River Pass under the west side of El Piveto. Hike up and over Cervus Mountain to reach the main pass.

Additional Info: IB 2001 p.25

West Basin: 3rd Class
From the main Cervus Creek-Wolf River Pass head directly up the prominent cirque on El Piveto's west face overlooking the pass. The ground gradually steepens with some exposed scrambling on 4th class terrain. Note the route on the way up for the descent. Cross a plateau to the summit overlooking the north glacier and north-east summit. Descend same route.

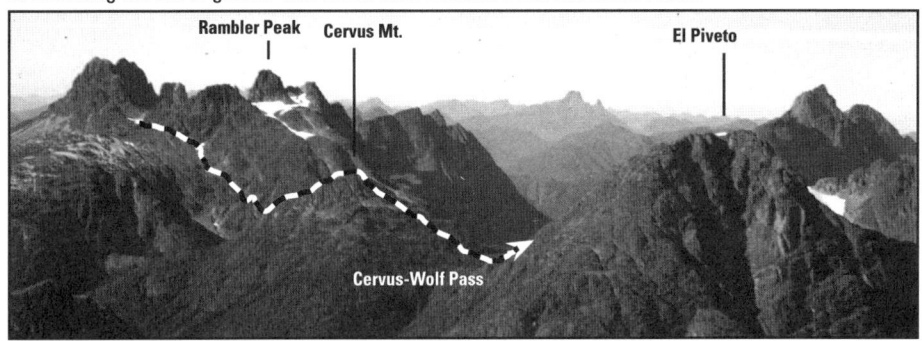

Mt. Colonel Foster (L) & Rambler (C) south aspect showing approach route to El Piveto (lower R), October.

250 El Piveto Mountain's hidden glacier at the head of Cathedral Creek

Cervus -Wolf Divide

Looking south along Cervus Creek East Divide from Mt. Cobb, August.

Cervus Creek-Wolf River Divide

The group of mountains that form the east divide of Cervus Creek are some of the highest on Vancouver Island, relatively accessible but among the least climbed. This has probably been due to the lack of trail access and the peaks' rugged nature. There are only a few possible approach routes out of Cervus Creek and they are tricky to locate in that deep secluded valley. The best way to climb the mountains on this divide is as a complete traverse of the range from north of El Piveto to Elk Mountain taking between 3 or 4 nights.

The recommended direction for the traverse is from south to north, approaching El Piveto via the Elk River Trail and Elk Pass and heading north to Elk Mountain. The route finding along the ridge is easier heading in this direction as several major obstacles present themselves rather than hiding as they do when travelling southward. The traverse is described this direction peak by peak.

The route description should translate fairly well for travelling north to south which admittedly would be more attractive for views.

Follow approach details as for El Piveto Mountain to the main Cervus Creek-Wolf River Pass. From the Cervus Creek-Wolf River Pass make a gradually rising traverse northward across the northwest flank of El Piveto. Cross scree or snowfields and some exposed heather slopes to gain a tight col at the foot of El Piveto's jagged north ridge. Gain the ridge crest and hike north on relatively easy ground (here is one of the most dramatic views on Vancouver Island looking across Cervus Creek at Mt. Colonel Foster framed by Rambler and Elkhorn's massive east faces). There are several good camping possibilities along this section of the ridge.

The south end of the Cervus-Wolf Divide and north col of El Piveto Mt. (R) west aspect, October.

Ptarmigan Pinnacles

Ptarmigan Pinnacles west aspect from Cervus Mountain, October.

Ptarmigan Pinnacles
5,900ft./1800m

A group of spiky pinnacles south of Mt. Haig Brown.

First Ascent: Unknown

Map Sheet: 92 F/13 Upper Campbell Lake - GR 0015

Approaches: From the col at the foot of El Piveto's North Ridge head north passing two high points on the ridge. Arrive at a point just west of the Ptarmigan Pinnacles where a long gully drops to the scree and meadow below. The ridgeline jogs east over the pinnacles before continuing north.

Crossing the pinnacles is very exposed and much more time consuming than the map would suggest but doing so is a highlight of the traverse. Tackle the first pinnacle on the ridge crest then drop onto the south-east flank. Conjure up a line through vegetated gullies and exposed bluffs. to the meadows south of Haig-Brown.

The gully off the south-west ridge offers a fast ascent line approaching from the north and is an ideal descent route off the ridge avoiding the pinnacles.

Either route leads into a magical alpine meadow with several alpine lakes below the south side of Mt. Haig Brown (Peak 6390).

Cervus Creek - Wolf River Divide

Mt. Haig Brown

Mt. Haig-Brown east aspect from Mt. Beadnell, August.

Mt. Haig-Brown
6,390 ft / 1,947 m

Mt. Haig Brown lies just south-east of Mt. Cobb. It is clearly visible from Buttle Lake through the Wolf River and Cathedral Creek valleys from where it strikes a formidable pose. However it is somewhat indistinct from many other angles. There are beautiful meadows on the south flank. The mountain is named after Roderick Haig-Brown a Campbell River author and naturalist.

First Ascent: Unknown

Map Sheet: 92 F/13 Upper Campbell Lake - GR 0216

Approaches: The easiest route up Mt. Haig-Brown is from the meadows below its south flank. Easy hiking weaves up open heather slopes to the summit. Approach from Cervus Creek using a

Wolf River - Cervus Creek Divide east aspect from Mt. Beadnell, August.

Mt. Haig-Brown north aspect from Mt. Cobb, August

bench under the Ptarmigan Pinnacles to reach the alpine or walk along the main Wolf-Cervus divide in either direction.

The Wolf River and Cathedral Creek provide access to the long routes up the East Face. From the north the North-East Ridge is a fun 3rd class scramble above an exquisite cirque and chain of lakes.

Travelling the Wolf-Cervus Divide over Mt. Haig-Brown is complicated by any desire to ascend Mt. Cobb. Mt. Cobb is a side trip from the main ridge.

To reach Mt. Cobb, descend 1,000 ft down the south side of Haig-Brown and traverse north-west around the base of some large rock pinnacles. Regain the ridge crest north of the pinnacles and continue to a col due south of the summit of Mt. Cobb. The summit is an easy hike from here.

To bypass Cobb and head directly to Mt. Filberg on the main ridge route descend the steep rocky North-East Ridge of Mt. Haig Brown to gain a scree filled gully. The gully leads down to an exquisite chain of lakes in a deep cirque below Mt. Cobb. A crucial gully leads out of this cirque to a shoulder east of the Mt. Cobb summit.

Additional Info: IB 1992 p.31

CC- Cathedral Couloir: AI2 4th class 700m (III)
Climbs the long gully that drops off the east face of Mt. Haig Brown down into the Cathedral Creek valley. Approach from Buttle Lake at the Wolf River outlet. Hike up the valley on the north bank of the river and make a horrific bush thrash into Cathedral Creek. Ascend the gully on snow and some rock scrambling. Join the North-East Ridge and follow it to the summit.
FA: Chris Barner, 1977

FB- Flying Buttress: 5.8 A1 700m (V)
Approach from Buttle Lake as for Cathedral Couloir. Climb the stacked buttresses up the centre of the East Face to the summit.
FA: Chris Barner, 1978

Mt. Haig-Brown (L) & Ptarmigan Pinnacles (R) south-west aspect from Mt Colwell, August

Mt. Cobb

Mt. Cobb north aspect from ERT Rd. February

Mt. Cobb
6,663ft / 2,031m

Mt. Cobb is a huge dome of basalt on the Cervus Creek-Wolf River divide north-west of Mt. Haig Brown. Climbing Mt. Cobb while following the Cervus-Wolf traverse is essentially a side trip. Notable are several impressive waterfalls that drain the rocky dome east of the summit tower. In winter these falls form thick ice pillars and are unclimbed. There is a improbable chockstone cave feature on the north side of the summit. The northeastern high point is the summit. Mt. Cobb is named for Charles Cobb who managed the Elk River Timber Co. in the 1930s and 1940s in gratitude for all the favours he showed the 1935-1936 survey party.

First Ascent: Unknown

Map Sheet: 92 F/13 Upper Campbell Lake - GR 0218

Approaches: Mt. Cobb is a very easy hike from the col, due south of the summit, connecting it to Mt. Haig-Brown (Peak 6390). This col can be reached from the south following the Wolf-Cervus Divide from Mt. Haig-Brown or from the north from Mt. Filberg via the lake chain between Cobb and Haig-Brown and then hiking direct from the lakes up to the col.

Mt. Cobb (far left) and Mt. Haig-Brown (far right) south aspect, August.

Mt. Cobb **255**

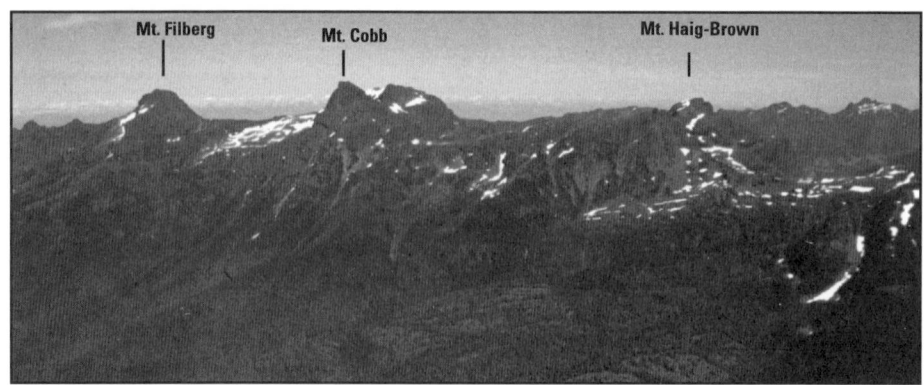

Wolf River - Cervus Creek Divide south-west aspect from Cervus Mountain, August.

The forested southwest slopes of Mt. Cobb rising from Cervus Creek have several good lines and may be used as an entry point to and from this divide.

To continue the Cervus-Wolf divide from the summit of Mt. Cobb you must retrace your steps down to the lake chain to Mt. Cobb's south-east. Hike eastward descending the lake chain to the west shore of the larger, easternmost lake. From the northwest tip of the lake rises a steep boulder choked gully almost 1,500ft.

Mt. Haig Brown to Elk Mountain south-east aspect from Mt. McBride, June.

This gully is highly visible from the summit of Mt. Haig-Brown. If heading south from Mt. Filberg, locating the top of this gully is tricky. Their are some slight folds in the contours of the topo map indicating the top of the gully at GR 039186 but the lower section is not apparent on the map. Climbing the gully is a strenuous scramble with overnight packs with 4th class and occassional low 5th class, a rope maybe required and in spring or early summer expect snow.

Having climbed the gully from the lake chain you arrive on a bench and scree/snow slope below the steep butt end of the rocky ridge east of the Mt. Cobb summit. (A gully up this butt end looks like a possible, but unconfirmed, route to the summit when it is full of snow.) Traverse the scree/snow slope northward to a narrow col due south of Mt. Filberg.

Mt. Filberg north aspect from Mt. Flannigan, May.

Mt. Filberg

Mt. Filberg east aspect from Lupin Mountain, June.

Mt. Filberg
6,677 ft. / 2,035 m

Mt. Filberg is the highest point on the Cervus Creek - Wolf River Divide and the most popular summit. Named after Robert Filberg a resident of Comox and head of the Comox Logging Company.

Map Sheet: 92 F/13 Upper Campbell Lake - GR 0320

Approaches: Mt. Filberg can be reached from Highway 28 at Lady Falls up the Cervus Creek valley Hike up the trail to the Lady Falls viewpoint. A path breaks off to the left at the viewing platform. Follow this rough trail to meet the creek at a long S bend. Keep to the the east bank of the creek around the S bend then leave it taking a sharp left into the forest trending southeast to gain the toe of Filberg's north-west ridge.

A long and bushy ascent eventually leads into open alpine. Avoid a group of pinnacles easily on the south-west side to the toe of Filberg's North Buttress. A short low 5th class scramble up this buttress leads onto the summit. Or from further back on the approach ridge descend eastward on to a bench and traverse around to the southeast flank of the mountain from where it is an easy hike to the top.

If approaching Mt. Filberg from Mt. Cobb, traverse a scree/snow slope north from the east flank of Cobb to a narrow col due south of Mt. Filberg. Climb one of several steep vegetated gullies up from the col to gain an open ridge south of the peak. Traverse eastward and then head up an easy slope on the south-east side to the summit. The easiest descent is back down the south-east side.

Filberg Creek is another option but its steep canyon walls in the lower valley should only be considered with an eye to the bush therein.

Additional Info: IB 1994 p.22, 23

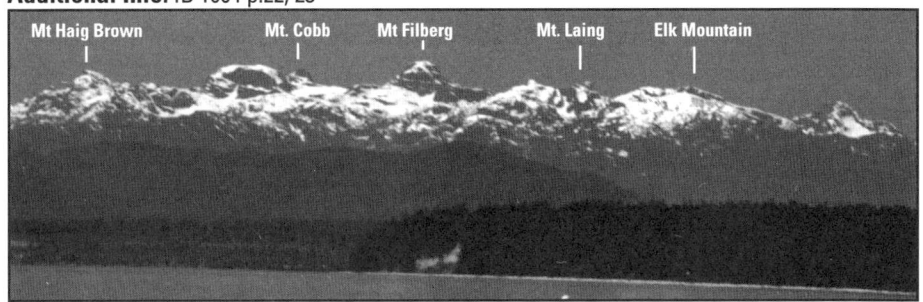

The Cervus-Wolf divide as seen from near Cortes Island, May.

Mt. Laing

Mt. Laing north-west aspect from Crown Mt., July.

Mt. Laing
5,900 ft. / 1,798 m

A small, dramatic peak toward the north end of the Cervus-Wolf divide. Mt. Laing is an infrequently climbed peak, overshadowed by its loftier neighbours and easily bypassed on the El Piveto-Elk Mountain traverse. Named after Hamilton Mack Laing (1926-82) a naturalist and writer who lived in Comox.

First Ascent: Unknown

Map Sheet: 92 F/13 Upper Campbell Lake - GR 0522

Approaches: Laing can be reached from the north via logging roads high on the northern slopes of Elk Mountain off Highway 28. These roads are gated and are on private land owned by Timberwest. Permission to use these roads should be obtained from the landowner. Hike from the highest road spur up the narrowing ridge direct to Peak 5205. Continue south over a second peak and on to the top of Elk Mountain. Descend a wide chute off Elk Mountain south into a small basin, with a boulder field at the base, north-east of Mt. Laing. A fine line up this basin leads to the east side of the mountain where a traverse may be made to reach the south-east ridge.

From Mt. Filberg hike northeastward along the height of land across the narrow Filberg Creek-Cathedral Creek pass and onto Mt. Laing's south ridge. Continue north bypassing obstacles on the ridge to gain Laing's south-east ridge which can be followed with some 3rd class to the summit. Descend same route. To continue on to Elk Mountain, descend from the summit to a bench at 5,400 ft and follow it northward and then descend a boulder field in a pass between Mt. Laing and up an open chute on Elk Mountain's south slope.

Mt. Filberg (L) & Mt. Laing (R) south-east aspect from Mt. Beadnell, August.

Elk Mountain

Elk Mountain north-east aspect from Highway 28, March.

Elk Mountain
5,700 ft / 1,737 m

Elk Mountain is a wide tapered mountain that sits on the south shore of Upper Campbell Lake at the crux where the west arm of the lake joins the main body of water. The bulk of the mountain falls outside the Strathcona Park boundary and is privately owned by Timberwest who have built logging roads almost to the treeline in recent years. The roads are gated and future vehicle access uncertain. The roads offer a very fast approach to the summit of Elk Mountain. The peak forms the northern terminus of the Cervus Creek-Wolf River Divide and provides the major route to or from the range of mountains south of it on that divide.

First Ascent: W.R. Kent, W.W. Urquhart, Einar Anderson 1913 or 1914

Map Sheet: 92 F/13 Upper Campbell Lake - GR 0524

Approaches: Permission to enter the Elk Mountain area should be obtained from TimberWest who own the mountain. Leave Highway 28 opposite the Big Den Rest Area. If vehicle access on the logging roads has been arranged drive up the logging road switchbacking up the flanks of Elk Mountain. If the road gate is locked park at the Big Den Rest Area or nearby, and hike the roads. From the highest road spur hike up the crest of a tapering ridge direct into the alpine above on Peak 5205. Continue southward over a sub-peak and on to the top of Elk Mountain.

If approaching from the south along the Cervus-Wolf divide, from the pass between Elk Mountain and Mt. Laing hike up the open heather/snow chute on the south side of Elk Mountain to the top. Continue on the height of land over a couple of lower sub-peaks. Descend to the logging roads and down them to Highway 28.

Elk Mountain and Mt. Laing north-west aspect from Crown Mountain, July. Note logging roads in lower left.

Mt. Titus

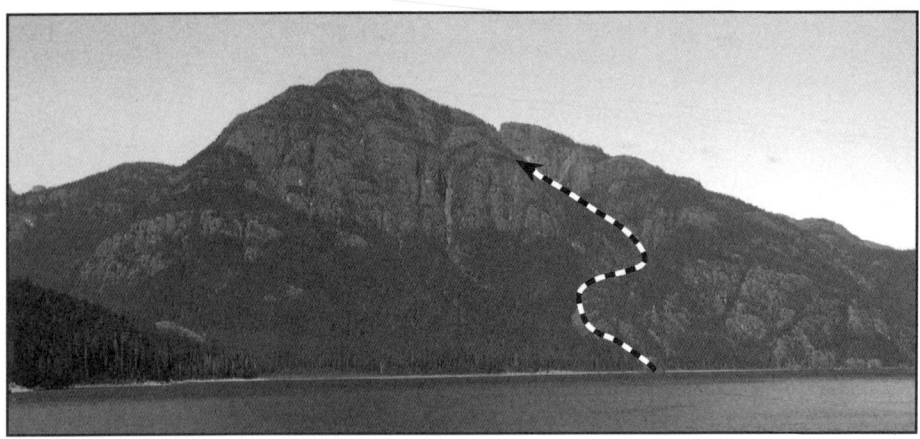

Mt. Titus south-east aspect from Buttle Lake, August.

Mt. Titus
4,860 ft / 1,481 m

Mt. Titus is a low but prominent mountain on the west shore of Buttle Lake, on the north side of the outlet of the Wolf River. It has great views of Buttle Lake and the mountains to the south and west including the Golden Hinde, Mt. McBride and the whole Cervus-Wolf divide.

First Ascent: Norman Stewart survey party 1936

Map Sheet: 92 F/13 Upper Campbell Lake - GR 0917

Approaches: Mt. Titus may be climbed from Buttle Lake up the long open gully that separates the Main Summit from the north summit- the Throat of Titus. This route is best climbed in spring when remaining snow makes travel up this boulder choked creek bed a much better proposisition than after the snow has melted away. Cross Buttle Lake by boat to the Mt. Titus marine campsite. Hike up through the forest directly into the base of the gully which is visible above the campsite. Hike up the gully to the notch and then trend south up to the summit.

Although the long north-east ridge looks appealling from Buttle Narrows it is a sucker ridge bluffing out on the north summit at an impassable gap where the Throat of Titus joins the summit ridge.

Additional Info: IB 1998 p.24, IB 1999 p.32

Mt. Titus south-west aspect from Mt. McBride, June.

Mt. Con Reid

Mt. Con Reid east aspect from Mt. Beadnell, August.

Mt. Con Reid
5,721 ft./ 1,744 m

A series of rocky summits dividing the Wolf River valley from Cathedral Creek, north-east of El Piveto Mountain. Likely one of the most infrequently climbed summits in Strathcona due to the access difficulties and it being surrounded by much higher and more attractive peaks. However its situation adds to the allure for its views of the El Piveto Glacier and north side of the Golden Hinde. There are also some exposed karst features along the ridge which join it to El Piveto. And of course the promise of a good bushwhack has an allure all of its own!

First Ascent: W.R. Kent, W.W. Urquhart, Einar Anderson 1913 or 1914

Map Sheet: 92 F/12 Buttle Lake - GR 0213 (see also 92 F/13 Upper Campbell Lake)

Approaches: Given that forest travel doesn't deter your mountaineering ambitions Mt. Con Reid can be reached from Buttle Lake via the Wolf River valley. Cross Buttle Lake by boat from the Buttle Lake Parkway. From the north bank of the river locate an old blazed route up the valley bypassing the small but steep canyon where Wolf River empties into Buttle Lake.

Follow a bushy (B3+) route up the valley on elk trails to the most prominent fork in the Wolf River south of the summit and ~8 km from Buttle Lake GR 0411. Ascend the steep forested hillside to reach a col south-west of the summit. From here it is an easy climb up the south-west ridge to the top.

Alternatively, try your luck on the Neave-McCoubrey route via Cathedral Creek to the steeper central peak. Cathedral Creek is the major tributary flowing into the Wolf River 4 km from Buttle Lake. Follow the creek up steep ground into the magical hidden valley and trend south-west under the south face of Mt. Haig Brown. From the small lake in the valley floor strike up the hillside and up gullies on the north side of the mountain. traverse to the west where the central summit can be climbed up a 250 m rock face.

Marble Peak

Marble Peak & Marble Meadows east aspect from Syd Watts Peak, August.

Marble Peak
5,797 ft / 1,767 m

Marble Peak overlooks the west shore of Buttle Lake and forms the eastern edge of the popular Marble Meadows alpine plateau. The views of Buttle Lake are great and Marble Peak is a perfect vantage point from which to become familiarized with the Marble Meadows area. The peak is overshadowed by Mt. McBride to its north-west but makes for a good distraction while visiting the meadows, especially if an ascent of McBride is not in the plans.

Map: 92 F/12 Buttle Lake - GR 1207

Approaches: Marble Peak is best reached via the Marble Meadows Trail from Buttle Lake (see Mt. McBride approach details). From a small col between Globe Flower Lake and Marblerock Lake hike up the mountain's south-west ridge. A few short but exposed rock steps, one through a tight notch in the ridge leads to the summit and the awesome view down to Buttle Lake.

The Wheaton Hut, Marble Meadows

Marble Peak (L) & Wheaton Ridge, Marble Meadows (R) north aspect from Mt. McBride, June.

Mt. McBride

Mt. McBride south-west aspect from the Golden Hinde, February.

Mt. McBride
6,829 ft. / 2,081 m

A distinctive landmark from Buttle Lake and along the Buttle Lake Parkway. Mt. McBride from the north-east takes on the apearance of a transplanted peak from the Rockies. The proliferation of limestone around the mountain enhances this effect. Throughout Marble Meadows and Marblerock Canyon steep limestone cliffs secret some great climbing. The whole Marble Meadows area is a remarkable corner of Strathcona Park and is a must-see part of the park. The maze of lakes and meadows illuminated by wildflowers are stunning. In winter and spring Mt. McBride is an ideal ski ascent from the Wheaton Hut which makes a perfect base from which to explore the area on skis. Mt. McBride is named after Sir Richard McBride British Columbia Premier at the time Strathcona Park was established in 1911

First Ascent: Possibley Leroy Stirling Cokely 1926
Map Sheet: 92 F/12 Buttle Lake - GR 0810

Mt. McBride north-east aspect from Mt. Beadnell, August.

264 Fred Michaud sneaks in some late spring turns on Mt. McBride.

Mt. McBride south-east aspect from Syd Watts Peak, August.

Approaches: To reach Mt. McBride, the best route is via the Marble Meadows trail on the west shore of Buttle Lake. Cross the lake from either the Augerpoint Day Area or the Karst Creek Boat Ramp to the north bank of Phillips Creek at its outlet into the lake. The trail climbs up steep switchbacks and is one of the longer such trail ascents in the area, reaching the plateau finally at 1,400 m. Hike north-west across the meadows to a col at the toe of Marble Peak's south-east ridge overlooking Marblerock Lake. Continue around the lake and to the Wheaton Hut at GR106077. From the hut hike up to the top of Wheaton Ridge from where a clear view can be had of Mt. McBride and the route ahead.

Head west across a wide pass between Phillips Creek to the south and Marblerock Creek to the north. Hike up a slope to the crest of the ridge between Mt. McBride and Morrison Spire. Hike north to a col at the foot of the south ridge of Mt. McBride. Either continue up the ridge (3rd Class) or traverse northwestward from the col at the base of the ridge around a prominent basin to gain the west side of the mountain and the McBride Glacier above.

Additional Info: IB 1997 p.22, WIM #21 p.18

Routes

MG- **McBride Glacier:** AI1
From the col at the foot of the South Ridge make a traverse left (north) across snow/scree above a deep basin. As the ground above eases hike upward on scree or snow to reach the wide open McBride Glacier. Walk up snow, or exposed ice in late summer or fall, to the summit ridge. Walk along the ridge admiring the exposure off the South Face to the summit cairn. The glacier may also be approached directly from Buttle Lake up the Wolf River. A B4 bushwhack up the valley is worth it for the ski turns down the full length of the glacier.

SR- **South Ridge:** 3rd class
Approach from Marble Meadows. From the col at the base of the South Ridge continue directly up the crest of the South Ridge with some 3rd class scrambling. Join the McBride Glacier near the top.

North-East Ridge: 3rd class
Climbs the left hand skyline as seen from Buttle Lake. Approach from the Wolf River outlet into Buttle Lake. A long hike up forested slopes leads to the rocky ridge crest. Some 3rd class scrambling along the ridge leads to a snow gully on the upper north face. Climb this gully on to the summit ridge.

Mt. McBride south-west aspect from Mt. Judy, Phillips Ridge, August.

Morrison Spire

Morrison Spire east aspect from Marble Meadows, August.

Morrison Spire
5,905 ft./ 1,800 m

Morrison Spire overlooks Marble Meadows from the west and is a familiar landmark to anyone who's spent time at the Wheaton Hut. It sits on the divide between Phillips Creek and Wolf River on the hiking route from Phillips Ridge to Marble Meadows. The Marble Meadows area is an excellent destination in any season and one of the true gems of Strathcona Park. Wildflowers and karst topography litter the landscape in summer and in winter the relatively benign terrain makes a superb ski touring destination with the bonus of a hut to base out of, if you can find it!

Map Sheet: 92 F/12 Buttle Lake - GR 0707

Approaches: Can be reached in a comfortable day trip from any of the popular camps in Marble Meadows. Follow the description for approaching Marble Meadows under Mt. McBride. From the slight col at GR 0908 due south of and overlooking Copper Brush Lake hike up on to the ridge crest on either the north or south side of the Spire. From the west side it is an easy hike on to the top.

The East Ridge is a nice scramble with some 5.6 moves over some blocky steps.

Golden Hinde & Morrison Spire from Wheaton Ridge, February.

Phillips Ridge

Looking north along Phillips Ridge to the Phillips-Burman pass and the Golden Hinde beyond, October.

Phillips Ridge
5,692 ft./ 1,732 m

Phillips Ridge is the alpine ridge dividing the lower reaches of the Myra Creek valley from the Phillips Creek valley. The western high point of the ridge is Peak 1732 which could be considered the summit of the ridge. The eastern high point is Mt. Phillips. The ridge system forms a huge 'E' shape with the top branch joining Mt McBride; the middle branch is Greig Ridge which protrudes into Phillips Creek; and lastly the bottom branch runs out to the summits of Mt Phillips. A complete high ridge traverse right around the Phillips watershed is one of the best backpacking/ski touring trips in Strathcona. The excellent trail access from the Westmin-Boliden mine makes the ridge a perfect day-hike destination too. For other extended expeditions in this area, Phillips Ridge plays a key role in access, especially to the Golden Hinde and on to the Elk River Trail.

Map Sheet: 92 F/12 Buttle Lake - GR 0797

Approaches: The Phillips Ridge trail from Westmin-Boliden offers some of the least strenuous alpine access out of the Elk River-Buttle Lake valley system. The Buttle Lake Parkway terminates at the parking lot on the far (west) side of the Westmin-Boliden Myra Falls mine site. Just 30m along the gravel on the Powerhouse Road the Phillips Ridge Trail heads off to the right (north) to wind up in series of switchbacks a scant 900m (2,800ft) to Arnica Lake. Take care to minimize your impact at Arnica Lake as it is a high use area. There are tent platforms a bear cache and outhouse at Arnica Lake.

At Arnica Lake you are in the middle of Phillips Ridge which runs in a line from Mt. Phillips in the east to Peak 1732 to the west. To climb Mt Phillips head east along the ridge from Arnica Lake (see Mt. Phillips approach details). For Peak 1732 follow the well-established route around the east shore of Arnica Lake then continue hiking westward on the gentle, open ridge crest as it arcs northward to the top of Peak 1732. Both Peak 1732 and Mt. Phillips are strenuous day trips from Westmin-Boliden return.

Looking south along Phillips Ridge to Peak 1732 from near Mt Judy, August.

Looking across Phillips Ridge from the Golden Hinde, February.

Phillips Watershed traverse: From Peak 1732 the ridge system turns 90° and runs north up and over a number of small mountains to eventually reach the south ridge of Mt. McBride and join the Marble Meadows Trail. Thus a circuit can be completed around the whole Phillips Creek watershed with a number of options to consider: To complete this high traverse around the Phillips Creek watershed clockwise you can start at either Westmin-Boliden on the Phillips Ridge Trail, as described above, or at Buttle Lake by boating across from the Karst Creek boat ramp on the Buttle Lake Parkway and gaining the alpine on a route up to the north peak of Mt. Phillips (see Mt. Phillips approach details). The latter is the preferred option for the complete traverse and the former works best for taking the route as far as the col south-east of Carter Lake, heading toward the Golden Hinde and/or the Westmin-Elk River traverse.

Peak 1732 is easily bypassed on the south-west flank by the main route along Phillips Ridge through a high col and onto the next high point on the ridge to the west. Phillips Ridge then swings north leaving its boundary with the Myra Creek valley to the south to form the divide between the Burman River and Phillips Creek. Continue hiking north over a series of humps on the ridge and then descend to the Phillips-Burman pass at GR 0599. (See photo on page 238).

The Phillips-Burman pass is the best point from which to leave the ridge if heading north-west to the Golden Hinde and/or the Elk River Trail. Make a gradually descending traverse northward across the west flank of the ridge to Carter Lake immediately south of Schjelderup Lake to take this route (see Mt. Burman and Golden Hinde approach details).

To continue around the Phillips Watershed traverse, hike up directly north out of the Phillips-Burman pass and keeping to the crest of the ridge follow the well marked route over several more high points to the summit of **Mt. Judy** 1,720m at GR 0401. The views of the Golden Hinde and the Wolf River valley north of Mt. Judy are awesome! Here the ridge system takes a little jog eastward to **Crystal Mountain** 1,720m (GR 0602) where Greig Ridge branches off farther east protruding into the Phillips Creek valley and splitting it in to two major forks. The terrain continues to offer superb hiking if a bit strenuous with numerous ups and downs!

At Crystal Mountain the ridge swings back to a north-south line and a short descent is needed down to the Phillips-Wolf pass a.k.a. 'Gallstone Col'. From the pass another short climb leads up to the top of **Tibetan Mountain** 1,800m (GR 0603) and the hardest work is left behind. Easier hiking northward arrives at **Limestone Cap** 1,753m one of Strathcona Park's most distinctive features. The Cap is a bent bottle cap-shaped band of limestone perched above the more prevalent basalt. The top is a wide open area of karst pavement heavily eroded by water and carpeted in pockets of wild flowers in summer.

Drop off Limestone Cap to the north-east into Rainbow Pass, another of the park's truly exquisite places. Morrison Spire is easily climbed from this pass up the south ridge. Either continue on the height of land past Morrison Spire toward Mt. McBride or swing around below the east side of the spire on a series of benches that lead north-eastward into Marble Meadows. Join the Marble Meadows trail at Wheaton Ridge and take it back down to Buttle Lake. Cross Phillips Creek to retreive your boat if that is how you arrived.

Mt. Phillips

Mt. Phillips north summit (R) over Buttle Lake, north-east aspect, May.

Mt. Phillips
5,652 ft./ 1,723 m

Mt. Phillips is a low alpine summit overlooking the south end of Buttle Lake on the south side of the outlet of Phillips Creek into Buttle Lake. The peak marks the east terminus of the extensive Phillips Ridge system which leads in a figure 'E' pattern to Greig Ridge, Marble Meadows and Mt. McBride.

First Ascent: W.R. Kent, W.W. Urquhart, Einar Anderson 1913 or 1914

Map Sheet: 92 F/12 Buttle Lake - GR 1399

Approaches: Mt. Phillips may be climbed as an easy hike from Westmin up the Phillips Ridge trail to Arnica Lake. From here most hikers head west toward the Golden Hinde, Marble Meadows or even through to the Elk River. Leave the beaten path and head east up a sub alpine slope to more open country on an alpine knoll at GR 1297. From here descend slightly to the east as the ridge makes a right angle shift and then again turns to the north. Continue through lightly forested alpine northward to the open slope on Mt. Phillips' south side. Hike the short steep slope to the summit.

Mt. Phillips may also be reached from the outlet of Phillips Creek into Buttle Lake. Cross Buttle Lake by boat from the Karst Creek boat ramp and secure your vessel on the south side of the creek. Find a route up the forested hillside to the alpine at Mt. Phillips north summit. Follow the ridge crest to Mt. Phillips. Descend either: back to Buttle Lake the way you came, go down the Phillips Ridge Trail to Westmin-Boliden or continue right around the Phillips Watershed Traverse to the Marble Meadows trail and take that back down to the lake cross the creek mouth to retreive your boat (4-7 days).

Mt. Phillips Main Summit (L) & North Summit (R) north-east aspect from Syd Watts Peak, August.

Mt. Burman

Mt. Burman (L) & the Golden Hinde (R), south aspect from Phillips Ridge, October.

Mt. Burman
5,761 ft./ 1,756 m

Mt. Burman is a granite dome located just south of the Golden Hinde and Burman Lake, between two forks of the Burman River. Its importance derives not so much from its own stature, being overshadowed by the illustious neighbour to the north, but beacuse of the role it plays in access to and from the Golden Hinde. There are many sporty granite crags around Mt. Burman particularly on its north-west flank along the shore of Burman Lake.

First Ascent: W.R. Kent, W.W. Urquhart, Einar Anderson 1913 or 1914

Map Sheet: 92 F/12 Buttle Lake - GR 0200

Approaches: A good route and a perfect way to take in the summit of Mt. Burman en route or returning from the Golden Hinde is to traverse the mountain via the east and north ridges. Approach from Westmin-Boliden up the Phillips Ridge Trail (see Phillips Ridge approach details) to the Phillips-Burman Pass (see photo page 238). Make a descending traverse from the pass down to Carter Lake. The east ridge rises from the south end of Carter Lake at GR 0499 south of Schjelderup Lake. It is an easy if steep hike on the crest of the ridge. This route is clearly shown on the photo above.

Alternatively, if following the route to or from Burman Lake across the north-east cirque of Mt. Burman, the summit can be climbed as a side trip up the easy north ridge. Note that in winter the north-east cirque is exposed to avalanche and is best avoided by using a lower route through the meadows at the head of the Wolf River just north of Schjelderup Lake to come and go from the Golden Hinde.

Mt. Burman east aspect from Syd Watts Peak, August.

Golden Hinde

Golden Hinde east aspect from Mt. Judy - Phillips Ridge, August.

Golden Hinde
7,219 ft./2200m

The Golden Hinde is Vancouver Island's highest peak and one of the more remote mountains on the island. Formerly known as the Rooster's Comb for its appearance the peak was renamed in 1939 to celebrate the voyage of Sir Francis Drake to the waters off British Columbia in his vessel the Golden Hinde. The Hinde is situated in the centre of Strathcona Park between the east and west branches of Wolf River which drains into the west shore of Buttle Lake, and Burman River which flows to the west coast at Matchlee Bay.

Most of the obvious features on the mountain have been climbed over the years and the Golden Hinde enjoys the attentions of several ascents annually due to its status as the island's highest mountain. Most of the technical routes are short compared to some other peaks in the neighbourhood but the remoteness of the Hinde puts alpine flavour to every ascent. There are some intriguing buttresses and gullies along the mountain's east face, the east face of the Comb and the peak at the far end of the north ridge.

First Ascent: Einar Anderson, W.R. Kent, 1913 or 14

First Winter Ascent: Robin Slieker, Philip Stone, Chris Barner 24 February 1993

Map Sheet: 92 F/12 Buttle Lake - GR 0104

Approaches: Climbers typically approach the Golden Hinde from Boliden-Westmin at the south end of Buttle Lake in the Myra Creek valley, via the Phillips Ridge Trail. Hike up the trail from the parking lot at Westmin to Arnica Lake. Continue westward along the height of land, following a well worn and marked route up through the treeline and higher ground. North of Peak 1732, Phillips Ridge takes a near 90° turn to the north. Follow the ridge crest northward and choose a route down to the Burman valley and Carter and Schjeldrup lakes to the west.

By far the best route is one of the least used, taking a descending traverse from the Phillips-Burman Pass down to Carter Lae. (See photo on page 238). From Carter Lake either hike up Mt. Buman's east ridge to the top and then descend Burman's north ridge to Burman Lake; or head over to Schjeldrup Lake and make an exposed traverse on a bench across Burman's north-east cirque to join the north ridge down to Burman Lake. In winter drop down into meadows below and to the north of Schjeldrup Lake to avoid avalanche exposure in the north-east cirque of Mt. Burman.

Golden Hinde north-east aspect from Mt. McBride, June.

The Golden Hinde may also be reached from Marble Meadows. Gain the ridge south of Morrison Spire and hike southward over Limestone Cap, Tibetan Mountain and Mt. Judy to a col at GR 0401. Descend west to the north shore of Schjelderup Lake and pick up the route up and down Mt. Burman's north ridge from there.

From either route head for the tiny canyon at the east tip of Burman Lake at the toe of Mt. Burman's north ridge. Pick up the well travelled route north-westward to a tarn at the base of the Golden Hinde's South Face. Expect to take on average two to three days to reach here.

The Hinde can also be reached from the Elk River Trail via Elk Pass and Mt. DeVoe. See descriptions for Rambler Peak and Mt. DeVoe. A complete traverse from Westmin to Elk River taking in an ascent of the Golden Hinde is a popular option.

Additional Info: IB 1994 p.35, IB 1996 p.6, IB 1998 p.18, IB 2001 p.27, WIM #1 p.10, WIM #9 p.9

Routes

SE- **South-East Couloir:** 4th class, AI1/2 250m (II)

The standard climb up the mountain and the fastest descent for other routes. Approach from the small tarn at the base of the South Face from either Burman Lake from the south or the south shoulder of the Behinde from Elk River and the north.

Head right (east) around the tarn and hike up snow/scree slopes to gain one of a number of gullies that lead out of the south basin and onto the South-East Ridge. Continue up traversing rightward to the base of the prominent South-East Couloir. Depending on seasonal snow cover climb steepening snow and/or rock ribs to the left and then right of the couloir until forced into the gully proper. Climb up the snow to steep boulders before the top.

FA: Einar Anderson, W.R. Kent, 1913 or 1914

Golden Hinde (R) & Behinde (L), south aspect from Schjelderup Lake, February.

Golden Hinde

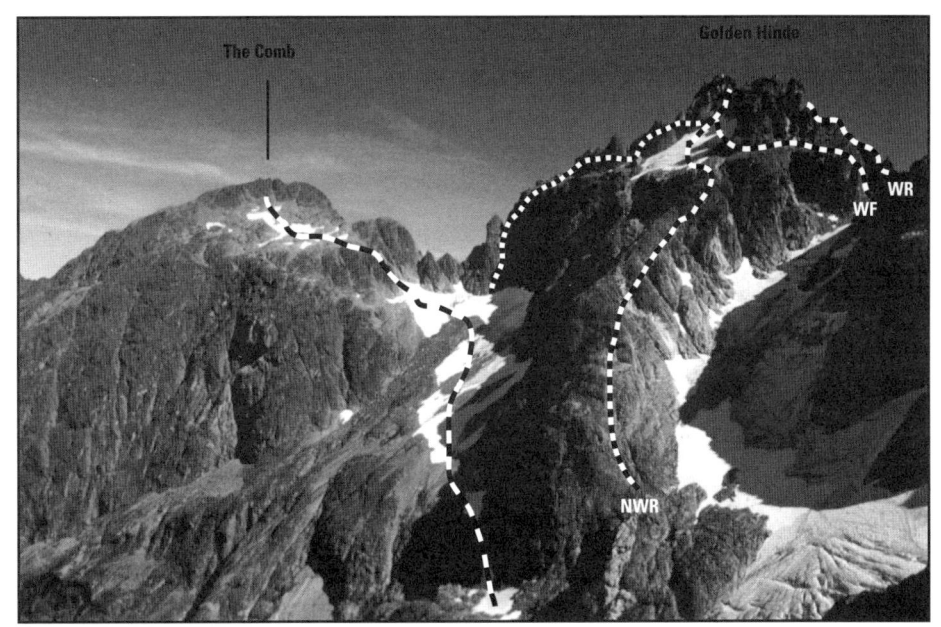

Golden Hinde, north-west aspect from North Glacier, September.

SF- South Face: 5.4 300m, 5pitches, (II)
Start up a left trending vegetated ramp at the left (west) side of the South Face following it to the end. Climb direct, crossing a leftward sloping corner through an obvious line of weakness to a ledge. Easy climbing heading right into a groove, continue up the groove then leave it left to another ledge. Head right to a band of granite and traverse farther right on a ledge which joins the West Ridge route above. Climb the granite to the base of a gully and head up the gully on to the West Ridge. Follow the ridge to the summit.
FA: Jim Sanford, J. Gresham, D. Newman, 30 July 1983

WR- West Ridge: 4th class 500m (II)
Climb from the toe of the ridge in the col between the Golden Hinde and Behinde starting up a short gully. Traverse snow/scree at the top of the gully and then up broken rock to the foot of a steep slab just right of the ridge crest. Easier climbing continues above, a pinnacle can be avoided on the right on a ledge on the South Face. Head right along this ledge to the base of a gully which can be climbed to return to the crest of the ridge. Follow the ridge crest to the summit.
FA: Dennis Davis, Brian Foan, John Gibson, Karl Lund August 31, 1969

WF- West Face: 4th Class 300m (II)
From the col between the Golden Hinde and Behinde descend in to the large glaciated cirque to the west of the Golden Hinde and drop around the toe of the West Ridge. Gain a line of weakness which leads up to a wide bench that can be traversed out onto the upper glacier. Climb the glacier to the narrow col just below the summit and scramble loose blocks to the top.
FA: Jim Rutter, Steve Smith, Tony Hunter June 30, 1978

NWR- Northwest Ridge: 4th Class 400m (II)
An excellent, straightforward route up the mountain on an impressive, low angle feature. Approach the Golden Hinde-Behinde col from the tarn below the South Face. From the col descend on to the west glacier keeping right close to the base of the rock cliffs. Start at the toe of the North-West Ridge.

Climb directly up the ridge crest with easy and fun 3rd class to the upper glacier. Continue up the glacier to a col just west of the summit. Climb through the col to the south-east side of the mountain. Finish up loose boulders on the south side of the mountain to the top. Descend same route or South-East Couloir.
FRA: John Roberts, October 1993

274 Chris Barner and Robin Slieker stop for a water break on route to winter ascent of the Golden Hinde

Golden Hinde (L) Behinde (C) & Mt. DeVoe (R) north-west aspect from Rambler Peak, August.

NR- **North Ridge:** upto 5.9 S 300m (III)
Approach from the Golden Hinde-Behinde col, descend on to the west glacier until a traverse can be made around the toe of the North-West Ridge. Hike up snow/scree to the col between the Comb and the North Ridge of the Hinde. Some superb climbing direct on the ridge crest from the col leads to easier ground and then a series of steep pinnacles. Traverse out on to the west side of the largest pinnacle and several stiff pitches above. From a saddle below a cluster of rotten boulders traverse right on to the upper glacier and climb a gully to a col below the summit. Finish up loose boulders to the top.
FA: Joe Bajan, Paul McEwan, August 1979

The Comb
6,693 ft. / 2040 m

The Comb is the high peak one kilometre north of the Golden Hinde's summit along the Hinde's north ridge. It is easily climbed from the col between the Behinde and the Golden Hinde and is a superb vantage point from which to view the surrounding terrain. From the Hinde-Behinde col, descend under the north-west face of the Hinde and then up a series of large snowfields on the south-west flank of the Comb toward the col that separates the Comb from the Golden Hinde. Just below the col trend left (north) up to the top of the Comb with a little 3rd class. (see photo page 263).

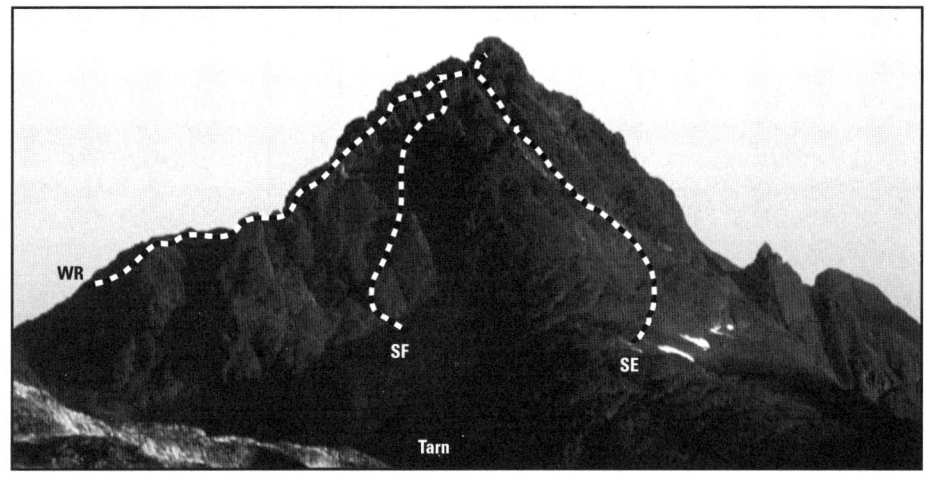

Golden Hinde south aspect from Mt. Tom Taylor, September.

Golden Hinde, east aspect from Mt. Washington, February.

Winter

South-East Couloir: AI2 250m (II)

Follows the standard South-East Couloir summer route from the tarn at the base of the South Face. The most practical approach in winter is via Phillips Ridge to Schjelderup Lake. Depending on conditions a number of options for descending off Phillips Ridge may be considered. Of note however is a route due west from the high point on the ridge at grid reference 0597 westward into the Burman valley. Head north up the valley through a flat meadow and across Carter Lake to reach Schjelderup Lake.

From Schjelderup Lake the normal summer route via Mt. Burman's north ridge is inadvisable and a less exposed alternative is to descend at the outlet of the lake 240m to a meadow at GR 0302. Cross the meadow then climb up a forested slope to the east snout of Burman Lake and the regular route. Gain the shoulder on the lower South-East Ridge from the tarn up one of a number of gullies. Cross the wide snowfield below the South-East Couloir and head up into the couloir. Dependng on snow conditions and cover, climb steep snow and exposed rock ribs. The couloir narrows and steepens higher up to a final step through a boulderfield and up to the summit. Descend same route.

FA: Chris Barner, Robin Slieker, Philip Stone 24 February, 1993.

Chris Barner, Robin Slieker, Philip Stone on the summit of the Golden Hinde on the first winter ascent.

The Behinde

The Behinde east aspect as seen from the Comb, October.

The Behinde
6,525 ft./ 1,989 m

The Behinde is a satellite peak of the Golden Hinde just to the west of the Island's highest mountain on the Burman-Wolf River divide. It is an impressive mountain from some aspects and basks in the glory of its larger sibling.

First Ascent: Mike Walsh 1966

Map Sheet: 92 F/12 Buttle Lake - GR 0004

Approaches: The Behinde may be reached by any of the approach routes to the Golden Hinde from Phillips Ridge, Marble Meadows or the Elk River. From the south, hike from the tarn below the South Face of the Golden Hinde north-west to the col between the hindes. Continue to the base of the South-East Ridge.

The base of the South-East Ridge may also be reached from the north. From Mt. DeVoe continue southward gaining the alpine ridge west of the Behinde. Follow the well trodden route along the crest of this ridge descending south-east at the south end of the ridge into a bushy alpine pass between the Wolf and Burman Rivers. Cross the pass and hike up the north-west of the Behinde to the shoulder on its south-west. Continue around to the base of the South-East Ridge which may be followed to the top on extremely loose rock.

The Behinde west aspect as seen from tarns on Ucona-Wolf divide, August.

Nine Peaks and Beauty Lake

Strathcona Park South

Greg Shea bouldering on the summit ridge of Mt. Tom Taylor.

Strathcona Park South
Contents

Mt. Myra	**285**
Mt. Thelwood	**287**
Peak 1805	**289**
Moyeha Mountain	**290**
Big Interior Mountain	**292**
Nine Peaks	**295**
Mt. Septimus	**296**
Mt. Rosseau	**298**
The Misthorns	**301**
Mt. Tom Taylor	**302**
Mariner Mountain	**306**
Ursus Mountain	**308**
Abco Mountain	**309**

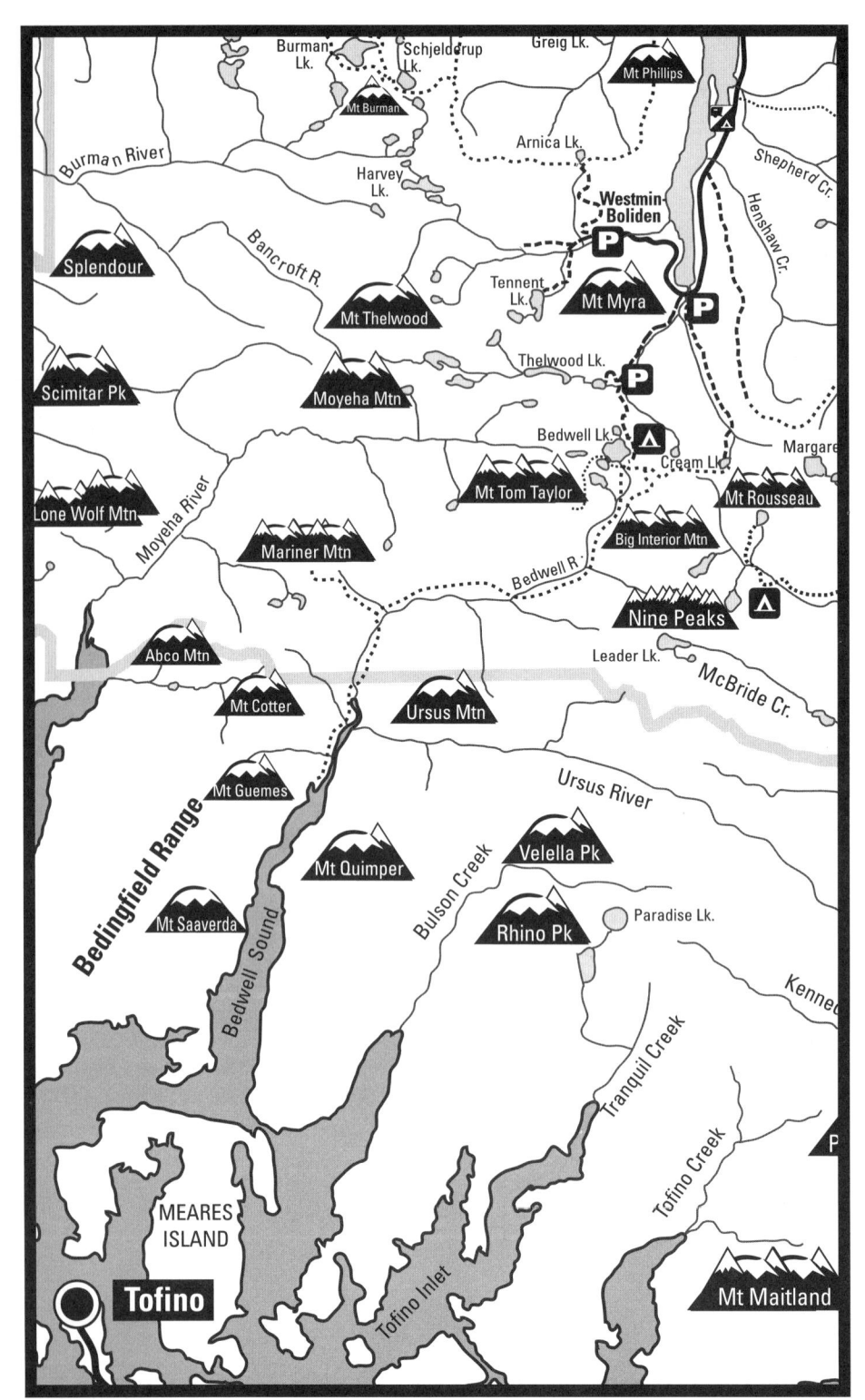

Strathcona Park South - Map

Strathcona Park South

The peaks of southern Strathcona Park have a unique character among Vancouver Island mountains. The majority of the peaks in this area are granitic batholiths shaped by heavy glaciation. The remnants of the once huge glaciers that carved the mountains and valleys still drape over the highest parts of the south Strathcona mountains and are some of the largest glaciers left on the Island. The close proximity of the Pacific Ocean at Clayoquot Sound and the long inlets, Bedwell Sound and Herbert Inlet bring moisture laden air in off the ocean replenishing the ice with massive winter snowfalls each year. Even in high summer it is not unusual for a salty mist to settle over Bedwell Lake.

The granite rock that gives these peaks their form also provides some excellent climbing. The Mt. Myra and Thelwood Creek area is simply littered with granite bluffs suitable for bouldering sessions around camp or packing a rope for some multi pitch lines. Mt. Tom Taylor's south face secrets the finest granite climbing on Vancouver Island with a series of impressive 1,000 ft / 300 m buttresses that have only a handful of routes and much more potential.

Curiously, there is an operating mine in this part of Strathcona although it is not technically within Strathcona Park per se, as the area around the mine has been designated a separate park Westmin-Strathcona. The mine's activities have had a significant impact on Myra Creek, Tennent Lake and Thelwood Creek with roads, dams, hydroelectric penstocks and of course some large, gaping holes in the ground. For the most part however, and particularly since noise reduction measures were taken with the installation of huge ventilation fans, the mine's presence does nothing to diminish the experience of visiting the exquisite alpine in this area.

Map Sheets: 92 F/12 Buttle Lake • 92 F/5 Bedwell River • 92 F/6 Great Central Lake

Boundaries: north: Myra Creek, **east:** Price Creek & Ash River, **south:** Ursus Creek & McBride Creek, **west:** Moyeha River & Herbert Inlet.

Major Access Routes: The main road access into southern Strathcona is **Buttle Lake Parkway** from Highway 28 at Buttle Narrows. Leave the highway at the Buttle Narrows junction and continue straight, southward, up the east shore of Buttle Lake. At the south end of the lake the road crosses a bridge above Thelwood Creek and then winds up into the Myra Creek valley where it runs right through the extensive mine facility to a well signposted parking lot.

Jim Mitchell Lake Road: At the south end of Buttle Lake on the west side of the Thelwood Creek bridge, just before the Parkway climbs the hill to the mine site in Myra Creek, a gravel road heads south into the Thelwood valley. The Jim Mitchell Lake Rd. services Westmin's hydro electric dam at Jim Mitchell Lake and the generating station lower down the valley. It is gated and usually open and clear through the summer but may be locked and unplowed during the winter. The road passes the Bedwell Lake trailhead and the provides access to the upper Thelwood valley from Jim Mitchell Lake.

Powerhouse Road: A much shorter gravel road continues past the parking lot at Westmin-Boliden to service the hydro electric facility on East Tennent Creek. This road is gated and even if open shouldn't be driven. It saves only a little time walking to the start of the Mt. Myra and Upper Myra Falls trails and doesn't compensate for the hassle of returning to your vehicle and finding the gate now locked. Park at the lot.

Trails

11- Price Creek: The Price Creek Trail is the historical route between Buttle Lake and Port Alberni. From the east side of the Thelwood Creek bridge, on the Buttle Lake Parkway, an old gravel logging and prospecting road heads south-east across the wide open lower Thelwood valley until narrowing into a trail and heading into the narrow Price Creek valley. The trail continues along the east bank of the creek, often up on the slope a hundred feet or so above the creek but occasionally dropping to follow the creek side. After 8 km the trail reaches a popular campsite and then crosses the creek. From here the trail continues up a steep hillside to eventually cross an open avalanche path under Mt. Septimus and make the final pull up to Cream Lake. The Price Creek Trail is no longer maintained by the Park's Dept. in deference to the more popular Bedwell Trail which now provides a cleaner line to Cream Lake. A circuit through these two trails is good option if you can deal with the gravel road from the Bedwell Trailhead to or from Buttle Lake. From the crossing of Price Creek, a rough route leaves the trail and heads up the upper part of Price Creek to Green Lake and Price Pass below the dramatic north-east face of Mt. Rousseau.

12- Bedwell Trail: The piece de resistance of Strathcona trails. The Bedwell Trail is a highly engineered route from the Jim Mitchell Lake Road to Bedwell Lake. Suspension bridges, boardwalks and even steel stairs combine to provide some of the fastest alpine access options in the park. From the west side of the Thelwood Creek bridge on Buttle Lake Parkway turn south onto the Jim Mitchell Lake Road. Drive for ~7 km to the clearly signposted trailhead and park. Hike the incredible trail up to Bedwell-Thelwood Pass and then on to the first campsite at Baby Bedwell Lake.

The trail continues along the south shore of Baby Bedwell Lake over a small ridge, and then down to Bedwell Lake. One of the approaches to Mt. Tom Taylor leaves the trail here crossing the creek that connects the two lakes. Follow the trail around the south shore of Bedwell Lake to a second campsite. From here the route to Cream Lake, Big Interior Mountain and Mt. Septimus leaves, as well as the Oinimitis trail down the Bedwell valley to the West Coast at Bedwell Sound.

13- Upper Myra Falls: Park at the lot at the west end of Westmin-Boliden. Walk down the gravel powerhouse road past the Phillips Ridge trailhead and to the start of the Upper Myra Falls trail just before the bridge over Myra Creek to the powerhouse. A short 40 minute hike through huge old growth forest leads to a lookout above the spectacular waterfall on the north fork of Myra Creek. This trail also starts the route up the Myra Creek valley to Mt. Thelwood which breaks off before the viewing platform to cross the north fork below the falls and above its confluence with the main south fork.

14- Mt. Myra: Park at the lot at the west end of Westmin. Walk down the gravel powerhouse road past the Phillips Ridge and Upper Myra Falls trailheads. Cross the bridge over Myra Creek to the powerhouse and locate the trailhead immediately on the other side of the bridge. The trail follows a steep cat road that Westmin used to construct the dam and penstock at Tennent Lake. The road is prone to erosion but recent work on the trail and alder clearing has improved it significantly.

Hike the trail up to the dam at Tennent Lake. To reach Mt. Myra follow the less distinct route which swings south-east to cross open meadows then climbs up a steep gully to Sandbag Lake and onto the south-west ridge of Mt. Myra. Alternatively, to head west toward Mt. Thelwood, bushwhack around the north side of Tennent Lake to gain a short bushy gully which leads up to more open meadows and lakes beyond. Continue on this ridge to Mt. Thelwood.

Forest Service & Mine Company Offices

Campbell River Forest District - 370 South Dogwood Street, Campbell River, B.C. V9W 6Y7 Ph: (250) 286-9300
Westmin-Boliden - 250-287-9271

Other Information Sources:

- **Hiking Trails III** - Northern Vancouver Island & Strathcona Park - (9th ed. 2002 Richard K. Blier, ed.) VITIS
- **Beyond Nootka** - A Historical Perspective of Vancouver Island Mountains by Lindsay Elms,
- **BC Parks web site:** http://wlapwww.gov.bc.ca/bcparks/explore/parkpgs/strathco.htm

Special Thanks:

Thanks to Lindsay Elms and Chris Barner for assistance in preparing this chapter.

Mt. Myra

Mt. Myra north-east aspect from Buttle Lake, June.

Mt. Myra
5,938 ft./ 1,810 m

Mt. Myra overlooks the south-west corner of Buttle Lake above the Westmin-Boliden mine in the lower Myra Creek valley. The mine's activities are concentrated both underground beneath Mt. Myra and above ground on its north and west flanks. Myra remains an excellent alpine hiking and climbing destination. It is an easy hike and scramble to the summit. The surrounding ridges and meadows are littered with short granite crags ideal for bouldering and sport climbing.

The Thelwood-Myra divide which runs west from Mt. Myra is a superb hiking route toward Mt. Thelwood and Moyeha Mountain with numerous lakes and granite crags for diversions en route. The terrain around the mountain makes an excellent ski touring destination and there are even a few waterfalls in the vicinity which freeze up in winter for some rare island waterice climbing.

First Ascent: W.R. Kent, W.W. Urquhart, Einar Anderson 1913 or 1914

Map Sheet: 92 F/12 Buttle Lake - GR 1190

Approaches: Best reached by the Mt. Myra Trail from Westmin-Boliden via Tennent Lake. Park at the signposted lot at the west end of the mine facility. Walk down the gravel road to the bridge over Myra Creek and locate the trailhead before the noisy powerhouse at the end of the road. The trail takes an old cat track steeply up the hillside to the dam at Tennent Lake which feeds the hydro electric powerhouse below. The route from the dam becomes less distinct (than a cat road!) and swings south-east to cross open meadows then climbs up a steep gully past Sandbag Lake and onto the south-west ridge of Mt. Myra. Follow the ridge keeping to its south side over a knoll and then down into a col below the final summit dome.

Myra may also be reached from the old road to the Westmin-Boliden ventilation shaft on the north-east flank of the mountain. The road leaves Jim Mitchell Lake Rd. just above the Thelwood Creek Powerhouse.

Mt. Myra (L) and connecting ridge to Mt. Thelwood (R) north-east aspect from Syd Watts Peak, August.

Mt. Myra north-west aspect from Phillips Ridge, February.

Routes

Hikers' Route: 3rd Class and or AI2 100m
Approach on the Mt. Myra Trail via Tennent Lake. From the col below the summit either scramble up an exposed gully right above the col or traverse further round to the south side of the summit and scramble up steep but less exposed ground to the summit.

NW - North-West Ridge: AI1 600m (III)
Leave the Mt. Myra trail before crossing the pipeline bridge over East Tennent Creek. Hike up the steep, timbered slope to gain open ground above. Continue along the crest of ridge to north glacier and on to the summit.

North Glacier: AI1 600m (III)
Approach from the ventilation shaft road, ascending the timbered slope up the north-east ridge to the north glacier. Walk up the glacier with some great exposure to the summit.

*** The Happy Warrior: WI4 90m
Takes the free falling waterfall just left (east) of the steep gully that the hikers route climbs to Sandbag Lake. The waterfall is the drainage from Sandbag Lake. Climbed in two pitches, the lower pitch varies from year to year and may fill out to a wide based pyramid by late season. The upper pitch takes a fantastic, slender ice pillar to a rock belay. Descend by rappel.
FA: Lyle Fast, Phil Stone, March 1990

Other Climbing: The Tenement Walls are hidden in trees on the north side of cat track just 200m before reaching Tennent Lake. A variety of ice climbs have been done from slabby ice to vertical pillars. The wall is ~30m high and looks to have incredible summer cragging potential as well. Higher up along the Mt. Myra trail, and especially on the granite knoll overlooking Sandbag Lake, numerous one and two pitch sport lines have been climbed.

Mt. Myra north-east aspect from Syd Watts Peak, August.

286   Mt. Myra

Mt. Thelwood

Mariner Mt. (L), Moyeha Mountain (C), and Mt. Thelwood (R) north aspect from Phillips Ridge, February.

Mt. Thelwood
5,679 ft./ 1,731 m

Mt. Thelwood is a dome-shaped, glaciated granite peak on the Myra-Thelwood Creek divide 9 km west of Mt. Myra. The hiking terrain along the connecting ridge from Tennent Lake and Mt. Myra is superb with a maze of granite crags and alpine lakes scattered along the way. Thelwood is one of the best 2-4 day objectives in Strathcona and is ideal on foot or on skis. The mountain and adjacent valley is named for Ethel Wood, wife of J.G. Wood M.L.A. for Port Alberni.

First Ascent: Norman Stewart survey party 1937

Map Sheet: 92 F/12 Buttle Lake - GR 0290

Approaches: The Tennent Lake trail provides quick access to Mt. Thelwood. Follow description under Mt. Myra to Tennent Lake then skirt the north shore of the lake and hike up a bushy gully to reach more open terrain and a long alpine ridge beyond McNish Lake. Continue west along the ridge crest or stay to the north side of the high knoll GR 0590 to Crystal Pass. From here Thelwood is a hike up steep snow or heather slopes. If heading west to Mt. Thelwood from Mt. Myra, follow the height of land between Carwithen and McNish lakes joining the route from Tennent Lake just west of McNish Lake.

Alternatively, as part of a horseshoe circuit, start up the Upper Myra Falls Trail and just 100m or so before the falls drop left, down to the junction of the two branches of Myra Creek. Cross the north branch (below the falls) to gain the toe of the ridge which separates the two branches. Hike up the crest of this ridge to a couple of skanky alpine pools where a camp is possible. Continue along the ridge as it turns south, until a traverse into the north-east cirque of Mt. Thelwood is possible. Hike up to the col at the back of the cirque between Mt. Thelwood and Peak 1805. From here Thelwood can be climbed via the north ridge, crossing the small glacier to reach the summit. Or from just above the skanky ponds traverse south to Crystal Pass and follow the description above from there. There is potential for some fine cragging in the north-east cirque of Mt. Thelwood.

Moyeha Mountain (L) & Mt. Thelwood (R) north-east aspect from Syd Watts Peak, August.

288 Lindsay Elms looking over the Thelwood valley toward Mt. Tom Taylor from the Thelwood-Myra divide.

Bancroft Peak

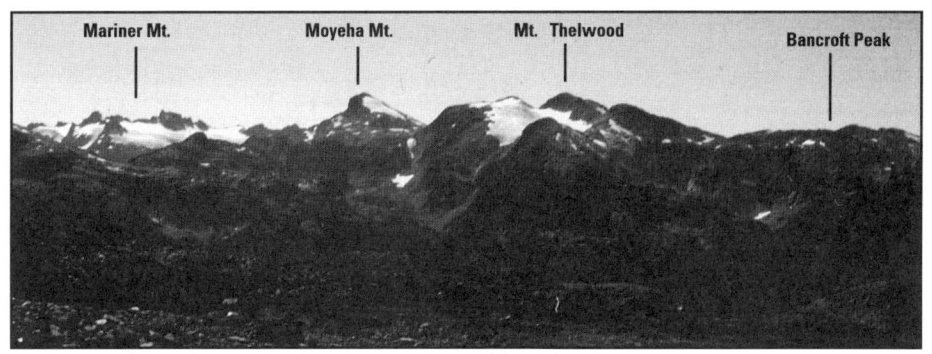

Mt. Thelwood (L) and Bancroft Peak north aspect from Phillips Ridge, October.

Bancroft Peak - 'Peak 1805'
5,265 ft./ 1,605 m ?

Spotting this peak on the topo you might think it was the 'big one that got way'! At 1,805 m this peak would be just shy of 6,000 feet ranking it up there with the highest of Island mountains. Sadly on closer inspection of the adjacent contours it seems that the '1805' is a typographical error (or is that a topographical error?) and it is probably closer to 1,605 m. Either that, or Peak 1805 is one heck of a spire, so slender as to be all but invisible! As it is, Bancroft Peak is a low granite dome three kilometres north of Mt. Thelwood offering open alpine terrain to explore on foot or on skis with a commanding view over the Bancroft and Burman valleys to the west.

First Ascent: Unknown

Map Sheet: 92 F/12 Buttle Lake - GR 0193

Approaches: Best reached from the route up the ridge between the two forks of Myra Creek off the Upper Myra Falls Trail. Follow the approach details for Mt. Thelwood to the col separating Mt. Thelwood from Bancroft Peak. Traverse north-westward under the cliff band until easier ground allows you to climb up to the open alpine plateau. Head across the plateau to a last short climb up to the summit. Other options which might be incorporated into a traverse of the peak include the east and north ridges. The Bedwell Lake - Burman Lake Traverse crosses this peak.

Additional info: Hiking Trails III

Mt. Thelwood east aspect from Flower Ridge, May.

Moyeha Mountain

Moyeha Mountain south aspect from Mariner Mountain, July.

Moyeha Mountain
5,918 ft./ 1,804 m

Moyeha Mountain sits at the head of three major drainages: the Moyeha River to its south, Thelwood Creek to the north and east and Bancroft Creek, a major tributary of the Burman River, to the north and west. The mountain sports twin granite buttresses on its south aspect and a distinctive convex glacier cloaks the north side. Moyeha Mountain is named for the river valley at whose head the peak sits. Despite the surrounding granite there is little in the way of good climbing on Moyeha Mountain.

First Ascent: Unknown

First Winter Ascent: Doug Wale 1999

Map Sheet: 92 F/12 Buttle Lake - GR 0188

Approaches: Moyeha Mountain is best climbed on its east and south-east flank. It is reached from the Thelwood-Myra Creek divide via the Mt. Myra Trail and Tennent Lake from Westmin-Boliden. Follow the approach description for Mt. Thelwood either as far as the small lake at GR 058903, from where a good route leads down to the east end of Upper Thelwood Lake and Greenview Lake, or continue to Crystal Pass from where a tricky & bushy descent may be made to the Mt. Thelwood-Moyeha Mountain col (Thelwood-Bancroft pass).

Moyeha Mountain north aspect from Mt. Col. Foster, August.

Moyeha Mountain north-east aspect from near Mt. Thelwood, September.

From the east end of Upper Thelwood Lake head south past Greenview Lake to a chain of small lakes in Moyeha's south-east cirque. The south-east cirque may also be reached from Crystal Pass via the Mt. Thelwood-Moyeha Mountain col. From the col make a wide traverse south-east in to the cirque.

Another alternative approach to Moyeha is from Jim Mitchell Lake right up the Thelwood valley. This has the benefit of close road access on the Jim Mitchell Lake Rd. from Buttle Lake Parkway but comes at a high price. The bushwhack up the Thelwood valley is a trying feat of endurance with sustained B3 throughout the valley. If the road is ploughed during winter or early spring and the lakes are still frozen this would be a perfect route for a ski approach.

East Ridge and North Glacier: AI1 500m (II)
Gain the mountain proper up a gully from the larger of the lakes in the south-east cirque or along the north-east ridge from the col to the north of the lake if approaching from Mt. Thelwood. Continue up with no technical difficulty along the East Ridge to the glacier. Enjoy the exposure and wild situation of this convex feature! Easier ground leads to the top.

South-East Gully: AI1/3rd class 500m (II)
An easy scramble up the gully between the twin buttresses on the south face. Snow or scree depending on the season. Approach directly from the south-east cirque.

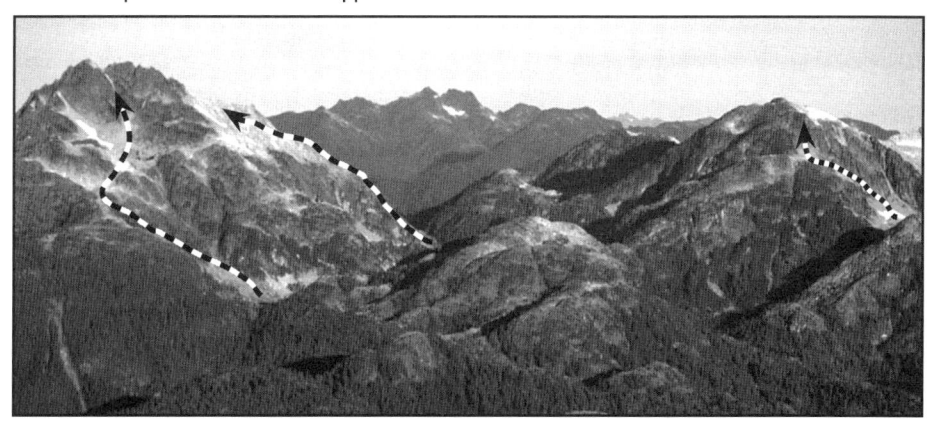

Moyeha Mountain (L) & Mt. Thelwood (R), south-east aspect from Mt. Tom Taylor, September.

Big Interior Mountain

Big Interior Mountain west aspect from Mt. Tom Taylor, September.

Big Interior Mountain
6,109 ft./ 1,862 m

Big Interior Mountain is located on the divide between the Bedwell River to its west and Drinkwater Creek to the east. Its glaciers have receded dramatically in recent years but it still retains some of the character of its glaciated neighbours. Big Interior is a popular summit due to its proximity to the Bedwell Trail. The mountain has a rich history of mining exploration and many artifacts and mine shafts litter its upper reaches. Big Interior Mountain is named for its character and location!

First Ascent: Joe Drinkwater 1899

Map Sheet: 92 F/5 Bedwell River - GR 1381

Approaches: By far the best way to reach Big Interior Mountain is from Buttle Lake via the Bedwell Trail. Drive from Campbell River up Highway 28 to Buttle Narrows. Pass the junction to Gold River leaving Highway 28 and continue south on the Buttle Lake Parkway along the shore of Buttle Lake. At the south end of the lake cross the bridge over Thelwood Creek and immediately turn left onto Jim Mitchell Lake Rd., a gravel road at the base of the hill which leads up to the Westmin-Boliden mine. This road services the hydro electric facility in Thelwood Creek which provides power to the mine and follows the creek up to Jim Mitchell Lake. Access to this road can be seasonal and it is often locked or left unplowed in winter.

Drive up the road for 6 km to the clearly signposted trailhead. Hike up the Bedwell Trail past the camp at Baby Bedwell Lake to the campsite at Bedwell Lake. From here a well marked route to Cream Lake leads south-east up a ridge to a gunsight notch, the Bedwell-Drinkwater Pass. Leave the route to Cream Lake and cross the creek to gain the ridge on the south side. Hike up the ridge on a well flagged and cairned route, trending right to locate a bench system which leads down into the base of the main north cirque below the north glacier.

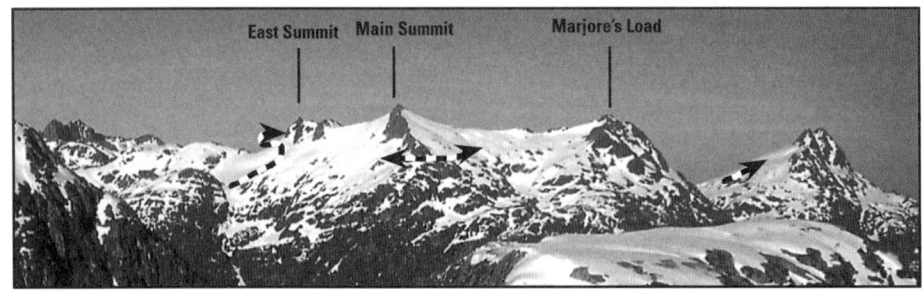

Big Interior Mountain and Nine Peaks (R) north-west aspect from Bedwell-Moyeha divide, June.

Big Interior Mountain north aspect from Bedwell Lake, September.

    The base of this cirque makes an excellent campsite. Cross the cirque and ascend the moraine to the toe of the glacier. Depending on seasonal snow cover, and resulting exposure, either traverse under the north side of the North-East Summit to less exposed ground on the south-east side of the ridge or in late season head directly up the glacier on the west side of the North-East peak to gain the ridge just below the main summit. It is a short, exposed hike to the summit along the ridge.

    Big Interior Mountain can also be reached from a point 2 km west of Cream Lake by traversing into a gully that leads up to a col at GR 148837. From here an opposing gully leads straight down to the base of the north cirque. The route up the north glacier can be picked up from there.

    The summit south of the mountaiin is called Marjore's Load. It is a sporting objective with some steep rock scrambling or a short steep climb up the small glacier/snowpatch on its north face. The mountain sweeps south-east past Marjore's Load to Bear Pass below the north side of Nine Peaks. Nine Peaks can be reached from here as can the picturesque Della Lake with a short descent from the pass. Della Lake is the source of Della Falls the highest waterfall in Canada. There is a rich history of mining around the lake and indeed all over Big Interior Mountain evidence of which can be seen scattered among the wildflowers.

    The elegant ridge that rises on the north side of Della Lake and sweeps around the mountain's south-east cwm to join the main summit ridge offers a superb route around the mountain via Della Lake (and with an optional side trip to Nine Peaks).

    There is also a treacherous but historic route up from the Drinkwater valley alongside Della Falls. Approach from Great Central Lake up the Della Falls Trail and locate the seriously exposed route on the left (south) side of the cascades.

Bedwell Lake from Mt. Tom Taylor, October.

Big Interior Mountain

294 Corrie Wright hiking near Cream Lake with Nine Peaks and Della Falls behind.

Nine Peaks

Nine Peaks north-west aspect from Bedwell-Moyeha divide, June.

Nine Peaks
6,043 ft / 1,842 m

Nine Peaks is the 'poster peak' of Strathcona Park having adorned the covers of brochures, magazines and posters promoting Strathcona Park for many years. The view of Nine Peaks from Cream Lake has to be considered the quintessential Strathcona vignette and the many hikers who make the trek each year will attest to its beauty. Nine Peaks is also source to the fabled Della Falls, reputedly the highest waterfall in Canada. At 440m, or over 1,500 feet, the falls in full flow are a sight to behold.

First Ascent: Unknown

Map Sheet: 92 F/5 Bedwell River - GR 1578

Approaches: The easiest approach to Nine Peaks is from Buttle Lake via the Bedwell Trail and Big Interior Mountain. It may also be approached from Great Central Lake via the Della Falls Trail. Leave the trail 9 km from the lake heading up the south-east ridge to the glacier. Pick up the Standard Route to the summit. Also may be reached from Bedwell Sound via the Bedwell Trail and You Creek to Bear Pass.

* Standard Route: AI1 3rd class
From Bear Pass ascend the glacier to the short gully on the west side of the summit (third from west), care with bergschrunds in summer. Scramble up rock steps to summit and awesome views!

ST- *** Summit Traverse: 5.6 600m (III)
A highly recommended traverse across all nine summits. Approach from Bear Pass up the west edge of glacier. First Summit is hard to reach. Continue over all nine summits with some sharp pinnacles in between. A couple of rappels required including from Main Summit.
FA: Chris Barner, Paul Rydeen, Darren Wilman, Nick Elson, August 2001

Nine Peaks north-east aspect from Syd Watts Peak, August.

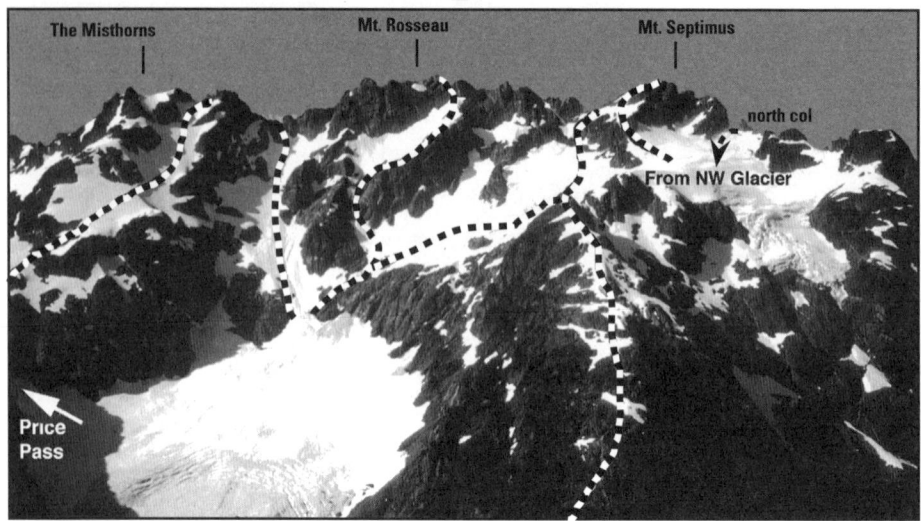

Mt. Septimus

Mt. Septimus and Mt. Rosseau north-east aspect from Flower Ridge, August.

Mt. Septimus
6,070 ft./ 1,850 m

Mt. Septimus-Rosseau is the most dramatic alpine feature in southern Strathcona. A craggy series of summit pinnacles rise in a fin form, dropping steeply off into deep glaciated cirques on all sides. The massif rises between the Ash River and Price Creek to the north and Drinkwater Creek and Great Central Lake to the south. Mt. Septimus offers some excellent alpine climbing in striking surroundings. Septimus is named after Septimus Evans, a surgeon on the S.S. Beaver.

First Ascent: Unknown

Map Sheet: 92 F/5 Bedwell River - GR 1783

Approaches: The most direct approach to Mt. Septimus is up the Bedwell Trail from Buttle Lake to Cream Lake and from there up the North-West Glacier to either the north col or the west shoulder.

Alternatively, approach via the Price Creek Trail to Green Lake, where the lower north-east ridge, North Face of Mt. Rosseau and the Misthorns can be reached. Cream Lake, the Septimus Glacier and routes on the west side of the massif may also be reached from the Price Creek Trail.

Additional Info: IB 1996 p.19, IB 2000 p.11

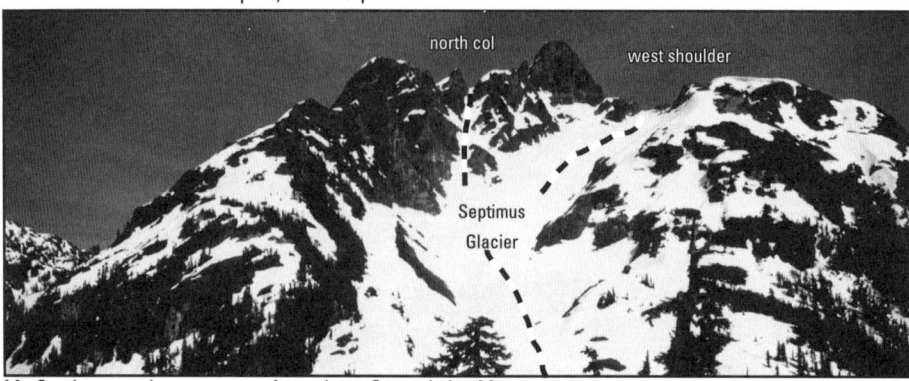

Mt. Septimus north-west aspect from above Cream Lake, May.

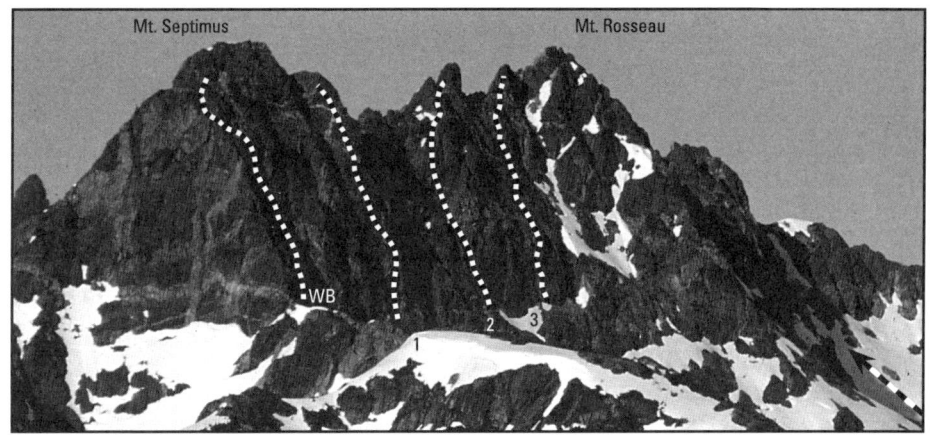

Mt. Septimus & Mt. Rosseau west aspect from Bedwell-Moyeha divide, June.

Routes

WB - ** **West Buttress:** low 5th Class, 300m as 5-6 pitches, (III)
From the west shoulder climb the prominent buttress crest direct to a subsidiary summit. It is difficult to reach the actual summit from here. Descend by rappelling and downclimbing the route.
FA: Unknown

1 - **Route 1:** 5.7 225m (II)
Hard climbing up the prow of an areté to the small summit south of Septimus from where an easy traverse can be made to the top.
FA: Chris Barner 1985

2 - **Route 2:** 5.4 200m (II)
Great scrambling up gullies and grooves to a sharp pinnacle summit.
FA: Chris Barner 1985

3 - **Route 3:** 5.6 225m (II)
Takes a wandering line up steps and ledges to the sharp summit north of Rosseau.
FA: Chris Barner 1985

** **North Glacier Route:** AI2, 800m (III)
From Cream Lake hike up the Septimus Glacier to the base of the steep gully that breaks off prominently to the left halfway up the glacier. Climb steep snow AI2, or nasty loose scree to the north col and the north glacier. Continue up and across the glacier heading south-east to an upper snowfield or rock slab and the summit. The lower north ridge can also be reached at Green Lake.

Septimus-Rosseau Traverse: 4th Class 1,700m
Originally started from Price Pass up the Misthorn Glacier to the Misthorn summits. Head north keeping to the exposed ridge crest on rotten rock. Bypass difficulties on the west side. One rappel north of the summit of Rosseau. Great views of the surrounding glaciers and Green Lake. First ascentionists descended from Septimus down North Glacier to Green Lake but other routes are possible.
FA: Paul Rydeen, Darren Wilman, Jim Tansky September 1999

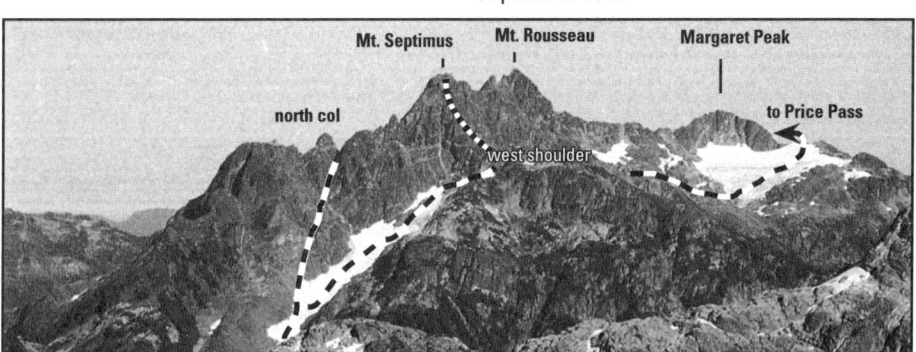

Mt. Septimus & Mt. Rosseau west aspect from Mt. Tom Taylor, September.

Mt. Rosseau

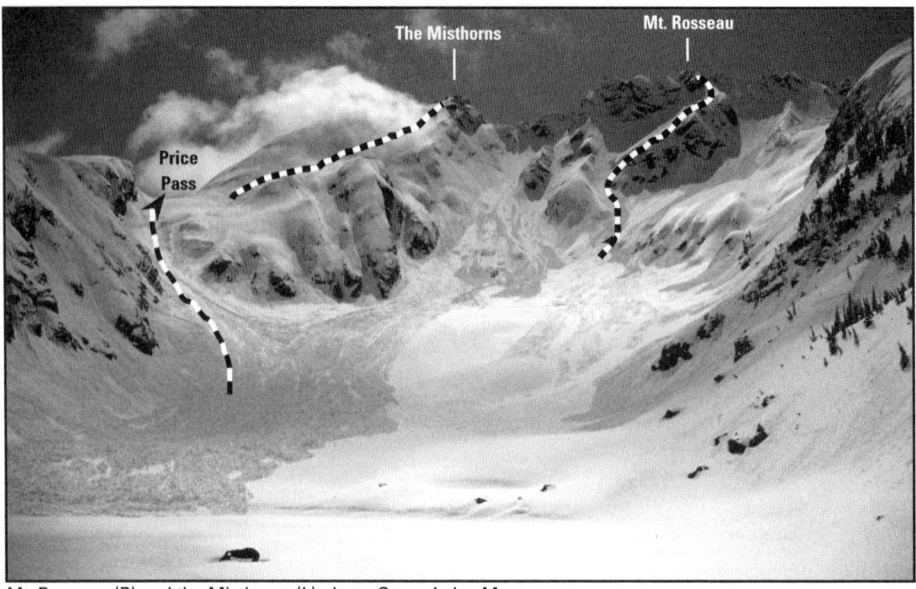

Mt. Rosseau (R) and the Misthorns (L) above Green Lake, May.

Mt. Rosseau
6,437 ft./ 1,962 m

Mt. Rosseau is the highest summit on the Septimus-Rosseau massif and is located south of Price Creek and to the north of the Drinkwater Creek valley. The summit is a much less difficult climb than Mt. Septimus which is probably why it seems overshadowed by its smaller neighbour to the west. A complete circuit around the massif from Cream Lake over the west shoulder across to the south cirque of Mt. Rosseau, up the pocket glacier to the toe of the south-east ridge and around to the glacier above Margaret Lake and Price Pass and Green Lake to finish is a superb alpine trip allowing each of the summits on the massif to be climbed. The mountain is named for Ralph Rosseau an early Port Alberni mountaineer who died on the peak in 1954.

First Ascent: Unknown

Map Sheet: 92 F/5 Bedwell River - GR 1883 (see also 92 F/ Great Central Lake)

Approaches: Mt. Rosseau may be reached from any of the Mt. Septimus approaches. From the west shoulder a long traverse may be made across an open snow-scree slope above Love Lake to a cirque below the South Face of Mt. Rosseau. A pocket glacier on the Misthorns north-west side feeds a small tarn which makes a perfect base from which to reach the South-West Gullies.

The north side of Mt. Rosseau may be approached from either the Price Creek or Flower Ridge trails to Green Lake.

Mt. Rosseau - Mt. Septimus north-east aspect from Beaufort Range, June.

Mt. Septimus (L) & Mt. Rosseau (far R) south-east aspect from Margaret Peak, July.   photo: Sandy Briggs

Routes

* South-West Gullies: low 5th Class, 350m (II)
From the south cirque ascend easier lower slopes to steeper gullies which gradually focus into one major gully. This gully's top is at a narrow col between Rosseau and a pinnacle to the east. Head left (west) up a final steep scramble to the very exposed summit.

**North-East Ridge: AI 1, 4th class, 350m (II)
Climbs directly up an arcing ridge and glacier above Green Lake to the summit.
FRA: Sandy Briggs, Don Berryman, 1 July 1980

C.O.L.T. students on glacier below Margaret Peak.

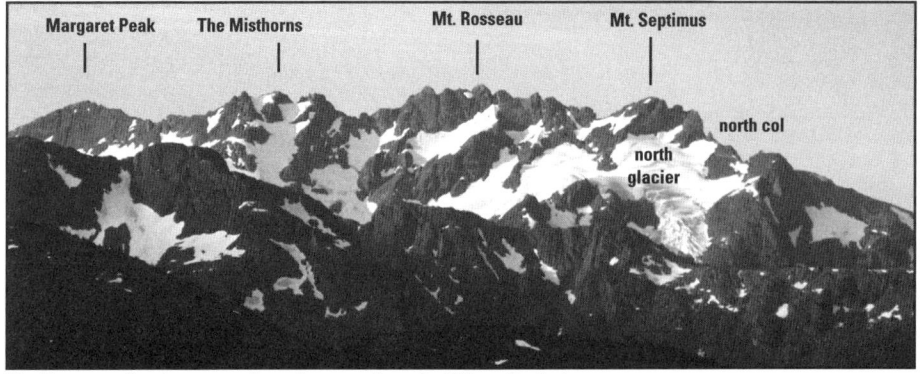

The Rosseau -Septimus massif north aspect from Syd Watts Peak, August.

Mt. Rosseau   299

Chris Motlock and Nikolai Galadza setting camp in a November downpour.

The Misthorns

The Misthorns north-east aspect from Central Crags, Flower Ridge, June.

The Misthorns
6,168 ft./ 1,880 m

The Misthorns are a group of 'generic' summits just east of Mt. Rosseau overlooking Price Pass and Green Lake. The Misthorn Glacier is one of the steeper such icefields on the Island and a fun summer climb.

First Ascent: Unknown

Map Sheet: 92 F/ Great Central Lake - GR (see also 92 F/5 Bedwell River)

Approaches: Approach the Misthorn Glacier from either Green Lake or Price Pass, (see Mt. Rosseau approaches). The steeper south side may be reached from Cream Lake and the west shoulder of Mt. Septimus. Follow the approach details for Mt. Septimus & Mt. Rosseau South-West Gullies. From the tarn south of Mt. Rosseau head directly up the pocket glacier and moraine to the South Face.

Misthorn Glacier: AI1, low 5th class, 300m, (II)
From Price Pass head directly up to the toe of the glacier. Traverse right into the main glacier chute that leads up to a col between the two summits. Scramble onto either summit with some exposed low 5th class moves.

Margaret Peak & Great Central Lake north-west aspect from Mt. Rosseau, September.

The Misthorns **301**

Mt. Tom Taylor

Mt. Tom Taylor main summit north-east aspect from east end of summit ridge July.

Mt. Tom Taylor
5,833 ft./ 1,778 m

Mt. Tom Taylor is a beautiful, glaciated mountain at the eastern end of the Moyeha-Bedwell River divide. Its symmetrical form of gentle sweeping arm-like ridges and cloak of glacial ice are a familiar sight from many peaks to the north in Strathcona Park. The short exposed granite towers on the north side of the summit ridge belies the splendid granite buttresses that are secreted on the south side of the peak. Mt. Tom Taylor has become a popular climb from Bedwell Lake.

First Ascent: Unknown

Map Sheet: 92 F/5 Bedwell Lake - GR 0883

Approaches: Mt. Tom Taylor may be approached from Bedwell Lake via the Bedwell Trail from Jim Mitchell Lake Road. From the inlet of the short creek draining Baby Bedwell Lake into Bedwell Lake cross the creek and hike up through the forested hillside to below a knoll overlooking an unnamed alpine lake at GR 1085. Continue up the south-east ridge on open granite bluffs to the snowfield and summit ridge above.

To reach the main summit continue along the crest of the summit ridge at class 3, move to the glacier and cross the snow/ice above the south ridge then regain the summit ridge before the pinnacle just east of the main summit. Descend slightly into the east col at the toe of the final east ridge. From here the south face, main summit and western half of the Taylor Glacier can all be reached.

Mt. Tom Taylor north aspect from near Mt. Myra, July.

Mt. Tom Taylor south aspect from Big Interior Mountain, October.

Alternatively, from the campsite at Bedwell Lake hike a few hundred metres down the Oinimitis Trail south-west toward Bedwell Sound. Leave the trail and head north to cross the Bedwell River just below its outlet from Bedwell Lake. Pick up a flagged route which leads around into the lower south cirque of Mt. Tom Taylor. Cross the meadows at the base of the cirque to gain the lower end of the sweeping South Ridge. After a bushy start, hike up the open ridge keeping close to the crest as the ridge steepens. Some class 3 leads to a seasonal snow/scree slope that can be hiked to join the summit ridge and the Taylor Glacier on the north side of the mountain. Continue west to the col just east of the main summit.

Routes

East Ridge: low 5th class, 100m, (I)
From the col just east of the Main Summit climb exposed rock ribs and gullies on the crest of the East Ridge. An exposed traverse left leads to easier moves up the final steps above the South Face

North Face: AI2, low 5th class. 150m (I)
From the col just east of the Main Summit descend onto the Taylor Glacier down the wide glacial chute and westward underneath the north side of the Main Summit. Climb back up the glacier to reach the base of some exposed rock steps, 4th class up rock and seasonal snow patches to the summit.

C.O.L.T. students on the Taylor Glacier, September

Mt. Tom Taylor north-east aspect from Baby Bedwell Lake, June.

304 Greg Shea leads off the first pitch of Indian Summer, Mt. Tom Taylor

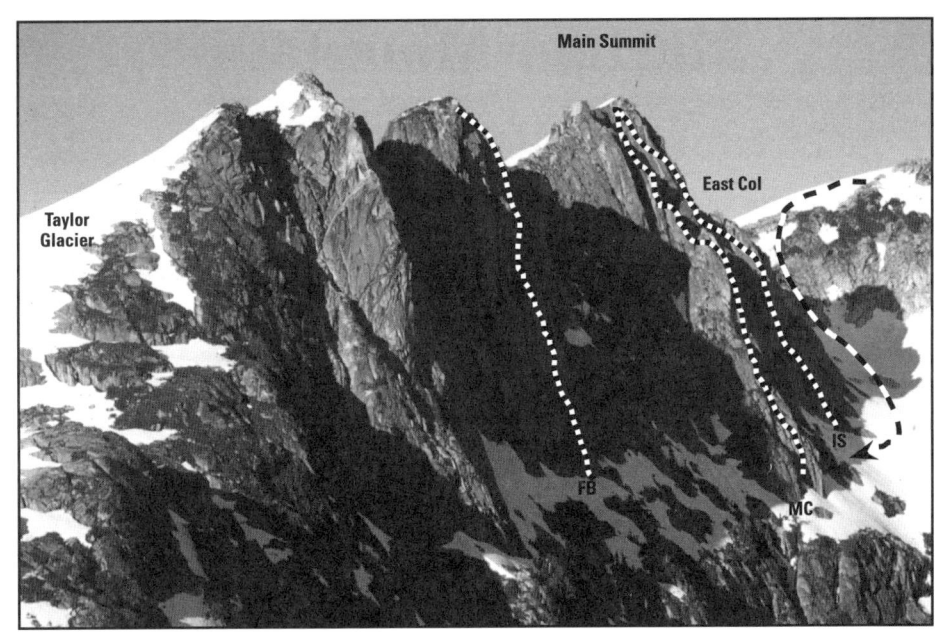

Mt. Tom Taylor South Face southwest aspect from near Mariner Mountain, June.

South Face: The steep granite buttresses that drop off the south face of Mt. Tom Taylor and the pinnacles west of the summit have some of the finest granite climbing on Vancouver Island. The base of the South Face is easily reached from the east col below the main summit. From the col, descend snow or scree to the bottom of a shallow cirque. Traverse south-west out of the cirque on a narrow snow-scree slope beneath the buttresses.

IS- ** Indian Summer: 5.9 300m (II)
Climbs the buttress below the main summit on the mountain's south face. Start at the foot of the righthand (easternmost) buttress. Climb 4 pitches with well protected cracks and corners to some positive, runout face above. A wide ledge marks the end of the difficulties and an optional finish to the route by traversing off right to the east col. To continue on to the main summit climb up directly from the ledge with easier class 4 scrambling.
FA: Greg Shea, Phil Stone, September 1998.

MC- ** Peering Through the Meat Curtain: 5.10 350m (II)
The route takes a sharp buttress line just left of Indian Summer to the main summit. Start at an obvious fist-sized crack that goes straight up for 15-feet and then angles dramatically to the right with increasing difficulty. Continue climbing on the buttress crest to an impressive right-facing dihedral. Climb the dihedral then step out onto the face and climb an easier crack to 4th class ground onto the summit above.
FA: Andrew Findlay, Ned Habedus, July, 2002

FB- ** Finnagan's Buttress: 5.9 300m (II)
Start at the toe of the prominent middle buttress west of the main summit. Climb a short right facing corner to gain a long chimney stemming on spectacular chicken heads 5.8. Climb steep cracks above belay for 10m then angle up and right over 5.8 face moves to belay at base of steep left facing corner. Jam and stem up beautiful corner 5.9. Higher easier ground & belay on large ledge below a white scar on south-east face of buttress. Follow obvious easiest broken ground through blocks and cracks 5.6. Continue following main weakness over broken ground into a narrowing gulley/chimney to a belay below two cracks 5.8. Avoid obvious overhanging corner, angling left on fantastic cracks and face. A short pitch on positive holds and cracks leads to the summit ridge.
FA: Jan Neuspiel, Andrew Findlay, 5 August, 1998.

Mariner Mountain

Mariner Mountain north-east aspect from Flower Ridge, May.

Mariner Mountain
5,833 ft./ 1,778 m

Mariner Mountain is a heavily glaciated and sprawling mountain situated on the Moyeha-Bedwell River divide west of Mt. Tom Taylor. The glaciers cloaking Mariner are probably the largest on Vancouver Island this and its proximity to the west coast make Mariner one of the most attractive peaks in Strathcona Park. Mariner Mountain is clearly visible from Tofino and around Clayoquot Sound where its south glacier (one of very few such south facing icefields) dominates the inland skyline.

First Ascent: Norman Stewart survey party 1938

Map Sheet: 92 F/5 Bedwell River - GR 9982

Approaches: Mariner Mountain may be reached from the Bedwell River valley via an old miners trail in Noble Creek. From Bedwell Sound, which may be reached from Tofino by air or sea, hike up the Oinimitis trail which runs initially up the north side of Bedwell River. After 9 km locate the Noble Creek trail. Noble Creek may also be reached from Buttle Lake via the Bedwell Lake Trail 15 km down river from Bedwell Lake.

Hike up Noble Creek northward through forest then into a deep moraine covered cirque. Continue hiking up the scree to a col at GR 9980. From here depending on the season either snow or open rock slabs lead up to the south glacier. Ascend the glacier to a col between the two main peaks.

Mariner may also be reached from Mt. Tom Taylor along the connecting ridge with one major descent through a pass between the Bedwell and Moyeha valleys. This is a superb 2-4 night trek, taking in some of the best of the glaciated terrain in southern Strathcona Park.

Mariner Mountain north-east aspect from Syd Watts Peak, August.

Mariner Mountain east aspect from Bedwell-Moyeha divide, June

Routes

North Face: AI 1 3rd class
From the south glacier hike through the col between the main summit and the east peak to the Mariner Glacier. Traverse around to the north side of the main summit and climb it on easy snow, or bare rock in later season.

South Face: 4th class
Approach the south face directly from Noble Creek up the south glacier. Climb a shallow gully to the summit.
FA: K. Denman, R. Eppler, P. Erickson, R. MacDonald, July 1985

Additional Info: IB 1992 p.18, WIM #7 p.10

Mariner Mountain east peak north-east aspect.

Mariner Mountain south-west aspect from Tofino, April.

Mariner Mountain **307**

Ursus Mountain

Ursus Mountain north-west aspect from Noble Creek, June

Ursus Mountain
4,826 ft./ 1,471 m

Ursus Mountain sits in the north crux of the meeting of the Ursus Creek and Bedwell River valleys. It has superlative views of Bedwell Sound and Mariner Mountain which is opposite Ursus Mountain across the Bedwell valley.

First Ascent: Unknown

Map Sheet: 92 F/5 Bedwell River - GR0375

Approaches: Reaching Ursus Mountain is directed by the path of the Bedwell (Oinimitis) Trail (see approach details for Big Interior Mountain as far as Bedwell Lake). Continue past Bedwell Lake on the signposted trail toward Bedwell Sound. Just before Ashwood Creek the old road the trail follows crosses Bedwell River. You can leave the trail here and thrash along the river bank crossing Blaney Creek. Strike up the hillside west of Blaney Creek to gain a horseshoe ridge which wraps around to the summit of Ursus Mountain.

Alternatively, and if approaching from Tofino by way of Bedwell Sound, leave the Bedwell Trail at GR 0177 and head northeastward up a forested ridge directly to the summit.

Ursus Mountain (C) and Bedwell River valley north-east aspect from Big Interior Mountain, September.

Abco Mountain

Abco Mountain north-east aspect from Mariner Mountain South Glacier, June.

Abco Mountain
5,006 ft./ 1,526 m

Abco Mountain is located south-west of Mariner Mountain on the Bedwell-Moyeha divide overlooking the head of Herbert Inlet. It is the highest point in the **Bedingfield Range** which runs along the west shore of Bedwell Inlet and includes **Mt. Cotter**, **Mt. Guemes** and **Mt. Saavedra**. The mountain is named for the American British mining company which operated its claim in Cotter Creek to the south of the mountain.

First Ascent: Unknown

Map Sheet: 92 F/5 Bedwell River - GR 9378

Approaches: Abco Mountain may be reached from Tofino by air or boat to Moyeha Bay at the head of Herbert Inlet. On the east side of the inlet head, Cotter Creek drains into Moyeha Bay. Try your luck locating old mining roads and trails up Cotter Creek. 2 km east from the inlet Abco Creek joins Cotter Creek. Follow Abco Creek north into a cirque east of the summit. From the stunning lake in the base of the cirque climb to a col north of the summit. Head south up to the summit.

Abco Mountain may also be reached from the Bedwell River valley via Noble Creek and the approaches to Mariner Mountain including a complete traverse from Mt. Tom Taylor along the Bedwell-Moyeha divide. Follow the approach descriptions for Mt. Tom Taylor and Mariner Mountain to the Noble-Mariner col at GR 9980. Head south over the jagged summit south of the col or avoid it by traversing on the west side. Turn south-west and then west keeping to the height of land over several alpine knolls. Drop down to the lake in the high cirque at the head of Abco Creek to avoid some rocky pinnacles on the ridge crest. From the lake climb back up to the col north of the summit. Head south on the north ridge to the summit.

The Bedingfield Range and Bedwell Sound north-east aspect from near Mt. Tom Taylor, June.

310 Corrie Wright en route to Splendour Mountain, Matchlee Bay

Strathcona Park West

Scimitar and Scissors Peak from near Mariner Mountain.

Strathcona Park West
Contents

Mt. Donner	317
Matchlee Mountain	318
Quatchka Ridge	321
Mt. Kent - Urquhart	322
M.S. Mountain	323
Popsicle Peak	323
Splendour Mountain	324
Scimitar Peak	325
The Scissors	326
Hygro Peak	326
Lone Wolf Mountain	327
Shelbert Mountain	327
Jacklah Mountain	328
Megin Mountain	328
Pretty Girl Peak	328
Sydney Cone	328
Mt. Gore	329
Mt. Rufus	329
Mt. Crespi	329
Mt. Albemarie	329
Mt. Lombard	329

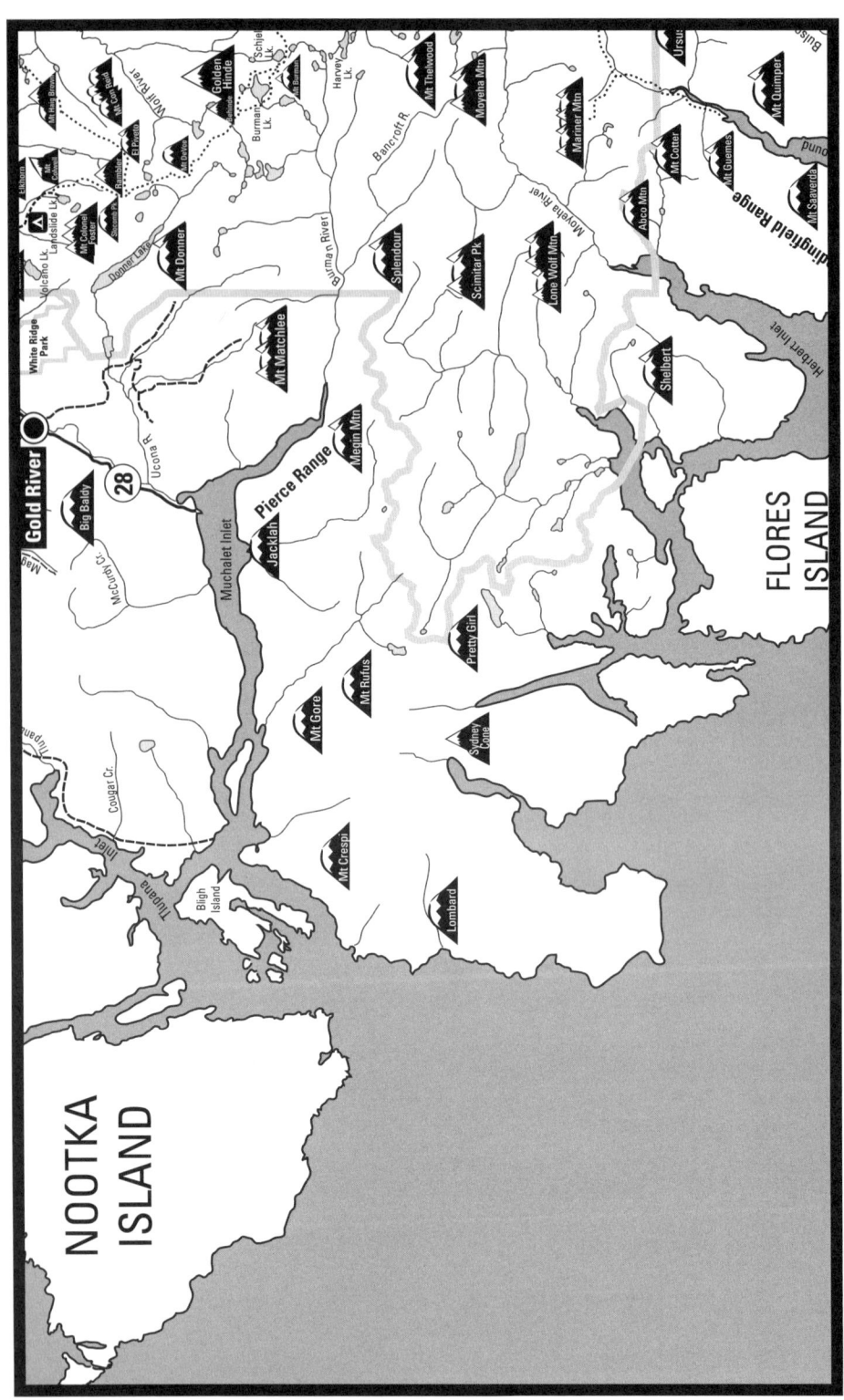

314 Strathcona Park West - Map

Strathcona Park West

The western region of Strathcona Park is some of the more remote territory within the park with few road links to the rest of Vancouver Island. Although logging roads do cover much of the region west of the park boundary they are isolated other than access by water or air. The area features vast tracts of old growth forest in some of the last remaining intact watersheds on Vancouver Island namely the Megin and Moyeha valleys. With the exception of Matchlee Mountain and the peaks close to Gold River the mountains of western Strathcona are rarely visited and offer one of the most remote wilderness experiences on the Island.

The alpine peaks of interest in this area are concentrated in three areas 1) west of Donner Lake centred around Matchlee Mountain, 2) a linked ridge system running south from Matchlee Bay and Splendour Mountain to Lone Wolf Mountain and Moyeha Bay at the head of Herbert Inlet, and 3) the mountains on the peninsula between Nootka and Clayoquot sounds. Such close proximity to the west coast and open Pacific Ocean gives these mountains a special character with spectacular views down long inlets to Nootka and Clayoquot Sounds.

Map Sheets: 92 F/12 Buttle Lake • 92 F/5 Bedwell River

Boundaries: north: Gold River, **east:** Kowus Creek, Ucona River , **south:** Moyeha River & Herbert Inlet, **west:** Pacific Ocean

Major Access Routes: The only way to access the western part of Strathcona Park is by air or water or to make a long overland traverse from access points in Strathcona off Highway 28 or the Buttle Lake Parkway. There are no roads linking the region to the main highway system on Vancouver Island. This of course adds immeasurably to the allure of the region The best options for reaching the area are water taxi or floatplane from either Tofino to the south or Gold River to the north.

From Tofino fly or boat into Shelter Inlet to the mouth of the Megin River. The Megin River can be followed up to Megin Lake on a rough trail. In late summer a canoe or kayak can be lined up the river to the lake.

From Gold River, fly or boat into Matchlee Bay which is closer and less expensive than travel from Tofino. From the old log dump on the north side of the bay pickup the old overgrown logging road and follow it along the bank of the Burman River. In low water a canoe or kayak can be lined up the Burman River with relative ease.

Forest Service & Logging Company Offices:

Campbell River Forest District - 231 Dogwood Ave. Campbell River BC V9W 2Y1 Ph: 287-2194

Western Forest Products -#118 – 1334 Island Hwy. Campbell River, BC V9W 8C9 Ph: 250 286-3767

Other Information Sources:

• **Hiking Trails III** - Northern Vancouver Island & Strathcona Park - (9th ed. 2002 Richard K. Blier, ed.) VITIS

• **Written By The Wind** by Randy Stoltmann

Special Thanks:

Thanks to Sandy Briggs for assistance in preparing this chapter.

Fred Put on the North West Ridge of Matchlee Mountain. photo: John Put

Mt. Donner

Mt. Donner (L) & Mt. Kent-Urquhart (R) north aspect as seen from Puzzle Mountain, June.

Mt. Donner
5,948 ft./ 1,812 m

Mt. Donner overlooks the south west shore of Donner Lake opposite the west face of Mt. Colonel Foster. During much of the year Donner is adorned with a long open snow field that cloaks its north east slopes enticing skiers but foiling them with the tricky access.

First Ascent: W.R. Kent, W.W. Urquhart, Einar Anderson, 1913 or 1914

Map: 92 F/12 Buttle Lake - GR 9107

Approaches: Donner may be reached from logging roads in the Pamela Creek valley which run along the mountain's west flank.

The west terminus of the Elk River Timber Co. road is in the high hanging valley between Donner Lake and Pamela Creek at the Strathcona Park boundary. The E.R.T. Ucona Rd gives access to the long north west ridge above Donner Lake (see photo below) and the upper part of the valley which continues up to Mt. Donner on the west flank. Reaching the E.R.T. Ucona Rd from Kunlin and Donner Lakes has been difficult for some time since the Heber River bridge was removed and the spur logging road which links it to Gold River and the Ucona Road (U-7) is in poor condition.

Mt. Donner & Donner Lake east aspect from Mt. Colonel Foster.

Matchlee Mountain

Matchlee Mt. east aspect from Mt. Colonel Foster, August

Matchlee Mountain
5,925 ft / 1,806 m

Matchlee Mountain is found on the Ucona-Burman River divide, south of the community of Gold River, at the head of Quatchka Creek. Its glaciated summit plateau is surrounded by steep rock buttresses that provide some fine alpine routes. Through the 1980s, then Gold River residents, John & Fred Put built excellent access trails and established some fine climbs on Matchleee. The peak and surrounding area was subsequently added to Strathcona Park. The name is a derivative of 'Muchalet' the name of the nearby inlet and means 'fish on top of water' referring to the historical salmon runs of the area.

First Ascent: Norm Stewart survey party 1938

First Winter Ascent: Rick Johnson, John Gresham, Don Newman, January 1987

Map Sheet: 92 F/12 Buttle Lake - GR 8501

Approaches: From Gold River, head south on the Ucona Road and follow it into the Quatchka Creek valley. Near the end of the road look for a rough path leading down into a small stand of old-growth around the creek. In this stand pick up the overgrown Matchlee trail and follow it through thick bush into an avalanche basin below the mountain. Two options lead up to the glacier. To the left a long wide snow/scree gully and to the right a narrow trail which winds up an exposed rock rib and steep forest to the glacier above.

Matchlee Mt. east aspect from Mt. Colonel Foster north col, August

Matchlee Mt. east aspect from Mt. Colonel Foster, May

Routes

E- * East Ridge: 5.6 350m (II)

The East Ridge sweeps off the main summit to a col with the East Peak. Avoid a steep section on the left to start. Return to ridge crest, climbing face and over ledges. Continue up a 5.5 slab and blocky rock to a chimney and a distinctive band of rock above. From here easier climbing leads to the summit.
FA: John Put, Fred Put, 1983

NB- *** North Buttress: 5.7 250m (III)

Begin at the base of the prominent buttress up cracks and face on the prow of the buttress. Pass a series of ledges to several pitches of grooves and corners keeping just left of the crest. A groove leads to a series of flakes and easier ground to the top.
FA: John Put, Fred Put, 6 July, 1985

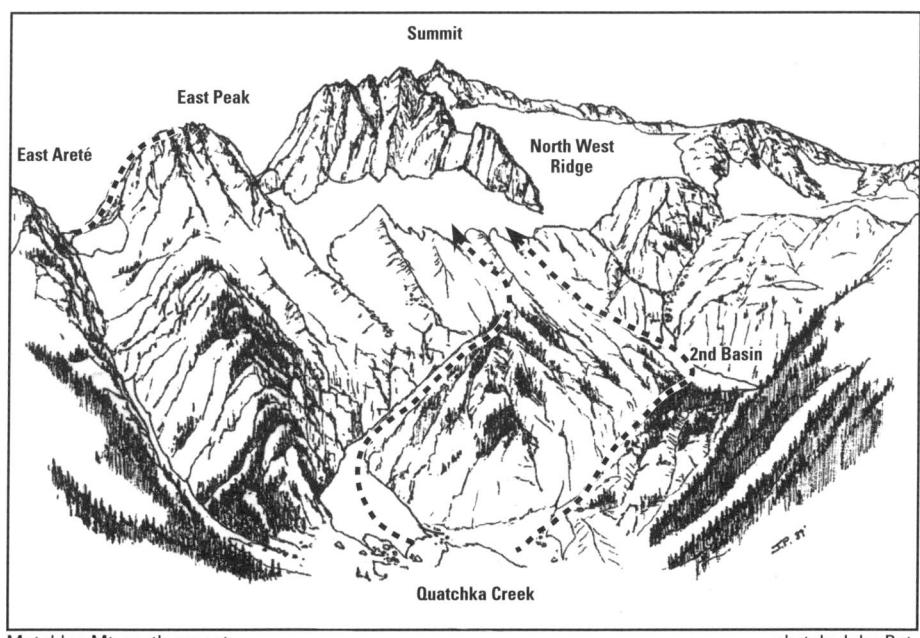

Matchlee Mt. north aspect. sketch: John Put

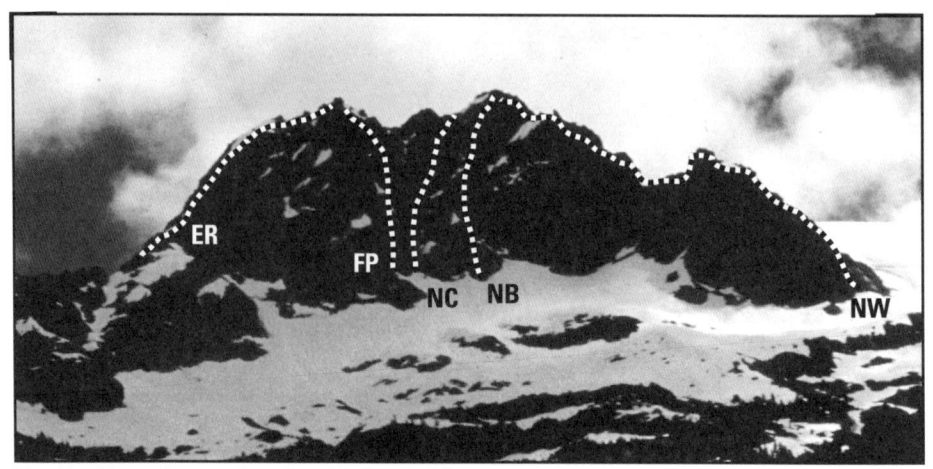

Matchlee Mt. north aspect from Quatchka Creek, July.

NW- ** **North West Ridge:** low 5th class, 450m (II)

A classic and easy scramble with a couple of low 5th class pitches, lots of 4th class and good exposure! Start at the toe of the ridge climbing up ledges and a short buttress followed by a prominent corner. 4th class terrain leads to a descent onto the snow. Cross the snow to regain the rock and an exposed class 3-4 traverse along the arete. Head out onto the north face and finish up a ramp to the summit.
FA: John Put, Fred Put, 29 June, 1985

FP- *** **Fickle of Pickle:** 5.7 250m (III)

Takes the buttress left of the prominent North Couloir. Start up a vegetated ramp at base of North Couloir heading left onto a ridge crest. Pass a large alcove through a chute above to reach a slab then cracks and an arete to finish.
FA: R Johnson, D. Newman, 13 July, 1986

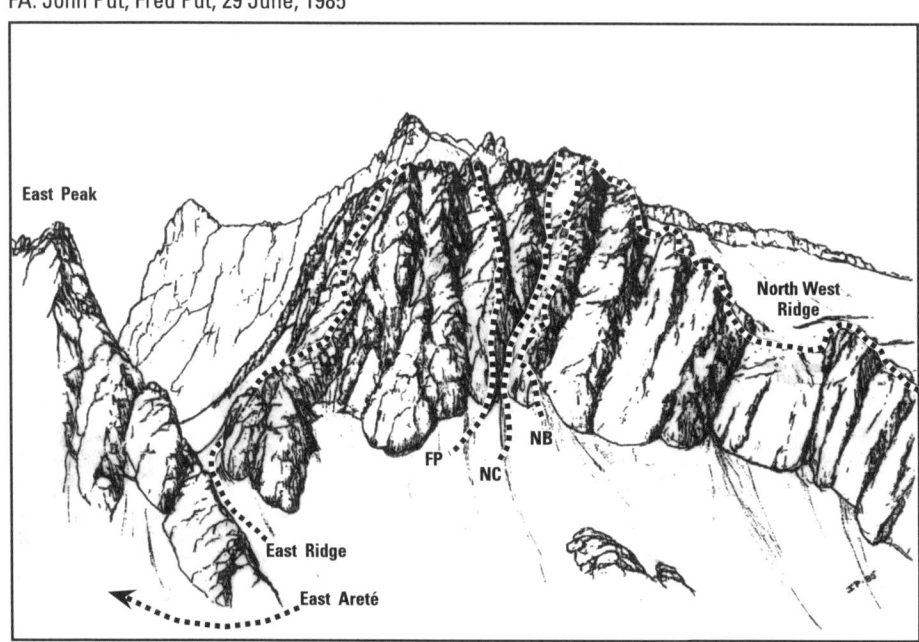

Matchlee Mt. north aspect. sketch: John Put

320 Matchlee Mountain

Matchlee Mt. north east aspect from King's Peak, January.

Winter Routes

NC- ** **North Couloir:** AI2/3 250m (III)

Climbs the prominent gully between the North Buttress and Fickle of Pickle. Climb the couloir direct with a few steep bulges.
FA: R. Johnson, D. Newman, January 1987

Additional Info: IB Fall 1987 (15:4) p.7

Quatchka Ridge south east aspect from below Mt. Matchlee, July.

Quatchka Ridge
4,882 ft / 1,488 m

A gentle alpine ridge running north west from Mt. Matchlee between Quatchka Creek and Matchlee Bay.

First Ascent: Unknown.

Map Sheet: 92 E/9 Muchalet Inlet - GR 1604 (see also 92 F/12 Buttle Lake)

Approaches: From logging road spurs off Ucona Road on the north flank of the mountain. May be used as an approach to Matchlee Mountain and neighbouring Crumble Mountain.

Mt. Kent - Urquhart

Mt. Kent-Urquhart north aspect from Volcano Lake, June.

Mt. Kent - Urquhart
5,942 ft./ 1,811 m

Mt. Kent-Urquhart lies on the divide south west of Mt. Donner between Pamela Creek and the Ucona River valley. As with the other summits on the Burman-Ucona divide the views into Strathcona Park from the top is superb. The mountain was named for surveyors W.R. Kent, W.W. Urquhart who between 1913 and 1914 surveyed and climbed most of the major peaks of Strathcona Park.

First Recorded Ascent: Lindsay Elms, Brian McClure, 5th September 1989

Map Sheet: 92 F/12 Buttle Lake - GR 9106

Approaches: Mt. Kent-Urquhart may be approached from Gold River via logging roads in Pamela Creek a tributary of the Ucona River or from roads in the hanging valley between Pamela Creek and Donner Lake. From Pamela Creek ascend steep hillside to the north west of the summit. Hike up easy ground to gain the pronounced north west ridge which may be followed to the top.

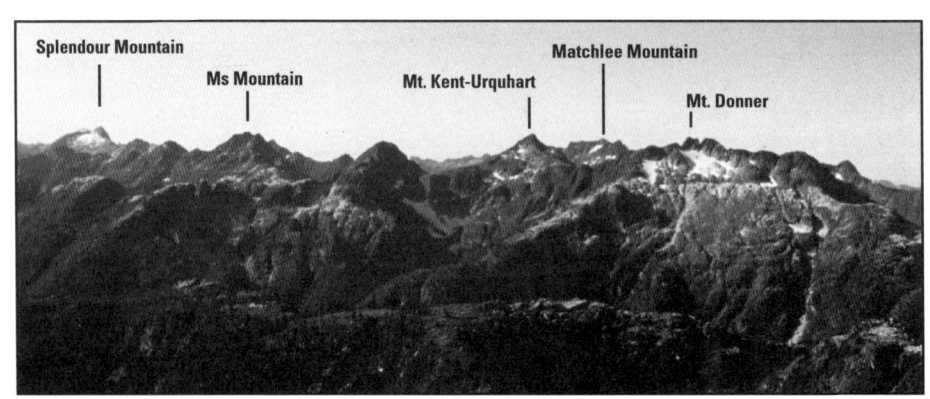

Ucona-Burman divide north east aspect from Rambler Peak, September.

M.S. Mountain - Popsicle Peak

Ms Mountain & Popsicle Peak north east aspect from Elkhorn, August.

M.S. Mountain
5,430 ft./ 1,655 m

M.S. Mountain is found at the head of Pamela Creek, a major tributary of the Ucona River. It overlooks the Burman River to the south and two parallel tributaries of the Burman flank M.S. Mountain to the east. To the west is Popsicle Peak. It is named for the two M.S.'s that made the first ascent.

First Ascent: D. Coombes, A. Harrison, D. Kanachowski, M. Symon, M. Spokes May 1975

Map Sheet: 92 F/12 Buttle Lake - GR 9102

Approaches: Logging roads in Pamela Creek which can be accessed from Gold River provide the best approach to both M.S. Mountain and Popsicle Peak.

Additional Info: IB 1995 p.18

Popsicle Peak
5,518 ft./ 1,682 m

Popsicle Peak lies just south west of Ms Mountain between the Burman River and Pamela Creek.

First Ascent: D. Coombes, B. McLean, M. Symon, M. Taylor 1980

Map: 92 F/12 Buttle Lake - GR 8900

Approaches: Read description for M.S. Mountain. From the pass at the head of Pamela Creek between Popsicle Peak and M.S. Mountain (GR 9001) hike westward to gain the west face of Popsicle Peak.

Popsicle Peak & M.S. Mountain south east aspect from Mt. Tom Taylor, September.

Splendour Mountain

Splendour Mountain north east aspect from Mt. Colonel Foster, August.

Splendour Mountain
5,794 ft./ 1,766 m

Splendour Mountain is a splendid sight from central Strathcona Park. Lying on the Burman-Megin River divide Splendour overlooks Matchlee Bay a scant 10 km from tidal waters.

First Ascent: Surveyors 1930s

Map Sheet: 92 F/12 Buttle Lake - GR 8994

Approaches: Splendour Mountain can be reached from Matchlee Bay, Muchalet Inlet via the Burman River Valley. From Gold River depart for Matchlee Bay by air or water to the old log dump on the east shore of the bay. Follow the old and very overgrown logging road east for ~8 km where a rockslide cuts off the river. Cross the Burman River and continue upstream on gravel bars avoiding dense second growth forest in the boggy valley floor.

Eventually you are forced to tackle the valley flats. Keep to the west edge of the flats to reach the old growth and cross the creek that drains Splendour's north west side. Continue south east to gain the prominent, forested north ridge. Keep to the ridge crest avoiding bluffs on the ridge crest by a ramp to the left. Hike up to treeline to a bench on the ridge below the upper north ridge. There are campsites at 880 m and 1240 m at GR 8896.

It is also possible to ford the river at gravel bars near the confluence with the creek draining the north west basin of Splendour Mt.. Then ascend the bushy forest of the north west ridge above said creek, eventually joining the other route. Continue south east to below the summit tower then traverse left (east) to reach the Splendour Glacier. Wrap around to the east ridge on the glacier and head up the ridge. Difficulties on the ridge crest can be avoided on the south side or up steep ramps on the north side up to low 5th class. Descend east ridge with one rappel back to the Splendour glacier.

Additional Info: IB 1993 p.18

Splendour Mountain north west aspect from Matchlee Bay, November.

Scimitar Peak

Scimitar Peak & Scissors Peak east aspect from the Bancroft-Moyeha divide, July. photo: Sandy Briggs

Scimitar Peak
5,498 ft./ 1,676 m

Scimitar Peak and its satellite Scissors Peak are a dramatic sight on the western skyline of Strathcona. Their resemblance to the Golden Hinde from certain aspects adds to the allure of these remote summits.

First Recorded Ascent: Sandy Briggs, Dave Whitehead, 1 September 1993

Map Sheet: 92 F/12 Buttle Lake - GR 8990

Approaches: The approach route of the first ascentionists was from the north branch of upper Kowus Creek en route along the Westmin-Elk River traverse. Ascend a gully directly to the Scissor–Scimitar saddle – class 4 at the top. Climb Scimitar by the glacier on the north west side of the mountain and then swing around the east side to a gully left of upper east ridge. Alternatively, approach Scimitar Peak from Matchlee Bay, Muchalat Inlet via Splendour Mountain and the connecting ridge which runs south from Splendour to join the north ridge of Scissors & Scimitar. This requires losing a fair amount of elevation to bypass the Scissors.

Additional Info: IB 1993 p.38

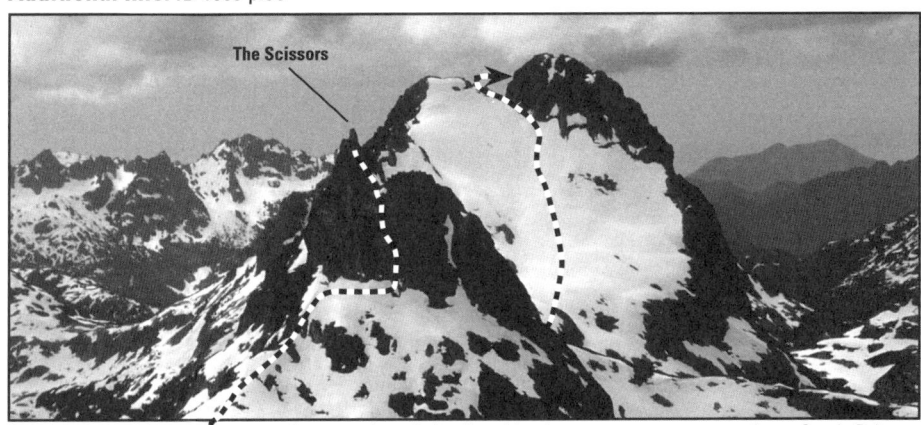

Scimitar Peak & The Scissors north aspect from Splendour Mt., June. photo: Sandy Briggs

The Scissors

Scimitar Peak & The Scissors north east aspect from Golden Hinde, February.

The Scissors
5,240 ft / 1,597 m

Prominent double summitted rock tower immediately north of Scimitar Peak.

FRA: Don Berryman, Sandy Briggs, Gerta Smythe, Dave Whitehead, 12 June 1993

Map Sheet: 92 F/12 Buttle Lake - GR 8990

Approaches: Follow approach details for Splendour Mt. & Scimitar Peak from Matchlee Bay (best) or Westmin. From the north climb the elegant ridge to a balcony overlooking the Scimitar Glacier. Two pitches of 4th/low 5th class leads to north summit.

Additional Info: IB 1993 p.18

Scimitar Peak (L), The Scissors & Splendour Mountain (R) north east aspect from the Golden Hinde, February.

Hygro Peak
5,343 ft / 1,628 m

The dome shaped mountain with a small pyramid summit between Splendour and Scimitar.

First Ascent: Sandy Briggs, Don Berryman, Dave Whitehead, Gerta Smyth, Valerio Faraoni, and Reinhard Illner, 13 June 1993

Map Sheet: 92 F/12 Buttle Lake - GR 9093

Approaches: From the north west via Splendour Mountain or from the south east from the Kowus - Bancroft divide from Westmin-Boliden via Moyeha Mountain.

Additional Info: IB 1993 p.18, p.38s

Lone Wolf Mountain

Lone Wolf Mountain north east aspect from Mt. Colonel Foster, August.

Lone Wolf Mountain
4,858 ft./ 1,481 m

Lone Wolf Mountain is a low sprawling series of rocky summits just 5 km north of tidal waters in Moyeha Bay, Herbert Inlet. Its situation so close to the ocean as well as being on the divide between the Moyeha and Megin Rivers, two of only a handful of intact watersheds on Vancouver Island's west coast makes Lone Wolf a very special mountain.

First Ascent: Unknown

Map Sheet: 92 F/5 Bedwell River - GR 8983

Approaches: The best access to Lone Wolf Mountain is from Herbert Inlet. Arrive at the head of the inlet in Moyeha Bay by air or water and prepare to engage the rainforest!

Shelbert Mountain
3,959 ft./ 1,207 m

Shelbert Mountain lies west of Moyeha Bay between Herbert and Shelter Inlets. It is the high point of the MacGregor Range which runs along the spine of the peninsula that separates the two inlets.

First Ascent: Unknown

Map Sheet: 92 F/5 Bedwell River - GR 8378 (see also 92 E/8 Hesquiat)

Approaches: The best approach looks to be up the valley west of the peak from Shelter Inlet.

Pierce Range

Looking north east toward Shelbert Mountain from the Whaler Islets, Clayoquot Sound.

Jacklah Mountain
4,593 ft / 1,400 m
At the north end of the Pierce Range overlooking Jacklah Bay and Matchlee Bay.

Map Sheet: 92 E/9 Muchalet Inlet - GR 0800

Approaches: From Muchalet Inlet up the north ridge from Jacklah Bay.

Megin Mountain
4,855 ft / 1,480 m
The highest point in the Pierce Range which runs parallel to the west shore of Matchlee Bay. Megin Mountain is between Megin River valley and Talbot Creek.

Map Sheet: 92 E/9 Muchalet Inlet - GR 1391

Approaches: May be climbed up the long gentle east ridge from Megin River.

Pretty Girl Peak
3,346 ft / 1,020 m
Overlooks Pretty Girl Lake.

Map Sheet: 92 E/9 Muchalet Inlet - GR 0090

Approaches: Best up the south east ridge from Pretty Girl Lake.

Sydney Cone
3,268 ft / 996 m
A prominent cone at the head of Syndey Inlet.

Map Sheet: 92 E/9 Muchalet Inlet - GR 9488

Approaches: Approach from the head of the inlet to a col south east of the summit. Hike direct up the south ridge to the top.

Escalante Range

Mountains of Escalante Range behind church at Yuquot, Nootka Island.

Mt. Gore
3,675 ft / 1,120 m
Map Sheet: 92 E/9 Muchalet Inlet - GR 8998

Approaches: From the log dump at Silverado Creek navigate logging roads up the north flanks.

Mt. Rufus
3,543 ft / 1,080 m
Lies west of Irving Lake on the divide between Mooyah River and Sydney River.

Map Sheet: 92 E/9 Muchalet Inlet - GR 9096

Approaches: From the major logging camp at Mooyah Bay up Mooyah River or Sydney Inlet.

Mt. Crespi
3,018 ft / 920 m
A deforested knoll at an outstanding position above Anderson Point overlooking Nootka Sound.

Map Sheet: 92 E/9 Muchalet Inlet - GR 8397

Approaches: From the lake in the deep basin to the south west of the peak.

Mt. Albemarie
3,412 ft / 1,040 m
A heavily logged peak in the head of the north fork of Escalante River.

Map Sheet: 92 E/9 Muchalet Inlet - GR 8394

Approaches: Escalante Main runs from Mooyah Main under the south flank of the mountain.

Mt. Lombard
3,018 ft / 920 m
A knoll above the north bank of Escalante River. Great views over Nootka Island & Pacific Ocean.

Map Sheet: 92 E/10 Nootka Island - GR 8094

Approaches: From the east off Escalante Main.

Jagged Mountain & Mt Waddington from Mt Cain

Northern
Vancouver Island

332 Ryan Stuart soaking up some silky powder in the Abel Creek valley.

Northern Vancouver Island
Contents

Sutton Range	336
Tlupana Range	374
Johnstone Strait	392
Haihte Range	416
Nimpkish Lake - Quatsino Sound	440

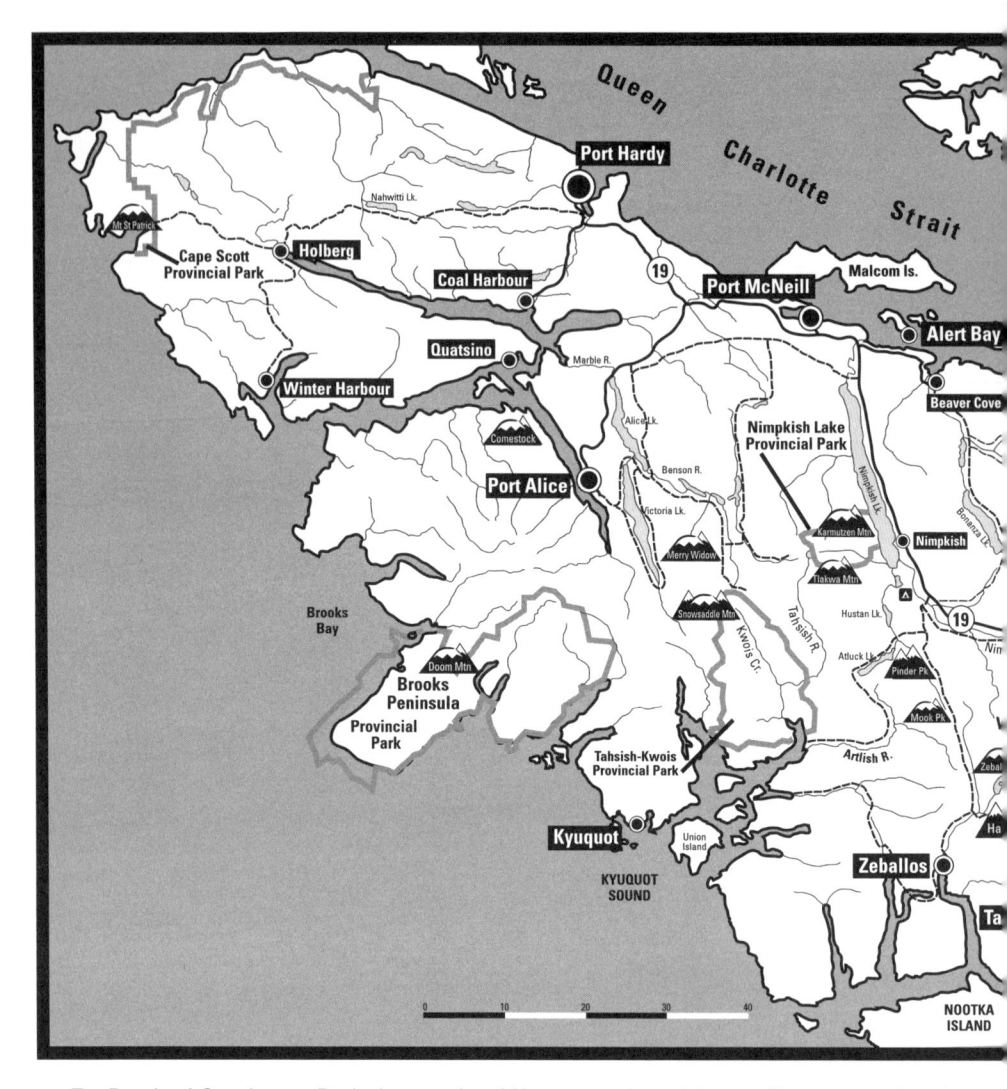

North of Strathcona Park the terrain of Vancouver Island is equally as rugged and mountainous. In this region mountains span the whole width of the Island from west to east coasts. Most, if not all, of the Crown Land in this half of the island is held in Tree Farm License tenures by private forestry companies. Logging roads and expansive clearcuts grace most valleys providing good access to the mountains but at the cost of their character and environmental integrity.

There are several Provincial Parks that are home to some of the finer alpine peaks, Schoen Lake, Woss Lake, Nimpkish Lake and Tahsish-Kwois Provincial Parks. Beyond the logging infrastructure there is little in the way of extensive trails even within the parks. Most of the travel through these mountains is on rough routes and a sense of pioneering in wilderness prevails in the North Island.

Map Sheets: 92 E/16 Gold River • 92 L/1 Schoen Lake • 92 L/8 Adam River • 92 K/5 Sayward • 92 L/7 Nimpkish • 92 L/2 Zeballos • 92 L/3 Kyuquot • 92 L/ Brooks Peninsula • 92 L/5 Mahatta River • 92 I/9 San Josef River

Boundaries: north: Queen Charlotte Strait, **east:** Johnstone Strait, **south:** Salmon and Gold Rivers, **west:** Pacific Ocean

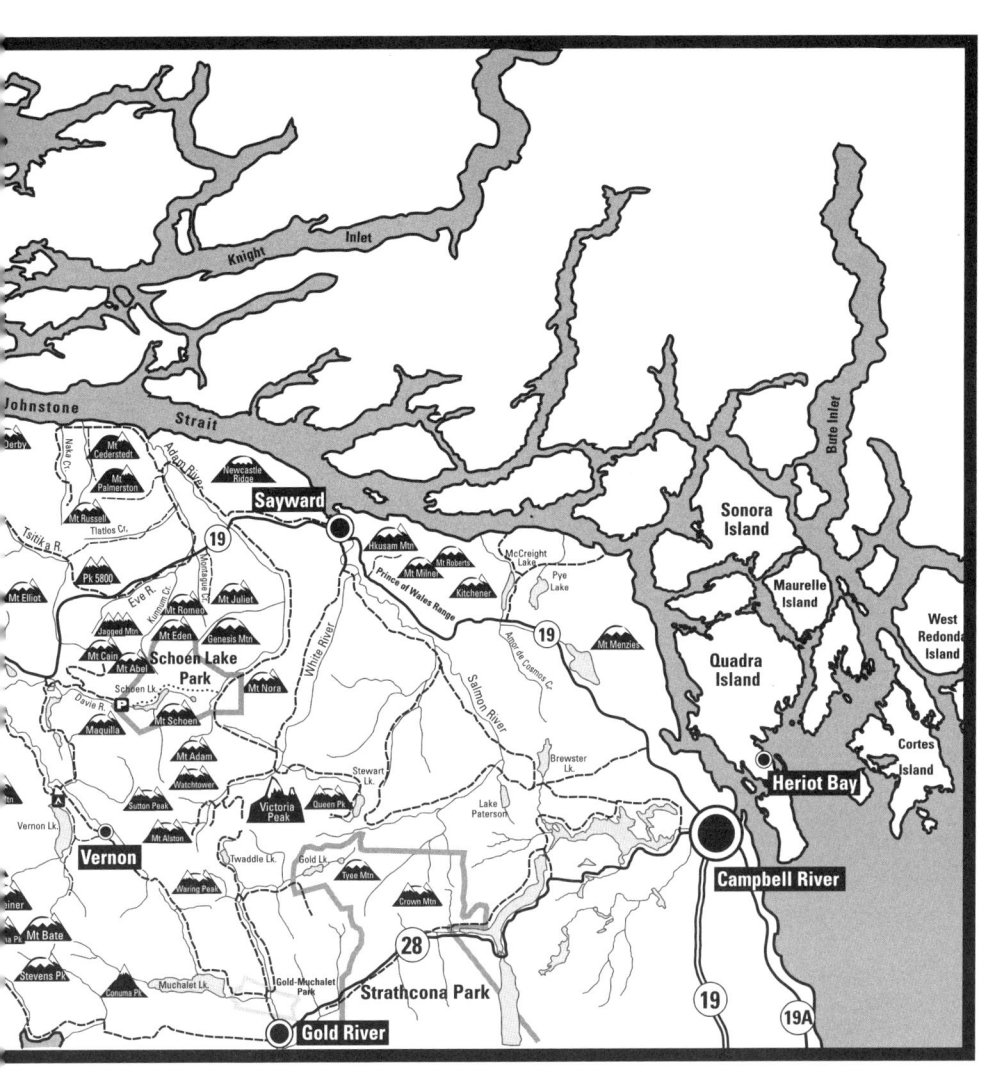

Major Access Routes: The Island Highway continues north from Campbell River taking an inland route weaving through the North Island mountain valleys to Port Hardy. Major public gravel roads link Gold River to Tahsis, Gold River and Woss and Woss to Zeballos. A paved secondary road links Port Hardy to Port Alice and the other small communities around Quatsino Sound.

Forest Service & Logging Company Offices

Campbell River Forest District - 370 South Dogwood Street, Campbell River, B.C. V9W 6Y7
Ph: (250) 286-9300

Port McNeill Forest District - 2217 Mine Road Port McNeill, BC V0N 2R0
Ph: 250 956-5000 eMail: Forests.PortMcNeillDistricOffice@gems3.gov.bc.ca

Timberwest - 5705 North Island Highway, Campbell River, BC V9W 5C5 Ph: (250) 287-9181

Western Forest Products - 1594 Beach, Port McNeill BC V0N 2R0 Ph: 250 956-4446

Other Information Sources:

• **Hiking Trails III** - Northern Vancouver Island & Strathcona Park - (9th ed. 2002 Richard K. Blier, ed.) VITIS

Northern Vancouver Island **335**

336 Victoria Peak and the White River.

Sutton Range

Includes: Schoen Lake Provincial Park

338 Ryan Stuart with Victoria and Warden Peaks.

Sutton Range
Contents

Mt. Nora	**343**
Queen Peak	**344**
Kokummi Mountain	**345**
Victoria Peak	**346**
Warden Peak	**351**
Waring Peak	**353**
Mt. Alston	**354**
Sutton Peak	**355**
Watchtower Peak	**356**
Mt. Adam	**357**
Maquilla Peak	**358**
Mt. Cain	**359**
Mt. Abel	**365**
Mt. Sarai	**366**
Mt. Abraham	**367**
Mt. Hapush	**368**
Mt. Eden	**369**
Mt. Schoen	**370**
Mt. Juliet	**372**
Mt. Romeo	**372**
Genesis Mountain	**372**
Jagged Mountain	**373**

340   Sutton Range - Map

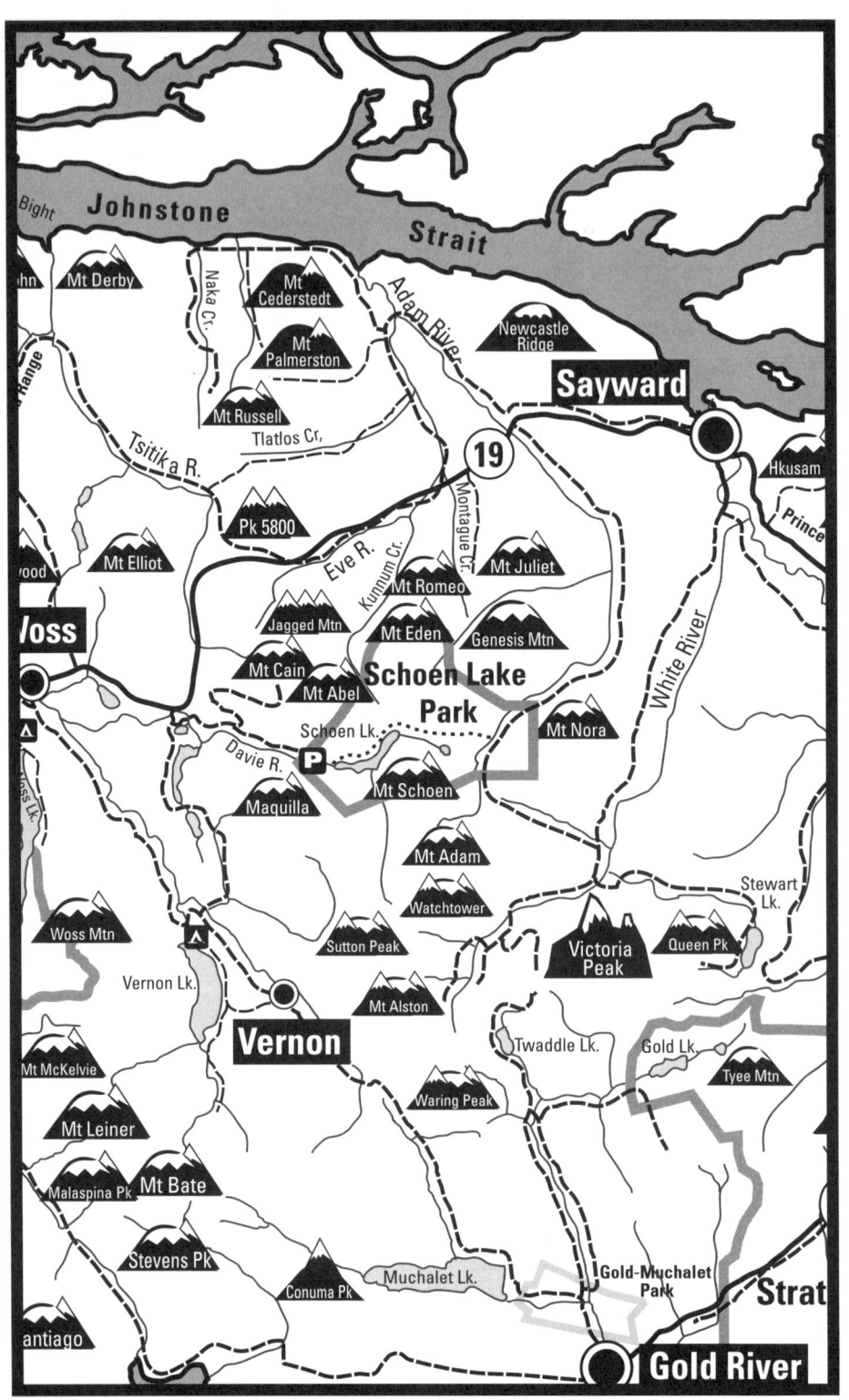

Sutton Range

From the Salmon River valley northward, mountains span the entire Island between the west and east coasts. The wide coastal lowlands that characterize the landscape from the Cowichan Valley to Campbell River along the east coast are replaced by a maze of deep river valleys and mountains. The Sutton Range is the natural extension of the Island backbone north of Strathcona Park and runs from Strathcona and the Salmon River valley north to the Tsitika River and the community of Woss. This range has some of Vancouver Island's highest peaks including the only summit over 7,000 feet outside of Strathcona Park, Victoria Peak and the Island's finest ski area Mt. Cain.

Most of the area is Crown land under tree farm licenses to private logging companies. There are several smaller Provincial Parks and numerous Forest Service recreation sites scattered throughout the area. Parks in the Sutton Range include Schoen Lake Provincial Park and Mt. Cain Regional Park.

The mountains have a very distinct character. Unlike the topography to the south in Strathcona the mountains in the Sutton group are for the most part separated from one another by deep passes and valleys, with few stretches of high continuous ridgelines. So the peaks become individual destinations rather than part of longer traverses. The rock in this range is predominantly volcanic basalt and offers fantastic climbing. The potential for technical routes in the Sutton Range is astounding.

Map Sheets: 92 L/1 Schoen Lake • 92 L/8 Adam River

Boundaries: north: Tsitika River & Island Highway 19, **east:** Adam & Eve Rivers & Island Highway 19, **south:** Salmon River - Strathcona Park, **west:** Gold & Nimpkish Rivers

Major Access Routes: The **Island Highway 19** provides paved road access along the eastern side of the Sutton Range between the communities of Sayward and Woss. Logging road mainlines branch off from the Island Highway into the White River, Adam River, Eve River and Davie River valleys and all can be used to approach the mountains.

White River Main: Leave the Island Highway at the Sayward Junction, 64 km north of Campbell River. Turn left and keep straight at the sudden right fork. Cross the White River to the gas station and turn right. Turn right yet again at a junction and after 200 m turn left uphill on the newly designated White River Main. Halfway up the valley a sharp right leads down to the White River and a bridge. White River Main crosses the bridge and continues upriver on the west side (on the east side is Victoria Main, a good 2WD road). About 30 km from the highway is a T-junction with Stewart Main. For Victoria Peak and Warden turn right, whence you will soon cross Consort Creek and then the White River.

Upper Adam Main: Heads south 10 km north of Sayward off the Island Highway into the east side of Schoen Lake Park. Joins Moakwa Main through Gerald Creek & links on to the White River Main.

Nimpkish Road: A public gravel road running along the west side of the Sutton Range between Gold River and Woss. This road has several spurs which provide access into the Sutton Range including: East and West Mains, Lower Alston Road, Murlock Road, Stuart Road, Fiona Road the Mt. Cain access road and Davie Main into the west side of Schoen Lake Park.

To reach the south end of Nimpkish Road drive to Gold River on Highway 28, 90 km west of Campbell River. To reach the north end of Nimpkish Road drive north on the Island Highway from Campbell River to the Schoen Lake-Mt. Cain junction 119 km north of Campbell River and 21 km south of Woss.

Forest Service & Logging Company Offices:

Campbell River Forest District - 370 South Dogwood Street, Campbell River, B.C. V9W 6Y7 Ph: (250) 286-9300

Timberwest - Beaver Cove Operation -P.O. Box 2500, 5705 North Island Highway, Campbell River, BC V9W 5C5 Ph: (250) 287-9181

Weyerhaeuser - North Island Timberlands -P.O. Box 6000, 8010 Island Highway, Campbell River, BC V9W 5E1 Ph: 250-287-5000

Other Information Sources:

• **Hiking Trails III** - Northern Vancouver Island & Strathcona Park - (9th ed. 2002 Richard K. Blier, ed.) VITIS

Special Thanks:

Thanks to Lindsay Elms, Chris Barner, Paul Kendrick & Sandy Briggs for assistance with this chapter.

342 Curtis Lyon on the steep chimney pitch of 'The Sceptre', Victoria Peak.

Mt. Nora

Looking up the west ridge of Mt. Nora, May. photo: Lindsay Elms

Mt. Nora
5,406 ft / 1,648 m

Mt. Nora is located between the Adam River to its west and the White River to its east. The mountain stands on its own surrounded by deep river valleys on every side giving it added stature in an area of larger peaks.

First Recorded Ascent: Lindsay Elms 1st June, 2002

Map Sheet: 92 L/1 Schoen Lake - GR 0659

Approaches: Mt. Nora is easily climbed from the Adam River Main which leaves the Island Highway just west of Keta Lake rest area 74 km west of Sayward. Drive in the Adam River Main to the parking pullout for Nisnak Meadows in Schoen Lake Park. Head up the forested slope on the east side of the road to gain the west ridge of Mt. Nora. Follow the west ridge to the summit skirting a sub peak on its south side.

Queen Peak

Queen Peak north-west aspect from Mt. Nora, May.　　　　　　　　　photo: Lindsay Elms

Queen Peak
5,383 ft / 1,640 m

Queen Peak lies in the shadow of Victoria Peak which is a scant 3.5 km to its west on the opposite side of Consort Creek. The mountain maybe the remnant rim of a volcano crater.

First Ascent: Unknown

Map Sheet: 92 L/1 Schoen Lake - GR 1147

Approaches: Approach Queen Peak from the White River Main. Cross the White River bridge and continue south on Stewart Main, leaving it shortly after the bridge turning right onto ST1 which follows the west bank of Consort Creek. Drive up a spur road onto the lower north ridge of Queen Peak. Hike from the road end at 3100 ft through a heli-logging block and gain the crest of the north ridge. Climb a difficult gully through a rock band to the top of the first high point on the ridge, some parties may require a roped belay through this gully. Descending the other end of this bluffy bump (down a gully on the left) also offers difficulties belied by its innocent appearance on the 1:50,000 topo. Continue along the beautiful, narrow ridge as it winds around to the summit. Descend same route taking care to locate the gully off the first high point as mentioned above.

Alternatively, continue up Stewart Main past Stewart Lake. Take the uphill spur into the upper reaches of Consort Creek, south of Queen Peak, to about 2300 ft and roughly 44 km from the Island Highway. Ascend a large steep clearcut on the south-east flank of the mountain to gain a steep forested hillside and eventually the friendly east ridge of Queen Peak. The summit is an easy ramble from here, and offers spectacular views of the eastern aspect of the Victoria-Warden massif.

Queen Peak north-west aspect from Kokummi Mountain, December.

Kokummi Mountain

Kokummi Mountain north aspect from Mt. Adam — photo: Lindsay Elms

Kokummi Mountain
5,300 ft / 1,615 m

Kokummi Mountain is a small forested, and deforested, mountain overlooking the north side of the upper White River valley between the White River and the Moakwa Creek valleys. While its southern flanks are broad gentle slopes crisscrossed by high logging roads the northern aspect of the mountain drop precipitously into Moakwa Creek. Kokummi Mountain makes a good day trip destination on foot or on skis giving great views of the surrounding high peaks in the upper White River.

First Ascent: Unknown

Map Sheet: 92 L/1 Schoen Lake - GR 0453

Approaches: Kokummi Mountain is easily climbed from logging roads that climb high on its southern flanks from the White River. Drive from Sayward along the White River Main to the junction with Moakwa Creek Main. Drive north a few kilometres then turn left (west) on to branch road MC12. Drive the road, which wraps around the east ridge of Kokummi to the south side, as far as you can then continue on foot. From the highest spur of the road continue up through the slash to the old growth on the south aspect of Kokummi Mountain. Easy route finding leads to the summit ridge.

Alternatively, continue driving on White River Main to the junction with Kokummi Main. Head north on this road into Kokummi Creek. Hike up through the forest on the broad south ridge of the mountain to the summit ridge.

Additional Info: IB 1998 p.16

Victoria Peak

Victoria Peak north aspect from Warden Peak, June. photo: Bill Readings

Victoria Peak
7,095 ft / 2,163 m

Victoria Peak and its satellite Warden Peak are distinctive landmarks from Campbell River and the adjacent Discovery Islands. They rise high out of the White River with no mountains of comparable elevation nearby. The peaks have excellent rock and an alpine scale and character unrivalled outside of Strathcona Park. The high logging road access particularly from the White and Gold Rivers make Victoria Peak a viable day trip objective at the high cost of the once splendid forests that filled the surrounding valleys.

The Victoria-Warden massif is the remnants of an extinct volcano's lava core. The rock on the peak, not surprisingly, is very solid offering superb climbing. Many of the obvious lines have been climbed but there are still some great routes to be done especially in winter. The Victoria Glacier makes an excellent short ski tour with some long descents.

First Recorded Ascent: Otto Winning, Syd Watts et al 1950's
Map Sheet: 92 L/1 Schoen Lake - GR 0748

Warden and Victoria Peak North west from Mt. Schoen, Sept.

Victoria Peak west aspect from WR500, August.

Approaches: Victoria Peak can be reached either from Sayward along the White River Main logging road or from Gold River near Twaddle Lake on the East or West Main. Logging roads (branch WR500) climb to around 3,500 ft from the White River side and from the Gold River side to 4,000 ft on branch W-79 of West Road. Access on these roads will vary with seasonal snow cover and logging activity. From either WR500 or W-79, a short steep hike through the remaining forest reaches the crest of Victoria Peak's south ridge. The south ridge is a beautiful hike in its own right with small alpine lakes and incredible views of Strathcona Park, Nootka Sound and back toward Campbell River.

To reach the Victoria Glacier and Warden Peak, the fastest access is now from branch WR380 which is currently at an elevation of around 2,700 ft. A long traverse is still required from this road so while it may save elevation gain it may still be faster just to head directly up to the glacier from WR381 on the old route. New logging roads in Consort Creek now open this original route to the mountain to quick access.

Additional Info: IB 1993 p.28, IB 1995 p.15, IB 1999 p.24, WIM #9 p.18

Routes

SF- * South Face: 4th class 300m (II)

The standard route up Victoria Peak. Approach along the lower south ridge. Follow the ridge almost to the "notch", a well cairned route descends slightly on the east side down to a large snowfield below the south face of the mountain. Traverse the snowfield to reach the base of a ramp system that leads far to the right, across the lower part of the face.

Continue up the ledges until a route back left is possible on easier ground. Climb up snow patches or 3rd class rock to one last steep step before the top. Descend the same route. Rappel anchors in place at the corner.

The original approach was from Consort Creek, usually by flying into Stewart Lake (then Consort Lake). New logging roads in the upper Consort Creek valley now reopen this option up as a quick alternative to the south ridge approach.
FA: Syd Watts, Otto Winning et al 1950's

SE- * South-East Ridge: 4th class 300m (II)

Climbs the right hand skyline of the peak when viewed from the south ridge approach. Follow the approach details for the South Face route. From the snowfield below the South Fave traverse right across the snow to the base of the South-East Ridge. Climb a straightforward scramble up the ridge crest on to the north-east summit. Make an easy traverse across the upper boulder field to the main summit.

ER- **East Ridge: low 5th class 1500m (III)

Approach from Consort Creek to the long sweeping East Ridge. Climb up through the old growth to the base. Scramble up bluffy rock steps until route gives way to good rock and excellent climbing higher up. Continue on crest of ridge to north-east summit. Scramble across upper boulder field to Main Summit.
FA: Chris Barner, F. Somner 1977

348 North-East Buttress and North Face of Victoria Peak as seen from the Victoria-Warden col.

South aspect of Victoria Peak from Elbow Creek divide, July.

NE- *** North-East Buttress: 5.8 400m (III)

Approach the base of the buttress from Victoria Glacier. Climb eight pitches direct up the steep buttress crest with good protection and solid rock. Incredible exposure, views toward Campbell River and big alpine character. Finish on north-east summit. To reach the main summit traverse boulder field across ridge crest. Descend route by rappel back to Victoria Glacier or take the South Face route down to the lower south ridge. It is possible to drop down the west side off the lower south ridge and traverse back to the Victoria Glacier under the west face if camping on that side.
FA: Greg Foweraker, Don Newman, 1986

WR- ** West Ridge: 4th class 800m (III)

A long and easy scramble, wild exposure and lots of loose rock. Best reached from White River approach. Little info on this route.
FA: Unknown

S- *** The Sceptre: 5.8 600m (III)

Climbs the awesome couloir that splits the west face of Victoria Peak. Can be reached by heading up direct from WR500 or via the south ridge and descending slightly to traverse in to base of the route. Scramble up ledges to the base of the chimney. Start up a ramp system on the left. Several steep pitches with progressively wilder exposure lead direct up the chimney separated by good belay ledges. Near the top the couloir narrows to a tight chimney, break off left avoiding the chimney to finish up a steep headwall joining the West Ridge just below the main summit.
FA: Curtis Lyon, Philip Stone, August 1997

SR- *** South Ridge: 5.8 500m (III)

Approach as for the Sceptre. Start up the right side of the west face to gain the crest of the South Ridge above the 'notch'. Continue along the crest of the ridge with two pitches of 5.8.
FA: Mike Norton, Scott Jackson, 12, June 2000

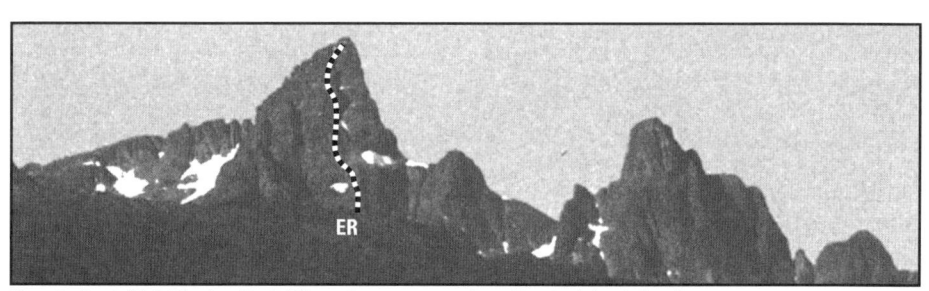

Victoria Peak (L) & Warden Peak (R) south-east aspect from Quadra Island, October.

Victoria and Warden Peaks north aspect from Kokummi Mountain, December.

Winter Routes

NF- *** **North Face:** 5.10 AI4 300m (IV)

Approach the Victoria Glacier either by hiking directly up the timbered slope on the flagged route from WR381 or traversing across the west flank of the mountain from WR380. Hike up the glacier to the centre of the North Face to start. Steep mixed climbing up ice falls and rock bands leads in to a narrow chimney with a 5.10 pitch near the top. Route tops out in a high gap between the two peaks. An exposed traverse across the South Face leads to the main summit.
FA: Rick Johnson, Don Newman, Matt Lunney January 1986

Note: "A serious attempt still incomplete. The party chose not to take bolts and was unable to protect the final difficult pitch (chimney with chockstone blocking the way). Several pitches of steep snow, short steep bands of verglass-covered rock to about 5.7/8. Some protection."

-Rick Johnson

Victoria Peak west aspect as seen from Sutton Peak, June.

Warden Peak

South aspect of Warden Peak from Victoria Glacier, May.

Warden Peak
6,460 ft./ 1,969 m

Warden Peak is a columnar basalt tower north-east of Victoria Peak overlooking the White River valley. Although much lower than Victoria Peak, Warden Peak is notable for its pillar-shape, incredible rock quality and exposure down into the White River thousands of feet below.

First Ascent: P. Guilbride, P. Perfect, K. Pfeiffer July 9, 1968.

First Winter Ascent: Don Newman, Sandy Briggs, Claire Ebendinger, Valerio Faraoni 30, January 1994

Map Sheet: 92 L/1 Schoen Lake - GR 0749

Approaches: Warden Peak is best approached from Sayward along the White River Main logging road off branch WR381 found on the left after crossing the White River bridge. Drive as far down this spur as possible then park and continue on foot. A flagged route leaves near the end of this spur and climbs up through the steep forest to the open alpine basin below the Victoria Glacier. Ascend rock slabs and snow to gain the glacier and the Victoria-Warden col.

An alternative route to the Victoria Glacier is from branch WR380 which is currently at an elevation of around 2,700 ft. below the west face of Victoria Peak. A long traverse north-eastward is required to reach the glacier. Ascend slabs and/or snow to the Victoria-Warden col.

Additional Info: IB 1996 p.9, IB 1995 p.26

Routes

North Face: 4th class 150m (II)

From the Victoria-Warden col head left (north) up a steep snow/scree slope to the shoulder at the foot of the south side of Warden's summit tower. Traverse left around to the west side of the tower and then begin climbing up the tower on solid rock, 4th class difficulties and incredible exposure! Keep trending leftward to the north side of the summit as you continue up to the top. Often, even in summer, there is a snow couloir to cross on the north-west side, for which a rope and ice-axes can be useful.

Victoria & Warden Peaks east aspect from Queen Peak, October.   photo: Peter Rothermel

Warden Peak south-west aspect from foot of Victoria Peak west ridge, May.

Warden Peak (L) & Victoria Peak (R) north-west aspect from Mt. Schoen, September.

Waring Peak

Waring Peak north-east aspect from Mt. Schoen, September.

Waring Peak
5,252 ft./ 1,601m

Waring Peak is a series of summits connected by sweeping ridges above Twaddle Lake between the Gold River and White River valleys. It is the southern end of the Sutton Range overlooking the Gold River valley which runs south of Waring Peak. Named after Harry L. Waring a cook with the Slocomb West Coast survey party. He was hurt in the field and later died in August 1947.

First Ascent: Alfred Slocomb survey party 1947

Map Sheet: 92 E/16 Gold River - GR0139

Approaches: Waring Peak is best approached on the west side from logging roads in Waring Creek. Around 27 kilometres north of Gold River on Nimpkish Road (Woss-Gold River Road) turn east onto Waring Road. The road curves back to the south-east and a branch to the left crosses the creek to the slopes below Waring's west side. Park as close to the foot of the south-west ridge as possible. Hike through slash to timber and ascend the steep ridge to the alpine below Waring Peak's west ridge. Scramble up the ridge on the crest to the summit with some 3rd class.

Sutton Peak (L) Mt. Alston (C) & Waring Peak (R) west aspect from Muchalet - Sebalhall divide, August.

Mt. Alston

Mt. Alston north-east aspect from Kokummi Mountain, December.

Mt. Alston
5,720 ft / 1,743 m

Mt. Alston sits at the head of the White River between it and the Nimpkish Valley to the west. Like its neighbours Alston is comprised of steep basalt cliffs and deep, glacier carved cirques. The pinnacle at the north end of the mountain is called 'Alston Fin'.

Map Sheet: 92 L/1 Schoen Lake - GR 9844

Approaches: Mt. Alston is most easily reached and climbed from the Nimpkish valley where logging roads branch high into the valley to the south-west of the summit. From the end of the road hike up regenerating forest to gain the south-west ridge. Follow the ridge with no technical difficulties to the summit.

A route across to Sutton Peak may be traversed by dropping north past 'Alston Fin' to the col below the south side of Sutton Peak. Climb the south ridge on to the top of Sutton Peak. Two pitches of 4th class rock to gain the summit ridge.
FA: Lindsay Elms, Jamie Gamble, 1990

Mt. Alston east aspect from south ridge of Victoria Peak, August.

Sutton Peak

Alston Fin (L) & Sutton Peak (C) north-east aspect from Kokummi Mountain, December.

Sutton Peak
6,109 ft / 1,862 m

Sutton Peak is a large massif between the Nimpkish River to the west and the White River to the east. High ridges connect from the west and north to an impressive summit tower which plummets on the south-east side in a series of high rock buttresses. Sutton is easily reached from high logging roads and makes an attractive destination for hiking and ski touring trips with lots of room to explore. The remarkable lakes around the mountain should attract the curious.

First Ascent: Unknown

Map Sheet: 92 L/1 Schoen Lake - GR 9846

Approaches: The best approach to Sutton Peak is from the logging roads in Maquilla Creek that rise onto the mountain's west flank. If drivable these roads provide outstanding access with only a 30 minute hike to the alpine. From the Island Highway, 55 km north of Sayward and 15 km south of Woss, turn off at the Mt. Cain - Schoen Lake Park junction. Take the first right onto the public gravel road to Gold River, the Nimpkish Road. Drive 30 km then turn left onto Stuart Road. Continue along Stuart Rd. and then turn right on Fiona Road. Turn onto a spur road which climbs high on the hillside due west of the summit.

On the crest of an obvious ridge park and hike through the clearcut to reach old growth which can be followed up to treeline and a series of satellite peaks west of the summit. Hike along the height of land over another broad sub peak and on to the North-West Ridge of the summit tower.

Sutton Peak has also been approached from the White River following the creek and lake chain on the north side of the mountain into a huge cirque below the north side of the summit. Climb the superb rock up the indistinct North Ridge to a false summit then along the crest to the summit proper.

Additional Info: IB 1993 p.47

Sutton Peak east aspect from Victoria Peak, August.

Watchtower Peak

Watchtower Peak (R) & Sutton Peak (L) south-east aspect from Victoria Peak, August.

Watchtower Peak
5,708 ft / 1,740 m

Watchtower Peak is a long jagged ridge top of rocky summits between the head of the Schoen Creek valley to the west and the White River to the south and east. There seems to be significant climbing potential on Watchtower especially on the north-east face.

First Ascent: J. Gibson, S. Watts, July 1975

Map Sheet: 92 L/1 Schoen Lake - GR 9851

Approaches: Watchtower Peak is reached from the White River valley. From Sayward head south on the White River Main. Pass the junction to the bridge over the White River staying on the west bank of the river. From branch roads off the Kokummi Road gain the remaining timber on the prominent south-east ridge of the mountain. Follow the ridge into the alpine avoiding any difficulties on the left (west) side of the ridge.

Front to back: Mt. Adam, Watchtower Peak, Sutton Peak & Mt. Alston north aspect from Mt. Schoen, Sept.

Mt. Adam

Mt. Adam north aspect from Mt. Schoen, September.

Mt. Adam
5,673 ft./ 1,729 m

Mt. Adam is a broad and elegant mountain with three long sweeping ridges running north, south and east from the summit. It is located to the east of Schoen Creek at the head of Moakwa Creek, a tributary of the White River.

First Ascent: A.J. Campbell survey party 1932

Map Sheet: Schoen Lake 92 L/1 9855

Approaches: The Upper Adam River Road forms a loop from the Island Highway through the Adam River valley into Gerald Creek (here called Moakwa Main) and joins the White River Main which also connects to the Island Highway. Approach Mt. Adam by driving in on either road to Moakwa Main.

~8 km north of the junction of the White River and Moakwa Mains turn west on Upper Adam Main which runs in to the valley on the north side of Mt. Adam. From near the end of the road climb a gully system which leads past a couple of high alpine lakes and onto the summit ridge just north of the top. Hike south along the ridge crest to the top. This gully route is best in spring snow cover.

Alternatively, from spurs off Upper Adam Main gain the east end of the east ridge at Peak 4375 at GR 0455. Hike westward over several false summits along the long ridge system to the summit.

Mt. Adam north aspect from Mt. Nora, May. photo: Lindsay Elms.

Maquilla Peak

Maquilla Peak north aspect from Mt. Cain, February.

Maquilla Peak
5,974 ft / 1,821 m

Maquilla Peak is a very attractive mountain located opposite Mt. Cain on the south side of the Davie River.

First Ascent: A.J. Campbell survey party 1931

Map Sheet: 92 L/1 Schoen Lake - GR 9054

Approaches: Logging roads all but encircle Maquilla Peak providing access to most aspects of the mountain. The most straightforward approach and climb is from Chuckan Road which winds up the west flank of the mountain from Nimpkish Road a few kilometres south of Lower Klalakama Lake. From Chuckan Road hike through slash to reach remaining old growth on the south-west ridge of Maquilla. Ascend the ridge directly to the summit.

Additional Info: IB 1995 p.14

Unnamed satellite peak east of Maquilla Peak north aspect from Mt. Cain, February.

Mt. Cain

Mt. Cain West Peak west aspect from West Ridge, January.

Mt. Cain
5,918 ft./ 1,804 m

Mt. Cain is a series of blocky summits at the headwaters of the Tsitika River. The central main peak is slightly higher and more difficult to climb than the west peak which is more often climbed. To the east is the Sunflower Tower and a lower outlying East Peak. Mt. Cain is home to Vancouver Island's finest ski hill which bears its name. The ski area is serviced by two T-bars from a base area which includes: parking, a day lodge, private cabins and all the trappings of a small community skihill. Most activity is unsurprisingly concentrated during the winter months but with fine road access Mt. Cain is an ideal alpine destination at any time of year. An number of fine summer rock and mixed winter routes have been established on each of the towers.

First Ascent: Rick Eppler, John Simpson, January 1977

Map Sheet: 92 L/1 Schoen Lake - GR 9067

Approaches: From the Island Highway, 55 km north of Sayward and 11 km south of Woss, turn off at the Mt. Cain - Schoen Lake Park junction. Follow the clearly posted signs for Mt. Cain to the base of the ski lift area, taking about 40 minutes from the highway depending on seasonal road conditions. From the parking lot hike (or in winter take a ride up the T-bar) to the top of the Upper T-bar. To reach the west peak hike up the west ridge. For the main peak traverse across the 'East Bowl' below the south face of the west peak. The South Face is the most popular route to the west peak.

Mt. Cain West Peak south-west aspect from top of Upper T-Bar, February.

Summer Routes

* SF- South Face: 150m AI2/4th class

Approach from the top of the Upper T-bar. Hike directly up behind the lift shack and on to the crest of the west ridge above the 'East Bowl' (note that the 'East Bowl' is only east from the ski area and in fact is more accurately the south-west bowl of Mt. Cain). Continue along the west ridge over a series of small humps to below a steep rock wall. Traverse right out on to an exposed ledge above the South Face to gain the central couloir which runs right up the South Face. Climb up the remainder of the couloir to the summit of the west peak.

** Ten: 100m 5.7

Climbs a direct line on superb rock up a clean rock face on the south-west side of the main peak, overlooking the col between the west and main peaks. Approach by traversing from the upper T-bar across to the far side of the 'East Bowl'. Continue under the west peak to a gully that leads up to a col between the west and main peaks.

Start up a diagonal leftward leaning crack. As it reaches the left side of the face trend back right to gain the prominent weakness splitting the centre of the face. Descend down the gully on climbers' right of the climb.

FA: Timo Saukko, Paul Kendrick, August 1996

Col between west (L) and main (R) peaks.

Mt. Cain Main Peak and Sunflower Tower south-west aspect from South Ridge.   photos: Paul Kendrick

West Peak summit and route of Frosted Flakes from top of 'Ten' on Main Peak. photo: Paul Kendrick

** Sunflower: 100m 5.8
Takes the prominent open-book corner on the south side of the Sunflower Tower. Approach by traversing right across the East Bowl below the South Face of the West and main peaks. Scramble up an easy rib to the right end of a leftward trending ramp that leads to the base of the corner. Belay and climb directly up the back of the corner to a small but strenuous roof. Belay and climb easier ground to the top.
FA: Timo Saukko, Paul Kendrick, July 1997

Miller Time: 100m 5.8
Takes a series of shallow corners in a leftward trending line to two upper dihedrals on the north-west face of the west peak. Approach by descending off the West Ridge into the North Bowl. Head down to just right of the middle of the face to start. An easier first pitch leads to a second pitch through dihedrals at 5.8 (crux).
FA: Paul Kendrick, Gene Rumley, Aug. 1995

Pie In The Sky: 75m 5.6
Climbs the left side of an open corner/groove system up the west face of the west peak from the west ridge. One 5.6 pitch taking a crack system up the groove.
FA: Gary Robinson, Paul Kendrick, Aug 1992

The Sunflower Tower. photo: Timo Saukko

Mt. Cain **361**

Paul Kendrick on Sunflower. photo: Timo Saukko

Mt. Cain West Peak south-west aspect from ski area, January.

Winter Routes

Frosted Flakes: 175m AI2
Climbs the prominent corner-like gully on the east side of the west peak from the col between the west and main peaks. Approach by traversing the 'East Bowl' from the Upper T-Bar. Continue under the west peak to a gully that leads up to a col between the west and main towers. Start up the gully on the left above a prominent overhanging prow. Climb direct to the summit. Descend the South Face route.
FA: Timo Saukko, Paul Kendrick,

CC- Central Couloir: 200m AI2
Takes the prominent gully that splits the centre of the South Face of the West Peak. The route is clearly seen from the upper T-bar station. Approach by traversing the East Bowl from the upper station directly to the base of the route. Climb 3 or 4 pitches with 2 difficult steps. Difficulties vary with conditions.

Wedgie: 100m AI2
This fun route takes a leftward trending line of corners and ramps up the north-west face of the west peak. Approach by descending off the west ridge into the north bowl. Head down to the middle of the face to start. Climb the gully-like line in two pitches. Described as awkward, strenuous and hilarious for the second through an A2 crux.
FA: Timo Saukko, Paul Kendrick, January 1998

Mt. Cain West Peak north-west aspect, January.
photo: Paul Kendrick

364 Skiers in the 'Dream Chute' between Mt. Cain and Mt. Abel.

Mt. Abel

Mt. Abel west aspect from Mt. Cain ski area, March.

Mt. Abel
5,905 ft./ 1,800 m

Mt. Abel is a familiar sight to visitors of Mt. Cain as it dominates the view from most parts of the skihill. Abel is a tempting figure for climbers with an imposing west face. It also hides a secret bowl on its south-west slopes which is an excellent backcountry ski destination.

First Ascent: John Clarke, J. Gibson, Syd Watts, 1971

Map Sheet: 92 L/1 Schoen Lake - GR 9165

Approaches: Easily reached from logging roads on the south-west flanks of the mountain. From the Island Highway, 55 km north of Sayward and 11 km south of Woss, turn off at the Mt. Cain - Schoen Lake Park junction. Follow the clearly posted signs for Mt. Cain as far as a major logging road junction at the first switchback. Take the right hand road, the Abel Main, and follow it up as far as you can drive. Continue up the road on foot to the end of the road. Traverse rightward into a small patch of remaining old growth and hike up through this timber to the bottom of a large basin south-west of the summit. Either head right up the basin or take the more scenic ridge along the right (east) flank of the cirque and follow it to the summit.

It is also possible to approach from the Mt. Cain lift area by traversing the whole basin connecting the two mountains and finishing up a wide gully between Mt. Abel's main and west summits.

Mt. Abel south-west aspect from Abel Creek road, March.

Mt. Sarai

Mt. Sarai north-west aspect from Mt. Abel, March.

Mt. Sarai
5,400 ft./ 1,646 m

Mt. Sarai lies on the north-west boundary of Schoen Lake Provincial Park between two branches of Abel Creek to the west, and a tributary of Schoen Lake to the east. The mountain is a narrow series of four domed summits dropping off steeply on both north and south flanks.

First Ascent: Unknown

Map Sheet: 92 L/1 Schoen Lake - GR 9264

Approaches: Mt. Sarai may be reached from logging roads on its north side in the branch of Abel Creek between Mt. Abel and itself. From the Island Highway take the Mt. Cain turn off 11 km south of Woss and follow the signs for Mt. Cain ski area. Turn right onto the Mt. Abel Main at the bottom of the first major switchback. Follow the road as far as you can drive or park on the Mt. Cain Road and hike or ski up the Abel Main (Adam Road). Follow the road into the high valley on the west side of Mt. Sarai. New logging blocks are planned for this area so road access may change. Climb the mountain by gaining the summit ridge up the easy ground on its south flank.

Mt. Sarai (L) & Mt. Abraham (R) west aspect from Abel Creek Rd., March.

366 Mt. Sarai

Mt. Abraham

Mt. Abraham north-west aspect from Abel creek meadows, March.

Mt. Abraham
5,500 ft./ 1,676 m

Mt. Abraham is located at the west edge of Schoen Lake Provincial Park overlooking the north side of Schoen Lake. The south-east flank of the mountain makes a very steep drop between the summit and the lake shore. To the north the, Abel Creek headwaters begin in a high hanging valley with an exquisite alpine lake chain. The hiking and ski touring terrain in the meadows around this valley is excellent. The Abel Creek meadows are easily reached from the Mt. Cain skihill access road which may help to make this beautiful alpine area more popular than it currently is.

First Ascent: Unknown

Map Sheet: 92 L/1 Schoen Lake - GR 9462

Approaches: There is very fast access into the upper Abel Creek valley from the Mt. Abel logging road which leaves the Mt. Cain road at the first major switchback (just past a bridge over a small but fast moving creek). The road may be drivable between the spring and fall but is snow covered during the winter. Follow the road as far as you can drive or park on the Mt. Cain Road and hike or ski up the Abel Main. Keep right on the roads until a long gentle hill leads down into the main Abel Creek valley. Follow the road to the end and then hike through the remaining forest inside Schoen Lake Park boundary up to the first of the lakes in an exquisite chain under the north face of Mt. Abraham.

Climb Mt. Abraham by either east or west ridges gained directly from the meadows below the north face. See photo above.

Mt. Hapush

Mt. Cain (L) and Mt. Hapush (R) east aspect from Hkusam Mt., October.

Mt. Hapush
5,800 ft./ 1,767 m

Mt. Hapush is located 2 km north of Mt. Cain on the divide between the Tsitika River and Kunnum Creek, a tributary of the Eve River. Hapush presents an imposing north face from Highway 19 at the head of the Eve River valley although it is quite indistinct when viewed from the Mt. Cain ski area.

First Ascent: Unknown

Map Sheet: 92 L/2 Schoen Lake - GR 9068

Approaches: Easily approached from the Mt. Cain ski area. From the parking lot at the base hike up the lower Ridge Run and follow the old cross country ski trails northward into the base of the West Bowl. The base of the bowl may also be reached directly off the ski area access road about 1km below the parking lot. Cross the base of the West Bowl under a subsidiary peak, passing some alpine lakes and an old A-frame cabin. Hike up a tight valley to a chain of tiny lakes south of Mt. Hapush's summit (GR 8968) and on to the south col. A steep gully leads up between the summit and Peak 5579. Climb this gully until a traverse may be made leftward across the south face of Mt. Hapush. A line of weakness leads off this ledge to the top.

Additional Info: IB 2001 p.7

Mt. Hapush south aspect from south col, March.   photo: Peter Rothermel

Mt. Eden

Mt. Eden
photo: Lindsay Elms

Mt. Eden
5,331 ft / 1,625 m

A steep series of rock pinnacles clustered on the massif just north of Schoen Lake Park to the east of the head of Kunnum Creek. The complete closure of the logging road into Kunnum Creek and Mt. Eden's proximity to Schoen Lake Park conspire to make this mountain one of the more challenging peaks to reach outside of Strathcona Park. The views from Mt. Eden are also superb with great perspectives on Mt. Schoen and the peaks around Mt. Cain.

First Recorded Ascent: Lindsay Elms October 22, 1999

Map Sheet: 92 L/1 Schoen Lake - GR 9668

Approaches: Mt. Eden can be approached from the east side from logging roads in the Compton Creek valley.

Access is also possible from Kunnum Creek by hiking or skiing up the valley on the now debuilt logging road bed. Leave the Island Highway 19, 90 km north of Campbell River turning left (south) on South Main in the Eve River valley. Drive parallel to the highway, westward 2 km to a bridge over Kunnum Creek. Park across the bridge and start up the debuilt roadbed southward up the Kunnum Creek valley. From the upper part of the valley gain the north ridge of Mt. Eden and follow it to the summit.

Additional Info: IB 1999 p.25

Mt. Schoen

Mt. Schoen west aspect from Schoen Lake, December.

Mt. Schoen
6,109 ft / 1,862 m

Mt. Schoen is the highest mountain in the Sutton Range next to Victoria & Warden Peaks. It is located within Schoen Lake Provincial Park between Schoen Creek which flows via the Davie River westward into the Nimpkish and the Adam River which flows to the east. Its situation above Schoen Lake and Nisnak Meadows is one of the most beautiful on Vancouver Island.

First Ascent: Mike Walsh, Bill Perry 1968

Map Sheet: 92 L/1 Schoen Lake - GR 9759

Approaches: Mt. Schoen is best reached from the east side of Schoen Lake Park through which the Adam River Main logging road runs en route to Gerald Creek and the White River Main. From the Island Highway 10 km north of Sayward (74 km north of Campbell River), near the Keta Lake rest area, turn south onto the Adam Main and continue along the gravel road 25 km to Schoen Lake Park. Park at a pullout among tall old growth trees.

Hike the flagged route across the Adam River and Nisnak Meadows to the east shore of Nisnak Lake. From here the best route heads south up a steep valley to the east of the mountain. From the col at the head of this valley turn west and begin climbing onto the south ridge of Mt. Schoen.

Additional Info: IB 1995 p.17

Mt. Schoen North-East aspect from Adam River, April.

Mt. Schoen south-east aspect from Kokummi Mountain, December.

Routes

South Ridge: 4th class
Approach from Adam River through Nisnak Meadows to the upper Nisnak Creek which drains a tight valley east of the summit. Hike south up the steep valley to a col at GR 000581. Turn north and continue up a steep, narrow, forested ridge. Turn 90° and hike westward along the south-east end of the summit ridge over the first of a series of summits. (At the first col a route leads down into the large east cirque bypassing the rocky sections along the ridge and rejoining the route at the col below the main summit's South Ridge.)

Continue along the South Ridge from the col and climb up the narrow ridge onto the next large summit at GR 986585. Descend the west side of this summit and follow the crest as it turns again to the north. Scramble over a series of pinnacles, with some exposed 4th class or low 5th class ,past the south summit to a col below the toe of the South Ridge of the main summit. Continue up the rocky ridge to the top.

Variation: The South Ridge may also be started directly from Nisnak Meadows at its toe.

Direct Route: 4th class
Takes a steep, direct line to the upper east cirque and joins the South Ridge route at the col between the two summits. From Nisnak Meadows follow the Nisnak Trail toward Schoen Lake. Aim across the meadows to the base of a prominent gully that leads up between two rock towers under the main summit. Hike up this gully to the east cirque. Cross the cirque on snow and scree leftward (south) to the col between the south and main summits. Climb up the South Ridge to the top.

FA: Lindsay Elms, Jan Neuspiel, 25 June 1995

West Side: 4th class
From the now decommissioned campground at the outlet of Schoen Lake cross the outlet and hike logging road (formerly a forest footpath) to Schoen Creek. Cross the creek and climb a rib right of the stream draining the summit. Drift rightward into the steep gully immediately south of the summit. This is a straightforward snow climb in early season. Continue up south ridge to summit.

FA: Mike Walsh, Bill Perry, 1968

Mt. Schoen north-east aspect from Nisnak Meadows, September.

Mt. Schoen 371

Mt. Romeo & Mt. Juliet

Mt. Juliet
5,371 ft / 1,637 m

A small area of alpine culminates in the summit of Mt. Juliet, located north-east of Mt. Eden between Montague Creek and Capulet Creek. There are some pretty alpine lakes north of the summit and great views of Jagged Mountain and the hidden north side of Mt. Cain.

First Ascent: A.J. Campbell survey party 1932

Map Sheet: 92 L/8 Adam River - GR 0170 (see also 92 L/1 Schoen Lake)

Approaches: Both Mt. Juliet and Mt. Romeo may be reached from logging roads in Montague Creek. To reach Mt. Juliet from the Island Highway, turn south on the Rooney Lake Rd. 87 km north of Campbell River, 23 km north of Sayward. Stay left on RL 640 in to Capulet Creek. Ascend Juliet from spurs on the long timbered (and formerly more timbered) north ridge.

The north ridge may be reached from the Montague Creek side too by ascending a wide, mapped avalanche chute 'Shovelgate Gully' from the floor of the valley right to the ridge crest. This route is best with snow cover. FA: Lindsay Elms, Sandy Briggs, 20 February, 2000

Additional Info: IB 2000 p.26

Mt. Romeo
5,449 ft / 1,661 m

Located north-east of Mt. Eden between Kunnum Creek and Montague Creek.

First Recorded Ascent: Lindsay Elms 28th September, 1999

Map Sheet: 92 L/8 Adam River - GR 9970 (see also 92 L/1 Schoen Lake)

Approaches: Follow the description for Mt. Juliet on Rooney Lake Road. Keep to the Owens Lake Main, 4 wheel drive essential, into Montague Creek. Approach from the back of the valley gaining the south-east ridge and following it with no difficulties to the summit.

Genesis Mountain
4,876 ft / 1,486 m

Genesis Mountain is an isolated peak surrounded by the deep valleys on the north-east boundary of Schoen Lake Provincial Park. To the south-east is the Adam River, to the north Compton Creek while to the west are Nisnak Creek and other tributaries of Schoen Lake. Genesis Mountain offers some of the finest views of Schoen Lake Park and Mt. Schoen which looms across the Nisnak valley.

First Ascent: Unknown

Map Sheet: 92 L/1 Schoen Lake - GR 0063

Approaches: Although the terrain along the tapered north-east ridge invites ready access from logging roads out of Compton Creek and/or Schoen Lake Rd on the west bank of the Adam River, a more aesthetic approach may be had through the old-growth from Nisnak Lake.

From the Island Highway 10 km north of Sayward (74 km north of Campbell River), near the Keta Lake rest area, turn south onto the Adam Main and continue on the gravel road 25 km to Schoen Lake Park. Park at a pullout among tall old growth trees. Hike the flagged route across the Adam River and Nisnak Meadows to the east shore of Nisnak Lake. Continue around the north shore of Nisnak Lake to the outlet of a prominent creek draining the south flank of Genesis Mt. Keep to the east side of the creek and follow a line up steep forest to a col and sub-alpine lake at 3,800 ft / 1160 m just west of the peak. Turn eastward and hike up the easy west ridge to the summit.

Jagged Mountain

Jagged Mountain north-west aspect from Island Highway 19, February.

Jagged Mountain
5,580 ft./ 1,701 m

Jagged Mountain is a complex maze of rock pinnacles towering over the Eve River valley and Highway 19 north-east of Mt. Cain.

First Recorded Ascent: T. De Groot, E. Kellerhals, L. Paterson, S. Paterson, M. Taylor, 7 June 1982

Map Sheet: 92 L/8 Adam River - GR 9271

Approaches: Approach from ever rising logging roads on the north flanks out of the Eve River valley. Just south of the Eve River rest area on Highway 19, 90 km north of Campbell River, is a junction to turn onto the Eve River South Main. Drive along the South Main paralleling the highway. Turn south on spur S 65 and follow it as high as you can drive into a narrow valley between Jagged and Peak 5008. A couple of routes options lead up the steep timbered slopes to the head of this valley in a col. Climb up the south ridge to the summit.

Jagged Mountain south-west aspect from the summit of Mt. Cain, January.

Jagged Mountain **373**

374 Mt. Grattan from Perry Creek valley.

Tlupana Range

Mt. Alava above Alava Lake.

Tlupana Range
Contents

Big Baldy Mt.	**380**
Conuma Peak	**381**
Stevens Peak	**382**
Leighton Peak	**382**
Mt. Bate	**383**
Mt. Alava	**385**
Malaspina Peak	**386**
Mt. Grattan	**387**
Thumb Peak	**388**
Mt. Leiner	**389**
Peak 5150	**389**
Mt. McKelvie	**390**
Tahsis Mountain	**390**
Santiago Mountain	**390**
Woss Mountain	**391**
Peak 5005	**391**

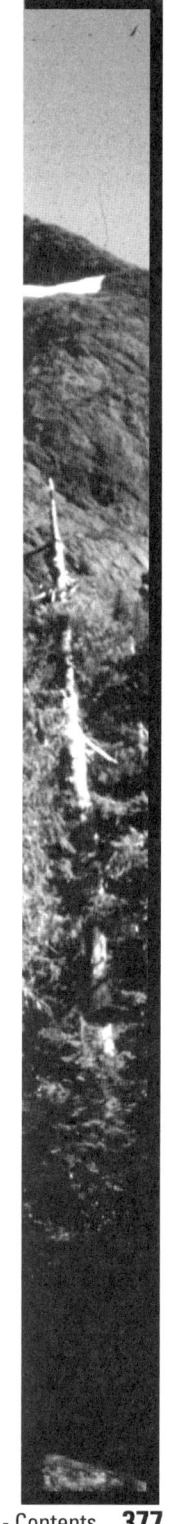

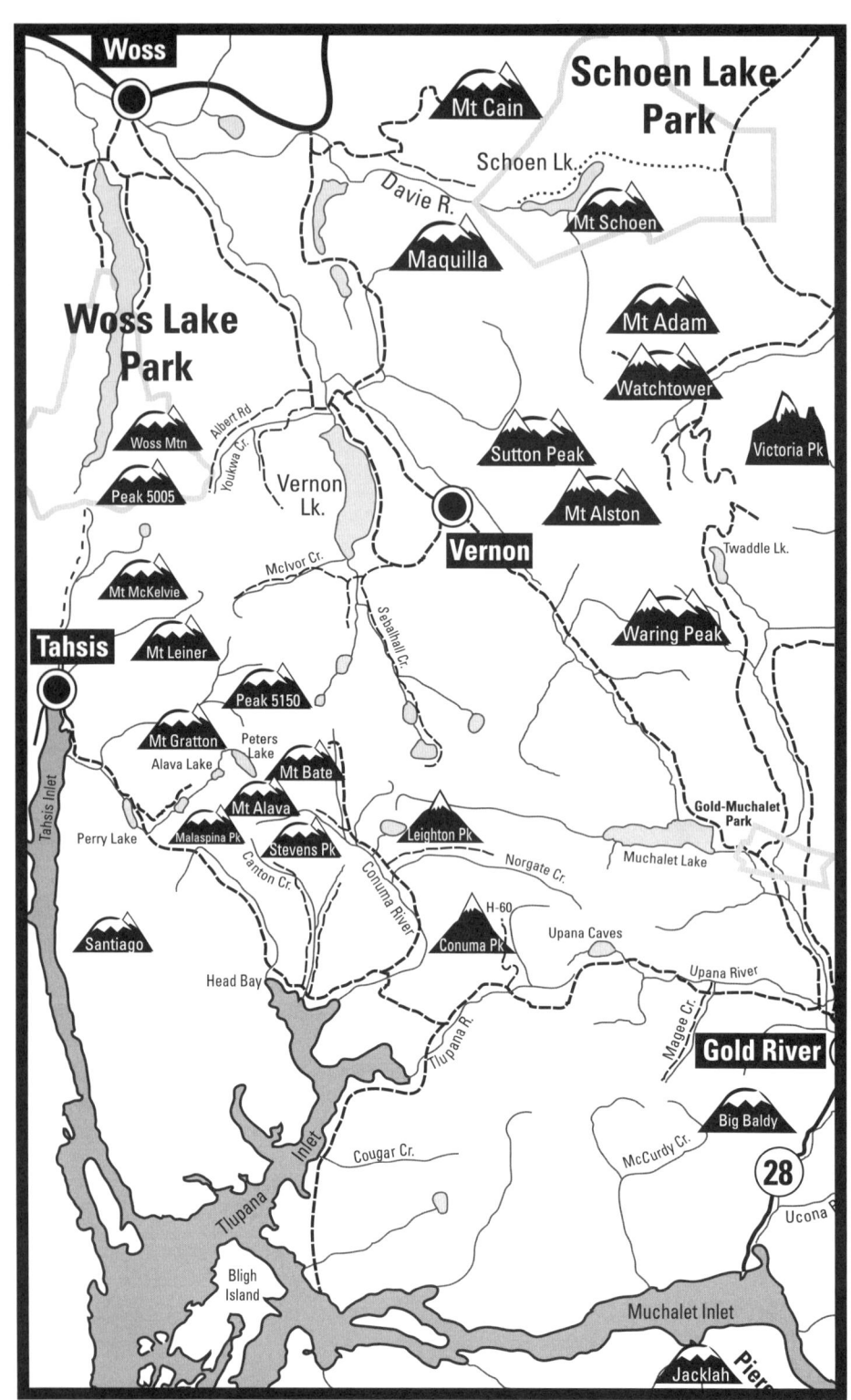

Tlupana Range - Map

Tlupana Range

The Tlupana Range is one of the least explored and most picturesque of all alpine areas on Vancouver Island. The climbing history of the range is in its infancy with most first ascents having taken place as recently as the 1990s. There are still several summits that have no recorded ascents and the climbing potential of this area is vast . One of the Tlupana Range's most striking features is the low elevation of the treeline which in places is as low as 3,000 ft. This gives the mountains in the range a character expected of much higher alpine peaks. The Tlupana Range is also one of the widest areas of alpine terrain on the island spanning with its main ridge stretching over 5 km in width in some places. Tlupana was a Nootka chief who lived in Mooacha village in Nootka Sound. He was visited by Capt. Vancouver and Brgdr. General Alava in 1794.[1]

There are several longer high traverses possible through the Tlupana Range. The Vancouver Island Backbone route makes use of the main spine and is an incredible hiking route through some of the wildest terrain on the Island. The rugged nature of the Tlupana Range and the difficult access complicate trip logistics somewhat and it is unlikely to ever become a high use area. The deep wilderness and pristine character of the mountains here offers a unique experience that those who have visited the area come to greatly respect. This respect manifests itself in a will to preserve the character and integrity of the Tlupana mountains with strict no-trace visits being de rigeur.

Map Sheets: 92 E/16 Gold River • 92 E/15 Zeballos • 92 L/2 Woss Lake

Boundaries: north: Nimpkish River, **east:** Nimpkish River, **south:** Tlupana Inlet, Nootka Sound, **west:** Tahsis Inlet, Tahsis River & Woss Lake.

Major Access Routes: The Tlupana Range may be reached from two main public gravel roads. The first is **Nimpkish Road** a.k.a. Woss-Gold River Road which follows the course of the Gold River to Muchalet Lake and from there north along Nimpkish River to join Highway 19 just east of the village of Woss.

The other major road is the **Head Bay Forest Service Road** which leads west from the town of Gold River over the Upana Pass to Tlupana Inlet and along the Perry and Leiner Rivers to the community of Tahsis at the head of Tahsis Inlet.

Conuma Main: Heads north off the Head Bay Rd. west of Gold River. Branch roads off Conuma Main come close to Mt. Bate, Stevens Peak and Leighton Peak.

Canton Main: Runs up Canton Creek west of Gold River from the Head Bay Rd. Accesses Stevens Peak, Malaspina Peak and Mt. Alava.

Perry Main: An overgrown and deactivated road which is still useful for reaching Malaspina Peak Mt. Grattan and Mt. Alava. The bushwack to Peters Lake up Perry River is well renowned!

Sebalhall Road: A major artery off Nimpkish Road at Vernon Lake. Sebalhall Rd. gives access to the north-east side of the Tlupana Range and has been used to reach Mt. Bate, Thumb Peak and Mt. Grattan.

From Nimpkish Road a long ridge line winds from Tolnay Creek westward along the divide between the Sebalhall and Conuma Rivers to the Tlupana Range. This ridge is an arduous hike but along with the main Tlupana Range forms one of the longest continuous alpine ridge systems on the island.

Forest Service & Logging Company Offices:

• **Campbell River Forest District** - 370 South Dogwood Street, Campbell River, B.C. V9W 6Y7
Ph: (250) 286-9300

• **Western Forest Products** - #118 – 1334 Island Hwy. Campbell River, BC V9W 8C9
Ph: 250 286-3767

Other Information Sources:

Nootka Sound and the Surrounding Waters of Maquinna by Heather Harbord (1996)

Special Thanks:

Thanks to Sandy Briggs, Chris Barner and Lindsay Elms for assistance in preparing this chapter.

Big Baldy Mountain

Big Baldy Mountain south-east aspect from south col of Mt. Colonel Foster, May.

Big Baldy Mt.
5,282 ft./ 1,610 m

Big Baldy Mountain overlooks the north shore of Muchalet Inlet just west of the town of Gold River. Valleys radiate off Big Baldy in every direction like spokes on a wheel. The mountain has a surprisingly impressive east face but no climbing routes have been reported on this feature.

First Ascent: Alfred Slocomb survey party 1947

Map Sheet: 92 E/16 Gold River - GR 0615

Approaches: To climb Big Baldy approach the mountain on logging roads in Magee Creek. From Gold River head west toward Tahsis on the Head Bay Forest Service Road. The gravel road climbs a steep grade up the Upana valley. After ~6 km look for the junction where branch H 11 heads south up Magee Creek. Cross the bridge over Magee Creek to its east bank and continue up with a high valley due west of Big Baldy's summit as the objective. Hike up this valley heading south to a col west of the summit.

From the col head east up a ridge which gradually becomes indistinct above treeline. The ground levels on the summit plateau and the last hike to the top is at a casual angle up the south-west ridge.

Big Baldy Mountain east aspect from Crest Mountain, August.   photo: Sasha Kubicek

Conuma Peak

Conuma Peak south-west aspect from Head Bay Road near Moutcha Bay, June.

Conuma Peak
4,860 ft./ 1,481m

A sharp needle which looms over Nootka Sound. The mountain is a cultural icon to the Nootka First Nation who give Conuma Peak its name.[2] Despite its diminutive elevation it is an imposing summit, dropping steeply off on all sides. It is located on the divide between Conuma River to the west and Norgate Creek a tributary of the Conuma to the north and east. To the south, the Tlupana River runs along with the Head Bay Forest Service Road which parallels the river. There is a rumour that a helicopter has flown through the large stone arch just below the summit.

First Ascent: Historically climbed by Mowachaht people.

Map Sheet: 92 E/16 Gold River - GR 9322

Approaches: Conuma Peak is best approached from branch logging roads in the upper Tlupana River valley on the south-east side of the mountain. At the bottom of a steep hill ~20 km west of Gold River the Head Bay Forest Service Road crosses the bridge over Tlupana River then turns right (north) on to branch H-60. Drive up the road system to the highest spur on the south ridge of Conuma Peak. Once on foot aim for the crest of the timbered south ridge and hike north toward the mountain. Ascend the south ridge to the summit keeping to the west side on lower angle ground near the top.

The north ridge is also a fine scramble from a pleasant tarn-strewn bench above treeline.

Additional Info: IB 1997 p.17

Conuma Peak south aspect from lower south ridge.   photo: Sandy Briggs

Stevens Peak

Stevens Peak north-east aspect from Conuma-Sebalhall divide, August.

Stevens Peak
4,952 ft / 1,509 m

Stevens Peak is located at the southern end of the main Tlupana Range cradled between two branches of Canton Creek to the south and west and Conuma River to the north and east.

First Ascent: Alfred Slocomb survey party 1947

Map Sheet: 92 E/16 Gold River - GR 8225

Approaches: The mountain may possibly be reached along the connecting ridge from south of Mt. Alava. Or more directly approach from logging roads in Canton Creek. A prominent ridge running south from the summit offers one route from Canton West Main from a point on the road after it crosses to the east bank of the west fork of the creek. Or try the long ridge running west to the peak from the pass at GR 8625 from East Canton Main. Watch for a canyon in the forest en route to the pass.

Leighton Peak (L) north-east aspect from Sutton Peak, June

Leighton Peak
4,632 ft./ 1,411 m

A lower twin to Conuma Peak and just to the north of it on the Conuma-Muchalet divide, Leighton Peak has a profile similar to that of its more impressive neighbour.

First Ascent: Unknown

Map Sheet: 92 E/16 Gold River - GR 9126

Approaches: Leighton Peak might be approached from the Conuma Main road in the Conuma River valley. From 5 km up the Conuma look for a branch road on the north side of the river heading toward Leighton Lake. Hike toward the mountain from the lake up the prominent west ridge.

Mt. Bate

Mt. Bate north-west aspect from Peter Lake, August.

Mt. Bate
5,511 ft./ 1,680 m

Mt. Bate is the highest peak in the Tlupana Range. Its east snowfield is a familiar sight on the western skyline from many peaks in Strathcona Park for much of the year. The peak is an impressive from most angles and climbing it is not without challenge.

First Ascent: Rob Macdonald and Paul Erickson, 18 September 1982

Map Sheet: 92 E/16 Gold River - GR 8129

Approaches: Mt. Bate may be reached from the Head Bay Forest Service Road via branch road P-15 in upper Perry River. Follow the road to the back of the valley and then head up through dense bush alongside the rushing creek. A steep sided canyon lined with B4 slide alder makes for great sport, thrashing up to an open slab of rock down which the creek tumbles. Weave a crafty line up the rock slabs to Alava Lake. Cross Perry River and continue up the valley to Peter Lake. The lake can be skirted on the west shore but is pretty awkward. Some parties have opted to avoid the bush and difficulties getting around the lake by flying in by helicopter. Larger fly-in parties also fly out their human waste to preserve this pristine alpine area.

Alternative approach routes to Mt. Bate come in from the south and east. From the south, approach up logging roads in the Conuma River valley. Take the spur road into the west branch of Conuma

Mt. Bate (R) south-east aspect from Victoria Peak, August.

Mt. Bate **383**

Mt. Bate west aspect from Mount Alava, June. photo: Sandy Briggs

River. Hike up the steep sided valley along the east flank of the mountain to the small lakes at the foot of the north ridge, known as Shangri-La.

From the east a very long approach may be made from Nimpkish Road at Tolnay Creek. Head up the branch roads on the north side of Tolnay Creek on the flanks of a horseshoe shaped peak at GR 9236. Be sure to hike up the southern-most of the two arms of the horseshoe to avoid getting bluffed out on the pinnacle on the north arm. Follow the divide west and south between the Sebalhall and Muchalet valleys to the Sebalhall-Conuma Pass at GR 8532 taking 2-3 days. From the pass traverse around the south side of a round knoll to the foot of a long ridge which leads up into the alpine just north-east of Peter Lake. Head south to Mt. Bate keeping to the east on the huge snowfield.

Additional Info: IB 1995 p.18, IB 1998 p.5

Routes

East Face: 5.5 (III)
From the Shangri-La lakes traverse a wide ledge system under the East Face. Scramble up to gain the south-east ridge which links Bate to the incorrectly named summit to the south-east. Continue up the ridge leaving it to traverse out onto the snowfield below a sub-summit. Climb up the snow on a diagonal line to a notch below the right side of the summit tower. Climb a black dike 5.5 to a belay. 3rd class leads to a couple of 5th class moves onto the tiny summit. Consider rappelling on the descent.

** North-East Ridge: 5.6 1500m (III)
Approach the toe of the ridge from Shangri-La lakes. Climb an east facing coulior to gain the crest of the ridge. Continue along ridge over the gendarmes. Bypass the last tower on the east side to notch below summit. Follow description for East Face to summit.
FA: Chris Barner, Mike Dwinnell, Gerald Cobbold, Chris Perreault, 1998

Mt. Alava (L) & Mt. Bate (R) south-east aspect from Conuma River, August.

Mt. Alava

Mt. Grattan (L) Thumb Peak (C) & Mt. Alava (R) south-west aspect from Malaspina Peak.   photo: Sandy Briggs

Mt. Alava
5,085 ft./ 1,550 m

Mt. Alava lies on the south side of the upper Perry River valley just west of Mt. Bate. The alpine around Mt. Alava is some of the most expansive and exquisite alpine on Vancouver Island. There are terrific views from Mt. Alava southward into Nootka Sound. The proximity to the coast and the subsequently harsher climate keep the treeline close to 3,000 ft giving the Bate-Alava area a distinctive character. Named for Brigadier-General Don José Manuel Alava last commander of the Spanish base in Nootka Sound. In 1795 he handed it over to the British in settling the Nootka Convention.[3]

First Ascent: Rob Macdonald, Paul Erickson, 11 July 1980

Map Sheet: 92 E/16 Gold River - GR 7929 (Mt. Alava is incorrectly labelled on the map)

Approaches: The area around Mt. Alava and Mt. Bate can be reached from the Head Bay Forest Service Road via branch road P-15 in upper Perry River. Follow the road to the back of the valley and then head up through dense bush alongside the rushing creek. A steep sided canyon lined with slide alder makes for great sport thrashing up to an open slab of rock down which the creek tumbles. Weave a crafty line up the rock slabs to Alava Lake. Cross Perry River and continue up the valley to Peter Lake. Climb up the prominent ridge which leads up to a col on the east side of Mt. Alava between Alava and 'Little Alava' (the falsely named summit to the south-east). From the col scramble up 4th class ground on the mountains east side to the summit. Little Alava is an easy scramble from the col.

A long timbered gully on the east side of the upper Perry River, near the unnamed lake, gives an alternate route to the mountain through a pass at GR 7827. Cross the high basin on the south-west side of Mt. Alava and use a gully up the west side of the south ridge to reach the route on the east side of the mountain as described above. This route also accesses Malaspina Peak from the pass.

Mt. Alava west aspect from head of Canton Creek, August.

Malaspina Peak

Malaspina Peak north-east aspect from near Mt. Alava, August.

Malaspina Peak
5,160 ft./ 1,573 m

A high summit of rocky pinnacles just above and to the east of the Head Bay Forest Service Road between Gold River and Tahsis. The mountain is encircled by Perry River to the north, Canton Creek to the east and Sucwoa River and the adjacent Head Bay Road to the west. It is a steep climb up to Malaspina Peak and a trip to Mt. Alava makes an overnight trip to the area worthwhile. Awesome views of Nootka Sound and Esperanza Inlet. Named after Captain Alexandro Malaspina 1754-1809, one of the more romantic early European navigators to visit the British Columbia coast.[4]

First Ascent: Unknown

Map Sheet: 92 E/15 Zeballos - GR 7726

Approaches: From the Head Bay Forest Service Road via branch road P-15 in upper Perry River gain the spur road which weaves up the north-west ridge of the mountain. Follow this ridge toward Peak 4961 which is incorrectly named as the summit. The now-deactivated Perry River main gives access via a southward spur that climbs in rough and vegetated fashion to 600m on the north-west ridge of Malaspina's second-highest peak (4,986 ft / 1,520 m). The bridge to this spur has been removed, so ford the creek. Hike off the end of this spur road and ascend a rib to the extreme upper right of the clearcut at nearly 700m. An animal trail leads up into the verdant old-growth and becomes indistinct on a small bench. Ascend through friendly forest leads to a band of bluffs at about 1000m. These can be surmounted by an upward right route followed by a leftward traverse along a ramp below a rock wall. The ridge crest, which immediately follows, is open with many small ponds. The south summit (1520m) is a steep hike from here. Strike north-east toward the Main Summit. Make a 4th class scramble or climb a steep snow gully Avoid a steeper chimney-gully to the left.

An alternative approach is from the Head Bay Forest Service Road up branch road WC-1 which can be reached in Head Bay taking a left off West Canton Main. Follow WC-1 into the tight, high valley on the south-east side of Malaspina Peak. Gain the prominent ridge on the west side of the valley and hike up it to the alpine at a satellite summit at GR 7824. Continue along the ridge toward the summit

Malaspina Peak (R) north-west aspect from the Haihte Range, March.

Mt. Grattan

Mt. Bate (L) Mt. Grattan (C() & Mt. Alava (R) north-west aspect from Rugged Mountain, March.

Mt. Grattan
5,085 ft./ 1,550 m

Mt. Grattan is a twin peaked pyramid-shaped mountain on the north side of Peter Lake and north of Mt. Bate. It is named after Noel Grattan, a soldier killed in action May 31, 1942. The mountain lies on the divide between the Leiner River to the north-west, the Conuma River to the south-east and the Perry River to the south-west. Mt. Grattan has a dramatic north face dropping steeply off into a south fork of Leiner River. It is a popular objective for the few climbers that make it into this area each year because of its great rock, its proximity to Peter Lake, and the outstanding position of the peak and the resultant views and atmosphere surrounding it.

First Ascent: Rob Macdonald, Julie Henderson, Paul Erickson, Rick Eppler, 5 October 1991

Map Sheet: 92 E/16 Gold River - GR 8031

Approaches: Mt. Grattan can be reached from the Head Bay Forest Service Road, follow the approach details for Mt. Alava to Peter Lake. From the south-east corner of Peter Lake hike up a draw toward a col at GR 8130 above and just south of the Shangri-La lakes. This col can also be reached via the Shangri-La basin from the upper Conuma River road system in under six hours. Follow the lower South Ridge of Thumb Peak to just below 'the Thumb' gendarme. Turn west descending slightly to the foot of the East Ridge of Mt. Grattan. For the West Ridge approach from the north-west shore of Peter Lake at the outlet of Perry Creek. Scramble up a narrow but easy ridge above the lake.

*** **East Ridge:** 5.6 (III) 175m
Superb climbing on excellent rock up the crest of the well defined ridge. Approach from Shangri-La.

*** **West Ridge:** 4th class 300m
Follows the crest of this superbly exposed ridge. Approach from Peter Lake.

Mt. Grattan south aspect above Alava Lake, August.

Thumb Peak

Mt. Grattan (L) and Thumb Peak (R) south-east aspect from Shangri-La, July. photo: Sandy Briggs

Thumb Peak
5,298 ft / 1,615 m

A rounded peak north-east of Mt. Grattan with a prominent thumb-shaped southern gendarme called The Thumb.

First Ascent: Paul Erickson, Karl Erickson, Rob Macdonald, Julie Henderson, Rick Eppler, 1 July 1995

Map Sheet: 92 E/16 Gold River - GR 8131

Approaches: Thumb Peak is easily climbed from the Shangri-La basin on snow or rock up its east ridge, which becomes a little steep higher up. To climb 'the Thumb' gendarme, follow approach details for Mt. Grattan and continue along the South Ridge of the main Thumb Peak keeping to the right (east) to minimize difficulties (low 5th). The last pitch is a low-fifth class chimney/gully.

Additional Info: IB 1995 p.18, IB 1998 p.5

South Ridge: 4th class 200m+
A fine scramble up an elegant arete. Climb 150 m of class 4 to easier ground. A long 50 m traverse out on a ledge across the east face ('the Thumbnail') leads to a short 15m, 4th class step on to the summit.
FA: Paul Erickson, Karl Erickson, Rob Macdonald, Julie Henderson, Rick Eppler, 1 July 1995

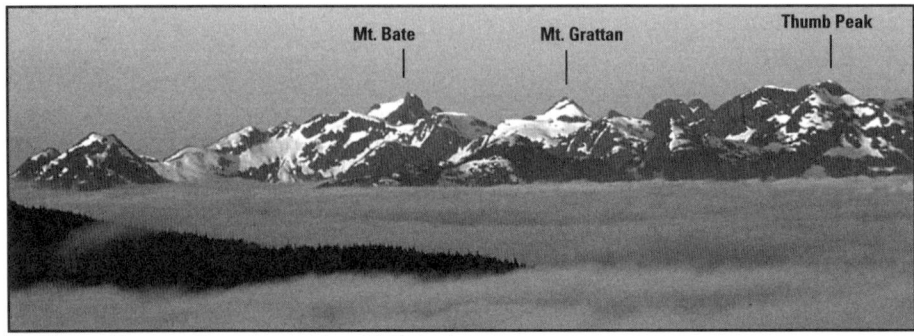

The Tlupana Range north-east aspect from Mt. Cain, June.

Mt. Leiner

Aerial view from the north-west into the Tlupana Range, March.

Mt. Leiner
4,783 ft / 1,458 m

Mt. Leiner is a rocky mountain surrounded by steep bluffy flanks. It sits on the divide between McKelvie Creek on its north side and the Leiner River to the south.

Map Sheet: 92 E/15 Zeballos - GR 7437

Approaches: A flagged route begins off the Head Bay Forest Service Road along the short section between the Leiner River estuary and the entrance to the village of Tahsis. The route is flagged only a short way at time of writing but starts you up a route on the south-west ridge which can be followed with a long hike to the summit. Consider a traverse around to Mt. McKelvie from Tahsis if you have a few days to spare.

Mt. Leiner might also be reached from logging roads in McIvor Creek south-west of Vernon Lake. Drive to Vernon Lake south from the Island Highway at the Schoen Lake - Mt. Cain junction following signs for Gold River. At Vernon Camp turn west on Vernon Lake Road then left (south-west) on Sebalhall Road. After 3 km turn right (west) and cross Sebalhall River. Turn right (north-west) on to McIvor Rd. and follow it as far back into the valley as is drivable. Hike to the mountain from the north-east over Peak 4750.

Peak 5150
5,150 ft / 1,570 m

Peak 5150 is a high mountain of several steep pinnacles jutting to the west of the main Tlupana Range ridge. The mountain juts into the Leiner River valley which drains all aspects of the peak.

Map Sheet: 92 E/15 Zeballos - GR 7934 (see also 92 E/16 Gold River)

Approaches: Peak 5150 may be reached from Peter Lake. Follow the approach descriptions for Mt. Alava and Mt. Grattan to Thumb Peak. Continue north along the ridge crest past Thumb Peak. The steeper ground over Thumb Peak may be avoided by crossing the cirque around the lake at GR 8130 and hiking due north up the back of the cirque onto the ridge crest. From a cluster of small lakes at GR 8034 head west toward Peak 5150.

Mt. McKelvie

Mt. McKelvie north-west aspect from the Haihte Range, March.

Mt. McKelvie
5,350 ft / 1,630 m

Mt. McKelvie is an isolated mountain separated from the main Tlupana Range by a low pass between the Leiner River and McIvor Creek. It is one of the higher peaks in the range and is notable for one of the few glaciers in the Tlupana Range which graces its north flank.

Map Sheet: 92 E/15 Zeballos - GR 7339

Approaches: A route from Tahsis leads up the long gentle south-west ridge. This route is flagged partway. Pickup this route 1km up McKelvie Creek. This drainage is the water supply area for the village of Tahsis. Permission may be needed to travel up the short road to the water intake area. Once underway hike up the flagged route to a knoll Peak 3868. Tragically decend almost 1200 ft to a timbered pass at GR 7038 and then pickup the upper extension of the ridge which leads to a summit west of Mt. Mckelvie's main summit. Keep to the north side of the mountain savouring views over Woss Lake and climb to the top with no technical difficulty. An ideal option with several days at hand is to do a horeshoe traverse around McKelvie Creek from Mt. McKelvie to Mt. Leiner right from Tahsis.

Tahsis Mountain
4,300 ft / 1,310 m

Tahsis Mountain is a collection of low craggy summits on the east shore of Tahsis Inlet.

Map Sheet: 92 E/15 Zeballos - GR 7124

Approaches: Logging roads run high all over the mountain, try T-60 from Tsowwin Main.

Santiago Mountain
4,236 ft / 1,291 m

Santiago Mountain is a surprisingly impressive peak on the east shore of Tahsis Inlet with commanding views of Esperanza Inlet and Nootka Sound.

Map Sheet: 92 E/15 Zeballos - GR 7219

Approaches: Best from spurs of Tsowwin Main off Head Bay Forest Service Rd to Tahsis try T-60.

Woss Mountain

Woss Mountain south-west aspect from Haihte Range, March.

Woss Mountain
5,230 ft / 1,594

Woss Mountain is a gentle open summit on the south-east end of Woss Lake. Despite its rolling plateau of a summit the flanks of the mountain are steep and bluffy. The height of land over Woss Mountain forms the boundary to Woss Lake Provincial Park. The views of Rugged Mountain and the Haihte Range is a superlative Vancouver Island mountain vista.

Map Sheet: 92 L/2 Woss Lake - GR 7447

Approaches: Try your hand reaching Woss Mountain by boat from Woss Lake. Use the boat ramp at the Woss Lake Forest Service Recreation site or drive further down the east shore of the lake to its furthest drivable point and hoof a canoe or kayak down to the lake from there. Boat down the lake to the outlet of a prominent creek draining the west flank of the mountain. Bushwhack up along the north bank of this creek and skirt a ridge north of Woss Mt. to reach a lake at GR 7348. Hike up the north-west ridge from the lake to the summit.

Logging roads in Youkwa Creek come close to the east side of Woss Mountain. Drive south from the Island Highway on Nimpkish Road. After crossing the railway line and bridge over the Nimpkish River turn right to Vernon Lake Forest Service Recreation site. Go right heading west and then left (west) on to Albert Road on the north bank of Youkwa Creek. Drive as far as possible on the road then continue on foot up the very steep hillside to a pass at GR 7445. Head north-west along the open ridge to the summit.

Peak 5005
5,005 ft / 1,525

Peak 5005 sits at the very south end of Woss Lake on the east shore.

Map Sheet: 92 L/2 Woss Lake - GR 7143

Approaches: Approach from Woss Lake, the Tahsis River trail or even from logging roads in Youkwa Creek, see Woss Mountain approach details.

392 Mt. Ashwood & Claude Elliot Lake.

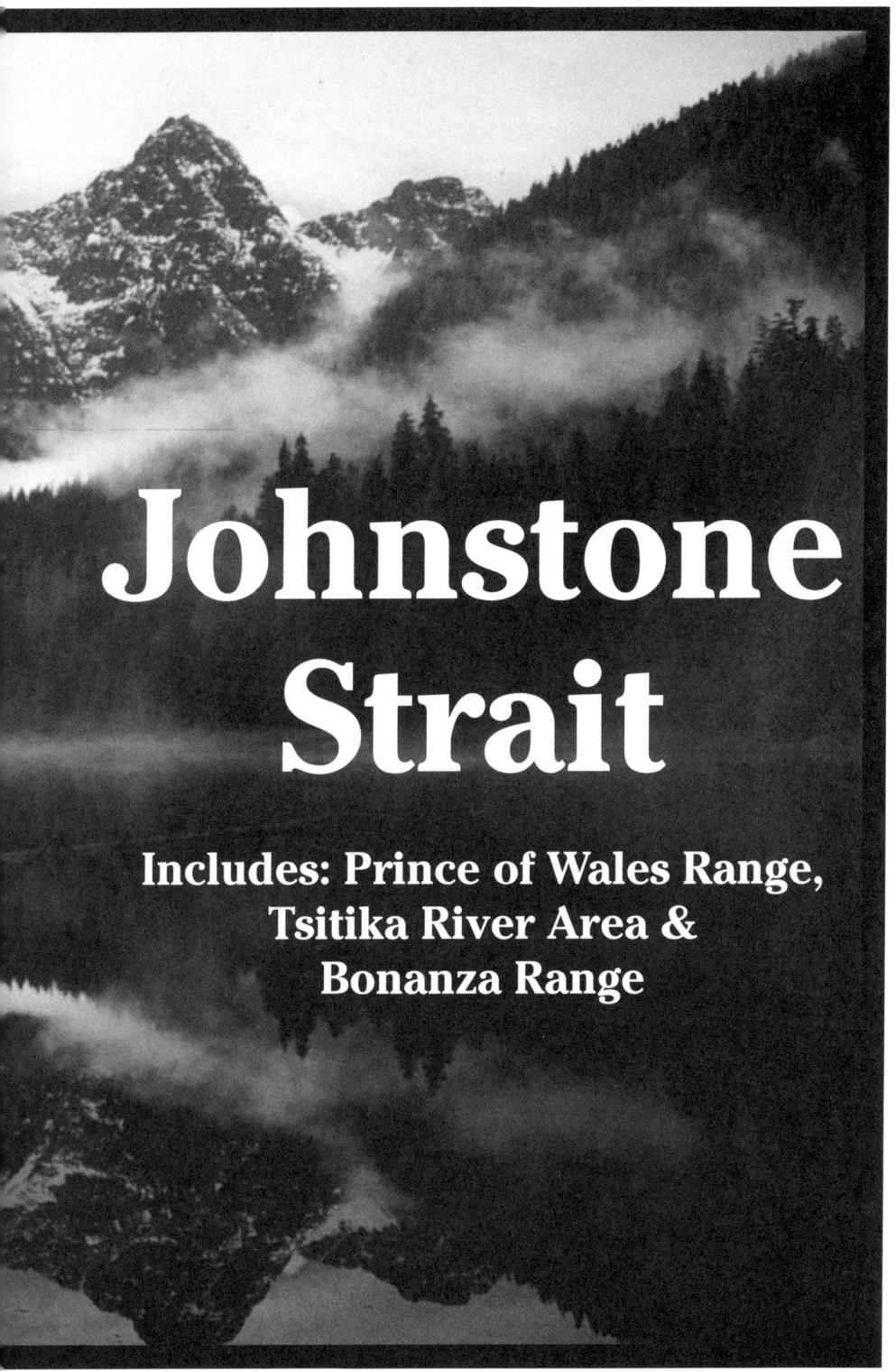

Johnstone Strait

Includes: Prince of Wales Range,
Tsitika River Area &
Bonanza Range

Bleached wood from the huge forest fire on Mt. Hkusam.

Johnstone Strait
Contents

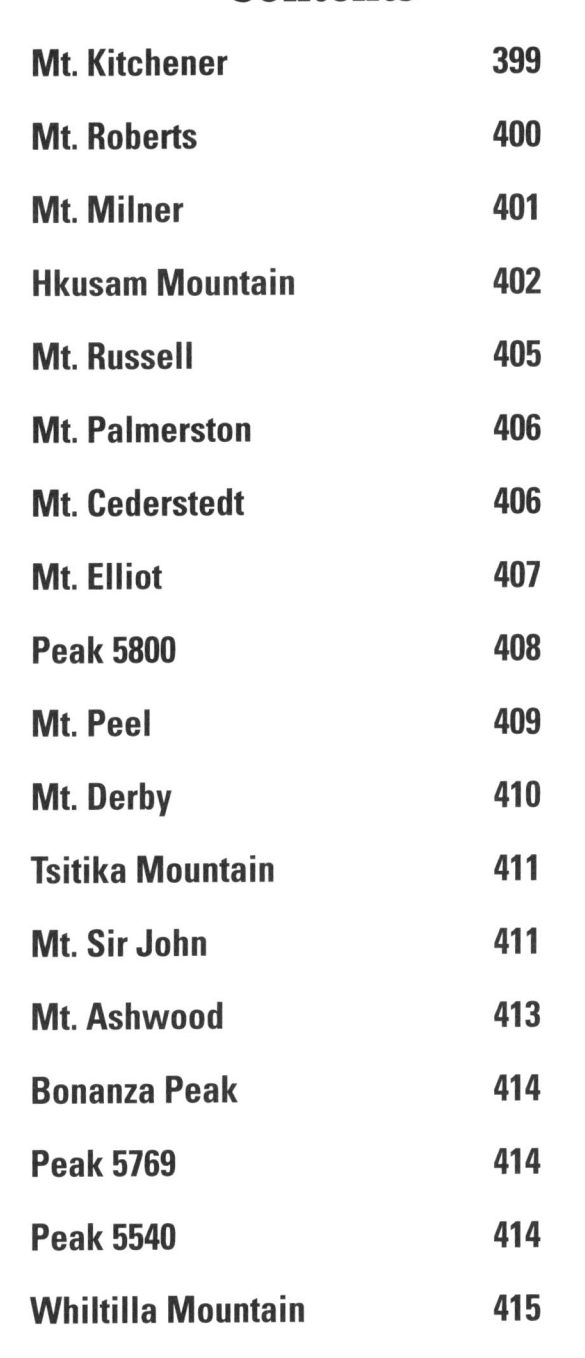

Mt. Kitchener	399
Mt. Roberts	400
Mt. Milner	401
Hkusam Mountain	402
Mt. Russell	405
Mt. Palmerston	406
Mt. Cederstedt	406
Mt. Elliot	407
Peak 5800	408
Mt. Peel	409
Mt. Derby	410
Tsitika Mountain	411
Mt. Sir John	411
Mt. Ashwood	413
Bonanza Peak	414
Peak 5769	414
Peak 5540	414
Whiltilla Mountain	415

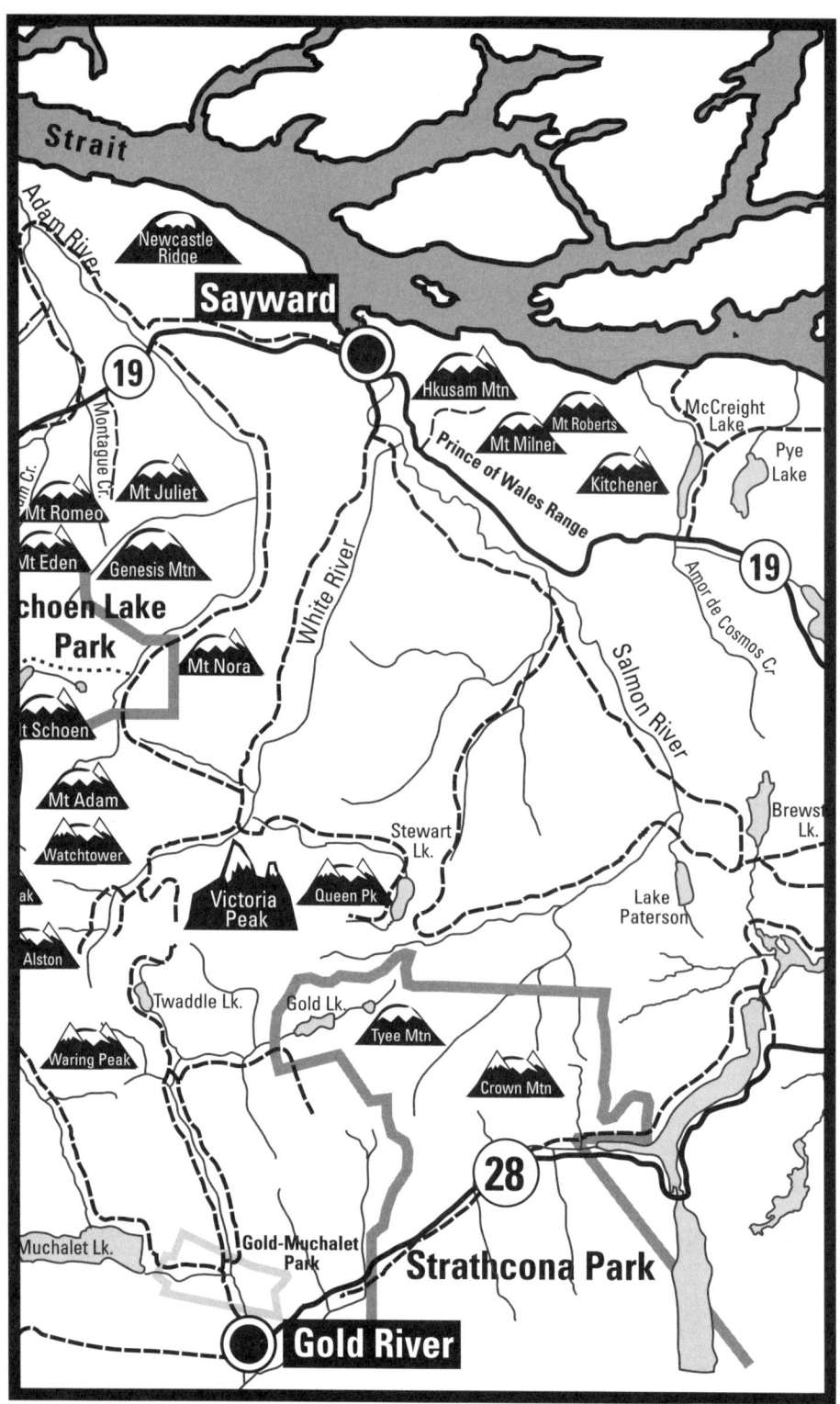

396 Prince of Wales Range - Map

Prince of Wales Range

Prince of Wales Range west aspect from Mt. Russell, September.

The Prince of Wales Range is a small tightly clustered group of mountains overlooking the village of Sayward and the mighty Salmon River valley. The views of the Vancouver Island mountains and Johnstone Strait are superlative. These peaks are one of the only alpine areas on the Island that is close enough to the mainland Coast Range mountains to feel 'connected' to them with views right into the range. The mountains & valley surrounding Sayward is one of the few places on Vancouver Island that can be considered a 'mountain village'. Hkusam Mountain dominates the skyline from Sayward and it along with the rest of the range has played a huge role in the life of the village. The timber from the mountains' slopes, the micro-climate created by the enclosure of the valley and the freshwater from the salmon bearing rivers all contribute to the abundance and vitality of the Sayward valley.

Hkusam Mountain is the obvious first destination to experience these mountains and an excellent trail system around and over the mountain adds to the attraction. Hkusam is by in large a day objective with little to recommend for an overnight stay. To the south-east around Mt. Roberts however, is found more expansive areas of alpine attractive for an overnight trip. The continuous and high connecting ridge along the Prince of Wales Range suggests a complete traverse on foot or on skis from Mt. Kitchener to Peak 5261 would be a very worthwhile 2-4 day trek.

Boundaries: north: Johnstone Strait, **east:** Amor de Cosmos Creek, **south & west:** Salmon River & Highway 19.

Map Sheets: 92 K/5 Sayward

Major Access Routes: The Island Highway runs along the south-west foot of the Prince of Wales Range. Logging roads from the highway into the valleys on the south-west aspect provide the principle access into the mountains.

Big Tree Main: Leaves the highway 46.5 km north of Campbell River and gives access to Mt. Roberts and Mt. Kitchener.

Dyers Main: Leaves the Island Highway 19 close to Sayward on the north side of the Stowe Creek bridge 62 km north of Campbell River off Timber Road. Take the road out of the logging company yard up the Stowe Creek valley to the trails on the east and north sides of Hkusam Mountain

Forest Service & Logging Company Offices:

Campbell River Forest District - 231 Dogwood Ave. Campbell River BC V9W 2Y1 Ph: 287-2194

Weyerhaeuser - North Island Timberlands -P.O. Box 6000, 8010 Island Highway, Campbell River, BC V9W 5E1 Ph: 250-287-5000

Special Thanks:
Thanks to Lyle Fast and Lindsay Elms for assistance in preparing this chapter.

398 Lyle Fast descending the gully off Hkusam Mountain to the Stowe Creek trail.

Mt. Kitchener

Mt. Kitchener south-east aspect from Rock Bay Forest Service Rd., September.

Mt. Kitchener
4,781 ft / 1,457 m

Mount Kitchener forms the eastern end of the Prince of Wales Range. It overlooks McCreight Lake and Amor de Cosmos Creek to the east, Johnstone Strait to the north, Mt. Roberts and the rest of the Prince of Wales Range to the west and Big Tree Creek and the Island Highway to the south. As with the other peaks in the Prince of Wales Range Mt. Kitchener is a surprisingly impressive mountain with four distinct summits. Its expansive, forested lower flanks hide, steep buttresses, ice filled gullies, ski chutes, and rocky needles and reportedly the wreckage of a WW II bomber higher up. Consider Mt. Kitchener and the rest of the area in any season. Cragging, ice climbing, skiing and snowboarding are all possible among these mountains. The mountain is named after Earl Kitchener (1850-1916) Great Britian's Secretary of War at the outbreak of WW1.[1]

First Ascent: A.F. Swannell survey party 1949

Map Sheet: 92 K/5 Sayward - GR 0774

Approaches: High road access into this micro-alpine playground is from the Big Tree Main logging road. Big Tree Main leaves the Island Highway 46.5 km north of Campbell River. Drive up this road, as far as your vehicle and road conditions allow, along the south side of the creek which drains the valley on Kitchener's north-west side. Hike from the end of the road up a gully between Mt. Kitchener and Peak 4781. Continue up the easy ridge to the top.

Additional Info: IB 1995 p.8

Views from the Prince of Wales Range over Johnstone Strait, Discovery Islands and Coast Range mountains.

Mt. Roberts

Mt. Roberts north-west aspect from Hkusam Mountain, October

Mt. Roberts
4,800 ft / 1,463 m

Mt. Roberts and Needle Peak are the next summits north-west of Mt. Kitchener on the Prince of Wales Range. The tops come the closest in this range to the tidal waters of Johnstone Strait and have superb views over Humpback Bay and the rest of the strait. Named for Lt. Henry Roberts a cartographer who accompanied Captain Cook on his second and third voyages. Roberts was initially due to lead the expedition that eventually became Captain George Vancouver's command during which Vancouver made the famous circumnavigation of Vancouver Island. [2]

First Ascent: Unknown

Map Sheet: 92 K/5 Sayward - GR 0676

Approaches: Mt. Roberts is best reached from Big Tree Main, see Mt. Kitchener approach details. Hike off Big Tree Main below the south side of the mountain. Head up to a col south-east of the summit. Continue along the easy hiking ridge to the summit of Mt. Roberts.

Alternatively, drive up the Venus Main logging road which runs up the north side of the Big Tree Creek valley. Locate Venus Main off the Island Highway 47 km north of Campbell River, just north of the Big Tree bridge and rest area. Gain the alpine from spur roads in the basin below the mountains west ridge. Follow the ridge over Peak 4660 and around to Mt. Roberts.

Hiking the ridge system right around the head of Big Tree Creek makes a great extended route to see the eastern end of the Prince of Wales Range. Approach either Mt. Roberts or Mt. Kitchener and keep to the height of land hiking the connecting ridge between the two summits. A few additional bumps get climbed en route and a side trip to the fabled **Needle Peak** north-east of Mt. Roberts adds a possible distraction. Worth an overnight stop and consider a complete traverse of the Prince of Wales Range on foot or on skis.

Needle Peak   photo: Lindsay Elms

Mt. Milner

Mt. Milner south-west aspect from Sayward Junction, September.

Mt. Milner
4,824 ft / 1,470 m

Mt. Milner is located in the centre of the Prince of Wales Range to the east of the Stowe Creek headwaters. Milner is somewhat overshadowed by the attractions of Hkusam Mountain and its trails but should be considered especially as part of a traverse from Hkusam around the Stowe Creek headwaters or as a short side trip on a complete traverse of the Prince of Wales Range. Named after Viscount Alfred Milner (1854-1925) a British statesman and administrator. [3]

First Ascent: F. Nash survey party 1949

Map Sheet: 92 K/5 Sayward - GR 0077 (incorrectly marked)

Approaches: Best reached directly from Stowe Creek. Drive north on the Island Highway 19 from Campbell River. Turn right (north) after 62 km on Timber Rd. Drive straight into the logging company yard and out on the old road in the back left corner. Follow this road up into the Stowe Creek valley. The road is ditched requiring a good clearance two-wheel drive vehicle. Drive ~7.5 km to an old and now indistinct junction in the road where a bridge over the Stowe Creek has been removed. Park and cross the Stowe Creek. Either: 1) Follow the old road into the east fork of Stowe Creek and from the end of the road continue south-east to a col at GR 0177. Hike up the east ridge to the summit. Or 2) Take the lower road across to the south ridge of the mountain. Hike through regenerating forest to old growth on the south ridge and continue directly to the top.

This col can also be reached from the main backbone of the Prince of Wales Range if travelling along the range or around the Stowe Creek headwaters. From the falsely named summit north-east of the peak simply descend south-west into the col and continue up the east ridge to the top.

Additional Info: IB 1998 p.14

Mt. Milner north-west aspect from Hkusam Mountain, October.

Hkusam Mountain

Hkusam Mountain south-west aspect from Keta Lake, September.

Hkusam Mountain
5,481 ft / 1,670 m

Hkusam (pron.- q'sum) is the highest summit in the Prince of Wales Range and a superlative vantage point from where to view Vancouver Island scenery. To the north lies Johnstone Strait and great views into the Mt. Waddington area on the mainland. To the south and west is the great Salmon River valley and the mountains of the Sutton Range, Strathcona Park and the North Island. A huge swath of Hkusam's south side and parts of the Stowe Creek valley were ravaged by a logging slash fire which ran out of control stripping the mountain's upper forest. A surreal landscape of bright red basalt and stark bleached standing snags remains. The open terrain left by the fire is slowly regenerating and gives glorious autumn colour, superb views and great skiing. The pastoral setting of the Sayward valley farms with a patchwork of green fields and livestock paints a scene reminiscent of mountain villages in the Alps. The scene is complete with a pub at the trailhead in Sayward for a cool beverage after a hot day on the sunny slopes of Hkusam. It is named for the Walatsumas First Nation of Kelsey Bay.

First Ascent: F. Nash survey party 1949

Map Sheet: 92 K/5 Sayward - GR 9779

Approaches: A network of trails on the north-west flank from Sayward and the east flanks from Stowe Creek logging roads offer a variety of hiking options on and around Hkusam Mountain.

The most direct route to the summit is from Stowe Creek. Drive north on the Island Highway 19 from Campbell River. Turn right (north) after 62 km on Timber Road. Drive straight into the logging

Hkusam Mountain east aspect from the upper Stowe Creek valley, October.

Peak 5261 and joining ridge to Hkusam Mountain south-east aspect from summit of Hkusam, October.

company yard and back out on the old road in the far left corner. Follow this road up into the Stowe Creek valley. The road is ditched but in good shape at the time of writing, requiring good clearance but is two-wheel drivable. Drive as far as your vehicle allows and then continue on foot to a large parking lot on an old landing about 10 km from the highway. Consider mountain bikes for this approach.

From the landing the road has been debuilt but an excellent trail follows the road bed into the north (left) branch of Stowe Creek. At a junction two trails continue up toward Hkusam.

1) The left branch, Lyle's Trail, continues along the road bed and then near the end of the road strikes up through regenerating clearcut on very forgiving terrain to old-growth. The trail then follows a forested gully up to a col joining the distinct south ridge of Hkusam at GR 9878. Turn right (north) and follow the south ridge on open terrain of red pillow lava and slopes of heather. Higher up, as the ridge steepens, keep to the left (west) side of the crest to avoid difficulties. A little 3rd class scrambling and a few exposed points on the hiking route add to the interest but present little challenge. A natural line leads back to the crest of the south ridge which is followed to the top.

2) The right branch, Bill's Stowe Creek Trail, follows the road bed into the upper valley to the north of Hkusam. At the end of the road an excellent trail continues up the valley through beautiful subalpine forest toward a col at GR 9780. From this col Bill's Trail takes a steep line down to Sayward village reaching the trailhead near the Coral Reef pub.

To climb up to Hkusam, leave Bill's Trail ~300 ft before the col, traversing south and up into the narrow bowl below Hkusam's north face. Cross the floor of the bowl and then climb up the major gully on the far left of the bowl, on scree or snow, to the ridge right below the summit of Hkusam. A short hike east takes you to the top.

A circuit can be completed by climbing Hkusam on Lyle's Trail and descending Bill's Stowe Creek Trail. The trick is being sure that the gully you descend is the right one and is in suitable condition for your party. The gully is the first cleft immediately below the summit, the scree is loose but not too steep.

An alternative, if you can arrange the transport, is to use Bill's Trail down to Sayward via the col at GR 9780. To locate the bottom of Bill's Trail in Sayward, leave the Island Highway at the Sayward junction and then turn right after the Coral Reef pub. Drive up this road which leads to the trailhead.

404 Bonanza Range - Tsitika Area - Map

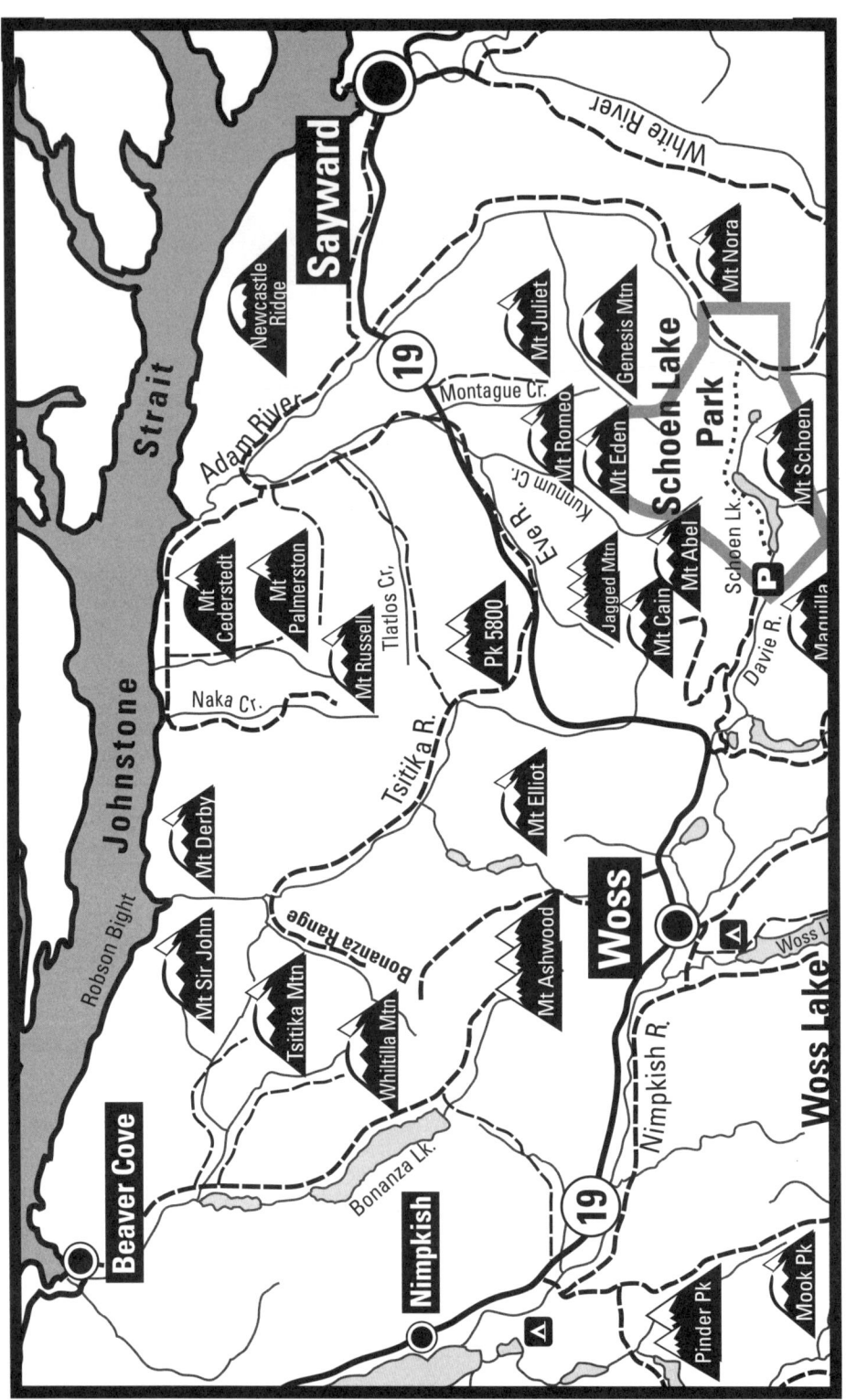

Mt. Russell

Mt. Russell north-west aspect from Peak 5,498, September.

Mt. Russell
5,470 ft./ 1,740 m

Mt. Russell is one of a number of summits on a high alpine plateau at the head of Tlatlos and Palmerston Creeks which drains the mountain's south and west sides. Palmerston Creek runs down to join the Adam River to the east of Mt. Russell, and Naka Creek and an adjacent unnamed valley form the north and west flanks. There are a couple of higher summits on this massif including one surveyed at 5,498 ft. Easily climbed as a day trip but worth an overnight stay combined with climbing Mt. Palmerston.

First Ascent: Unknown

Map Sheet: 92 L/8 Adam River - GR 8784

Approaches: Russell may be approached from Palmerston Creek or Tlatlos Creek. From the latter drive to the mountain's south flank up the highest currently drivable spur off Tlatlos North road which can be reached by leaving the Island Highway at the bottom of the steep hill north of Rooney Lake ~30 km north of Sayward. Turn north onto the Eve River East Main and follow this for 3 km and then turn left and cross the Eve River onto the Eve River West Main Line. Turn left on to Tlatlos North 6 km past the bridge and follow it to the end of the road.

A better approach is from West Palmerston Road which is found just a bit further north on the Eve River West Main from Tlatlos North. At the time of writing this road is drivable to the back of the valley by 2 wheel drive vehicles. From the end of the road continue up the main valley keeping in the timber on the north bank of the creek to avoid avalanche debris and bush. Climb a crafty line up a steep vegetated headwall or snow gullies to the ridge north-west of Mt. Russell and Peak 5498.

Mt. Russell (C) & Peak 5,498 (R) west aspect from Palmerston Creek valley, September.

Mt. Palmerston

Mt. Palmerston south-west aspect from Mt. Russell, September.

Mt. Palmerston
5,783 ft./ 1,763 m

Mt. Palmerston is an impressive but isolated summit overlooking Johnstone Strait and the Adam River estuary between Palmerston and Naka Creeks. Its south side hides a dramatic rock face which drops off the mountain's north side.

First Ascent: Geodetic Survey of Canada 1914

Map Sheet: 92 L/8 Adam River - GR 8987

Approaches: Leave the Island Highway at the bottom of the steep hill north of Rooney Lake, ~30 km north of Sayward. Turn north onto the Eve River Main and follow this for 3 km and then turn left and cross the Eve River onto the Eve River West Main Line. **Note** the lower Eve River bridge on East Main is now closed. After ~12 km cross the bridge over Palmerston Creek and then turn left on to West Palmerston Rd. Follow this road to the back of the valley. Hike from the end of the road into old growth and head up hill to a high timbered pass south-west of the summit. Continue up the ridge on the south-west side of the mountain to the top. Good to combine with a trip to Mt. Russell.

Mt. Cederstedt
4,525 ft./ 1,379 m

A low peak west of the Adam River estuary and north of Mt. Palmerston. Good views of Johnstone Strait with some high alpine and subalpine lakes on the narrow summit plateau and the pronounced subalpine bench on the east side of the mountain.

First Ascent: Unknown

Map Sheet: 92 L/8 Adam River - GR 8790

Approaches: Approach Mt. Cederstedt from the Naka 100 Rd. which can be found by following the approach description for Mt. Palmerston but instead of turning up Palmerston Creek, continue north to the sharp left turn onto Naka Main west along the Johnstone Strait shoreline. After ~10 km turn south onto Naka 100 which runs into the valley on Mt. Cederstedt's west flank. From spurs below the summit hike up the hill side to the alpine direct to the summit.

Mt. Elliot

Mt. Elliot south-east aspect from Mt. Abel, March.

Mt. Elliot
5,187 ft./ 1,581 m

A pronounced pyramid shaped summit west of the Tsitika River and the Island Highway 19. There is little alpine terrain around the summit but the views of Mt. Hapush and Mt. Cain are worth the trek.

First Recorded Ascent: Lindsay Elms, Charles Turner, 11 November, 2000

Map Sheet: 92 L/8 Adam River - GR 7873

Approaches: May be reached with ease from Claude Elliot Main in Lukwa Creek. ~ 8 km north of the Mt. Cain-Schoen Lake turn off and 4 km south of Woss on the Island Highway. Turn north onto North Nimpkish Rd. Then after just over 1 km turn left (north) on to Claude Elliot Main. At the second bridge stay on the east side of Lukwa Creek and drive up spur roads high up on to the west flank of Mt. Elliot. Head up the hillside directly to the west of the summit. The west ridge takes form higher up but eventually steepens into a buttress of rotten rock. Drop off the ridge and traverse the basin right (south-east) to gain the south ridge. Climb the south ridge with some 4th class to the summit.

Additional Info: IB 2000 p.24

Unnamed & unlisted peak east aspect from Mt. Russell, September.

Peak 5800

Peak 5800 (L) from Mt. Hkusam.

Peak 5800
5,800 ft./ 1,768 m

Peak 5800 is located due north of Jagged Mountain on the north side of the Eve River and the Island Highway. The mountain is easily identified travelling south on the Island Highway through the Tsitika-Eve River pass. There are a group of summits surrounding this peak which combine to make the area worth a day trip or even an overnight visit. The low elevation rock face on the north end of this group dropping into the Tlatlos Creek valley may be worth closer inspection!

First Ascent: Island Mountain Ramblers

Map Sheet: 92 L/8 Adam River - GR 9177

Approaches: The Island Highway and logging roads in the Tsitika and Tlatlos Creek valleys encircle Peak 5800 and its neighbours. To approach from the east, leave the Island Highway on the Tsitika Main and after ~5 km turn right (east) on Tlatlos South and 6 km further TS 120 breaks off south. Drive up TS 120 choosing any one of a number of nicely angled lines out of the valley and on to the south-east ridge. Hike along the south-east ridge and tackle the summit tower from the west.

A more direct route comes up the south-west flank of the peak from near the Eve River rest area on the Island Highway. Leave the highway at the rest area and locate a spur road on the hillside behind. Start up an open creek bed then forested ridges to reach the alpine south-west of the summit. Continue up to the summit along the west ridge.

Additional Info: IB 1997 p.26

Unnamed & unlisted peak east aspect from Mt. Russell, September.

408

Mt. Peel

Mt. Peel south-east aspect from Mt. Russell, September.

Mt. Peel
5,131 ft./ 1,564 m

Mt. Peel is located west of Naka Creek and east of Tsitika River just above the Vancouver Island shoreline along Johnstone Strait. There is little surrounding alpine around the summit which drops off quite steeply on every side into the valleys and Johnstone Strait of which there are great views.

First Ascent: Unknown

Map Sheet: 92 L/8 Adam River - GR 8091

Approaches: Mt. Peel may be reached from logging roads in either Naka Creek or Peel Creek. Drive from the Island Highway down the Eve River West Main Line. Continue past the old log sort at the Adam-Eve River estuary turning west along Naka Main, which follows the Vancouver Island shoreline. Turn south into Naka Creek on South Main or continue along the coast on Peel Main and tackle the steep forested hillside up the north side of the mountain to the top. Peel Main may be gated at the Naka Creek Recreation site where parking and even camping is possible.

Alternatively, drive up the Naka Creek South Main to branch road S 100 which climbs very high up the south flanks of Peak 4915 a few kilometres south of the summit of Mt. Peel (see photo above). Drive as far as possible up S 100 and then continue on foot to gain the south end of the connecting ridge to Mt. Peel at Peak 4915. Continue north, hiking up and over two additional summits, to reach the south ridge and the summit of Mt. Peel.

Mt. Peel south-east aspect from Mt. Russell, September.

Mt. Derby

Mt. Derby south-east aspect from Mt. Russell, September.

Mt. Derby
5,400 ft./ 1,646 m

Mt. Derby overlooks Robson Bight and Johnstone Strait from the east divide of the Tsitika River. This position gives Mt. Derby the distinction of commanding views over the only protected and therefore pristine river mouth on the east coast of Vancouver Island. The mouth of the Tsitika River is the only place on the east side of the island where the mountains can truly be said to touch the sea. It is also the site of summer gatherings of orcas (killer whales) who congregate in the Bight and adjacent Johnstone Strait to feed on the salmon runs and rub on the gravel beaches of the Bight. All in all Mt. Derby is an excellent mountain to climb if you can get there!

First Ascent: G.J. Jackson survey party, 1931

Map Sheet: 92 L/7 Nimpkish - GR 7490

Approaches: Consider approaching Mt. Derby from Johnstone Strait. With the added attraction of the orcas in summer this makes for a unique island mountaineering experience. Kayaks are ideal because they can be easily secured in the forest and don't require near impossible moorage in the turbulent waters of the strait or the logistical planning of a drop off and pick up. The closest put in is Naka Creek to the east. Reach Naka from the Eve River Main off the Island Highway. Paddle west up Johnstone Strait to the boundary of the Michael Bigg (Robson Bight) Ecological Reserve. Pull ashore on the beach on the west side of the creek mouth at GR 7795. No boats are permitted on the water inside the reserve and travel on foot inside the reserve is also discouraged. Head south up the gentle north ridge of Mt. Derby following the Tree Farm Licence and reserve boundary to the summit.

Mt. Derby (L) and Robson Bight from West Cracroft Island.

Tsitika Mountain

Tsitika Mountain and the west divide of the Tsitika valley north aspect from West Cracroft Island, July.

Tsitika Mountain
5,437 ft./ 1,657 m

Tsitika Mountain is a rocky, dome-shaped summit on the west divide of the Tsitika River. To its west are the Kokish and Bonanza Rivers. Catherine Creek which is a short tributary of the Tsitika runs below the steep forested (and deforested) eastern flanks of the mountain. Like the other peaks along the east coast of the island it has excellent views of Johnstone Strait and looks over the pristine lower Tsitika River valley and Robson Bight.

First Ascent: G.J. Jackson survey party 1931

Map Sheet: 92 L/7 Nimpkish - GR 6688

Approaches: From the Island Highway head north on the Tsitika Main logging road. Follow the road past the Tsitika Crossing recreation site and into Catherine Creek. Cross the bridge over Catherine Creek and park past a second bridge over the creek from Mudge Lake. Head up through the nasty clearcut slash to gain the forested upper reaches of the elegant east ridge. Continue up the crest of this ridge into a basin on the north side of the peak. Climb the North-East Ridge to the summit.

Additional Info: IB 2000 p.14

Mt. Sir John
4,690 ft./ 1,429 m

Highest point in the Franklin Range, which runs parallel to Johnstone Strait west of Robson Bight. Has the distinction of being the most northerly peak listed in this guide.

First Ascent: Unknown

Map Sheet: 92 L/7 Nimpkish - GR 6793

Approaches: Try logging road branch 256 off Kokish Main and report back!

Mt. Ashwood & Bonanza Peak north-east aspect from West Cracroft Island.

412 Tak Ogasawara climbing Mt. Ashwood, Bonanza Peak behind. photo: Peter Rothermel

Mt. Ashwood

Mt. Ashwood (L) & Bonanza Peak (C) north-east aspect from Claude Elliot Lake, November.

Mt. Ashwood
5,722 ft./ 1,744 m

Mt. Ashwood is the southern-most of twin peaks at the south end of the Bonanza Range. It overlooks Claude Elliot Lake and Claude Elliot Provincial Park. The mountain is named for Dave Ashwood a prospector in the Tsitika region during the 1930s.

First Ascent: Rick Eppler, J. Gibson, B. Peterson, Syd Watts, 1979

Map Sheet: 92 L/7 Nimpkish - GR 7074

Approaches: May be reached from Claude Elliot Main in Lukwa Creek. About 8 km north of the Mt. Cain-Schoen Lake turn-off and 4 km south of Woss on the Island Highway turn north onto North Nimpkish Rd. Then after just over 1 km turn left (north) on to Claude Elliot Main. At the second bridge cross to the west side of Lukwa Creek. Follow the road into the valley to the south-east of Mt. Ashwood. Park and hike up the slash and into the timber on the broad ridge above the south-west corner of Claude Elliot Lake. Continue up this ridge until it joins the south ridge of the mountain above a cluster of alpine lakes. Turn north and follow the north ridge past the lakes to the summit.

Mt. Ashwood may also be reached from the south and west up the Bonanza River via Steele Creek from Island Highway 19.

Bonanza Peak (L) and Mt. Ashwood (R) south-west aspect from near Woss Lake, July.

Bonanza Peak

Twin summits of Mt. Ashwood & Bonanza Peak (L) and Mt. Elliot (R) south-east aspect from Mt. Cain, February.

Bonanza Peak
5,800 ft./ 1,767 m

Bonanza Peak is the northern and higher twin of Mt. Ashwood at the south end of the Bonanza Range. The mountain is the highest summit in the Bonanza Range.

First Ascent: Rick Eppler, J. Gibson, B. Peterson, Syd Watts, 1979

Map Sheet: 92 L/7 Nimpkish - GR 7075

Approaches: Follow the approaches for Mt. Ashwood, climbing Bonanza by its south ridge or steeper north ridge.

Peak 5769
5,769 ft./ 1,758 m

Peak 5769 is the next mountain north of Mt. Ashwood-Bonanza Peak along the main Bonanza Range ridge system.

First Ascent: Unknown

Map Sheet: 92 L/7 Nimpkish - GR 6877

Approaches: Approach from the Bonanza River up the south-west flank.

Peak 5540
5,540 ft./ 1,688 m

Peak 5540 is just south of Whiltilla Mountain along the main Bonanza Range ridge system.

First Ascent: Unknown

Map Sheet: 92 L/7 Nimpkish - GR 6479

Approaches: Approach from the Bonanza River up the south-west ridge.

Whiltilla Mountain

Mt. Ashwood and the Bonanza Range south-east aspect from Mt. Cain, February.

Whiltilla Mountain
5,554 ft./ 1,693 m

Whiltilla Mountain is at the north-west end of the Bonanza Range. It overlooks Bonanza Lake to the west, Catherine Creek and the Tsitika River to the east and, to the north, the Kokish River. It is an impressive mountain viewed from the north in the Kokish valley. A large, high cirque sweeps around to the south-east of the mountain enclosing the headwaters of both Catherine Creek and Kokish River.

The mountain is named for a native word of the Kwakiool-Kwahi Sept First Nation meaning 'fire'. Also known as 'Porphry Peak'. To geologists this is a very hard purplish-red rock containing small crystals of feldspar.

First Ascent: G.J. Jackson survey party 1931

Map Sheet: 92 L/7 Nimpkish - GR 6381

Approaches: Logging roads come up each of the three main valleys around Whiltilla Mountain providing access to the north side from either Catherine Creek or Kokish River and to the south side from Bonanza River.

The easiest route up the mountain and the shortest drive on logging roads is from the Bonanza River. Leave the Island Highway heading east on Old Steele Main. Follow this road to BR 80 which takes you to the south end of Bonanza Lake. Cross the bridge over Bonanza River and join the Main Road South. Locate the highest drivable logging road spur on the south-west flanks of Whiltilla Mountain. Head up the gentle hillside to gain the south ridge. Hike along the south ridge to the summit.

From Catherine Creek to the north-east, leave the Island Highway on the Tsitika Main. Follow Tsitika Main past the Tsitika Crossing recreation site and into Catherine Creek where the road changes designation to Catherine Main. Keep on the east side of Catherine Creek and continue driving to the stunning but devastated upper valley around Warm Lake. From spur roads across the flanks of the adjoining horseshoe ridge, east of the summit, hike up to gain the crest of the ridge. Head south-west to join the main Bonanza Range spine and then turn north-west. Hike along the ridge crest to the south ridge of Whiltilla Mountain and on to the top.

416 Rugged Glacier - Haihte Range

Haihte Range

418 Camp at Nathan Creek col, Ya'ai Peak behind. photo: Sandy Briggs

Haihte Range
Contents

South Blades	423
Rugged Mountain	424
The Gendarmes	428
Merlon Mountain	429
Ya'ai Peak	431
Haihte Spire	433
North-West Outliers	435
Half Dome	435
Zeballos Peak	436
Grayback Peak	437
Peak 4400	438
Lukwa Mountain	438
Kaouk Mountain	439
Mamat Mountain	439

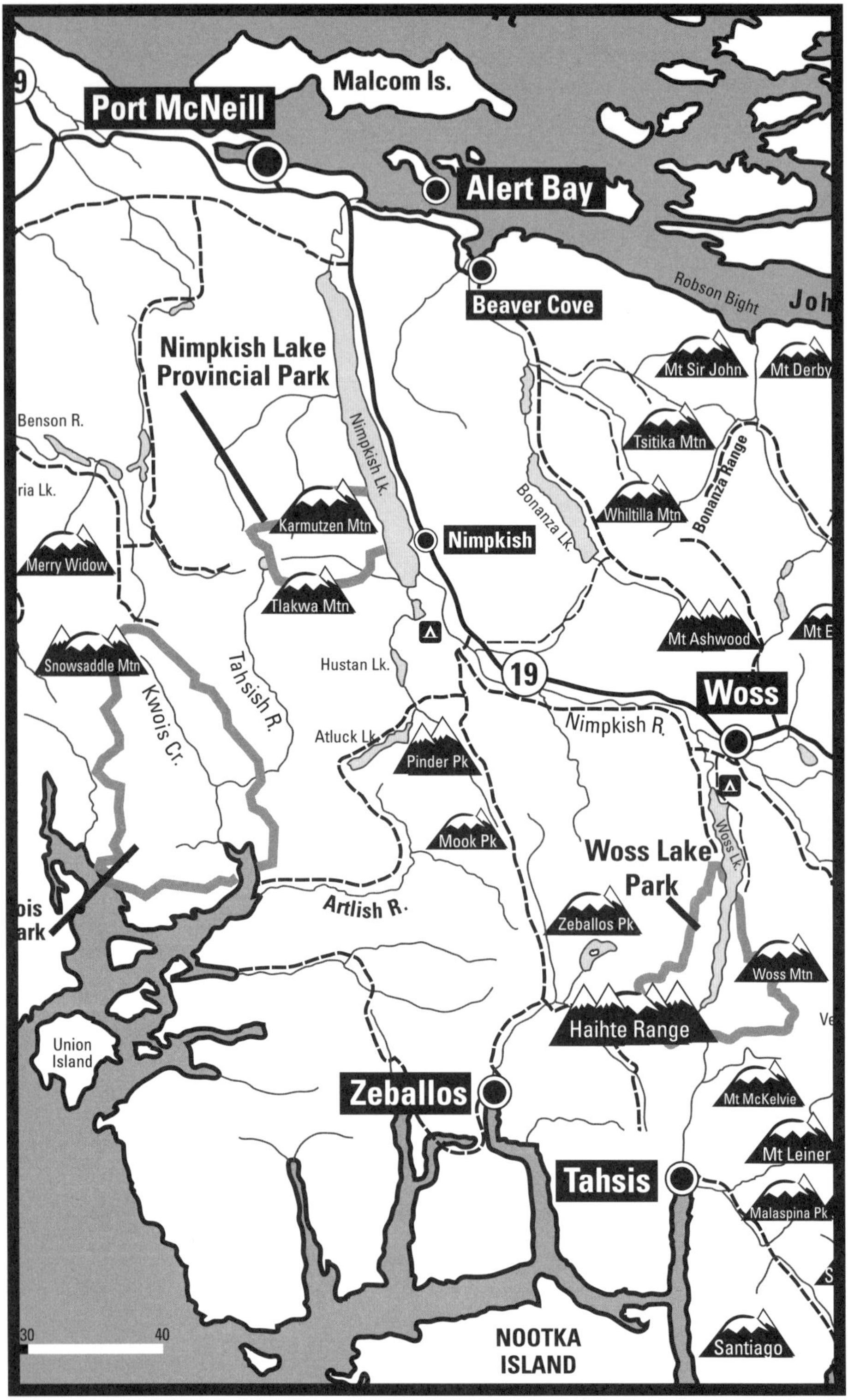

9
Port McNeill
Malcom Is.
Alert Bay
Beaver Cove
Robson Bight
Joh
Nimpkish Lake
Provincial Park
Mt Sir John
Mt Derby
Benson R.
Nimpkish Lk.
Tsitika Mtn
Bonanza Range
ria Lk.
Bonanza Lk.
Whiltilla Mtn
Karmutzen Mtn
Nimpkish
Merry Widow
Tlakwa Mtn
Mt Ashwood
Mt E
Snowsaddle Mtn
Tahsish R.
Hustan Lk.
19
Woss
Kwois Cr.
Nimpkish R.
Atluck Lk.
Pinder Pk
Mook Pk
Woss Lake
Park
Woss Lk.
ois
ark
Artlish R.
Zeballos Pk
Woss Mtn
Haihte Range
Ve
Union
Island
Zeballos
Mt McKelvie
Mt Leiner
Tahsis
Malaspina Pk
30
40
NOOTKA
ISLAND
Santiago

Haihte Range

The Haihte Range, (pronounced hī' te like the West Indies island) a.k.a. Rugged Range, is one of the most spectacular and rugged alpine areas on Vancouver Island. The range is found between the Nomash River to the south-west and Woss Lake to the north-east. Its close neighbours include Zeballos Peak and the Province Range which runs along the west side of Zeballos River and Pinder Creek. The bulk of the Haihte Range lies within Woss Lake Provincial Park.

Some of the largest remaining glaciers on the island are secreted in the Haihte Range. They are literally secreted as many features of this range do not appear accurately charted on the government topo map and are hidden from view from the highways and byways. The glaciers sit in a series of deep cirques ringed by a chain of serrated peaks. The glacial terrain is ideal for skiing and snowboarding and many great descents have been done in the range. The rock and ice climbing found in the range is superb and the atmosphere created by the many spires is a little like a mini-Patagonia.

Access to this area is notoriously difficult as the lower flanks of the range drop precipitously on all sides with few good lines of weakness up to the glaciers. In addition the routes that do exist are exposed to avalanches in conditions of poor snow stability. The Haihte Range's position so close to the west coast guarantees an inordinate number of cloudy days and much precipitation to feed the expansive icefields. In addition the range has gathered a reputation for its fierce winds which have simply crushed several camps. Haihte is a Native word meaning 'fishhead'.

Map Sheets: 92 L/2 Woss Lake • 92 E/15 Zeballos

Boundaries: north: Nimpkish River **east:** Woss Lake **south:** Nomash River **west:** Zeballos River

Major Access Routes: Originally the Haihte Range was approached by boat from Woss Lake. While that route is still possible and remains an excellent way to experience the unique coastal experience of approaching a mountain by water it has fallen out of favour in preference for the extensive logging road networks in the Nomash River and Zeballos River valleys.

Nomash Main: From the Island Highway, 151 km north of Campbell River and 21 km north of Woss, turn south on the Zeballos Forest Service Road (Atluck Main becomes Pinder then Zeballos Main). The Zeballos Road is a well maintained gravel road. It is one of the few 'mountain roads' on the Island cutting through narrow valleys along the flanks of Pinder and Zeballos Peaks. 33 km south of the Island Highway and a few kilometres north of the town of Zeballos turn left (east) on to Nomash Main. 7.3 km up the valley turn left onto N20 which winds high up below the south-west face of Rugged Mountain. This spur is not very driveable and is becoming overgrown in its upper parts. Drive then hike up this spur to locate the flagged, established route into Nathan Creek col.

Forest Service & Logging Company Offices:

Campbell River Forest District - 231 Dogwood Ave. Campbell River BC V9W 2Y1 Ph: 287-2194

Western Forest Products -#118 – 1334 Island Hwy. Campbell River, BC V9W 8C9 Ph: 250 286-3767

Other Information Sources:
- **Beyond Nootka** by Lindsay Elms
- **The Unknown Island** by Ian Smith (1973)

Special Thanks:
Thanks to Sandy Briggs for assistance in preparing this chapter.

422 John Roberts climbing 'the Chuck', Rugged Mountain.

South Blades

The Blades with Tahsis Inlet below north-west aspect from Rugged Mountain, March.

South Blades
5,499 ft./ 1,676 m

The Blades are a maze of serrated rock spires thrusting above a small (by Haihte Range standards) glacier due south of Rugged Mountain. It is this south end of the range which dominates the skyline from the community of Tahsis and has given rise to a local habit of calling the Blades as visible from Tahsis 'Rugged Mountain' even though Rugged Mountain is hidden from view from the town.

First Ascent: Mike Walsh, Joe Bajan 1975-1976

Map Sheet: 92 L/2 Woss Lake - GR 6741

Approaches: A prominent easy gully from near the end of the innermost spur of N20 leads to a terrace of small lakes west of the Blades which can be climbed from here, though rock climbing is involved. A narrow gully, snow-free in late summer, close to the face of Rugged Mountain leads upward and south, directly to the small Blades glacier. The Blades have also been approached from the Tahsis River.

Aerial view of the South Blades north-east aspect above Woss Lake, March.

Rugged Mountain

Rugged Mountain north-west aspect, July.

Rugged Mountain
6,151 ft / 1,875 m

Rugged Mountain is the apex of the Haihte Range and a dramatic summit to tread. It overlooks some of the largest glaciers on Vancouver Island which fill the huge cirques across the Haihte Range. Rugged offers superlative views of Woss Lake, Nootka Sound and the neighbouring Tlupana Range.

First Ascent: George Lepore, Chuck Smitson, September 1959

First Winter Ascent: Sandy Briggs, Dennis Manke, Don Berryman, G. Smythe, February 1992

Map Sheet: 92 L/2 Woss Lake - GR 6643

Approaches: Historically Rugged Mountain has been approached by boat down Woss Lake and up steep bluffy slopes onto the Rugged Glacier. In 1986 high level logging activity on the south-west side of the Haihte Range in the Nomash River saw roads built high on the flanks of the mountain. Currently the highest and most convenient road for access to Rugged is branch N 20 which climbs into the Nathan Creek valley below the south-west face of Rugged Mountain. A hiking route climbs up the steep north side of this valley to gain a ridge crest that butts into the two peaks north-west of Rugged. A long traverse on the south side of this ridge leads to the north col a.k.a Nathan Creek col.

Haihte Range north aspect from Mt. Cain, June.

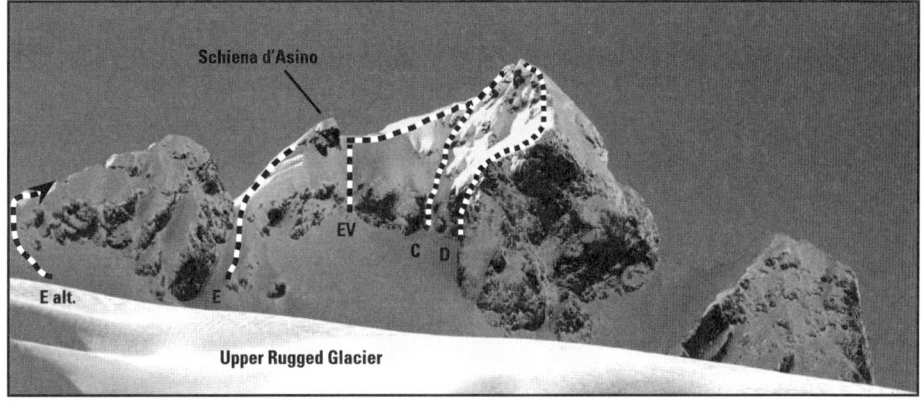

Rugged Mountain north aspect, March.

Routes

E ** East Ridge: AI2 low 5th class, 250m (II)
The original first ascent route and standard line to climb Rugged by. From the upper Rugged Glacier the route is short but with incredible alpine atmosphere.

From the upper shelf of the Rugged Glacier, south-east of the Nathan Creek col, approach the north side of the East Ridge. In winter/spring a snow gully leads right up onto the crest of the East Ridge. In summer/fall a jumbled bergschrund and moats need to be negotiated with care to reach rock slabs which can then be climbed to the ridge crest at a prominent notch.* Head up the ridge keeping to the south side over a small pinnacle (Schiena d'asino - the Donkey's back). Continue up directly on the ridge to the summit. Descend same route.

*If access to the ridge through the bergschrunds is too difficult then continue traversing to the very toe of the East Ridge (E alt) and gain the crest here. Climb over 'the Hump' and drop to the notch on the regular route, recommended!
FA: George Lepore, Chuck Smitson September 1959.

South Ridge: low 5th class, 300m (II)
From Blades Glacier ascend east to a notch on the main spine of Rugged Mountain just north of the spectacularly spiky south peak (1,680m, "The Pitchfork") Travel north avoiding the complex formations of the ridge by easy progress on the eastern snowfield and bypassing altogether the 1,779 m middle summit.

From the notch north of this summit a short descent is required (rappel or downclimb). Go left of the next pillar and regain the ridgeline. Climb toward the prominent orange blade 'Lama de Lepore'. An airy ramp leads around the blade to the right and the route joins easily with the east ridge route. Short sections of easy 5th class.
FA: Sandy Briggs, John Pratt, Rick Hudson, 25 August 1989

EV ** East Ridge Variation:
A short steep route onto the East Ridge avoiding the Schiena d'Asino
FA: Lindsay Elms July 1998

426 Don Berryman & Greta Smythe below the north-west face of Rugged Mountain. photo: Sandy Briggs

South-West Face of Rugged Mountain from N-20.

photo: Sandy Briggs

JN- * Johnson/Newman Route: 4th class up to 5.8 500m var. (III)
Ascend left of the Briggs/Berryman route aiming for just left and below the base of an arete. Climb mostly 4th and low 5th class, there is some loose rock, and poor protection. Climb right through a small cave and directly up the left hand skyline of the arete to about mid-way where there are exit ledges to the right. Scramble up to join with the South-West Face route. This pitch has no protection with difficulties at about 5.7-8. The upper pitches of the unclimbed arete look to be stiff mid 5th class.
FA: Rick Johnson, Don Newman 3-4 June1989

SW- * South-West Face:** 3rd class up to 5.6 700m (III)
Starts up easy slabs approached from the N 20 logging road spur in Nathan Creek. A long ledge leads right to a thin waterfall. Climb up on the left side of the waterfall trending left to gain a long prominent rib that sweeps up the upper part of the route to the summit.
FA: Sandy Briggs, Don Berryman 27 June 1987.

Additional Info: IB Fall 1987 (15:4) p.6

Rugged Mountain

Spires ringing the Rugged Glacier, March.

North-West Face: low 5th class 150m (II)
Access is from the upper Rugged Glacier. From the base of the west side of the main large gendarme on the north-west ridge, traverse onto a ledge system on the North-West Face. Continue diagonally upward to reach the skyline which is essentially the west ridge of the upper mountain. At a table-shaped rock one pitch from the summit a lovely corner crack leads to the top. Great scrambling on 4th class with a few 5th class moves.
FA: Mike Walsh, Ralph Hutchinson 1968

Winter Routes

C * The Chuck: AI2/3 150m (II)
A direct route to the summit climbing the gully formed where the East Ridge meets the summit tower. Start at the base of the obvious gully with a steep ice step. Easier climbing up a long steep snow gully joins the East Ridge just below the summit.
FA: Phil Stone, John Roberts, Tak Ogasawara March 1990

D ** Dan's Route: AI4 250m (II)
Climbs an impressive pillar of ice to start. Gain the upper north ridge & easier angled terrain to the summit.
FA: Dan ? March 1990

Additional Info: IB 1992 p.29, IB 2001 p.20

The Gendarmes
5,440 ft / 1,658 m

A double-topped sub-peak immediately north-west of Rugged Mountain (between Rugged and Merlon).

Merlon Mountain south spires, March

Merlon Mountain

Merlon Mountain north aspect from Rugged Creek col, March.

Merlon Mountain
5,898 ft./ 1,798 m

Merlon Mountain is something of a sleeper. When viewed from most angles within the Haihte Range it appears as just another bump on the skyline. However its north and south-west faces drop precipitously off in to the Nomash valley enticing climbers in every season. The mountain is comprised of three distinct summits south to north 1782 m/5846 ft, 1800 m/ 5906 ft, 1813 m/ 5948 ft.

First Ascent: Sandy Briggs, John Pratt, Dennis Manke, September, 1990

Map Sheet: 92 L/2 Woss Lake - GR 6544

Approaches: Merlon is best approached from the Nathan Creek col from where a simple traverse across the upper Rugged Glacier leads to a high point just below the east face. None of the three peaks requires more than a very short pitch of easy 5th class climbing.

Merlon Mountain south-west aspect from Nomash valley, September.   photo: Sandy Briggs

430 Climbers on Ya'ai Peak North-East Ridge, March. photo: Roseanne van Schie

Ya'ai Peak

Ya'ai Peak north-east aspect from the Unmapped Glacier, March.

Ya'ai Peak
5,695 ft / 1,736 m

Ya'ai peak is a striking looking mountain sitting on the ridge line between the Rugged Glacier to its south and the unmapped glacier to the north. The peak is comprised of a complex series of aretes, towers and snowfields.

First Ascent: Mike Walsh, Ron Facer, 7 August, 1968

Map Sheet: 92 L/2 Woss Lake - GR 6545

Approaches: Best reached from the regular approach to the Haihte Range from the Nomash River logging roads up to the Nathan Creek col. Drop down onto the lower Rugged Glacier heading north to locate a gully and pass, left of "the Sphinx", that leads on to the south edge of the unmapped glacier (see photo below right).

Routes

North-East Ridge: AI2 5.4, 200m (II)
A very aesthetic and airy line from the unmapped glacier to the summit. Conditions will vary widely with season. In winter expect exposed climbing on the upper snowfield.
FA: Mike Walsh, Ron Facer, 1968

West Ridge: 5.7 350m (III)
Takes the left skyline as viewed from Nathan Creek col. Approach directly across the upper Rugged Glacier. Start up huge chimney system to gain the ridge crest above. Some rappel gymnastics to reach a col below the second gendarme. Ledges lead to north-west side and a 20m corner crack (crux) toward the top.
FA: Chris Barner, Paul Rydeen June 1998

Ya'ai Peak east aspect from Rugged Glacier.

432 Haihte Spire and the terminal serac of the Unmapped Glacier.

Haihte Spire

Haihte Spire east aspect from the Unmapped Glacier, March.

Haihte Spire
5,597 ft / 1,706 m

Haihte Spire is found at the north end of the Haihte Range overlooking the unmapped glacier (Second Glacier) and Haihte Lake, neither of which appear on the 1:50,000 government topo. The spire is a dramatic peak from every angle but shows its needle shape most clearly from Haihte Lake

First Ascent: Sandy Briggs, Dennis Manke, John Pratt, Chris Wickham, March 21, 1992

Map Sheet: 92 L/2 Woss Lake - GR 6446

Approaches: Haihte Spire may be reached by approaching the Nathan Creek col from logging road branch N20 in the Nomash River. From the Nathan Creek col descend to the Rugged Glacier and hike through the small pass north-east of Ya'ai Peak on to the unmapped (Second) glacier. From the toe of the north ridge of Ya'ai Peak gain the crest of the ridge which runs into the south-east buttress of Haihte Spire. Climb the spire by the East Face.

Additional Info: IB 1992 p.23

NW- **North-West Ridge:**
Approach from another unmapped glacier (3rd glacier a.k.a. Haihte Glacier) immediately north of Haihte Spire. Drop north off the east arm of the unmapped glacier and descend toward the outlet of Haihte Lake. Hike up beside a small lake which drains into Haihte Lake. There are some fine pillow lava formations here. Climb the left (east) side of Haihte Glacier to a notch in the North-West Ridge (see photo below). The summit ridge is easy class 4 from the notch.
FA: Sandy Briggs, Claire Ebendinger, Chris Odgers, Dennis Manke August 1993

Haihte Spire north-east aspect from the Haihte Glacier, March.

434 Dave Sears on some camp side bouldering in the Nathan Creek col.

North-West Outliers

Haihte Spire (L) and the North-West Outliers (C) north aspect from Mt. Cain, June.

North-West Outliers
5,355 ft / 1,632 m

There are six peaks between Haihte Spire and Zeballos Lake that reach 5,000ft or higher. Collectively these peaks are known as the North-West Outliers. Four of these combine with Haihte Spire, Ya'ai Pk, and Merlon Mountain to form a cirque around the head of Rugged Creek. The remaining two lie north-west of a tiny isolated alpine lake. Peak 1,554 (5098ft) appears as a dramatic, craggy promontory from the road near the confluence of the Nomash and Zeballos Rivers.

First Ascent: (Peaks 1583, 1632, 1611, & 1595) Sandy Briggs, Valerio Faraoni, February, 1993
The other two, Peak 1524 mand Peak 1554 m are likely unclimbed at time of publication.

Map Sheet: 92 E/15 Zeballos - GR 5951

Approaches: Best from a camp on the south ridge of Peak 1583. The bottom part of the approach (from ca. 0.8 km before Rugged Creek on the Nomash main) is closely-spaced second growth which makes for slow travel.

Half Dome
4,478 ft / 1,365 m

The name suggests the shape of this most northerly summit of the Rugged group.

First Recorded Ascent: Sandy Briggs and Dennis Manke in August 1993.

Map Sheet: 92 E/15 Zeballos - GR 6247

Approaches: Easily reached from Haihte Lake.

The South Blades and Tahsis Inlet from Nathan Creek col, June

Zeballos Peak

Zeballos Peak west aspect from Zeballos Road, August.

Zeballos Peak
5,170 ft / 1,576 m

Zeballos Peak is a series of short towers rising from an island of alpine which plummets steeply down on all sides to the Zeballos River, Zeballos Lake and Kaipit Lake. Zeballos Peak is named after Lt. Ciriaco Cevallos an officer of Captain Malaspina's expedition to the West Coast on the corvettes Descubierta and Atrevida in 1791.

First Ascent: Syd Watts and John Gibson July 26 1983

Map Sheet: 92 E/15 Zeballos - GR 5951

Approaches: Zeballos Peak may be reached from Woss Lake along a long connecting ridge which runs north-east from the mountain. This route is a superb high ridge trek over 10 km long passing numerous alpine lakes, meadows and **Kaipit Peak 4,748 ft** en route. Leave the Island Highway at Woss and head through town toward Woss Lake. Turn left (south) on West Woss Main Road which runs down the west shore of Woss Lake. From either spurs in Clint Creek or Fiddle Creek (Budlite Rd) gain the ridge system near Peak 4484 and head south-west toward Zeballos Peak. Climb to the summit along the easy north-east Ridge.

A new logging road up Maraude Creek (N2) is reputedly headed around the north shore of Zeballos Lake giving access options up the south-east and east flanks of the mountain.

Zeballos Peak has also been tackled from the west off the Zeballos Road with varying degrees of success! Checkout the micro-mountain in the middle of Zeballos Lake. At 1,519 ft / 463 m.it stands 500 ft above the lake, no ascent records to date!

Additional Info: IB 1998 p.31

Zeballos Peak south-east aspect from Haihte Glacier, March.

Grayback Peak

The Nomash Slab on Grayback Peak. photo: Sandy Briggs

Grayback Peak
3,670 ft./ 1,119 m

This hill, 5.5 km south-west of Rugged Mountain on the opposite side of the Nomash valley, is a sloping plateau of exposed granite with intermittent islands of trees. The name appears in a 1940 paper of the Geological Society of Canada by M.F. Bancroft, who indicates that this peak is part of the Zeballos batholith, a formation of gray granodiorite and quartz diorite which cuts off the basaltic Karmutzen volcanics more common in this area. The steeper south-east face of this peak is a spectacular 400m sweeping apron of bare granite (the Nomash Slab) which attracts the eye from high on Rugged Mountain across the Nomash valley to the north-east. High quality multi-pitch rock climbs have been developed on this feature in recent years.

First Ascent: Likely prospectors or surveyors.

Map Sheet: 92 L/2 Woss Lake – GR 6240

Approaches: Access to Grayback is via the Nomash Main. After passing the N20 spur, which is the access road to Rugged Mountain, cross a bridge to the south side of the Nomash and ascend the N14 logging road. Park far enough off the road at the landing to give the logging trucks unrestricted access and no harvest trees are to be cut down or damaged during trail building.

Routes

Kevin Floyd and Dave Parsons started the first multi-pitch route on Grayback around 1988 and in 2000, 12 years later, Dave Lepard and Dave Parsons returned and pushed another 7–8 pitches on the route. In September 2001 they completed the 11th pitch which they graded at 5.10b. The first 10 pitches were rated between 5.6 to 5.8. This route they called 'Wapiti Mainline'.

In July 2001 Dave Lepard and Ryan Fisher put up a 4 pitch route on the same slab called 'Talladega Highbank' rated 5.10a

Peak 4400

Peak 4,400 (L) & Grayback Peak (R) across the upper Nomash River (L) from Rugged Mt., June.

Peak 4400
4,400 ft./ 1,341 m

Peak 4400 is the highest of the low, steep sided mountains south of the Nomash River. It has an interesting coastal character with sweeping, forested (and deforested!) ridges running away from the peak in a variety of directions. Views of the west side of the Haihte Range and Tahsis and Zeballos Inlets make this a worthy destination.

First Ascent: Likely prospectors or surveyors. The Zeballos area experienced a mini-gold rush in the 1930s and many claims were staked all over the area.

Map Sheet: 92 E/15 Zeballos — GR 6438 (see also 92 L/2 Woss Lake)

Approaches: From the Zeballos Road turn east onto Nomash Main. As for approaches to Rugged Mountain and the west side of the Haihte Range, drive up the Nomash Main through the valley on the east bank of the river. Cross the bridge over to the west bank of the river at the toe of the long north ridge of the mountain. Turn right and follow roads into the small valley west of the mountain (see photo above). Either strike up the hillside to gain the north ridge which may be climbed along its crest to the top. Or continue farther in to the back of the valley and make a short steep hike up to the pass at GR 6239 adjacent to some small lakes. Head east along the height of land toward the mountain joining the north ridge which is then followed to the summit.

Lukwa Mountain
3,749 ft./ 1,142 m

Lukwa Mountain is a nondescript mountain south-west of Rugged Mountain at the back of the Curly Creek valley, a tributary of the Nomash River.

First Ascent: Likely prospectors or surveyors.

Map Sheet: 92 L/2 Woss Lake - GR 5941

Approaches: The mountain is easily reached from overgrown logging roads in Curly Creek. From the Zeballos Road turn east onto Nomash Main. As for approaches to Rugged Mountain and the west side of the Haihte Range drive up the Nomash Main as it runs up the valley on the east bank of the river. Cross the bridge over to the west bank of the river and head north-west following a main spur road into the Curly Creek valley. Choose a line off the road up the hillside to gain the crest of the arcing north-west ridge of Lukwa Mountain. Hike up the timbered ridge to the summit.

Kaouk Mountain

Kaouk Mountain (L) and Peak 4041 (R) south aspect over Zeballos, August.

Kaouk Mountain
4,295 ft./ 1,309 m

Kaouk Mountain stands sentry over the small coastal village of Zeballos. The mountain lies on the west side of the Zeballos River just a few kilometres north of the town and tidal water at the head of Zeballos Inlet. It is the most striking of the small mountains on the west side of Zeballos River valley and has excellent views of the surrounding inlets.

First Ascent: Likely prospectors or surveyors.

Map Sheet: 92 L/2 Woss Lake - GR 5244

Approaches: Best climbed by the south ridge. From Zeballos cross the bridge and head west out of town following signs for Fair Harbout. At a major junction turn right (north) and drive back up the Zeballos River valley on the west side of the river. After 3 km turn left onto Z-10 and follow spur roads right high up on the south-east flank of the mountain. Hike off the road and head for the crest of the south ridge which may be followed as it steepens up to the summit.

Alternativley, and more sportingly, try the long sweeping east ridge (see photo above). Park 2 km before the bridge over Zeballos River on the Zeballos Road from the Island Highway. Head west up into the timber above the road and find the crest of the east ridge. Follow the ridge to the top.

Mamat Mountain
3,810 ft./ 1,161 m

Mamat Mountain lies on the west side of the Zeballos River just a few kilometres north-west of the town and tidal water at the head of Zeballos Inlet.

First Ascent: Likely prospectors or surveyors.

Map Sheet: 92 L/2 Woss Lake - GR 5041 (see also 92 E/15 Zeballos)

Approaches: May be reached and climbed from logging roads in Mamat Creek. Drive through Zeballos heading south then west, following signs for Fair Harbour. The road crosses a bridge over Little Espinosa Inlet where some impressive tidal rapids swirl with the ebb and flood. Cross the Mamut Creek and take spur F-20 northward along the west bank of Mamut Creek. From the valley gain either the south or west ridges which can be followed with no technical difficulty to the summit.

Paul Nimmon looking over the Nimpkish valley from Pinder Peak.   photo: Greg Shea

Nimpkish Lake
Quatsino Sound

Haihte Range from Pinder Peak.

Nimpkish Lake - Quatsino
Contents

Province Range	446
Pinder Peak	447
Barad-dur	448
The Stone Trolls	448
Mook Peak	449
Karmutzen Mountain	450
Tlakwa Mountain	451
Merry Widow Mountain	453
Kwois Peak	455
Mt. Renwick	455
Peak 4330	455
Peak 4225	456
Snowsaddle Mountain	457
Garibaldi Peaks	458
False Ears	458
Nunatak Mountain	459
Doom Mountain	459
Saxifrage Mountain	459
Mt. Seaton	460
Mt. Clark	460
Carter Peak	460
Mt. Wolfenden	461
Mt. Pickering	461
Comestock Mountain	461

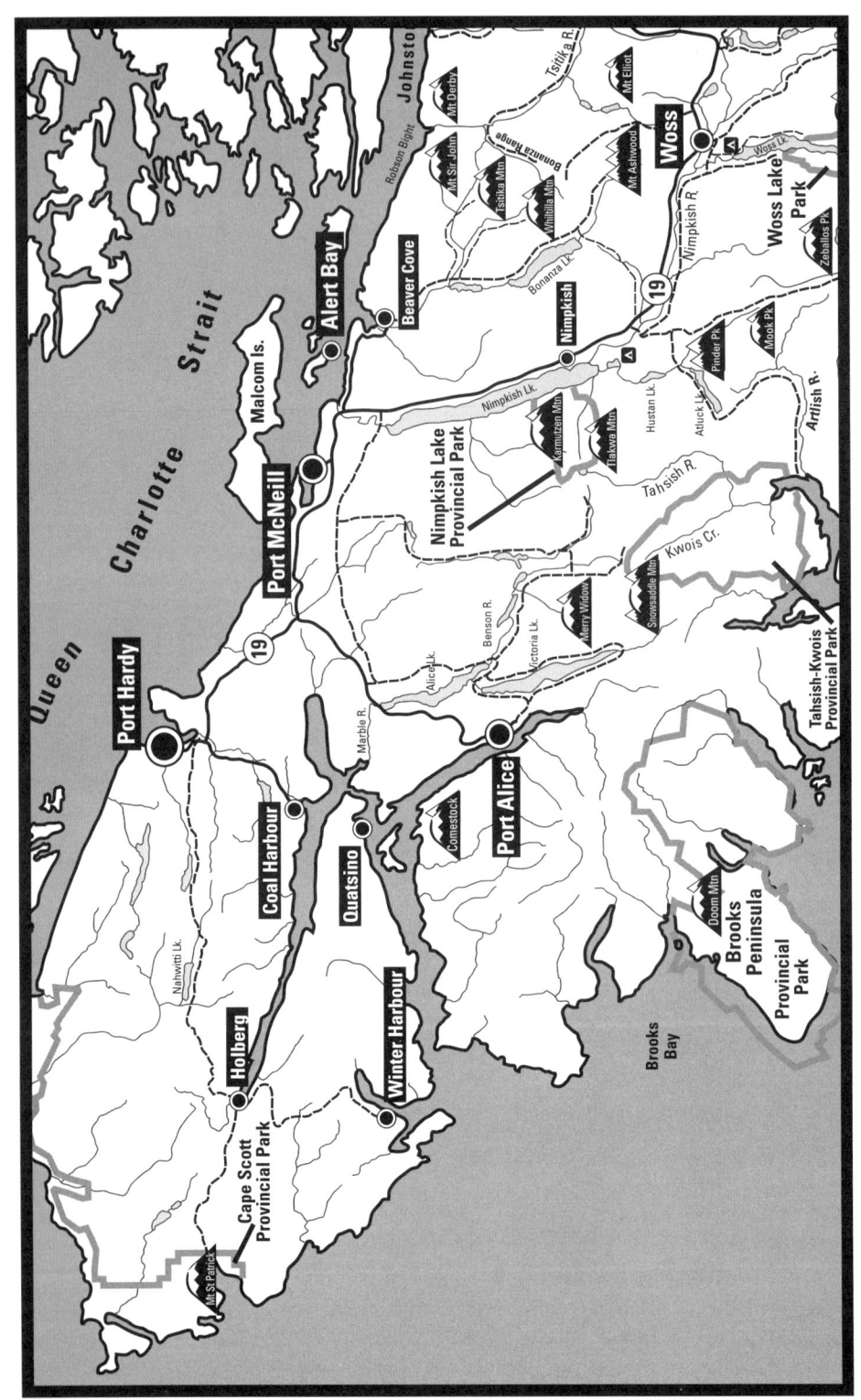

444 Nimpkish Lake - Quatsino Sound - Map

Nimpkish Lake - Quatsino

As the mountainous backbone of the Island's interior reaches the northern end of Vancouver Island it is terminated by the deep inlets of Quatsino Sound. Like Alberni Inlet far to the south the long fjords which branch off Quatsino Sound almost cut right across the island. The peaks of this region give spectacular views of Quatsino and Kyuquot Sounds along with Victoria, Alice and Nimpkish lakes. The mountains here are of lower elevation than the mountains to the south but they retain a noble character befitting of this rugged end of Vancouver Island.

Major logging roads provide excellent access high on the flanks of most of the mountains of the area making some of the peaks feasible day trip destinations from say Courtenay north. The extensive and intensive logging across northern Vancouver Island has created a landscape of vast clearcuts and regenerating forest.

Amongst the chaos of the timber harvesting are several significant Provincial Parks which are home to some of the more attractive mountains in the area. Tahsish Kwois Provincial Park protects a stunning valley of old growth forest ringed by mountains right to the ocean in Kyuquot Sound. Nimpkish Lake Park is home to some of the largest remaining Douglas Fir in the world and the Artlish Caves Park is well worth a visit for a sample of the magical world of limestone caves cloaked in old growth forest.

Map Sheets: 92 L/7 Nimpkish • 92 L/2 Zeballos • 92 L/3 Kyuquot • 92 L/ Brooks Peninsula • 92 L/5 Mahatta River • 92 I/9 San Josef River

Boundaries: north: Johnstone Strait, **east:** Nimpkish River & Pinder Creek, **south:** Kyuquot Sound, **west:** Pacific Ocean.

Major Access Routes: Through this most north and westerly region of Vancouver Island the **Island Highway 19** winds its way through the mountains in the middle of the Island north from Sayward, returning to follow the Johnstone Strait shoreline at Port McNeill. Main logging roads head west from the highway giving excellent road access to some of the mountains. From the Island Highway several of these gravel logging roads cut across the Island to communities and log dumps on the west coast where boat access is possible to the peaks closer to the coast.

Zeballos Road: The Zeballos Forest Service Road (Pinder Main) leaves the Island Highway 21 km north of Woss servicing the picturesque community of Zeballos.

The Artlish Main: Leaves the Zeballos Road giving access to the east side of Tahsish-Kwois Park.

Keogh (Benson) Main: runs from Port McNeill south to the north end of Tahsish-Kwois Park.

Alice Lake Main: From Port Alice the Alice Lake Main accesses the north and west side of Tahsish-Kwois Park, linking with the Keogh Main under Merry Widow Mountain.

Forest Service & Logging Company Offices:

• **Port McNeill Forest District** - P.O. Box 7000, 2217 Mine Road Port McNeill, BC V0N 2R0 Ph: 250 956-5000 eMail: Forests.PortMcNeillDistrictOffice@gems3.gov.bc.ca

• **Western Forest Products Limited** - 1594 Beach, Port McNeill BC V0N 2R0 Ph: 250 956-4446

• **Weyerhaeuser** - Port McNeill Ph: 250 956-5200

• **Timberwest** - Johnstone Strait Operation - P.O. Box 2500, 5705 North Island Highway Campbell River, BC V9W 5C5 Ph: (250) 287-9181

Province Range

Province Range north-east aspect from outlet of Nimpkish Lake, March.

Province Range

The Province Range a.k.a. Pinder Range runs south from the south end of Nimpkish Lake on the divide between Atluck Lake and the Artlish River to the west, and Pinder Creek and the Zeballos River to the east. Pinder Peak was named Province Peak by William Bolton for the Province newspaper which sponsored his 1896 expedition traversing the interior of Vancouver Island from Shushartie to Victoria. The name did not stick to Pinder Peak but in deference to Bolton's effort may be used to refer to the range which Pinder heads.

The summits along the Province Range are all distinct towers, separated by low passes between them. A complete traverse of the range is a possible option to visiting these peaks, with a little effort in vehicle logistics. Otherwise the four main peaks are readily accessible individually from logging roads in the Artlish Valley to the south-west.

Other recreational opportunities in the area include a visit to some of the outstanding caves in the area. Little Hustan Caves near Hustan Lake is worth a quick visit. For more, check-out the Artlish Caves Provincial Park accessible from the north via Artlish Main off Atluck Road or drive in from the south off the Zeballos Forest Service Road on the confusingly identically named Artlish Main.

Map Sheet: 2 L/2 Woss Lake

Camping & Accommodation: Excellent bases for exploration in this area are the Forest Service Recreation sites at Anutz Lake, Hustan Lake and Atluck Lake. For more salubrious accommodation try the Rugged Mountain Motel in Woss or Masons Motor Lodge in Zeballos.

Looking south from Pinder Peak over the Stone Trolls, Mook Peak and the Haihte Range beyond.   Photo; Greg Shea

Pinder Peak

Pinder Peak north aspect from Atluck Creek, August.

Pinder Peak
5,060 ft./ 1,542 m

Pinder Peak is known locally as the 'Matterhorn of the North Island'. Its dramatic profile dominates the skyline along Nimpkish Lake along with the jagged 'Province Range' that runs to its south-east along the divide between the Artlish and the Pinder/Zeballos valleys. Pinder Peak is easily climbed as a day trip from the road with little terrain to warrant a longer stay other than tackling a traverse of any of the other peaks to the south. There is great potential for more difficult technical routes on the steep clean rock buttresses that surround the summit particularly on the north side of the mountain. The views from Pinder of the lower Nimpkish valley, Kyuquot Sound, the Haihte Range and northern Vancouver Island are superb.

First Ascent: A.J. Campbell survey party 1931

Map Sheet: 2 L/2 Woss Lake - GR 4762

Approaches: From the Island Highway 19 turn south on the Zeballos Road 21 km north of Woss. After ~7 km a major junction signposted for Atluck Lake breaks right. Follow the Atluck Road to Atluck Lake from where Pinder Peak's west aspect is clearly seen rising over the lake. At the south-west end of Atluck Lake turn onto the Artlish Main and then locate the road which enters the short high valley on Pinder's south-west flank, Apollo Creek. Gain the south-west ridge using any remaining old growth forest and trend slightly north into the basin between the main peak and the horn to the south-east of the summit. Apparently, recent roads have advanced even further up Pinder's slopes.

Pinder Peak south-west aspect from approach, Aug.

Stay to the left (south-east) of the basin with a few exposed scrambling moves up a wide open slab to easier ground above. From just below the col between Pinder and The Horn strike directly across snow or scree to gain the final rocky section of the south-east ridge to the summit.

The Horn is the satellite peak to the south and is easily reached from the col as well with a little exposed 3rd class scrambling on to the summit.

Additional Info: WIM #5 p.10

Barad-dur & Stone Trolls

Barad-dur east aspect from Zeballos Road, August.

Barad-dur
4,938 ft./ 1,505 m

Barad-dur (named for the fictional castle of J.R.R. Tolkein's classic Lord of the Rings trilogy) is a steep rocky pyramid between Mook Peak to its south and the Stone Trolls to the north in the centre of the Province Range.

First Ascent: Heather Kellerhals, Marcus Kellerhals, Rolf Kellerhals, August 1981

Map Sheet: 92 L/2 Woss Lake - GR 5158

Approaches: As with the other peaks in the Province Range Barad-dur is best reached from the south-west out of the Artlish River valley. Follow the approach description for Pinder Peak but continue on the Artlish Main past Apollo Creek to close to the end of the road at the Artlish Caves Park and locate roads leading into Crystal Creek which drains the valley to the north-west of the peak. Hike east up the south-west flank of the mountain until the terrain moulds into a prominent south-west ridge which is followed with some scrambling near the top.

Barad-dur may also be reached from the north from the Stone Trolls via the connecting ridge and col between the two.

The Stone Trolls
4,849 ft./ 1,478 m

The Stone Trolls are two rock-dome summits south of Pinder Peak along the Province Range. Of the peaks in the Province Range there is more open alpine terrain around these summits than the others. The Trolls are easily combined as an objective along with Barad-dur.

First Ascent: Heather Kellerhals, Marcus Kellerhals, Rolf Kellerhals, August 1981

Map Sheet: 92 L/2 Woss Lake - GR 5060

Approaches: The Trolls may be reached from the Artlish River valley logging roads. Follow the approach description for Pinder Peak but continue on the Artlish Main past Apollo Creek to branch roads that climb very high on the south-west flanks of the Trolls. Hike up along the south-west ridge keeping to the right to avoid obstacles to the summit.

Additional Info: IB 1996 p.13, IB 2000 p.25

Mook Peak

Mook Peak north-east aspect from Zeballos Road, August.

Mook Peak
4,937 ft./ 1,505 m

Mook Peak forms the south-east terminus of the Province Range as a rocky dome overlooking the Zeballos road. Mook's north-east face drops right to the floor of the Pinder Creek valley creating one of the few real mountain passes through which public vehicle traffic travels on Vancouver Island.

First Ascent: Unknown

Map Sheet: 2 L/2 Woss Lake - GR 5257

Approaches: Unlike the other peaks in the Province Range Mook is best reached from the south-west from the lower Artlish Main which joins the Zeballos Road ~15 km south past the Atluck Lake junction and ~15 north of Zeballos. Turn west on to the Artlish Main and gain any one of a variety of spurs like A-27 or A-20 which climb up the south-west side of the mountain. Hike up the remaining forest to the summit ridge.

Note that because of the formation of Artlish Caves Park the Artlish Main does not connect through to Atluck Lake despite sharing the name with the road from that end of the valley.

Province Range east aspect from Mt. Cain, February.

Karmutzen Mountain

Karmutzen Range south-east aspect from Anutz Lake, July.

Karmutzen Mountain
4,680 ft./ 1,426 m

Karmutzen Mountain is the highest point of the Karmutzen Range which forms the divide to the west of Nimpkish Lake. Rising steeply from the lake it is, in part, responsible for the gorge effect that produces the reliable winds that Nimpkish Lake has become famous for among windsurfing circles. Karmutzen in the Kwa-kwala language means "waterfall".[1]

First Ascent: H.E. Whyte survey party 1931

Map Sheet: 92 L/6 Alice Lake - GR 8041

Approaches: Turn left (west) off the Island Highway at the north end of Nimpkish Lake on Kilpala Main. Drive across the bridge over the lower Nimpkish River and keep left at the junction with Hookup Rd. Drive south along the west shore of Nimpkish Lake. Kilpala Rd. then turns west away from the lake up Kilpala Creek. Turn left on to Karmutzen Main which runs south up Karmutzen Creek on the west side of Karmutzen Mountain. Turn left on to branch road KMR 1000 which winds up high on the west flank of Karmutzen Mt.. Drive as far as road conditions allow then continue on foot up a prominent ridge in to a basin with an alpine lake west of the summit. Hike up the back of the basin on to the ridge to the south of the summit and head north to the top. May be climbed from Tlakwa Creek too.

Additional Info: IB 1997 p.19

Karmutzen Mountain east aspect from Merry Widow Mountain, October.

Tlakwa Mountain

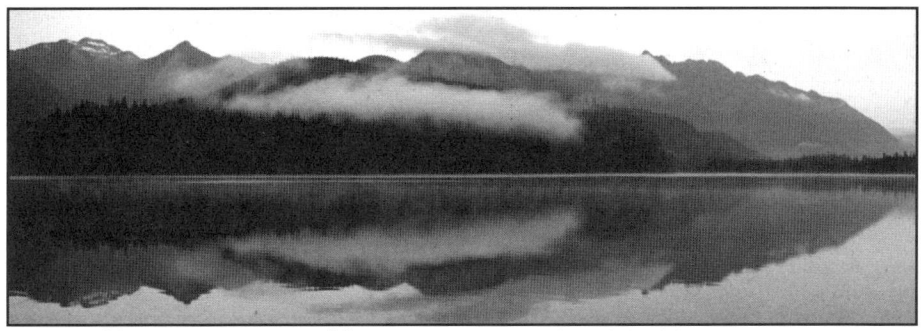

Tlakwa Mt. (L) & the Karmutzen Range (R) south-east aspect from Anutz Lake, July.

Tlakwa Mountain
4,779 ft./ 1,457 m

Tlakwa Mountain is found to the west of the south end of Nimpkish Lake on the divide between Tlakwa Creek and the Tahsish River. The tlakwa Creek is a protected area within the boundaries of Nimpkish Lake Provincial Park.

First Ascent: A.J. Campbell survey party 1931

Map Sheet: 92 L/6 Alice Lake - GR 3874

Approaches: Tlakwa Mountain may be reached from Nimpkish Lake up a tributary of Tlakwa Creek off the Tlakwa Main logging road. Drive north on the Island Highway, 21 km north of Woss (151 km north of Campbell River) turn left (south) on the Zeballos Road. After ~9 km turn right (west) on Atluck Main leaving the road to Zeballos. After 3 km turn right (north) to Anutz Lake. Tlakwa Main heads around the south end of Anutz Lake to the boundary of Nimpkish Lake Provincial Park. Drive as far as you can up the Tlakwa Main keeping right into a tributary to the south of Tlakwa Creek. Continue on foot to gain the south ridge of the mountain. Head north on the ridge crest to the summit, bushy!

Alternatively, approach Tlakwa Mountain from the west off Melanie Main, a branch road of Atluck Main. Continue past the turn off to Anutz Lake along Atluck Lake. Keep right at the junction with Artlish Main. The Atluck Main swings northward following the Tahsish River on its east bank. Turn right on to Melanie Main which runs up high on the west flank on Tlakwa Mountain. Drive as far as you can then continue on foot up the west ridge on easy hiking terrain to the summit.

Tlakwa Mt. east aspect from Merry Widow Mountain, October.

452 Ryan Stuart hiking through meadows below Merry Widow Mountain.

Merry Widow Mountain

Merry Widow Mountain west aspect from west bowl, October.

Merry Widow Mountain
4,600 ft./ 1,402 m

Merry Widow Mountain is situated to the south-east of Victoria Lake and the town of Port Alice. The Benson River runs to the east of the mountain linking a series of freshwater lakes which are some of the largest such lakes on the island. Merry Widow marks the northwestern-most extent of significant alpine terrain on Vancouver Island and its situation overlooking the large lakes and Neroutsos Inlet to the west gives sweeping views of the northern Island lowlands. The mountain has superb access from various logging roads on its east and north flanks and is a locals' favourite hike.

First Ascent: Possibly surveyors 1927

Map Sheet: 92 L/6 Alice Lake - GR 2277

Approaches: Approach Merry Widow off Keogh (Benson) Main from Port McNeill. Port McNeill is 194 km north of Campbell River on the Island Highway 19. Continue past the Port McNeill junction on the Island Highway 3.7 km north to a crossroads where Keogh Main crosses the highway. Turn left (south) on Keogh Main, keep left after 4.5 km at the junction with West Main. A long drive up the Three Lakes Creek valley 28 km past the West Main junction leads to a bridge over Raging Creek. Keep right where Raging Main leaves Keogh Main and cross the bridge. 2.5 km west of the Raging Creek bridge cross the Benson River bridge and then turn right on Alice Lake Main 1.2 km north on Alice Lake Main turn left onto Merry Trail Main (M1080).

Drive up Merry Trail Main which runs up the north side of Merry Widow Creek on the mountain's east flank. Turn right after 2 km and follow this branch road as high as current road conditions allow on the flanks of the north-east ridge. From the highest spur locate the signposted Merry Widow trail and hike west up the remaining forest to gain the alpine at Peak 4349. Head south-west along a beautiful open ridge to the foot of the short north ridge. A short exposed 3rd class scramble leads up the north ridge to the small exposed summit.

Merry Widow may also be reached from logging roads in Craft Creek to the north-west. Reach Craft Creek Main BR 90 from either the Keogh Main from Port McNeill or from Port Alice via the south-east and Alice Lake Main from Jeune Landing.

To reach Craft Creek from Port McNeill follow the directions above to the Merry Trail Main junction. Pass the junction staying on the Alice Lake Main. ~7.5 km past the Merry Trail Main the Alice Lake Main joins a road servicing a mine. Turn left down the mine road and immediately before a bridge over the Craft Creek turn right on to BR 90. BR 90 is deactivated but at the time of writing was simply ditched and drivable with a high clearance 2 wheel drive. Drive 3.6 km up BR 90 to a junction with a debuilt branch which continues to the left up to the back of the Craft Creek valley, park here.

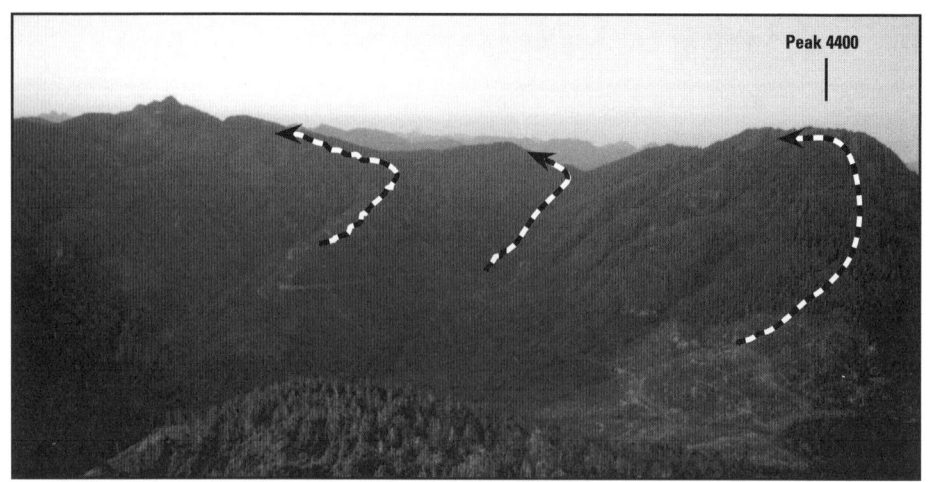

Merry Widow Mountain (L) & Peak 4400 over Craft Creek, north aspect from Peak 4217, October.

Hike along the debuilt logging road (90H1) to the back of the valley. The road crosses the creek and doubles back on the other side of the valley making a long switchback up onto the crest of a prominent ridge (see photo above). From the creek crossing upward, the road has been thoroughly decommissioned and is a chore to hike.

Consider heading off the road at the creek crossing and hike up alongside the creek-bed to a col at GR 1978. It is a very nasty bushwhack through the old clearcut to reach the remaining timber and a very steep climb up a crafty line on the right (west) side of the creek gully to reach the col. From the col turn south-east and follow the height of land over a forested knoll toward Merry Widow. Join the route from the 90H1 road which after winding up a prominent spur ridge heads up through the forest to a col at GR 2078.

Hike east along the beautiful alpine ridge over a knoll and on to a col below the foot of the north ridge of Merry Widow Mountain. A short exposed 3rd class scramble leads up the north ridge to the small exposed summit.

An alternative on this side of Merry Widow is to use the high, currently open roads in the saddle between Peak 4217 and Peak 4400 (see photo below) to hike up Peak 4400 at GR 1979 and follow the height of land around the headwaters of Craft Creek to Merry Widow. This route may require an overnight camp but would be well worth it for the beautiful alpine and views encountered along this ridge.

Peak 4217 south aspect across Craft Creek from near Merry Widow Mountain, October.

454 Merry Widow Mountain

Kwois Peak

Peak 4330 north aspect from Merry Widow Mountain, October.

Kwois Peak
4,181 ft./ 1,274 m

Kwois Peak stands sentry at the head of the Kwois Creek valley between this protected watershed and the conversely devastated Benson River valley. The summit is within Tahsish-Kwois Provincial Park and offers commanding views of the spectacular pristine west coast watershed found in Kwois Creek looking out to Kyuquot Sound.

Map Sheet: 92 L/3 Kyuquot - GR 2870

Approaches: Might be tackled from logging roads near Cross Lake off Atluck Main. A symmetrical tapering ridge rises from west of Cross Lake providing a route along the divide between Tahsish River and Benson River. Hike south-west up the tapering ridge from Cross Lake to the alpine. Descend to a col heading north-west up the south-west ridge of Kwois Peak passing a subsidiary peak en route.

An alternative approach might be attempted along the north ridge from the Benson River logging roads. Gain the alpine from the best of open logging spur roads off Benson Main. Hike the north ridge directly to the summit.

Mt. Renwick
3,736 ft./ 1,139 m

Mt. Renwick stands in the north crux where the Tahsish River joins Kwois Creek. The mountain is with in Tahsish-Kwois Provincial Park and offers commanding views of the spectacular pristine west coast watershed found in Kwois Creek.

Map Sheet: 92 L/3 Kyuquot - GR 3463

Approaches: Approach from the Tahsish River valley. Leave the Island Highway on the Zeballos Road and after ~9 km keep right leaving the Zeballos Road on Atluck Main. Drive around Atluck Lake and continue west into the Tahsish valley. Turn left (west) onto Lower Tahsish Main following signs for Tahsish-Kwois Provincial Park. Try the long south-east ridge direct from the parking lot.

Peak 4330
4,330 ft./ 1,319 m

Peak 4330 is found at the meeting of several valley systems. To the north-east runs Blue Ox Creek a tributary of the Benson River, to the north-west is Teihsum River which flows in to the east shore of Victoria Lake, the south and west flanks of this mountain are drained by the Kauwinch River.

Map Sheet: 92 L/3 Kyuquot - GR 2870

Approaches: Best reached from the north-east out of the Benson River valley. Try a route off B200 or B310 out of Blue Ox Creek or the next branch of Benson River to the south.

Peak 4225

Kwois Valley, Peak 4170, Snowsaddle Mountain & Peak 4225 north aspect from Merry Widow Mountain, October.

Peak 4225
4,225 ft./ 1,287 m

Peak 4225 is situated at the head of Kwois Creek between the Kwois to the east and the Kauwinch River to the west. The mountain has the form of double humps with a secondary summit, Peak 4170, to the east of Peak 4225. The twin humps are separated by a deep col. The north and east aspects of this mountain are fairly steep complicating access and require a circuitous approach.

Map Sheet: 92 L/3 Kyuquot - GR 2870

Approaches: The kinking north ridge looks to be the best route up this mountain from Benson River. To reach the north ridge approach off Benson Main up a long ridge east off Peak 4330. Descend southward to a col at GR 2570 and the toe of the north ridge of Peak 4225. Hike up the ridge to the top.

Alternatively, approach from Benson River up to the Benson-Kwois Col at GR 2770. Hike up and over the north-east ridge of Peak 4170 descending westward to the deep saddle between 4170 and 4225. Traversing south underneath the east face to join the south-east ridge to the summit is a promising but untested route.

Snowsaddle Mountain, Peak 4225 & Peak 4330 north aspect from Merry Widow Mountain, October.

Snowsaddle Mountain

Snowsaddle Mountain & False Ears (distant R) north aspect from Merry Widow Mountain, October.

Snowsaddle Mountain
4,593 ft./ 1,400 m

Snowsaddle Mountain lies a on the west divide of Kwois Creek in the Tahsish-Kwois Provincial Park. This park is one of the larger provincial parks on Vancouver Island notable for its intact temperate rainforest ecosystem and probably the most viable Roosevelt Elk herd on the Island. Access to Snowsaddle is somewhat complicated which combined with its remote situation has meant very few recorded ascents.

First Ascent: Rev. William Bolton, James Magee, J.J. Skinner, 24 July, 1894

Map Sheet: 92 L/3 Kyuquot - GR 2766 (see also 92 L/6 Alice Lake)

Approaches: Snowsaddle Mountain may reached from the north off Benson Main via the Keogh (Benson) Main from Port McNeill. 3.7 km north of Port McNeill junction on the Island Highway turn left (south) on Keogh (Benson) Main. Keep left after 4.5 km at the junction with West Main. A long drive up the Three Lakes Creek valley 28 km past the West Main junction leads to a bridge over Raging Creek. Keep right where Raging Main leaves Keogh (Benson) Main and cross the bridge. 2.5 km west of the Raging Creek bridge cross the Benson River bridge and then keep left on Benson Main and follow this road to the head of the valley.

From the end of the road hike south to the Benson-Kwois Pass at GR 2770. Head south-west up a long ridge to gain the alpine north-west of Peak 4170. Continue south along the ridge over Peak 4170 descending to a pass north of Snowsaddle. Ascend the north ridge to the summit.

Alternatively, approach from the Kwois Creek valley. Leave the Island Highway on the Zeballos Road and after ~9 km keep right leaving the Zeballos Road on Atluck Main. Drive around Atluck Lake and continue west into the Tahsish valley. Turn left crossing the Tahsish and then left again on the Lower Tahsish road. Drive to the end of the road close to the Tahsish-Kwois Provincial Park boundary. Hike west down the Tahsish River to its confluence with Kwois Creek. Cross to the west bank of Kwois Creek and follow elk trails north-west along the creek. Turn west up a small valley to the south of the peak and gain the ridge south of Snowsaddle Mountain. From a tight col continue up the south ridge over a satellite peak and on to the top of Snowsaddle.

Garibaldi Peaks

Garibaldi Peaks & Peak north aspect from Merry Widow Mt., October.

Garibaldi Peaks
4,054 ft./ 1,235 m

A group of forested summits overlooking the east side of Kauwinch River on the west boundary of Tahsish-Kwois Provincial Park.

Map Sheet: 92 L/3 Kyuquot - GR 2660

Approaches: Approach from Kashutl Inlet taking the main logging road up Kauwinch River. The condition of these roads is unknown but travel up the valley is only required a few kilometres before a valley under the south side of the peaks can be reached and a route from here forged up to the long summit ridge.

False Ears
3,486 ft./ 1,063 m

False Ears lie just south of Tahsish-Kwois Provincial Park overlooking the west side of Tahsish Inlet. It has fantastic views overlooking Kyuquot Sound.

Map Sheet: 92 L/3 Kyuquot - GR 3254

Approaches: Approach from Tahsish Inlet. Leave the Island Highway on the Zeballos Road and after ~9 km keep right leaving the Zeballos Road on Atluck Main. Drive around Atluck Lake and turn left (south) onto Artlish Main. Follow Artlish Main south then west all the way to the log dump in Tahsish Inlet. Cross the inlet by boat and tackle the Ears from the most convenient active road system.

Aerial view looking east across Kyuquot Sound toward the Family Humps, August.

Refugium Range

Refugium Range and Brooks Peninsula south-east aspect from Acous Peninsula, August.

Nunatak Mountain
2,984 ft./ 909 m

Nunatak Mountain is the highest point in the Refugium Range which forms a storm swept backbone ridge running out the centre of Brooks Peninsula. While the peaks of this range (also known as the Range of Doom) are of low elevation their singular situation and character demand a mention. The Brooks was missed by the last ice-age leaving the Refugium Range with a distinct form and giving the range its name.

Map Sheet: 92 L/4 Brooks Peninsula- GR 9361

Approaches: The Brooks Peninsula and thus the Refugium Range can be reached by boat or sea kayak with landing and moorage possible in a couple of superbly protected lagoons. Columbia Cove on the south-east shore of the peninsula and Cape Cook Lagoon on the north-west side. As the Brooks is an Ecological Reserve in which travel by people is discouraged access to the mountains is by permission from BC Parks only.

Doom Mountain
2,500 ft./ 762 m

A dramatic mountain in the midst of one of the wildest parts of Vancouver Island.

Map Sheet: 92 L/ 4 Brooks Peninsula - GR 8858

Approaches: The Brooks Peninsula is an Ecological Reserve in which travel by people is discouraged access to the mountains is by permission from BC Parks only.

Saxifrage Mountain
2,625 ft./ 800 m

A great situation at a constriction in the main Refugium Range with the land dropping steeply away from this low summit.

Map Sheet: 92 L/4 Brooks Peninsula- GR 9260

Approaches: The Brooks Peninsula is an Ecological Reserve in which travel by people is discouraged access to the mountains is by permission from BC Parks only.

Mt. Seaton

Mt. Seaton west aspect from Columbia Cove, Brooks Peninsula, August.

Mt. Seaton
3,141 ft./ 957 m

Mt. Seaton is found above the north-west shore of Ououkinsh Inlet in the Nasparti River Addition portion of Brooks Peninsula Provincial Park.

Map Sheet: 92 L/ Brooks Peninsula- GR 0558

Approaches: The Brooks Peninsula and Nasparti River Addition is an Ecological Reserve in which travel by people is discouraged access to the mountains is by permission from BC Parks only.

Mt. Clark
3,400 ft./ 1,036 m

Mt. Clark is on the divide between Teeta Creek and Cayuse Creek west of Port Alice and Neroutsos Inlet.

Map Sheet: 92 L/5 Mahatta River - GR 0579

Approaches: Easily reached from either the north on Teeta Main or from the south on Cayuse Creek. Look for the highest currently open logging roads on either side of the mountain.

Carter Peak
3,600 ft./ 1,097 m

Carter Peak is a forested pyramid at the head of Mahatta Creek.

Map Sheet: 92 L/5 Mahatta River - GR 9977

Approaches: Maybe climbed from the north-east where Klootchlimmis Main Road climbs over the ridge to link with Teeta Main.

Mt. Wolfenden

Peaks west of Neroutsos Inlet south-east aspect from Peak 4217, October.

Mt. Wolfenden
4,177 ft./ 1,273 m

Mt. Wolfenden looks over the village of Port Alice from the west shore of Neroutsos Inlet

First Ascent: H.E. Whyte survey party 1927

Map Sheet: 92 L/5 Mahatta River - GR 0186

Approaches: Approach from the west from logging road spurs off East Main in Klootchlimmis Creek.

Mt. Pickering
3,300 ft./ 1,006 m

Mt. Pickering is the high point of McKay Ridge which separates Klootchlimmis and Teeta Creeks on the west shore of Neroutsos Inlet opposite Port Alice. The mountain is also known as McKay Summit.

Map Sheet: 92 L/5 Mahatta River - GR 0280

Approaches: Mt. Pickering and the whole of McKay Ridge is encircled by logging roads. Teeta Main to the east, Klootchlimmis Main to the west and K 500 to the north-east. The mountain is best climbed from the south-west where Klootchlimmis Main climbs over the ridge to link with Teeta Main.

Comestock Mountain
3,600 ft./ 1,097 m

Comestock Mountain is at a commanding position overlooking Quatsino Sound. Although not the most northern peak on Vancouver Island (that distinction I believe goes to Mt. Sir John 4,690 ft) it can be considered the furthest 'up-island' peak over 3,500 ft.

Map Sheet: 92 L/5 Mahatta River - GR 0090

Approaches: Approach from the west from logging road spurs off East Main in Klootchlimmis Creek.

462 Aerial view of Rugged Mountain and Woss Lake

Appendix

Vancouver Island Backbone	465
Sources	469
Island Peaks Over 6000ft	470
Glossary	471
Index	473

464 Greg Shea & Phil Sera looking across the Conuma valley toward Mt Bate from Sebahall-Muchalet divide.

Appendix 1
Vancouver Island Backbone

The Vancouver Island Backbone is a wilderness hiking route that weaves over 300 km (200 miles) along the mountainous interior of Vancouver Island. The route links trails, rugged alpine ridges, logging roads, lush river valleys and lakes as it charts a course through the heart of the island. Although primarily a hiking route in concept, the Backbone covers terrain suitable for, mountain biking, ski touring and whitewater paddling.

Completing the whole route in a single expedition is an experience of world class calibre. However, the route is conveniently dissected into sections by roads and towns making much shorter trips possible. Within these sections, the Backbone traveller will find adventure to satisfy any level of ambition, whether that be; strolling the trails of Paradise Meadows, canoeing the rapids of the Nimpkish River or scaling the summit of Victoria Peak.

The Vancouver Island Backbone project began in the winter of 1991-92 as an initiative of the Western Canada Wilderness Committee, Mid-Island Branch, in Nanaimo. Roseanne van Schie guided its early development. In 1993 the WCWC secured funding in the form of a grant from the Mountain Equipment Co-op to contract the mapping and exploratory work. The author undertook this work and through that summer hiked some of the lesser known sections, accompanied by various volunteers from the WCWC membership.

The data collected during these exploratory hikes was plotted onto 1:50000 NTS maps along with accompanying 35mm slides, video and field notes. The result was the publication of a guidebook: 'A Guide to the Vancouver Island Backbone' published in 1995. This book is still available free of charge in an electronic pdf format from www.wildisle.ca/publications

Following the Vancouver Island Backbone celebrates the spirit of First Nations traders and early European explorers. We can only imagine the journey up the Nimpkish River, hauling canoes and goods across to Tahsis when the land was wild and empty. William Bolton describes such an undertaking in his journal as, initially accompanied by First Nations guides, he led an expedition traversing the Island from the mouth of the Nimpkish River to Victoria in 1896. Bolton's route is emulated and followed in part by the Backbone Route. However, the land that Bolton knew which had been inhabited by the First Nations people is now very different. Logging roads siphon out the Island's riches, and parks preserve its beauty in isolated pockets creating a landscape of incredible contrast.

This route provides a challenge unlike any other long distance hiking trail as no additional infrastructure has been constructed. To prevent more development and undue pressure on the fragile wilderness, no trails have been cut or even marked, beyond those that already existed. The Vancouver Island Backbone is more concept than trail. It is hoped this ethic is respected by those following the route in the future, thus helping to preserve this unique experience and landscape.

The Backbone Route crosses several Provincial Parks, and it is especially important to respect the conservation values and development plans for these parks by passing through leaving no trace. Similar care is needed while hiking through private land on the Beaufort Range and around Buttle Lake. We must ensure future access is not jeopardized by conflicting with the wishes of land owners.

Mountain Hemlock in the Vancouver Island alpine.

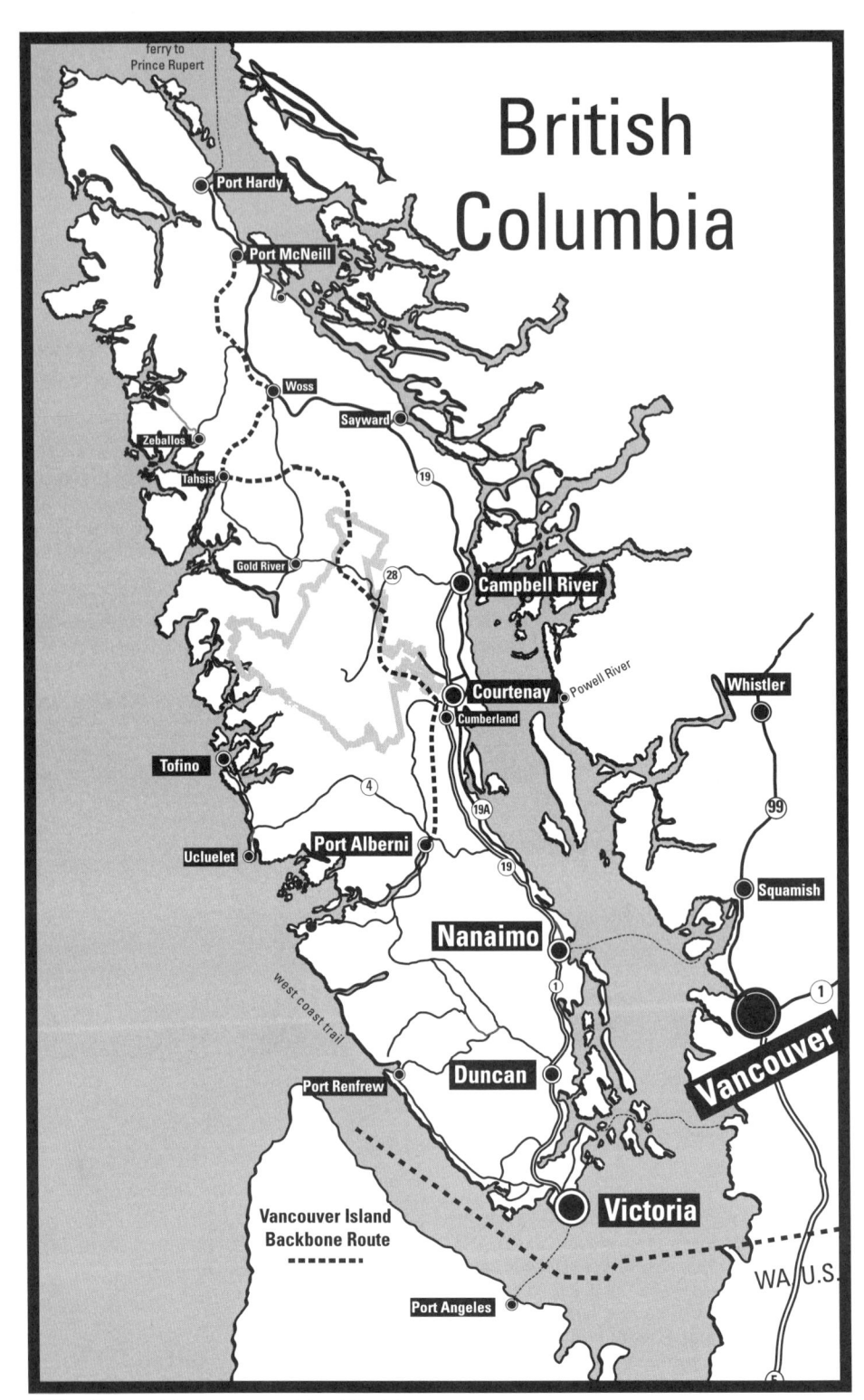

Route of the Vancouver Island Backbone

The Route of the Vancouver Island Backbone.

The exact line of the Vancouver Island Backbone weaves a crafty route through the Island mountains. In some areas the route avoids the true watershed divide between east and west coasts in respect to other values and access considerations. For example the route from Port Alberni to Buttle Lake doesn't take the early explorers route via Great Central Lake through Price Pass in deference to the conservation values and increasing pressure on Strathcona Park. Instead the route takes advantage of the greater ease of access to the Beaufort Range and the exisiting trails across Forbidden Plateau and Paradise Meadows to Augerpoint.

The only missing link is between Buttle Narrows and the Crest Mountain Trail where no practical alternative to Highway 28 exists. So one is left with the choice of either hiking the road or using vehicle transport to make the quick hop through the valley.

Broken down into eight sections the Vancouver Island Backbone takes the following route:

1-Beaufort Range
Port Alberni to Cumberland; 55km/32mi

2- Forbidden Plateau
Cumberland to Augerpoint, Buttle Lake; 36km/22mi

3- Buttle Lake
Augerpoint to Buttle Narrows; 30km/20mi

4- Gold Lake
Crest Mountain to Gold Lake; 28km/18mi

5- Victoria Peak
Gold Lake to Nimpkish Road; 31km/20mi

6- Tlupana Range
Nimpkish Road to Tahsis; 40km/25mi

7- Woss Lake
Tahsis to Woss; 35km/22mi

8- Nimpkish River/Karmutzen Range
Woss to Port McNeill; 65km/40mi

The details of each section are found in the Guide to the Vancouver Island Backbone but may just as easily be deduced by experienced backcountry hikers from the 1:50,000 NTS map sheets. Logging road development and debuilding is one of greatest variables with literally entire valleys having been logged and then closed in the ten years since the Backbone route was researched in 1993.

Craig Maxwell hiking the Backbone near Augerpoint.

468 Patrick Malloy on Indecent Exposure 5.9 Crest Creek Crags.

Appendix 2
Sources

- Intro
1- Beyond Nootka, Elms
2- Beyond Nootka, Elms
3- CAJ 1971
4- CAJ 1979
5- Toward the Unknown Mountains, Wood
6- CAJ 1990

- South Island
1- Amor De Cosmos - 1001 British Columbia Place Names, Akrigg & Akrigg

- Central Island
1- Mt Moriarty - British Columbia Coast Names, Walbran
2- Arrowsmith - 1001 British Columbia Place Names, Akrigg & Akrigg
3- Mt Maitland - - British Columbia Coast Names, Walbran
4- Mt Quimper - British Columbia Coast Names, Walbran

- Beaufort Range
1- Beaufort Range - British Columbia Coast Names, Walbran

-Strathcona Introduction
1- Toward the Unknown Mountains, Wood

- East Strathcona Park
1- Mt Washington - British Columbia Coast Names, Walbran
2- Siokum Mountain - Hiking Trails III
3- Comox - British Columbia Coast Names, Walbran

- Tlupana Range
1- Tlupana Range - British Columbia Coast Names, Walbran
2- Conuma Peak - British Columbia Coast Names, Walbran
3- Mt Alava - 1001 British Columbia Place Names, Akrigg & Akrigg
4- Malaspina Peak - - British Columbia Coast Names, Walbran

- Johnstone Strait
1- Mt. Kitchener - 1001 British Columbia Place Names, Akrigg & Akrigg
2- Mt. Roberts - 1001 British Columbia Place Names, Akrigg & Akrigg
3- Mt. Milner - 1001 British Columbia Place Names, Akrigg & Akrigg

- Nimpkish - Quatsino
1- Karmutzen Mt. - British Columbia Coast Names, Walbran

Island alpine legends Joe Bajan & Mike Walsh. Unnamed 15,000' peak in the Kohi Baba, Afghanistan, 1975

Appendix 3
Island Peaks Over 6,000 ft

1 **Golden Hinde** 7,219 ft / 2,201 m	p. 271	
2 **Elkhorn** 7,200 ft / 2,195 m	p. 218	
3 **Victoria Peak** 7,095 ft / 2193 m	p. 346	
4 **Colonel Foster** 7,000 ft / 2,134 m	p. 228	
5 **Rambler Peak** 6,900 ft / 2,104 m	p. 241	
6 **Albert Edward** 6,86,8 ft / 2,094 m	p. 150	
7 **Mt McBride** 6,829 ft / 2,082 m	p. 263	
8 **Kings Peak** 6,774 ft / 2,06,5 m	p. 214	
9 **Mt Celeste** 6,695 ft / 2,041 m	p. 158	
10 **Mt Filberg** 6,677 ft / 2,035 m	p. 257	
11 **Red Pillar** 6,665 ft / 2,035 m	p. 165	
12 **Mt Cobb** 6,663 ft / 2,031 m	p. 255	
13 **Behinde** 6,561, ft / 2,000 m	p. 277	
14 **Mt Colwell** 6,526, ft / 1,990 m	p. 225	
15 **Alexandra Peak** 6,503 ft / 1,983 m	p. 178	
16 **Argus Mtn.** 6,500 ft / 1,982 m	p. 163	
17 **Mt Harmston** 6,500 ft / 1,982 m	p. 164	
18 **Mt Regan** 6,500 ft / 1,982 m	p. 152	
19 **Iceberg Peak** 6,486 ft / 1,977 m	p. 159	
20 **El Piveto Mountain** 6,460 ft / 1,970 m	p. 249	
21 **Warden Peak** 6,460 ft / 1,970 m	p. 351	
22 **Mt Rosseau** 6,437 ft / 1,962 m	p. 298	
23 **Comox Glacier** 6,429 ft / 1,960 m	p. 162	
24 **Mt Haig Brown** 6,390 ft / 1,948 m	p. 253	
25 **Mt Frink** 6,300 ft / 1,921 m	p. 154	
26 **Shepherd Ridge** 6,299 ft / 1,921 m	p. 168	
27 **Peak 1920** 6,299 ft / 1,920 m	p. 156	
28 **Peak 1909** 6,262 ft / 1,909 m	p. 156	
29 **Mt George V** 6,178 ft / 1,884 m	p. 155	
30 **Tzela Mountain** 6,166, ft / 1,880 m	p. 167	
31 **Rugged Mountain** 6,151 ft / 1,861 m	p. 424	
32 **Mt Adrian** 6,135 ft / 1,870 m	p. 179	
33 **Mt Schoen** 6,109 ft / 1,86,3 m	p. 370	
34 **Big Interior Mtn.** 6,109 ft / 1,863 m	p. 292	
35 **Sutton Peak** 6,109 ft / 1,862 m	p. 355	
36 **Syd Watts Peak** 6,036 ft / 1,840 m	p. 175	
37 **Crown Mtn.** 6,057 ft / 1,847 m	p. 197	
38 **Nine Peaks** 6,042 ft / 1,842 m	p. 295	
39 **Siokum Mountain** 6,036 ft / 1,840 m	p. 157	
40 **Slocomb Peak** 6,036 ft / 1,840 m	p. 240	
41 **Mt Mitchell** 6,030 ft / 1,838 m	p. 176	
42 **Jutland Mtn.** 6,003 ft / 1,830 m	p. 149	

Production Notes

Island Alpine was composed on a G4 533 mhz Apple Macintosh computer. I used Adobe InDesign to layout the publication in 17 separate chapter files. The final data tally was over 3 gigabytes.

Adobe Photoshop was used to edit the photographs which were either scanned on an Apple Macintosh G3 266 with a Nikon Coolscan LS 10-E film scanner or with a UMAX S-12 hooked in to an aging but stalwart Power PC 7200/90.

All the maps were created in Adobe Illustrator with the patience of a saint.

The photographs were taken with a variety of cameras but principally a Minolta XG-M, Minolta 600si and more recently a Nikon F90x and a digital Olympus Camedia 3030 which produces some of the best results. My preference for film is Fuji Velvia but you take what you can get sometimes and there is picture in here taken on just about every type of major film type.

Proofs were printed on a Xanté PlateMaker and eventually 20 draft copies were output on a Xerox DocuTech. For pre-press handoff Island Alpine was distilled into press ready pdf files and shipped to Hignell Book Printing on CD.

Glossary

alpine: technically speaking 'alpine' is an abbreviated form of 'alpine tundra zone' however, colloquially it refers to both the mountain hemlock (subalpine) zone and the alpine tundra zone.

alpine tundra zone: describes the bio-geoclimatic zone found above 5,000 ft where no trees grow.

arete: a narrow fin or edge of rock or snow found at the crest of a ridge, often formed by glaciation.

aspect: a direction from which a feature is viewed. The north aspect means looking from the north southward to the north side.

basalt: prevalent volcanic rock formed from molten lava rising from the Earth's core underneath the sea. Rapid cooling forms a fine crystal structure in this reddish-coloured rock.

belay: a word of wide meaning in climbing rope techniques referring to the securing of climbers by rope and other climbing hardware to a rock, snow or ice surface. A belay station or fixed belay is a place where anchors and a rope paid out to a leading climber create essential security in a roped system. A running belay is a point where a piece of hardware such as a piton, stopper, camming unit or ice screw has a lead climber's rope running through it and provides essential secondary security on a roped climb. The act of paying out or reeling in rope to a climber through a braking device that may arrest a fall is called 'belaying'.

bergschrund: A gaping crack in snow or ice. Often formed at the base of mountain faces when the lower snow/ice settles, breaking away from that securely anchored to the steeper ground above.

chimney: a steep sided rock feature very similar in shape to a three-sided house chimney. Often require contorted manoeuvres to climb.

chockstone: a large boulder that has become wedged in a chimney, couloir or gully forming an obstruction that is often difficult to surmount.

cirque: a curved bowl-shaped formation carved by a glacier against a mountainside. May vary widely in size from a few hundred feet high to many thousands of feet on larger mountains.

clearcut: an area cleared of old-growth trees by commercial tree harvesting.

col: a low point or pass between two mountains or between smaller mountain features such as summits or pinnacles.

couloir: a steep gorge, ravine or gully running vertically up a mountain face. Often snow-filled and suitable for snow/ice climbing or skiing.

crevasse: a large crack in a glacier formed by stress in the ice as the glacier moves. Presents a serious mountaineering hazard requiring skilled navigation and specialized rope techniques to negotiate safely.

cwm: (koom) Welsh word for a cirque

gendarme: From the french word for policeman, a pinnacle of rock usually sticking out of a ridge.

glacier: a river of ice which as it slowly flows downhill, carves many common mountain features.

hanging valley: a geological feature formed by a glacier at higher elevation being intersected at roughly 90° by a second deeper glacier. As the ice retreats the higher valley is left with a steep drop off into the larger one giving rise to the term 'hanging'.

horn: a pinnacle of rock usually sticking out of a ridge.

massif: a self-contained portion of a mountain range. For example Mt. Albert Edward, Mt. Regan, Mt. Frink and Castlecrag could be though of as part of the same massif.

moat: A similar formation to a bergschrund formed during the annual thaw when snow and ice melts away from rock faces leaving a deep fissure between the two. Typically a later season phenomena.

mountain hemlock zone: describes the bio-geoclimatic zone between 3,000 and 5,000 feet where the predominate trees are mountain hemlock and yellow cedar.

old-growth: a forest which has not been logged and so is comprised of a wide variety of tree species at a range of ages. This is the native forest sometimes refered to as 'pristine'.

pfd: stands for personal floatation device. A vest of buoyant material secured to the torso during watersport activities for safety. Wearing one is now mandatory for boating in Canada.

pitch: the distance climbed between two fixed belays. Therefore a length no greater than the length of climbing rope employed (typically 50 m / 145 ft.). In practice a pitch may vary in length from a few feet to a hundred metres or more depending on the rope length and climbing undertaken.

rappel: to descend a climbing rope which is secured to a fixed belay anchor, with a retrievable system, by means of a friction device through which the rope passes under control.

rime: a coating of frost.

saddle: a low point between two high points (typically mountains) forming a saddle-shaped feature, akin to a pass or col.

satellite summit: a small adjacent summit to a larger peak. For example the Behinde is a satellite of the Golden Hinde.

scree: a field of frost or glacier created boulders or gravel usually found under a steep rock face or in gullies.

serac: the exposed end of a glacier separated from the rest of the glacier by a crevasse. Often seracs are jumbled piles of ice blocks which pose a serious risk to climbers below if they should break off.

slide alder: a tough relative to our common Red Alder tree which frequents the subalpine zone in avalanche paths and other steep areas where heavy snowfalls accumulate. Difficult to travel through in summer conditions.

snag: a dead standing tree.

subalpine: the zone found between 3,500 ft. and 5,000 ft which is the highest regions in which trees and many other alpine plants can grow.

switchback: a zig-zag up or down a slope. Many island trails follow a path of switchbacks as they zig-zag up the hillside to reduce the effort and rate of ascent.

talus: an area of frost or glacier created boulders found under steep rock faces.

tarn: a small mountain lake.

ungulates: an animal that has hooves.

ungulatesque: pertaining to ungulates.

verglass: thin ice which can coat rock and vegetation during and after freezing rain falls. Can make travel and climbing particularly treacherous.

Cam Powell among some fine rime and verglass on Rambler Peak's upper north gully.

Index

50-40 Peak	93	Buttle, Mt.	56
A Word on Ethics	28	Cain, Mt.	359
Abco Mountain	309	Camping and Accommodation	35
Abel, Mt.	365	Canoe Peak	97
Abraham, Mt.	367	Carter Peak	460
Adam, Mt.	357	Castlecrag Mountain	153
Adder Peak	90	Cat's Ears Peak	96
Adrian, Mt.	179	Cederstedt, Mt.	406
Alava, Mt.	385	Celeste, Mt.	158
Albemarie, Mt.	329	Centaur, The	100
Albert Edward, Mt.	150	Central Crags-Flower Ridge	169
Albert Edward - Flower Ridge Traverse	160	Cervus Creek-Wolf River Divide	251
Alexandra Peak	178	Chief Frank, Mt.	123
Alston, Mt.	354	Clark, Mt.	460
Apps, Mt.	121	Clifton, Mt.	123
Argus Mountain	163	Clubs	39
Arrowsmith, Mt.	73	Cobb, Mt.	255
Ashwood, Mt.	413	Cokely, Mt.	72
Augerpoint Mountain	171	Colonel Foster, Mt.	228
Augerpoint (Jack's) Trail	142	Colwell, Mt.	225
Augerpoint Traverse	170	Comb, The	275
Avalanches	31	Comestock Mountain	461
Bancroft Peak	289	Comox Glacier	162
Barad-dur	448	Con Reid, Mt.	261
Bate, Mt.	383	Conuma Peak	381
Beadnell, Mt.	180	Cotter, Mt.	309
Beaujest Peak	118	Crespi, Mt.	329
Becher Trail	142	Crest Mountain	192
Becher, Mt.	144	Crest Mountain Trail	187
Bedingfield Range	309	Crown Mountain	197
Bedwell Trail	284	Curran, Mt.	119
Behinde, The	277	De Cosmos, Mt.	61
Big Baldy, Mt.	380	Derby, Mt.	410
Big Den Mountain	189	DeVoe, Mt.	247
Big Interior Mountain	292	Donner, Mt.	317
Black Cat Mountain	161	Doom Mountain	459
BonanzaPeak	414	Douglas Peak	80
Brenton, Mt.	58	Drabble, Mt.	145
Brooks, Mt.	148	Ecological Reserves	31
Bueby, Mt.	161	Eden, Mt.	369
Burman, Mt.	270	El Capitan Mountain	54

El Piveto Mountain	249	Hkusam Mountain	402
Elk Mountain	259	Hooper, Mt.	57
Elk River - Westmin Traverse	248	Hornets	31
Elk River Trail	207	Horseshoe Mountain	201
Elkhorn Mountain	218	How To Get Here	35
Elliot, Mt.	407	Hygro Peak	326
Emergency Numbers	35	Iceberg Peak	159
False Ears	458	Idsardi Mountain	193
Filberg, Mt.	257	Irwin, Mt.	116
Flannigan, Mt.	191	Jacklah Mountain	328
Flat Top	100	Jack's Fell	173
Flower Ridge Trail	142	Jack's (Augerpoint) Trail	142
Forbidden Plateau	143	Jagged Mountain	373
Frink, Mt.	154	Joan, Mt.	117
Garibaldi Peaks	458	Judson, Mt.	199
Gemini Mountain	60	Juliet, Mt.	372
Gendarmes, The	428	Jutland Mountain	149
Genesis Mountain	372	Kaouk Mountain	439
George V, Mt.	155	Karmutzen Mountain	450
Gibson, Mt.	90	Kent-Urquhart, Mt.	322
Ginger Goodwin, Mt.	161	King'sPeak	214
Glacier Trail	142	Kitchener, Mt.	399
Gold Lake Trail	187	Klitsa, Mt.	89
Golden Hinde	271	Kokummi Mountain	345
Gore, Mt.	329	Kookjai Mountain	161
Government of B.C.	39	Kwois Peak	455
Grattan, Mt.	387	Laing, Mt.	258
Grayback Peak	437	Landale, Mt.	53
Green, Mt.	60	Leighton Peak	382
Grey, Mt.	57	Leiner, Mt.	389
Guemes, Mt.	309	Limestone Mountain	81
Haig-Brown, Mt.	253	Little Eiger	107
Haihte Spire	433	Logan Peak	58
Hal, Mt.	116	Logging Companies	39
Half Dome	435	Logging Road Travel	33
Hall, Mt.	94	Lombard, Mt.	329
Hannah, Mt.	91	Lone Wolf Mountain	327
Hapush, Mt.	368	Lukwa Mountain	438
Harmston, Mt.	164	Lupin Mountain	181
Heather Mountain	56	M.S. Mountain	323
Heber, Mt.	194	Mackenzie Peak	100
Henry Spencer, Mt.	122	Mackenzie Range	99
Hidden Peak	105	Maitland, Mt.	104

Malaspina Peak	386	Peak 5150	389
Mamat Mountain	439	Peak 5540	414
Maps	37	Peak 5769	414
Maquilla Peak	358	Peak 5800	408
Marble Meadows Trail	209	Pearl Peak	177
Marble Peak	262	Peel, Mt.	409
Mariner Mountain	306	Phillips Ridge	267
Marmot, Mt.	59	Phillips Ridge Trail	209
Matchlee Mountain	318	Phillips Watershed Traverse	268
McBride, Mt.	263	Phillips, Mt.	269
McKelvie, Mt.	390	Pickering, Mt.	461
McQuillan, Mt.	79	Pinder Peak	447
Megin Mountain	328	Pogo Mountain	102
Merlon Mountain	429	Popsicle Peak	323
Merry Widow Mountain	453	Pretty Girl Peak	328
Milner, Mt.	401	Price Creek Trail	283
Misthorns, The	301	Private Property	31
Mitchell, Mt.	176	Province Range	446
Mook Peak	449	Ptarmigan Pinnacles	252
Moriarty, Mt.	71	Publications	37
Morrison Spire	266	Puzzle Mountain	211
Moyeha Mountain	290	Quatchka Ridge	321
Mt. Myra Trail	284	Queen Peak	344
Myra, Mt.	285	Quimper, Mt.	109
Nahmint Mountain	92	Rambler Peak	241
New Route Information	13	Red Pillar, The	165
Nine Peaks	295	Redwall	101
Nora, Mt.	343	Rees Ridge	158
North-West Outliers	435	Regan, Mt.	152
Nunatak Mountain	459	Renwick, Mt.	455
Olsen, Mt.	58	Rhino Peak	106
Online Resources	40	Roberts, Mt.	400
Palmerston, Mt.	406	Rodger's Ridge	180
Paradise Meadows	146	Romeo, Mt.	372
Paradise Meadows Trail	141	Rosseau, Mt.	298
Patlicant Mountain	58	Rufus, Mt.	329
Peak 1805	289	Rugged Mountain	424
Peak 1909	156	Russell, Mt.	405
Peak 1920	156	Saaverda, Mt.	309
Peak 4225	456	Santiago Mountain	390
Peak 4330	455	Sarai, Mt.	366
Peak 4400	438	Saxifrage Mountain	459
Peak 5005	391	Schoen, Mt.	370

Scimitar Peak	325	Vancouver Island Backbone	467
Scissors, The	326	Velella Peak	108
Seaton, Mt.	460	Victoria Peak	346
Septimus, Mt.	296	Volcano Peak	213
Service, Mt.	55	Warden Peak	351
Shadowblade	101	Waring Peak	353
Shelbert Mountain	327	Washington, Mt.	147
Shepherd Ridge	168	Watchtower Peak	356
Sid Williams Peak	174	Water	30
Siokum Mountain	157	Whiltilla Mountain	415
SirJohn, Mt.	411	Whymper, Mt.	52
Slocomb Peak	240	Wildlife	30
Snowsaddle Mountain	457	Witch Hat	100
South Blades	423	Wolf Mountain	210
Spencer, Mt.	59	Wolfenden, Mt.	461
Splendour Mountain	324	Woss Mountain	391
Squarehead, The	118	Ya'aiPeak	431
Steamboat Peak	103	Zeballos Peak	436
Stevens Peak	382		
Stone Trolls, The	448		
Strata Mountain	148		
Strathcona Provincial Park	134		
Stubbs, Mt.	122		
Sutton Peak	355		
Syd Watts Peak	175		
Sydney Cone	328		
Tahsis Mountain	390		
Thelwood, Mt.	287		
ThumbPeak	388		
Ticks	31		
Titus, Mt.	260		
Tlakwa Mountain	451		
Tom Taylor, Mt.	302		
Trails	207		
Trails and Routes	30		
Trio Mountain	195		
Triple Peak	95		
Tsable Mountain	123		
Tsitika Mountain	411		
Tyee Mountain	200		
Tzela Mountain	167		
Upper Myra Falls Trail	284		
Ursus Mountain	308		